Trolling Before the Internet

Trolling Before the Internet

An Offline History of Insult, Provocation, and Public Humiliation in the Literary Classics

David Rudrum

BLOOMSBURY ACADEMIC
NEW YORK • LONDON • OXFORD • NEW DELHI • SYDNEY

BLOOMSBURY ACADEMIC
Bloomsbury Publishing Inc
1385 Broadway, New York, NY 10018, USA
50 Bedford Square, London, WC1B 3DP, UK
29 Earlsfort Terrace, Dublin 2, Ireland

BLOOMSBURY, BLOOMSBURY ACADEMIC and the Diana logo are trademarks of Bloomsbury Publishing Plc

First published in the United States of America 2025

Cover design by Jason Anscomb / rawshock design

Library of Congress Cataloguing-in-Publication Data
Names: Rudrum, David, 1974- author.
Title: Trolling before the internet : an offline history of insult, provocation, and public humiliation in the literary classics / David Rudrum.
Description: New York : Bloomsbury Academic, 2025. |
Includes bibliographical references and index.
Identifiers: LCCN 2024013963 (print) | LCCN 2024013964 (ebook) |
ISBN 9781501391538 (paperback) | ISBN 9781501391521 (hardback) |
ISBN 9781501391545 (ebook) | ISBN 9781501391552 (pdf)
Subjects: LCSH: Invective in literature. | Ridicule in literature. |
Humiliation in literature. | LCGFT: Literary criticism.
Classification: LCC PN56.I648 R83 2025 (print) | LCC PN56.I648 (ebook) |
DDC 809/.91–dc23/eng/20240516
LC record available at https://lccn.loc.gov/2024013963
LC ebook record available at https://lccn.loc.gov/2024013964

ISBN: HB: 978-1-5013-9152-1
PB: 978-1-5013-9153-8
ePDF: 978-1-5013-9155-2
eBook: 978-1-5013-9154-5

Typeset by Integra Software Services Pvt. Ltd.
Printed and bound in Great Britain

For my parents,
without whom …

CONTENTS

ACKNOWLEDGEMENTS

First of all, my thanks to everyone at Bloomsbury for taking on this project and seeing it through, and principally to Haaris Naqvi, whose patience with me during the many challenges of recent years has been more than magnanimous.

The idea of writing a literary history of trolling first came to me over drinks with my brilliant colleague James Underwood. It was probably as much his idea as mine. His inspiration and encouragement got this book off the ground, and I remain in his debt, especially for his encyclopaedic knowledge of all things Larkin.

Support for my research came from Jessica Malay and Merrick Burrow, who provided me with two invaluable semesters of sabbatical research leave – one at the book's inception, and one to bring it to fruition. I'm grateful to them for backing a project that must surely have struck them as quixotic, as well as to my colleagues and students at the University of Huddersfield for putting up with my absences. Jodie Matthews, Steve Ely, Michael Stewart, and Todd Borlik have all chipped in with thought-provoking comments. Ildiko Csengei's expertise on Byron deserves my special thanks.

I have benefitted immeasurably from the input of a remarkable squad of attentive readers, all of whom brought their considerable insights to bear on early drafts of these chapters. My profoundest gratitude goes to Jenny Marshall in particular, and to Julia Rudrum, Alice Brumby, Clémentine Beauvais, Amy Tinnion, Nicholas Gardiner, Helen Wright, Kerry Chippendale, Nicholas Howells, and, once again, James Underwood.

By taking (or affecting) a sceptical interest in my work on trolling, Ridvan Askin and Josh Toth have both goaded me along. Richard Eldridge provided much-needed encouragement at an early stage and Paweł Wojtas moral support later on. Tim Shaw's comments gave much-needed inspiration. Furthermore, I was helped along the way by innumerable conversations with my students and former students about the absurdities of my haphazard and reluctant entry into a digital age – too many to mention, though those with April Lodge, Henry Dale, and Liam Wilde left the deepest footprints.

Above everything, though, I need to thank my partner, Alice, and my family – especially my father, for teaching me how to argue, and my mother, for teaching me when not to. If nothing else, this book proves what a sorry pupil I have been.

PREFATORY NOTE ON CONTENT

This book is about some of the finest writings by some of the greatest authors in literary history; it is also about some of the most deplorable, offensive writings by some of the most abusive writers imaginable. If literature is amongst the best of what has been thought and said, then trolling is amongst the worst. Consequently, please be warned that readers will need to brace themselves for language of an extremely scatological and sexual nature, as well as misogyny, homophobia, racism (including anti-Semitism), and religious hatred.

I have endeavoured to keep this to a minimum wherever possible, using it only to illustrate key points as and when necessary. I have tried not to be gratuitous when doing so. But it is simply not possible to write a research study of trolling without having to deal with offensive material. It is also unwise to try: turning our faces away from the unpleasantness of trolling does not help us, as a society, to challenge it.

The downside of my approach, obviously, is that it involves reproducing – and therefore circulating, disseminating, and perpetuating – some utterly hateful and repugnant content. This raises clear ethical problems. They are not dispelled by pointing out that I have also included some relatively innocuous forms of trolling, and that the internet is awash with material immeasurably worse than even the most egregious examples of trolling cited herein.

One of my main arguments in what follows is that trolling should be confronted, not ignored. It follows that, whilst I am loath to give further publicity to content I find abhorrent, I fear that not doing so is also wrongheaded. It risks under-evidencing why trolling is such a problem. I have therefore tried to keep this content to a minimum, without shying away from the importance it has in demonstrating the nature and extent of this problem. But I recognize that this is not a perfect approach and that some readers will be exposed to material they may find upsetting – for which, wholeheartedly, I apologize in advance.

Introduction

Trolling in/and/as literature

In the beginning was the Lulz, and the Lulz was with God, and the Lulz was God ... Through him all trollings were made; without him nothing was trolled that has been trolled.

– ENCYCLOPEDIA DRAMATICA

Trolling is the most controversial genre of writing to have risen to prominence in the twenty-first century. Barely a week seems to go by without some trolling-related story making the news – the latest hapless innocent victim of an online mob, say, or some twisted prank perpetrated through the internet, or yet another celebrity forced off-line because of a targeted hate campaign against her social media accounts. Things like these are typically blamed on people known as trolls.

The public debate around trolls and their actions (basically, trolling) has at times become so heated as to verge on moral panic, and not without reason. After all, trolling can have far-reaching consequences for its readers and writers alike. It can cause lasting psychological damage to its victims, and has led to a disturbing number of well-documented suicides.[1] As

[1]Among too many others, the cases of 14-year-old Megan Meier (2006, USA), 15-year-old Natasha MacBryde (2011, UK), 15-year-old Amanda Todd (2012, Canada) and celebrity Charlotte Dawson (2012, Australia) stand out as landmarks that brought the issue to public attention in these countries.

for its perpetrators, it might result in a criminal record, even a jail sentence. In other words, though trolling is sometimes shrugged off as the pursuit of laughter by digital means, it's a deadly serious matter. Moreover, it is (bafflingly) seldom clear what trolls hope to gain or achieve from their trolling, except perhaps a risibly ephemeral notoriety. And yet, having said all this, trolling sometimes has its positives too: a witty riposte to a troll can easily turn victim into victor. Some researchers have even argued that trolling actually strengthens online communities, as group members rally round to defend themselves, one another, and their community from the disruptive antics of the trolls.[2] Indeed, later chapters will bring to light occasions when the tactics and techniques we call trolling have been harnessed in the service of good causes and noble purposes: in certain contexts, trolling is not always a bad or reprehensible thing.

Above all, the practice of trolling remains poorly understood, especially as a form of written expression – a genre of writing, if you will. Whether for good or ill, the discussion has thus far been dominated by politicians, campaigners, software and social networking companies, law enforcement agencies, and occasionally some social scientists. It needs to be widened. Genres of writing seldom emerge from nowhere, and this book will be arguing that a study of literary history can help us to understand the practice of trolling, the tactics behind it, and its effects on individual readers and writers, as well as on society as a whole. Trolling, that is, is too often regarded as a technological problem, confined to the internet. This book takes a very different approach: it regards trolling as a cultural problem with a long and venerable literary history.

To begin with, though, we'll need to tackle the basics. Firstly: what exactly is trolling, and why is it the occasion of so much acrimonious debate? Secondly: if trolling generally comes laced with obscenity and hate speech, if it's barely literate and often synonymous with verbal thuggery, then what can it possibly have in common with literature, the label we traditionally attach to the finer, more cultivated, more beautiful echelons of written expression? Indeed, how could there be a literary history of trolling, if, as is widely thought, it came into being only recently, with the digital age, and flourishes only in the anonymous and instantaneous environment of the internet? Answering these questions, I'm afraid, will not be easy.

---

[2]The clearest statement of this view is Angela Gracia B. Cruz, Yuri Seo, and Mathew Rex, 'Trolling in online communities: A practice-based theoretical perspective', *The Information Society*, vol. 34, no. 1, 2018, pp.15–26. See also Bryn Alexander Coles and Melanie West, 'Trolling the Trolls: Online Forum Users Constructions of the Nature and Properties of Trolling', *Computers in Human Behavior*, vol. 60, 2016, pp.233–44.

Trolling before the internet

Let's broach the second area of inquiry first. To establish that trolling predates the internet, and can be found in offline writing, we'll turn to a British report entitled *Social Media and Criminal Offences* by the House of Lords Select Committee on Communications. The 'Concluding Remarks' section of this surprisingly engaging read ends with this short paragraph:

> Just to show that nothing is ever really new, a man was convicted by magistrates in 1913 under section 4(1)(c) of the Post Office (Protection) Act 1884 for sending 'grossly offensive' postcards to officials in Leeds in which he described an Alderman as an 'insurance swindler'.[3]

The key point here is that this man was prosecuted for abusing the latest form of communications technology: the ha'penny postage stamp, as instituted by the Victorians. He *wasn't* prosecuted for libel or defamation – even though writing these messages on postcards meant they might have been read by other people, like the postman or the recipients' housekeepers, and even though under the Libel Act of 1843, knowingly and maliciously publishing a libel was theoretically a criminal offence (punishable by up to two years in prison and an unlimited fine). His crime wasn't the slander of a public official but rather the wrongful and wilful misuse of a public messaging service. In short, trolling.

In common parlance, trolling is taken to mean things as disparate as hurling abuse through social media; vandalizing Wikipedia pages with misinformation; disingenuously asking pointless questions in online discussion groups; posting inflammatory comments in response to a news article or YouTube video; disrupting a gaming community by asking idle questions whilst the game is in play; and using the internet to orchestrate co-ordinated pranks, bullying, or harassment. What *seems* to link all these things is their digital nature. But actually, that is incidental. The key to it is not something specific to digital technology but rather something about the way it is written; how it manipulates language to heighten feelings and elicit reactions, or how it deploys certain textual strategies to create a transformative impact – in other words, the very things we expect literary texts to do. If this seems too much of a stretch, then all I need you to grant me for now is that 'a questioner can troll a political meeting, and academics troll each other in committees when they are bored; and a newspaper

---

[3]House of Lords Select Committee on Communications, *Social Media and Criminal Offences*, 1st Report of Session 2014–15, 2015. Available at: https://publications.parliament.uk/pa/ld201415/ldselect/ldcomuni/37/37.pdf

columnist may be a profit-troll towards a whole city', as Rachel Barney has it. 'And it is clear from this that there can be trolling outside the internet'.[4]

In an insightful study of the trolling subculture, Whitney Phillips remarks that 'every aspect of modern trolling culture has had some basic behavioral precedent'.[5] She's quite right, and she adduces a body of evidence for the claim that stretches as far back as the early 1990s, with primitive online platforms such as Usenet. In this chapter, we'll be going much further back – as far as ancient Greece, and stretching right up to the dawning of the digital age in the 1980s. In what follows, we'll be going back around a thousand years, beginning with Anglo-Saxon and Norse literature, and ending with the early twentieth-century avant-gardes. By breaking down the troll phenomenon into its constituent parts, and exploring the literary ancestry of each, we'll see that none of the features of modern trolling is entirely new or unprecedented. But there is no single genealogical line or literary thread that holds it all together – rather, trolling involves a disparate range of strategies, each with its own literary ancestry. Lord Byron, for example, cultivated a reputation most trolls would envy, precisely through outrageously contrarian writing, just as Oscar Wilde did after him, and any number of avant-garde writers after that. Contrastingly, Jonathan Swift responded to an impending humanitarian catastrophe with the sickest humour imaginable, possibly inventing a subgenre called disaster trolling in the process. Even using profane insults for purposes of public humiliation has been a staple of English literature in times gone by. By turning away from the contemporary moral panic about the internet, and investigating this range of literary precedents for contemporary trolling, we stand to learn a great deal.

With this in mind, let me introduce, as my Exhibit A, a piece of evidence to suggest that the words 'troll' and 'trolling' have been in colloquial usage since at least about 1540. A one-page ballad sheet from the time of Henry VIII, entitled *A balade agaynst malycyous Sclaunderers*,[6] uses a familiar term for the nasty deeds of these 'malicious slanderers'. The noun used to refer to their deeds is 'trollynges', the verb is to 'trolle', the participle of this verb is 'trollynge', and people who do this are 'trolles'. Remarkably, the usage of the term seems to carry virtually all of its present-day connotations, even though the ballad dates from almost 500 years ago.

We don't know who its author was – the ballad was anonymously written (like most of today's trolling, aptly enough). But we do know that

---

[4]Rachel Barney, '[Aristotle], *On Trolling*', *Journal of the American Philosophical Association*, vol. 2, no. 2, 2016, pp.193–5, p.194.

[5]Whitney Phillips, *This Is Why We Can't Have Nice Things: Mapping the Relationship Between Online Trolling and Mainstream Culture* (Cambridge, MA: MIT Press, 2015), p.18.

[6]Anon., *A Balade agaynst Malycyous Sclaunderers* (London: Iohn Gough, *c.* 1540).

it was written shortly after the death of Thomas Cromwell, and that it was printed 'at London in Lombard strete nere vnto the Stockes market at the sygne of the Mermayde by Iohn Gough'. Its explicit aim is to call out the reprehensible practice it calls trolling, and those responsible for it. The 'trolles' it targets are those malicious slanderers mentioned in the title: they were Catholic sympathizers who seemingly used Cromwell's execution for high treason as an opportunity to spread all manner of untruths about him and the Reformation he had spearheaded, presumably with the goal of discrediting or halting the break from Rome. The ballad seeks to expose their 'trollynge'.

These 'trolles' are said to speak craftily ('Is it thy facyon [i.e. fashion] thus craftely to saye?'); to tell lies ('thou lyest'); and to speak under 'pretence'. But perhaps its most revealing stanza begins 'I pray god thou be not fownde one of those / That peruarteth the people … / From redyng of gods worde' – that is, these trolls might well be perverting people into not reading, or misreading, the Holy Scriptures. Their traitorous words are feared to be strategies to this end: 'Thou traytor allurest them this fayre floure to defame'. Thus, these trolls are treacherously 'alluring' people with their 'malycyous sclaunders' – a vocabulary that clearly paints these 'trollynges' as dangerously deceptive, luring people into their trap. (We shouldn't forget how deadly a trap this was: some ways of reading the Bible could cost you your life during the Reformation.) This, as we'll soon see, is one of the most important senses attached to the word 'trolling' today.

And there's more. These 'trolles' are thoroughly reprobate characters. They have nothing but disregard for appropriate social and moral behaviour. In what sounds like an early precursor to a practice known as RIP trolling – of which more soon – they are said to speak ill of the dead by telling tales ('To tayle … on dead men'); to rail against their fellow Christians ('to rayle vpon a christen soule'); and to hold the law in contempt ('thou woldest deface / The kynges royall power / dispysyng the same'). The ballad upbraids these 'dronken' trolls, who have 'small charyte and lesse wytte', just as their twenty-first-century descendants do. This clearly anticipates another sense of the word 'troll' – an antagonistic, inflammatory individual, contemptuous and contemptible.

Whether a one-page ballad sheet of doggerel verse printed cheaply and hurriedly counts as enough evidence that the terms 'trolling' and 'troll' were already in circulation by 1540, and that their usage then was more or less what it is now, I do not presume to say. At the very least, though, it's a fascinating possibility. But perhaps most fascinating of all is the fact that the terms 'trollynge' and 'trolle' are often used indistinctly and interchangeably – much like how they're bandied about today – as in this stanza:

Thou makest a trollyng hyther and thyther
Somtyme thou trollest thou canst not tell whyther

But if all thy trollynges were gathered togyther
Thy trollynge might … tourne the[e] to blame
Wherfore trolle thou nowe into the way for shame.

It's hard to say here what 'trollynge' is, exactly. Trolling is clearly seen as something blameworthy and shameful, but why that is, and what is meant by it, seem less important than the term's status as a handy buzzword. And, as the next chapter demonstrates, that is precisely the situation that, nearly 500 years on, hampers researchers studying twenty-first-century trolling.

What does 'trolling' mean?

That's a good question. Finding a comprehensive definition of trolling has proved nigh-on impossible, for reasons the next chapter discusses. For now, let's start by looking at where the term comes from. Unfortunately, this isn't straightforward either: there are two conflicting accounts of the origins of this troublesome word.

The first is a widespread assumption that it's related to evil figures from Norse mythology called trolls. The word 'troll' in Old Norse is synonymous with 'demon' or 'fiend', and so trolls are a bit like monsters. They're typically aggressive, and seem to reserve a particular hatred for humankind. A tale from the thirteenth-century *Prose Edda* recounts how, long ago, a travelling bard named Bragi Boddason (who, as it happens, actually existed: he served as a court poet to several kings of ninth-century Sweden and is believed to have inaugurated the Scandinavian tradition of *skaldic* poetry) is waylaid in the woods late one evening by a troll woman. She accosts him, quite fiercely, and demands he answer her questions. Perhaps this is why, in later Scandinavian folklore, trolls lurk under bridges and ambush travellers, demanding they answer a question or solve a riddle before they can pass.

So: on this account of the word's origins, trolls are aggressive, misanthropic creatures who pounce on unsuspecting passersby, spitting cryptic, riddle-like messages and threats at them, which bewilder and frighten their victims. A history of trolls, then, would begin in the literature of the Viking age, pass from there into Scandinavian folk tales, and on into the well-known nineteenth-century fairy tale about three billy goats that was derived from those tales, before finding a home on the twenty-first-century internet.

The other version of the story has to do with – of all things – fishing. 'Trolling' is an established practice in which an angler drags one or, more typically, several baited hooks or lures behind a boat. It's looked down on by some anglers, who say it lacks the skill of, say, fly-fishing, where it is the dexterity with which the angler plays the line, rather than the slow plodding progress of a boat, that gives the lure of the illusion of movement that draws in the fish. Furthermore, since trolling often involves multiple fishing lines with multiple hooks, it might have an unfair advantage over more conventional forms of angling. But still, the metaphor seems pretty clear: trolling is a ruse. Though disapproved of by some, it's seen as fun by others. Its aims are to draw unsuspecting people in – to attract their attention and get them to follow you. Someone taken in by trolling has, quite literally, risen to the bait.

This sense of the word 'trolling' also goes back centuries: amongst its aficionados was one Robert Nobbes, who quite literally wrote the book on trolling long before me. Back in 1682, when he was thirty years old, Nobbes published *The Compleat Troller, or, The Art of Trolling, with a Description of All the Utensils, Instruments, Tackling, and Materials Requisite Thereto, with Rules and Directions How to Use Them: As Also a Brief Account of Most of the Principal Rivers in England, by a Lover of the Sport.*[7] It's a genuinely delightful read, from a time when quasi-scientific prose could sit cheek by jowl alongside poetry and genuinely warm, good-humoured personal anecdotes. Nobbes acknowledges his debt to Izaak Walton's much-loved classic *The Compleat Angler* (1653), a book he sees as decidedly incompleat, since Walton scarcely mentions the technique of trolling. In setting this to rights, Nobbes has much useful advice for would-be trollers: 'Old Fish are more wary and cunning', he warns: 'they are sooner taken with a Line laid for them all night, then by Trolling'.[8] No doubt this is as true on the internet today as it was on Nobbes's beloved River Avon in the seventeenth century.

So how did the usage of this word migrate from the context of angling to that of computing? It's been suggested that this might have come about through American military slang. 'Trolling for MiGs' seems to have been an expression used to describe how Cold War–era US fighter pilots would attempt to provoke Soviet warplanes into aggressive behaviour, so that they could then be shot down legitimately. It was an unauthorized tactic, and a plausibly deniable one. (Similarly, trolls almost never admit they're trolling.) There's a documented case of the word being used this way in 1972, during the Vietnam War.[9] Given how intertwined the history of electronic communications is with the history of the American military, it wouldn't be surprising if there was a connection here.

What we have, then, is two very different origin myths. Let's pause for a moment to contrast them. In the first, a troll is a specific kind of person; in the

---

[7]Robert Nobbes, *The Compleat Troller, or, The Art of Trolling, with a Description of All the Utensils, Instruments, Tackling, and Materials Requisite Thereto, with Rules and Directions How to Use Them: As Also a Brief Account of Most of the Principal Rivers in England, by a Lover of the Sport* (London: T. James for Thomas Helder at the Sign of the Angel in Little Britain, 1682).

[8]Ibid., p.61.

[9]See Andy Bodle, 'Trolls: Where Do They Come From?', *The Guardian*, 19 April 2012.

second, trolling is a particular kind of practice. In the first, a troll is someone who is cruel and aggressive by nature, 'an archetypical anti-social individual in online communities'[10] who targets unsuspecting victims. In the second, trolling is a leisurely pursuit, and although it's a blood sport, the emphasis is on guile, subterfuge, and duping rather than on naked aggression. The majority of scholars seem to think the likelier explanation involves anglers; the abundant witticisms about trolls that pepper the internet (comparing the bridges they live under to the mothers' basements in which all trolls are believed to reside, for example) suggest that lay users opt for the Viking explanation. Either way, it's worth pointing out this: which origin myth you find the more persuasive probably indicates a good deal about what you think of trolling. Either trolls are a thoroughly nasty bunch of people who threaten all the rest of us and need to be stopped, or trolling is supposed to be a piece of fun, albeit fun at its victims' expense. Probably, the truth of the matter lies somewhere between the two.

These two different understandings of what 'trolling' means obviously imply two very different sets of textual strategies and literary techniques. Both are confrontational, but one is explicitly so and the other surreptitiously so. The former entails a direct, abusive rhetoric, or what we call personal invective. The latter would seem to involve using language to string people along by provoking them, closer to what Cicero did in the law-courts of ancient Rome, or Socrates in the Athenian *agora*. Its deceptiveness also makes it a bit like dramatic irony, that device whereby everyone in the audience is privy to something a hapless character on the stage doesn't know. Let's see how these ideas work out in practice.

We're going to look, briefly, at some literary trolls. Both the examples I have in mind – one for each of these versions of what it means to troll – involve poetry. As it happens, they're (respectively) the earliest and the latest examples of trolling we'll look at in this book. The first was written some 2,700 years ago in faraway ancient Greece. The second was written in the north of England, in the city of Hull, just before the dawning of the modern internet age.

Aggressive trolling: Archilochus

The poet Archilochus has as fair a claim as any to be considered the founder of what we, in the twenty-first century, call poetry. He was the first poet we know of to draw primarily on his own feelings and emotions, and to write about his personal experiences, as opposed to singing the praises of gods and heroes through storylines everyone knew in advance. To do so,

[10]Cruz, Seo, and Rex, 'Trolling in Online Communities', p.16.

he broke completely with the rhythms and metres of Homer and the epic tradition. He pioneered the use of iambic verse – the same vehicle that drove the lines of Chaucer, Shakespeare, Milton, and Wordsworth, without any of them finding a way to improve upon it – instead of writing conventional Homeric hexameters. He might even have invented the tradition of elegy, and possibly that of satire too. The ancient Greeks clearly thought he was in the pantheon of the greats, often ranking him alongside Hesiod and Homer. When he fell in battle, the man who killed him was expelled from the temple of Apollo, Plutarch tells us, 'on the ground that he had killed a man sacred to the Muses' – even though the fight had been a fair-and-square, kill-or-be-killed scenario.[11] And yet Archilochus was as heinous and loathsome a troll as any you'll find on today's internet.

A concise version of the story is told (originally in Latin) by a scholar writing in the margins of an ancient Greek manuscript at some time during the Middle Ages:

> Lycambes had a daughter Neoboule. When Archilochus sought her hand in marriage, she was promised by her father but not given to him. In anger at this Archilochus wrote an abusive poem against him and the latter was so grief-stricken that he hanged himself along with his daughter.[12]

The bile and vitriol of Archilochus's poetry became, quite literally, the stuff of ancient Greek legend. After his death, a short piece of verse was written warning Cerberus, the fearsome three-headed dog that guards the underworld, to be wary of upsetting his ghost. It was said that the epitaph on his tomb warned passersby to hurry on with their journeys in case they stirred up his waspish ire. Apparently, a proverb later came about: if you'd upset someone known for their sharp tongue, a friend might warn you 'You have stepped on Archilochus', in roughly the same way they might say you'd stepped on a poisonous snake. We have it on the authority of one of the later cynic philosophers that Archilochus 'makes use of every kind of foul and unspeakable language against women, language which no man of discretion would even bear to hear'.[13]

Archilochus's work survives only in fragments – often, through short quotations of his lines found in the writings of other authors. Judging by what's left, it's probably just as well. His misogyny knows almost no bounds. The lines that have come down to us rail against women, with neither taste nor mercy. One is described as 'a revolting woman, fat about the ankles',

---

[11]See Plutarch, 'On the Slowness of Divine Vengeance', in *Greek Iambic Poetry*, ed. and trans. Douglas E. Gerber (Cambridge, MA: Harvard University Press, 1999), p.41.

[12]Pseudo-Acron, in *Greek Iambic Poetry*, ed. and trans. Gerber, p.53.

[13]Oenomaus, in *Greek Iambic Poetry*, ed., and trans. Gerber, p.45.

another as 'a public woman; a worker for hire'.[14] One is 'afflicted by lice', while another is polluted with the 'froth of defilement'.[15] Not all his poetry is this direct; some of it is more metaphorical. Though its meaning isn't spelled out quite so graphically, let's just say you don't have to be Sigmund Freud: 'you have received many blind eels', he sneers at another unfortunate girl.[16] Having said that, we can't tell, from these remaining fragments, whether the lines refer to another unfortunate girl or not, or even whether they're from different poems. For all we know, they could all be parts of one big, long, foul-mouthed rant against young Neoboule.

We know that in ancient Greece, 'public recitation was not only part of the education and training of a member of the Greek *polis*, it was also a form of publication – *the* form of publication'.[17] So, in all probability, Archilochus was reciting and singing these verses in public places. Once his fame had caught on, admirers of his poetic craft would be repeating them throughout the streets, markets, and *agora* all over Paros. Apparently, slandering Neoboule went viral, spreading abusive invective about a hapless target in the most public ways possible at the time. No wonder that, in a society where shame and dishonour were so stigmatized, Lycambes and his daughter (and, in some versions, his wife and two other daughters) felt driven to end their lives.

The parallels with modern trolling are abundantly clear. The nasty, personal derision in the tone; the filthy, sexually explicit language, surely a symptom of an almost hysterical fear of female sexuality; the uptake of it by a pernicious minority who circulate, to a merciless public, second-hand lies, innuendo, and smut about a girl who has done nothing wrong; even the subject matter (what are these lines, if not a blueprint for what we call 'slut-shaming'?) – all these flag up Archilochus's poetry as trolling. And, as if in a warning from history, there's the tragic outcome, directly caused by such wanton persecution, that anticipates the suicides of Megan Meier, Natasha MacBryde, Amanda Todd, Charlotte Dawson, and so many other victims of trolls. Perhaps the saddest part of the whole sorry tale is that later poets (mostly men) took to writing imaginary epitaphs for Neoboule and her poor, traduced sisters:

> We here, the daughters of Lycambes who gained a hateful reputation, swear by the reverence in which this tomb of the dead is held that we did not shame our virginity or our parents or Paros, pre-eminent among holy

[14]Archilochus, in *Greek Iambic Poetry*, ed. and trans. Gerber, p.221; p.223.

[15]Ibid., p.241; p.223.

[16]Ibid., p.205.

[17]Marshall McLuhan, *The Gutenberg Galaxy: The Making of Typographic Man* (Toronto: University of Toronto Press, 1962), p.85.

> islands, but Archilochus spewed forth frightful reproach and a hateful report against our family. We swear by the gods and spirits that we did not set eyes on Archilochus either in the streets or in Hera's great precinct. If we had been lustful and wicked, he would not have wanted to beget legitimate children from us.[18]

It's heartbreaking: no calls for vengeance, no pleas for justice, no angry lambasting of the man who wronged them – just a simple statement of the truth of this wretched matter. The contrast with the longest surviving fragment of Archilochus's verse couldn't be more stark or more sickening:

> Neoboule another man may take!
> She's doubly ripe ...
>
> the bloom is off her maidenhood,
> the charms she had are gone, for she
> can never get her fill ...
>
> but, frenzied, shows the measure of her shame.
> Crows take her! and
> may [Zeus ensure]
>
> that I shall never be the butt of neighbours' jokes
> for having one like her! ...
>
> she is sharp and takes
> a hundred [friends] –
>
> indeed I fear she'll bear litters premature
> and blind, for she's as eager as
> the fabled Bitch.[19]

The twenty-first-century internet is awash with outpourings of a similar nature, mostly written by men about the women who have (very sensibly) rejected them. The female dog metaphor isn't that different from its modern use in the English language – shortly, we'll come across Evelyn Waugh using it. There's a pretty clear consensus that 'trolling behaviors are gendered male', as Whitney Phillips puts it.[20] The extract above is a perfect example of the twisted logic of misogyny that fires today's trolls.

---

[18] Dioscorides, in *Greek Iambic Poetry*, ed. and trans. Gerber, p.49.

[19] Archilochus, in Anne Pippin Burnett, *Three Archaic Poets: Archilochus, Alcaeus, Sappho* (London: Bristol Classical Press, 1983), p.87.

[20] Phillips, *This Is Why ...*, p.42.

Incredibly, these lines that abuse a woman for being sexually promiscuous are, in the context of the poem in which they're found, *spoken to another woman,* with whom Archilochus is about to have sexual intercourse. She is 'a soft and pretty maid whose beauty / I call blameless'. And, straight after he has spoken the hateful lines cited above to this young girl, Archilochus boasts that 'I took the girl and couched her / Where the blossoms opened full'. He tells in graphic detail how his

> soothing hands ... claimed her breasts ...
>
> and then my fingers learnt her lovely body well
> before I let the white sperm go,
> touching golden hair.[21]

Perhaps there's one more detail that, under the circumstances, is even more shocking than this: he names her. She is 'Amphimedo's child'.

It's not just that, like so many men throughout history, Archilochus feels the need to take revenge on the woman who spurned him by casting aspersions about her sexual immodesty. Nor is it just that Archilochus, like so many men throughout history, feels the need to brag in the crudest terms about his sexual conquests. It's not even the obvious, bare-faced hypocrisy behind the incompatibility of the two positions – deriding one woman for sleeping around while, in the same breath, boasting at how easily he can get this girl to sleep with him. It's the fact that he does these things so very publicly, and so very crudely, naming and shaming real women for reasons that are so obviously malicious. If trolling, understood in the Viking sense of the term, is about aggressive comments directed at defenceless innocents for the sick pleasure of it, then this, surely, is trolling *avant la lettre*. It is a strange and sobering thought that the founding moment of what we call poetry was simultaneously the earliest instance of what we call trolling.

Deceptive trolling: Larkin

To illustrate the second kind of trolling, let's fast forward in time some twenty-seven centuries to the superbly curmudgeonly poet Philip Larkin. Larkin's legendarily dour outlook on the dross of modern life might lead us to suspect he'd view the age of the internet with impatience, even exasperation. But in point of fact, Larkin was quicker than most to realize the potential of computers. Later in life, at an age where stereotypical expectations would dictate he'd be growing impervious to new technologies,

[21]Archilochus, in Burnett, *Three Archaic Poets*, p.87.

he did the very opposite. In his role as university librarian at the University of Hull's Brynmor Jones Library, he oversaw the digitalization of the library catalogue and circulation records, making his the first library in Europe to install a state-of-the-art online GEAC system. He seems to have viewed the task with some ambivalence: on the one hand, his concern for the end-user experience was, by all accounts, far-sighted and exemplary; on the other hand, he wrote in one letter that 'Computerization proceeds apace, resembling a kind of lunatic professional hari-kiri. I've never knowingly destroyed a library before'.[22] That was way back in 1980. What he would have made of eBooks, let alone the world of social media, with its 'liking' and 'sharing' of the trivial and vapid, one shudders to think.

Larkin's trollish temperament is often on show in his letters. He cultivated a façade of brusque Englishness, dismissive of the 'foreign' to the point of xenophobia, especially literature written in 'foreign' languages. (For instance: when asked to comment on the similarities between his career and that of Jorge Luis Borges, the Nobel Prize–winning writer who also had a day job as a librarian, he simply replied, 'Who is Jorge Luis Borges?') And yet it is an established fact that Larkin read and was influenced by an impressive range of international writers. Most of all, he seems to have been taken with the poetry of Jules Laforgue, the nineteenth-century French symbolist writer: 'In the early 1950s he told Arthur Terry that Laforgue's "L'Hiver qui vient" was "the poem I've been trying to write all my life"'.[23] Twenty years later, in a letter to Anthony Thwaite, Larkin went so far as to call himself 'the Laforgue of Pearson Park'.[24]

In light of all this, we may well wonder how to make sense of the following extract from a letter that Larkin wrote to fellow poet and friend Robert Conquest on 7 May 1957: 'And if that chap Laforgue wants me to read his things, he'd better write them in English. Can't read his lingo, sorry. Don't expect he can read mine, if it comes to that'.[25]

For a start, Larkin knew perfectly well that by this time, Laforgue had been dead for a full threescore years and ten. The idea of a long-dead nineteenth-century poet suddenly writing new poems for a newly emerging twentieth-century poet, and changing the very language in which he wrote them to suit his reader's whims, is kind of amusing. And perhaps that's the best way to make sense of all this: as a joke. The brash overconfidence of a

---

[22]See James Booth, *Philip Larkin: Life, Art and Love* (London: Bloomsbury, 2014), p.430–31.

[23]John Osborne, *Larkin, Ideology and Critical Violence: A Case of Wrongful Conviction* (Basingstoke: Palgrave Macmillan, 2008), p.58.

[24]Philip Larkin, *Selected Letters of Philip Larkin, 1940–1985*, ed. Anthony Thwaite (London: Faber and Faber, 1992), p.460.

[25]Larkin, *Selected Letters*, p.274.

young poet (though Larkin was in his mid-thirties at this point) undercuts itself humorously with the barefaced ignorance it simultaneously reveals.

And yet Larkin doth protest too much, methinks. This isn't a casual one-liner. It turns into a tirade. Larkin bullishly flaunts his ignorance of foreign languages, then disparages Laforgue by insinuating that he's a fellow ignoramus, and then glibly implies a snide moral equivalence between these two ignorances. And the strange thing is that it's all completely groundless. For his part, Laforgue took English lessons from a woman named Leah Lee, whom he went on to marry, in a church in Kensington. His English would no doubt have been good enough to read the plain, direct language of a Larkin poem like 'This Be The Verse'. And as for Larkin, why did he own French language editions of Laforgue's poetry if he couldn't read the lingo?

A better way to make sense of the passage, then, is to realize that Larkin is trolling, that is, his comments about Laforgue are, in a Nobbesian sense, trollbait. They are deliberately crafted to make it unclear if they are brusque, xenophobic cluelessness, or just flippant, acerbic banter. It's a strategy for luring in readers that places Larkin in a win-win position: if you think he's joking, then you're giving him credit for his wit, irony, and sense of humour; if you think he's just clueless, then he gets to claim credit for hoodwinking you, and you've been successfully trolled. Either way, he gets to duck the charge of xenophobia with a Larkinesque snigger. No wonder trolling has become the favoured rhetorical strategy of bigots – they get to say all manner of risqué things in a way that remains practically risk-free.

Admittedly, what Larkin wrote in his private letters was just that – private. At the time, he likely had no idea that these words would be read by anybody other than Robert Conquest. Trolling, as I will argue later in this book, is typically more public-facing than this, and it's important to bear in mind that different genres of writing work in subtly different ways. What might amount to banter in a letter to a friend can easily become something else in a more public setting. So let's consider how this same strategy of trolling through affected cluelessness works in an environment intended for public consumption. In an interview that took place years after he wrote this letter, Larkin was pressed on the very point of his apparent xenophobia: the interviewer put it to him that his (public-facing) resistance to the cultures and literatures of other countries might amount to courting a social, personal, or national insularity. Larkin's response is the very stuff of trolling: 'Every man is an island, entire of himself, as Donne said'.[26]

You don't need to be an expert on the literature of the English Renaissance to know that what Donne wrote was, of course, 'No man is an island' – the phrase has passed into common usage and carries the force of a proverb.

[26]John Haffenden, *Viewpoints: Poets in Conversation with John Haffenden* (London: Faber and Faber, 1981), p.122.

Larkin was an exceptionally well-read poet: he knew this. So what was he doing? Slyly, surreptitiously testing the interviewer's knowledge? Hardly: the interviewer, John Haffenden, lectured in English literature at the University of Sheffield. Later in life, he would go on to edit William Empson's ambitious book on Donne and the literature of the renaissance.

Surely what Larkin is doing here is testing not the interviewer's knowledge or alertness but rather whether Haffenden is willing to risk the embarrassing social awkwardness of interrupting a distinguished poet, twenty-three years his senior, so as to correct his (probably deliberate) mistake. Larkin has put Haffenden on the spot: if he butts in, he seems rude and pedantic; if he keeps quiet, then the scholarly tone of his interview is marred with a glaring error. Either way, one can imagine Larkin privately laughing a smug, self-satisfied, laugh – the kind of sadistic laughter trolls call 'lulz', which we'll discuss later on. It's precisely the infuriating dilemma in which today's trolls place their victims, and Haffenden, like many of them, decided the lesser of two evils was not to feed the troll. Heads, Larkin wins; tails, Haffenden loses – here we can see the asymmetry of trolling, which we'll explore in later chapters.

Larkin's is amongst the most thoroughgoingly trollish writing not to have its own chapter in this book. But only in the angler's sense of the word. There's nothing of the verbal thuggery that characterizes the Viking sense of the term in Larkin. Whereas Larkin is angling for Haffenden to take his bait, Archilochus is confrontational, aggressive, and abusive. So a good question to ask would be whether we're talking about one phenomenon or two, when we talk about trolls and trolling.

Trolls and trolling: One thing or two?

One recent study sheds interesting light on this point.[27] Surveying a sample of posts (625 in all) by everyday internet users commenting in a range of online spaces – for example, in response to blogs, digital newspapers, or in an online forum – researchers discovered that 'trolling' can sometimes be considered a very different thing from 'being a troll'. A troll is typically seen as something nasty, vicious, even hateful. But trolling isn't. Trolling is sometimes seen as a legitimate activity, especially if it's directed at a legitimate target. And who would a legitimate target for trolling be? Trolls, naturally. Trolling in self-defence is, apparently, no offence; giving trolls a dose of their own medicine is seen as no bad thing, especially if you're protecting your online community. Disregarding the common wisdom that says, 'Don't

[27]Coles and West, 'Trolling the Trolls'.

feed the trolls', some people apparently take pride in the very opposite strategy – that of trolling the trolls. Strangely, there seems to be a belief that this doesn't make them trolls: rather, they 'behave in a trollish manner without becoming a troll themselves', suggesting 'that while trolling may be acceptable under certain circumstances, being a troll is not acceptable'.[28]

Perhaps this goes back to my earlier point that on one hand our key term can designate a kind of person but on the other, it can designate an activity. You might brush off someone's actions as 'just trolling' without any hard feelings, but if you dismiss a person as 'just a troll', you are implicitly writing off their moral character as a human being. This distinction has important consequence for this book: Martin Luther, Jonathan Swift, Oscar Wilde, and Émile Zola might have employed forms of trolling, but this doesn't mean they were 'just trolls'. The label defines neither them as authors nor their writings: there is far more to their work than trolling, thank goodness.

Tempting though this distinction between trolls and trolling is, it's also problematic. The simple fact is that these two usages, and indeed the two origin myths we've been tracing, are so intertwined in common parlance as to be inextricable. Differentiating between them – let alone establishing which is the 'true' origin and hence the 'correct' usage – is simply not feasible. As the next chapter demonstrates, the term 'trolling' is used so widely and contradictorily that it's become all but impossible to define. Scholars have argued that, as time goes by, the word is used in more and more contexts, so its meaning gets more and more confused. This is certainly true. But it's not as if anyone can remember a time when it was crystal clear what trolling was, and whether or not it was similar or different to being a troll – we've already seen that these lines were probably blurred as long ago as the 1540s.

Given all this, the best way of understanding what trolling is is to try comparing it with similar practices, especially its forerunners, to see what we can learn from analogies and contrasts. Literature offers us the perfect resource for doing just that. Besides being a vast cultural repository of verbal and rhetorical strategies, it also portrays and depicts a huge array of incidents and behaviours, some of which overlap with what, today, we'd call trolling. This can help us understand the trolls of our own time. As Whitney Phillips puts it, careful study of trolling can 'unearth the biases, hypocrisies, and deep inconsistencies that compose mainstream culture'.[29] And so, I'd add, can the study of literature.

Far from a dichotomy that says 'trolling – bad; literature – good', what's most revealing about studying literary examples of troll-type activities is that we soon see there isn't always a 'boundary between where the troll mess

---

[28] Ibid., p.241.

[29] Phillips, *This Is Why ...*, p.136.

ends and the mainstream mess begins'.[30] Otherwise put, literature has more in common with trolling than we might like to admit. In any case, Phillips remarks, because trolling is 'widely condemned as being bad, obscene, and wildly transgressive, [it] therefore allow[s] one to reconstruct what the dominant culture regards as good, appropriate, and normal'.[31] All I'd add is that it does so even better when read alongside mainstream literature.

To illustrate this point, we're going to turn now to some scenes in a well-known, highly regarded satirical novel, and, by comparing them with the sickening phenomenon that's come to be known as RIP trolling, we'll hopefully see that literature can shed light on trolling – and conversely. Specifically, we'll be looking at what trolls call 'lulz'. This term designates a specific form of malicious laughter often said (by trolls and scholars alike) to underpin trolling. I'm hoping to demonstrate that the novel shows how the kind of lulz involved in RIP trolling were already in use in the 1940s – and if I'm right about this, it should simultaneously show that trolling gives us a clearer, better defined conceptual framework through which to understand the novel. What follows, then, is an attempt to show the symbiotic relationship between trolling and literature, by which I mean the light that each can shed on the other.

Lulz: From Evelyn Waugh to Sean Duffy

Well over fifty years before the launch of Facebook, Evelyn Waugh's satirical novel *The Loved One* (1948) was published. The targets of its biting ridicule are the tackiness of the American film industry and the tastelessness of the American funeral industry – disturbingly, Waugh shows us how the two resemble each other to an uncomfortable degree.

The protagonist, Dennis Barlow, is an English expat living in Los Angeles. Having failed as a poet in England, and been let go from his job as screenwriter (of a biopic about Shelley) in Hollywood, Dennis has taken a job at a pet cemetery. As he explains to a customer, part of the aftercare package is that 'every anniversary a card of remembrance is mailed without further charge. It reads: *Your little Arthur is thinking of you in heaven today and wagging his tail*'. The customer is suitably impressed: 'That's a very beautiful thought, Mr Barlow'.[32]

Dennis's exploits take him to Whispering Glades, probably the most luxurious and exclusive graveyard in the world (the 'Happy Resting Place

[30]Ibid.

[31]Ibid., p.7.

[32]Evelyn Waugh, *The Loved One* (Harmondsworth: Penguin, [1948] 1958), p.20.

of Countless Loved Ones', as it styles itself). There, he meets, falls in love with, and courts Aimée Thanatogenos, a young cosmetician to said deceased Loved Ones, before losing her to her colleague Mr Joyboy, senior mortician at Whispering Glades. Feeling torn between these two suitors, Aimée turns to an advice columnist for guidance, but the advice he gives (now that he's been fired and got drunk) is that she kill herself – which she does, by injecting herself with Joyboy's embalming fluid, in his workshop, the night before their nuptials.

Panicking – as well you might when 'you have the poisoned corpse of your fiancée in the ice-box'[33] – Joyboy turns to his rival for help. In exchange for Joyboy's life savings, with which he intends to rebuild a life back in England, Dennis agrees to cooperate: 'She disappears on the eve of her wedding. It is known that I once favoured her with my attentions,' so, he reasons, 'What could be more plausible than that her natural good taste should have triumphed at the last moment and she should have eloped with her earlier lover? All that is necessary is for me to disappear at the same time'.[34] He then proceeds to dispose of Aimée's body in the pet cemetery's crematorium, after reciting (plagiarized) love poetry over her corpse. Finally, 'he entered the office and made a note in the book kept there for that purpose. Tomorrow and on every anniversary … a postcard would go to Mr Joyboy: *Your little Aimée is wagging her tail in heaven to-night, thinking of you*'.[35]

I first encountered this novel many years ago, in the summer before I started university. My English teacher had recommended it as a perfect book for the vacation, a light-hearted read to make me laugh. (It still strikes me as a strange recommendation for this purpose.) I wasn't much taken with the sneering tone of Waugh's humour. But this final twist, skilfully stored up by Waugh till the very last page, made me – quite literally – Laugh Out Loud. Yet it disturbed me, too. I was laughing not in spite of, but *because of* the distastefulness of Dennis's final prank. In short, Evelyn Waugh, who was writing four decades before the internet age, and whom I read a full three years before I first used the World Wide Web, had made me realize – and I was and remain deeply troubled by this realization – what the attraction of so-called 'lulz' is, and with it, perhaps *the* central feature of trolling.

'There is only one legitimate reason to be trolling: For the lulz' – so the Urban Dictionary informs us.[36] Whitney Phillips goes so far as to claim that this is 'the most critical concept within the subcultural troll space', because 'behaviors that fail to generate and/or celebrate lulz do not qualify as

[33]Ibid., p.120.

[34]Ibid., p.125.

[35]Ibid., p.127.

[36]Urban Dictionary, s.v. 'Trolling, 3 January 2014. Available at: https://www.urbandictionary.com/define.php?term=Trolling

trolling'.[37] Simply put, 'lulz' is an 'acute amusement in the face of someone else's distress, embarrassment, or rage'.[38] It is a form of laughter that 'celebrates the anguish of the laughed-at victim'.[39] In other words, it's 'similar to *Schadenfreude* ... but has much sharper teeth'.[40] Other researchers into the phenomenon of trolling concur, describing lulz as 'a concept virtually synonymous with sadistic pleasure'.[41] Hopefully, we'll be able to refine our understanding of this fundamental concept a bit further as we go along. For now, the point is that some scholars have claimed we need to understand the nature of this specific kind of laughter in order to understand trolling aright – a laughter, that is, that laughs all the louder when the source of humour is in poor taste, or when it causes offence, pain, humiliation, indignation, even moral outrage. But this, I maintain, is precisely the kind of laughter my teenaged self found so troubling in Evelyn Waugh.

In *The Loved One*, Dennis Barlow hijacks a well-meant innovation in communications technology and uses it maliciously (and, in Waugh's eyes, *humorously*) to automatically send offensive messages about the deceased in order to torment the bereaved. As we're about to see, it's exactly the sort of thing trolls do 'for the lulz'. Let's be clear: Waugh isn't trolling. But he *is* describing it, and in a way that glamourizes it at that. Moreover, at least some of the novel's first readers ranked this 'lulzy' laughter among the foremost of Waugh's writerly gifts: 'Rarely in fiction have such execrably bad taste and such cruel wit been combined in one short satirical novel. Its humors are ghoulish and its hyena laughter snarls obscenely', opined the reviewer in the *New York Times* – before writing in the very next sentence that 'Mr Waugh has never written more brilliantly'.[42]

Some six decades after *The Loved One* came out, a British troll named Sean Duffy was jailed for eighteen weeks after pleading guilty to offences against the Malicious Communications Act. He too had hijacked a well-meant innovation in communications technology and used it maliciously to send offensive messages about the deceased in order to torment the bereaved. In 2011, this took the form not of a postcard, but of comments, images, and films uploaded to the walls of Facebook memorial pages. The deceased were invariably teenagers: fourteen-year-old epilepsy victim Lauren Drew, sixteen-year-old car crash victim Hayley Bates, fourteen-year-old stabbing victim

---

[37]Phillips, *This Is Why ...*, p.12; p.25.

[38]Ibid., p.57.

[39]Ibid., p.27.

[40]Ibid., p.24. For a very insightful discussion of the nature of 'lulz', see Chapter 2.

[41]Erin E. Buckels, Paul D. Trapnell, and Delroy L. Paulhus, 'Trolls Just Want to Have Fun', *Personality and Individual Differences*, vol. 67, 2014, pp.97–102, p.98.

[42]Orville Prescott, 'Books of the Times – *The Loved One* by Evelyn Waugh', *The New York Times*, 23 June 1948.

Jordan Cooper, sixteen-year-old gunshot victim Sophie Taylor, and fifteen-year-old Natasha MacBryde, who committed suicide under a train, possibly as a result of online bullying. Examples of Duffy's comments included 'Used car for sale, one useless owner' (relating to Hayley Bates) or 'I fell asleep on the track lolz' (relating to Natasha MacBryde). Additionally, he uploaded images, including photographs of the victims that he'd doctored by crossing out the eyes and adding stab wounds (for Jordan Cooper) or bullet holes (for Sophie Taylor). More elaborately, he created a video entitled 'Tasha the Tank Engine' by superimposing Natasha MacBryde's face over that of Thomas the Tank Engine. It's hard to imagine anyone actually laughing at any of this. But the British press tended to report Duffy's actions as 'mockery' – in other words, as attempts at lulzy humour.[43]

Sean Duffy was not an isolated case. The following year, in 2012, a twenty-one-year-old man from Burton-on-Trent, Staffordshire, was formally cautioned by Staffordshire police (meaning he got to remain anonymous) for similar behaviour. Within hours of the death of Jordan Agar – a local lad who'd died in a tragic accident the day after his sixteenth birthday – this man had set up a fake Facebook tribute page and posted comments on it addressed to Jordan's grieving mother, purporting to be from her son. They included 'Mum I'm not really dead. I'm sat at the computer, I just ran away', and 'I've gone to hell'. This incident and the Duffy case gained much publicity, including parliamentary debates about trolling. They were, it's fair to say, the tip of an iceberg.

In her history of trolling, Whitney Phillips points to 24/25 February 2010 as some sort of watershed moment.[44] Two high-profile deaths which happened within hours of each other in the United States (those of Dawn Brancheau, killed in front of an audience at SeaWorld Orlando while performing with a trained orca, and Chelsea King, a sixteen year old from San Diego who disappeared while jogging and whose raped and murdered body was found a few days later) gave rise to large-scale outpourings of online grief, which were deliberately targeted by considerable numbers of trolls. The depravity of much of the content they posted does not bear repeating: suffice to say that it ranged from setting up a Facebook page entitled 'I Bet This Pickle Can Get More Fans Than Chelsea King' (as a rival to 'Chelsea's Light', a Facebook page set up to rally support in the search for the missing girl), on the one hand, to bestial pornography suggesting a sexual

[43]See, *inter alia*, 'Internet Troll Jailed After Mocking Deaths of Teenagers', *Guardian*, 13 September 2011; 'Internet "Troll" Jailed For Mocking Dead Teenagers on Facebook', *Telegraph*, 14 September 2011; 'Jailed for Online Abuse: Man Who Mocked Child Suicide Tributes', *Independent*, 14 September 2011.

[44]See Chapter 5 of Phillips's *This Is Why* ...: 'LOLing at Tragedy: Facebook Trolls, Memorial Pages, and the Business of Mass-Mediated Disaster Narratives'.

relationship between Dawn Brancheau and Tilikum the whale, on the other. The trolling of memorial pages on Facebook – RIP trolling for short – had become an overnight phenomenon.

How can we begin to explain such a bizarre and appalling thing? What would possess a human being to behave this way? Simplistically, it's as visceral an illustration of the vicious nature of 'lulz' as you could hope to find and demonstrates 'that the pursuit of lulz is, at the most basic level, objectifying. The trolls' targets aren't ends unto themselves, they're fetishized pawns in the trolls' game'.[45] But Phillips argues that the way mainstream media handled these incidents is arguably no less objectifying, quite possibly as fetishistic, and morally flawed in its own ways. Consider the subject matter: almost all the deceased were 'cute dead white girls', as Phillips calls them.[46] Three days before Chelsea King vanished, a teenage African American high school student named Jalesa Chantell Reynolds went missing in North Carolina (she remains unaccounted for at the time of writing, over ten years later). American TV news stations not only fixated on the search for pretty, blonde Chelsea King minute by minute, but they also found time to cover the 'human interest' angle, including her grades in school, religious beliefs, and her hobbies and pastimes. They interviewed her family and her schoolfriends and even covered the impact of the RIP trolls' antics. But they gave scarcely a mention to Jalesa Reynolds, not even once the search for Chelsea King had become a murder enquiry – while the search for Jalesa Reynolds was ongoing and hopes of finding her alive were beginning to dwindle.

Or take the case of Natasha MacBryde in England. Like King, MacBryde came from a middle-class background (some newspapers pointed out she went to a fee-paying grammar school) and was a conventionally pretty blonde girl. Is the suicide of a girl with 'so much to live for' more newsworthy than another death? For Phillips, this is no empty philosophical question. That's because there is a clear and proven link between reportage of suicide in the media and rises in suicide rates, especially among teenagers, and the broader and deeper the coverage, the higher the rise in suicide rates.[47] In other words, it's easily demonstrable that mainstream media coverage of the

---

[45]Ibid., p.36.

[46]Ibid., p.84.

[47]She cites a report into the phenomenon of 'copycat suicide' by the American Foundation for the Prevention of Suicide, which adduced over fifty scientific studies (some published in organs as reputable as the *New England Journal of Medicine*), and which was endorsed by (among others) the Annenberg Public Policy Center, the Centers for Disease Control and Prevention, and the UCLA School of Public Health. It gives recommendations to news organizations on responsible coverage of such stories, which, Phillips argues, are routinely and irresponsibly ignored. See Phillips, *This Is Why ...*, p.90.

Natasha MacBryde tragedy was likely to result in more copycat tragedies – and whilst there's no proof that a spoof Thomas the Tank Engine video mocking the deceased might deter future suicides, at least it is unlikely to encourage them. Moreover, Phillips remarks, whereas mainstream news organizations made a great deal of money from their sensationalist and irresponsible coverage of the MacBryde and King tragedies, trolls such as Sean Duffy don't actually profiteer from the misery of others. Yet the former was regarded as trustworthy, reputable journalism, while the latter was prosecuted and jailed. Hence, Phillips argues, trolling can show us a great deal that is wrong in our media, in our society, and in our values.

I'm uncomfortable with this conclusion. Partly, it seems to be one-sided (trolls routinely urge their victims to commit suicide, and quite graphically and explicitly at that), and partly, it smacks of a questionable moral equivalence (two wrongs don't make a right, as we tell our children). On top of that, Phillips herself is wary of ascribing simplistic political motives to the bizarre deeds of trolls:

> Just as it would be a mistake to dismiss participating trolls' behaviors as politically meaningless, the impulse to posit clear political meaning is similarly misguided.... [T]here is far too much variation within the behavioral category of trolling ... to affix any singular, unified purpose to constituent trolls' actions. Furthermore, the assertion that a given act of trolling is inherently political, or even politically motivated, suggests that a specific argument or politics is the trolls' intended outcome. Given trolls' anonymity, this assumption simply isn't verifiable. Of course this doesn't mean that specific instances of trolling can't be political, or that individual trolls can't be politically motivated. It just means that outside observers can't be sure if and when it happens. Whether or not trolls deliberately forward political or cultural critiques, however, political or cultural critiques can be extrapolated from the trolls' behaviors.[48]

Thus, much as we might like to conveniently explain RIP trolling away as an ideological critique of the likes of Fox News and the *Daily Mail* – our society's self-appointed 'tragedy merchants'[49] – doing so would be wishful thinking. Nevertheless, Phillips is probably right that RIP trolling reveals a great deal about our attitudes to death, grief, and mourning. And this, I maintain, is why it's worthwhile to return to Evelyn Waugh's *The Loved One*, a novel precisely about how these attitudes have been infected by crass for-profit sentimentalism. It's a far cry from Waugh to Sean Duffy, no doubt. But how wide is the gulf between what Duffy did and what Dennis Barlow did?

---

[48]Ibid., pp.6–7.

[49]Ibid., p.83.

Writing in 1948, the idea of automatically sending condolence cards to people you've never met on the anniversary of their pets' death apparently seemed grotesque enough to justify the cruelty of Waugh's derisive laughter. Note that Dennis turns the impersonality of the system to his advantage: the secretary who mails the card will never know who Mr Joyboy is or who Aimée was and will probably assume she was a pet dog (literally, a bitch). Precisely because Mr Joyboy is senior mortician at Whispering Glades, he has turned the cloying sentimentality of mourning into gainful employment, and so, Waugh seems to imply, has no moral right to indignation when a cog in the funerary machine automatically reminds him that (in trollspeak) his dead bitch preferred killing herself to marrying him. Waugh's novel implicitly asks: so what if Dennis misuses an impersonal system to target his personal enemy, when that enemy has turned death into such an impersonal business? In some respects, admittedly, RIP trolls are the opposite of Dennis Barlow: they target people they've never met and don't know (the victims' families are usually strangers to RIP trolls) by misusing communication systems that are, for most people, deeply personal (i.e. social networks, such as Facebook). But the distress felt by those who receive the messages, and the lulzy laughs laughed by those who send them, are surely much the same, whether they're in 1948 or 2011.

To evidence this, compare Dennis Barlow's message – 'Your little Aimée is wagging her tail in heaven to-night, thinking of you' – to messages once automatically and impersonally sent to bereaved people *through social media itself*. For example, memorializing the dead online quickly migrated from MySpace to Facebook, partly because the open access nature of the former made it embarrassingly 'easily subject to spam robots promoting pornography or diet pills, which pop up in between the heartfelt messages of friends'.[50] Yet on Facebook, prior to late 2009, you couldn't deactivate your Loved Ones' accounts when they died. 'Consequently', writes Phillips, 'the deceased's profile would occasionally show up in friends' suggestion boxes ("Reconnect with Bill by posting something on his wall!")'.[51] Thus, the original senders of truly insensitive, impersonal messages to the grieving were not trolls, but social media companies.

Evelyn Waugh, I'd suggest, might have seen the funny side. Facebook, understandably, didn't. Instead, it enabled the ring-fencing of certain pages as designated memorial sites. The move was announced in a message entitled 'Memories of Friends Departed Endure on Facebook'. As can be

[50]Tony Walter et al., 'Does the Internet Change How We Die and Mourn? Overview and Analysis', *Omega*, vol. 64, no. 4, 2012, pp.275–302, p.291.

[51]Phillips, *This Is Why …*, p.72.

inferred from its title, it's replete with precisely the kind of commercialized mawkishness that Waugh takes aim at. For example:

> When someone leaves us, they don't leave our memories or our social network. To reflect that reality, we created the idea of 'memorialized' profiles as a place where people can save and share their memories of those who've passed.... As time passes, the sting of losing someone you care about also fades but it never goes away. I still visit my friend's memorialized profile to remember the good times we had and share them with our mutual friends.[52]

To quote Phillips once more, 'Facebook was deliberately positioning itself as a potential grief space.... In mid-February 2010, Lisa Miller of *Newsweek* praised these changes, arguing that "this is how we collectively mourn: Globally. Together. Online"'.[53] In Waugh's terms, Facebook had set itself up as a Happy Resting Place of Countless Loved Ones.

It was a popular development: expressions of grief and condolence quickly became a trendy new form of online activity. Many were written by complete strangers, as in 'the much-ridiculed statement "I didn't know you but I'm very sorry you're dead"'.[54] Just days after Lisa Miller's aforementioned article, vast numbers of people had used Facebook to express their feelings over Chelsea King: eighty thousand of them within three days of her disappearance. Almost all were strangers, who had never met her or her family: this wasn't grief. Phillips regards it as online grief tourism; I prefer to think of it as a lachrymose, apolitical form of virtue signalling. In any case, it is against this backdrop that we must view RIP trolling: virtually overnight, social media went from having sent (impersonally and automatically) hurtful and offensive messages to the dead and bereaved, to being *the* space where thousands would flock to commiserate with strangers about the deaths of other strangers they'd never known, and where sending hurtful and offensive messages to the dead and the bereaved had suddenly become a criminal offence. Thus, the few scholars who have studied RIP trolling (Phillips; Walter et al.) suggest it's some kind of response to the travesty that passes for grief in the digital age, to the effrontery of social media companies in cashing in on it, and to the hypocrisy of society in embracing it. Well, perhaps.

---

[52]'Memories of Friends Departed Endure on Facebook', Facebook. Available at: https://www.facebook.com/notes/%20facebook/memories-of-friends-departed-endure-on-facebook/163091042130

[53]Phillips, *This Is Why* ..., pp.72–3.

[54]Ibid., p.84.

My question is: are we hypocrites if we laugh at Evelyn Waugh and condemn Sean Duffy? After all, there's plenty more in *The Loved One* that anticipates trolling. As I've already mentioned, goading their targets to suicide is a very common taunt amongst trolls: often, it's suggested (ironically, one hopes) as a solution to even the most mundane of everyday problems. But the goads get more vicious the moment the target seems vulnerable, especially if that target is female. The 2010 case of eleven-year-old Jessi Slaughter was a well-publicized instance, but the following comment, posted on the website of a research project investigating violence against women, is a fairly representative example: 'Bitch, please find the tallest skyscraper near you, and jump off it. You would be doing a great service to society'.[55] And what has this got to do with Evelyn Waugh? Well, Aimée Thanatogenos doesn't just kill herself because she's heartbroken at the turmoil in her love life. Nor are her reasons quite the same as Neoboule's, driven to suicide after the public calumnies and 'slut'-shamings Archilochus subjected her to. Aimée does it because she – an emotionally vulnerable female – has been goaded into it by a boorish, drunken, misogynistic man, who – like today's trolls – communicates with the public under a pseudonymous avatar (he styles himself 'Guru Brahmin' in his agony aunt-style newspaper column). Furthermore, Aimée is unable to detect any irony or drunkenness in his advice because, thanks to the latest communications technology, their conversation doesn't take place face to face, but impersonally, over the telephone. His exact words to her are 'I'll tell you what to do. Just take the elevator to the top floor. Find a nice window and jump out. That's what you can do',[56] before boasting to his male friends that 'I told her to take a high jump', and mocking her for her ridiculous surname. So not only does *The Loved One* anticipate RIP trolling, but the death itself resembles a cyberbullied suicide: a man Aimée has never met, and knows only by an alias, abuses the impersonal nature of communication technology to taunt her into suicide, and then brags about it. The *New York Times* called all this 'a macabre frolic filled with laughter' – so why wouldn't we describe Sean Duffy's work this way?

The obvious answer would be that Waugh is writing a novel: the objects of his baleful humour are fictional characters, not actually existing, emotionally vulnerable people. But this answer is suspiciously neat, and it's not quite true: the novel was, in fact, based on a real place (Forest Lawn Memorial Park, in Glendale, California), and real people are recognizably caricatured in it (cricketer-turned-actor Sir Charles Aubrey Smith is less than flatteringly depicted as Sir Ambrose Abercrombie, for instance). He, along with plenty of people working in film studios or funeral parlours, might well have felt

[55]F. Vera-Grey, '"Talk About a Cunt with Too Much Idle Time": Trolling Feminist Research', *Feminist Review*, vol. 115, no. 1, 2017, pp.61–78, p.71.

[56]Waugh, *The Loved One,* p.115.

stung or humiliated by Waugh. So let's look instead at how *The Loved One* works as a piece of writing.

How does Waugh get away with humour that's in such poor taste? Largely by making the targets of that humour seem even more repugnant. Consider how proud Aimée is of the fifty-dollar tip she gets from a widower who is thrilled that the body of his wife looks better and happier dead than it did alive, after Aimée has given the corpse a shampoo, blue rinse, and perm: 'I began to realize what a work of consolation it was', she says, in earnest.[57] Or the actress Baby Aaronson, who undergoes graphically described cosmetic surgery to relaunch her career as the smouldering Spanish starlet Juanita del Pablo, only to have to undergo even more of it, disfiguring her body further in order to reinvent herself as an Irish ingenue, to accord with the dictates of her film studio, Megalopolitan Pictures.[58] Simply put, Waugh depicts the media industry and the death industry as so grotesque that no blow Dennis can strike against them would be too low for the average reader: 'He has omitted no revolting detail ...', said the *New York Times*, 'of the false view of life which Mr Waugh finds so utterly repellent'. It was abundantly clear that his novel critiqued the pursuit of maudlin sentimentality for greed and profit: 'A deliberate effort to smother reality under trappings of irrelevant decoration and to distort values so that comfort, conformity and a perpetual adolescent euphoria pass for the only worthy goals arouses his nauseated contempt', the review put it, more wordily.

By the twenty-first century, online grieving has made this saccharin groupthink (or, better, groupfeel) even more pervasive, even more profitable, even more insincere. Did Sean Duffy simply fail to demonstrate this? But how could anyone fail to hit such an easy target? Or did he rather fail to make clear *what* point he was trying to make? Perhaps – but maybe 'fail' is the wrong word here: more likely he didn't even try. Take the 'Tasha the Tank Engine' video. Is this a calculated insult to the deceased or a jibe at Facebook's sick 'grief tourists'? Is its aim to taunt the grieving MacBryde family or rather the social media companies, who know their platforms play host both to gruesome content like this and to expressions of genuine anguish and sorrow, and who absurdly allow both to sit cheek by jowl? The problem is that it could be any, all, or none of the above. It could just as easily be some form of outlandish protest against the commodification of the Rev. Wilbert Awdry's *Thomas the Tank Engine* character into a merchandising brand – we can't tell. So it makes no sense to argue that, unlike the inappropriate spam that automatically popped up on MySpace memorial sites, Duffy's messages were intentionally hurtful: his video is so downright bizarre it's impossible to guess what the intention behind it was.

---

[57]Ibid., p.76.

[58]Ibid., pp.10–11.

Thus, whereas the *New York Times* ended its review of *The Loved One* with the lament that 'Evelyn Waugh, accomplished writer that he is, doesn't always know when to stop', we might conclude that Sean Duffy, a somewhat less accomplished writer, didn't know where to start.

Waugh's satire makes a clear point, though he takes it too far.[59] Lulz needn't have any point, nor even make a joke: from a troll's viewpoint, the laughable thing isn't just the video or images or comments; it also includes the moral uproar they caused in the press, and probably also the fact that, so many years on from such a small handful of thoughtless comments, they have merited inclusion in a book like this, alongside literature like Beowulf, Shakespeare, and Oscar Wilde – indeed, several pages of discussion at that. And perhaps this really is laughable. Thus, as Whitney Phillips explains:

> Lulz ... does not distinguish between friend and foe, and is as much enjoyed by the trolling spectator as by the active trolling agent. This makes lulz an extremely slippery term, one that implies active pursuit (lulz don't amass themselves, they have to be sought out), an object (the person, place or thing that has been designated as lulzy), and an aesthetic (that which marks a lulzy action or object as such).[60]

So, trolls like Duffy are both laughers-at and laughed-at; their trollings are inextricable from the mess they cause, yet nonetheless exist as distinct texts in their own right; and the trolls who laugh at antics like Duffy's could all be laughing at totally different things at once. Lulz are 'both plural and singular and passive and active and static and dynamic'.[61] And, as I hope I've begun to demonstrate, one of the best ways to understand trolls and their lulz is by reading them in comparison and contrast to the textual strategies we find in works of literature.

It's important to point out a basic methodological distinction between works of literature that *depict* instances of trolling (whether by describing it, portraying it, recounting it, etc.) and works of literature that arguably *constitute* instances of trolling. That is, some works, from *Beowulf* to Evelyn Waugh, include scenes that represent troll-like behaviours. They show it at work, rather than actually doing it. By contrast, Émile Zola's *J'Accuse*, for example, or Jonathan Swift's *A Modest Proposal,* or even Martin Luther's *Ninety-Five Theses* all actually deploy at least some of the tactics of today's trolls. Bluntly, they verge on trolling. They therefore reveal important things about what trolling is, and how it works.

---

[59]We'll unpack the difference between satire and trolling in a few chapters' time, with reference to the work of Jonathan Swift.

[60]Phillips, *This Is Why ...*, p.28.

[61]Ibid.

I hope, then, to have established what scientists call 'proof of concept' – that trolling predates the internet and can be found in various guises throughout a variety of literary texts over time. This done, we need to look closer and in more detail at what it is we're trying to study. It's time to refine what it is we mean by 'trolling', and explore some of the problems involved in trying to define it more precisely.

1

Trolling is …

Trolling and its definitions: What we (don't) know so far

Let's be clear from the outset: no one really knows what trolling is. We all seem to be bullishly confident in our ability to detect it – we feel we 'know it when we see it', as the saying goes. But (or, perhaps, therefore) we find it surprisingly difficult to spell out exactly what it consists in. Why is this?

Firstly, it's partly because trolling now occurs in a large (and increasing) number of different online environments, each of which brings a new context and imparts subtly different behavioural patterns. There's quite some difference, for example, between lambasting a celebrity through X (the platform formerly known as Twitter), and spreading misinformation by vandalizing a Wikipedia page.[1] Trolling has been studied in familiar spaces such as social networks,[2] or the online forums of newspapers and magazines,[3] yet it can also range from fairly inconsequential disruptions

---

[1]See Pnina Shachaf and Noriko Hara, 'Beyond Vandalism: Wikipedia Trolls', *Journal of Information Science*, vol. 36, no. 3, 2010, pp.357–70.

[2]See, for example, Jonathan Bishop, 'The Psychology of Trolling and Lurking: The Role of Defriending and Gamification for Increasing Participation in Online Communities Using Seductive Narratives', in Honglei Li (ed.), *Virtual Community Participation and Motivation: Cross-disciplinary Theories* (Hershey, PA: IGI Global, 2012), pp. 160–76.

[3]For newspaper forums, see Carlos Ruiz et al., 'Public Sphere 2.0? The Democratic Qualities of Citizen Debates in Online Newspapers', *International Journal of Press/Politics*, vol. 16, no. 4, 2011, pp.463–87. For magazine forums, see Amy Binns, 'DON'T FEED THE TROLLS! Managing Troublemakers in Magazines' Online Communities', *Journalism Practice*, vol. 6, no. 4, 2012, pp.547–62.

of online gaming[4] to disrupting more weighty matters, such as government e-petitions.[5] Simply put, the kind of trolling you'd find in a by-trolls-for-trolls space such as 4chan's notorious /b/ board, where porn and hate-speech-peppered outbursts can and do pass for everyday banter,[6] is a very different species of trolling from attempts to troll the online forum of a respectable, blue-blooded magazine such as *Horse and Hound*.[7] Thus, 'trolling is inherently contextual, since what constitutes trolling may vary across different sites',[8] and this is further complicated by 'the (ever-increasing) semantic scope of "trolling" as a term'.[9]

Secondly, scholars from a broad variety of academic backgrounds have tried to define trolling, and their different disciplines bring different perspectives to it. Just take the papers I've cited so far in this book. Their authors work on fields as diverse as linguistics (Claire Hardaker), psychology (Buckels, Trapnell and Paulhus), gender studies (Fiona Vera-Grey), journalism (Amy Binns), information science and management (Shachaf and Hara), political science (Shefali Virkar), philosophy (Rachel Barney), and cultural studies (Angela Nagle). On top of this, trolling is often regarded as a problem for computer science to solve.[10] Trolling has been studied through a great many different academic lenses (though, so far as I know, this is the first attempt at investigating it from the angle of literary history), and each brings with it a set of methodologies and terminologies, emphasizing different aspects of it. Sometimes, scholars who discuss trolling might even be talking about different things.

Thirdly, like most words, its meaning has changed over time. Jonathan Bishop, a leading authority on the subject, observes that 'Internet trolling as

---

[4]See Scott Thacker and Mark D. Griffiths, 'An Exploratory Study of Trolling in Online Video Gaming', *International Journal of Cyber Behavior, Psychology and Learning*, vol. 2, no. 4, 2012, pp.17–33.

[5]See Shefali Virkar, 'Trolls Just Want to Have Fun: Electronic Aggression within the Context of e-Participation and other Online Political Behaviour in the United Kingdom', *International Journal of E-Politics*, vol. 5, no. 4, 2014, pp.21–51.

[6]See Angela Nagle, *Kill All Normies: Online Culture Wars from 4chan and Tumblr to Trump and the Alt-Right* (Winchester: Zero Books, 2017).

[7]See Binns, 'DON'T FEED THE TROLLS!'.

[8]Angela Gracia B. Cruz, Yuri Seo, and Mathew Rex, 'Trolling in online communities: A practice-based theoretical perspective', *The Information Society*, vol. 34, no. 1, 2018, pp.15–26, p.21.

[9]Claire Hardaker, '"I Refuse to Respond to This Obvious Troll": An Overview of Responses to (Perceived) Trolling', *Corpora* vol. 10, no. 2, 2015, pp.201–29, p.224.

[10]See, for example, Paraskevas Tsantarliotis, Evaggelia Pitoura, and Panayiotis Tsaparas, 'Defining and Predicting Troll Vulnerability in Online Social Media', *Social Network Analysis and Mining*, vol. 7, no. 1, 2017, pp.1–15.

a term has evolved significantly in recent years'.[11] There are several reasons for this. For instance, the sheer number of different ways we misbehave online has ballooned as internet usage becomes more common and more sophisticated. Do we really know the difference between trolling and cyberbullying, for example? Are these two different things, or different aspects of the same thing? Is either or both of them distinct from or equivalent to cyberharassment? Is there a spectrum between these terms, or are they better defined in isolation from each other? No one really knows. One study confidently asserts that 'trolling has become equivalent with online harassment',[12] but others point out that cyberharassment involves repeatedly targeting a victim whose identity is usually known to the attacker – not so in the case of many trolls. Similarly, the term 'flaming', discussed in the next chapter, is sometimes used to describe particularly vitriolic or abusive exchanges online. It's not clear if this is a separate thing from trolling, or a subcategory of it, or if the two simply overlap to some degree. Even 'flaming' has been seen as an imprecise term: apparently, it's only flaming when you sound off in response to a provocation (although provocation, confusingly, is said to be a characteristic of trolling). If you fire off obscenities for no reason, that's what some people call 'e-bile'.[13]

The fact is that some of the characteristics that are said to define trolling simply don't differentiate it from other ways of misusing the internet. Shortly, we'll see that some scholars see intentionality as the key to trolling: trolling, they say, involves a malicious or aggressive intention. But so does doxing, for example (using the internet to circulate personal information about someone – typically address, phone number, workplace, etc. – often so as to intimidate them). So does hacking (breaching online security systems for malevolent ends). Whereas hacktivism (breaching online security systems in pursuit of social or political change) tends to be regarded as well-intentioned. Similarly, we're about to see other scholars arguing that trolling is defined by its deceptive nature, but that by itself doesn't differentiate it from, say, catfishing (the use of a fictional online persona to manipulate or defraud someone). When a friend of mine once told me she'd been a victim of trolling, what she described was a distressing case of revenge porn. Clearly, a great deal of anguish and mayhem is triggered by these abuses of the internet – but are they really all cases of trolling?

---

[11]Jonathan Bishop, 'The Effect of Deindividuation of the Internet Troller on Criminal Procedure Implementation: An Interview with a Hater', *International Journal of Cyber Criminology*, vol. 7, no.1, 2013, pp.28–48, p.45.

[12]Tsantarliotis, Pitoura and Tsaparas, 'Defining and Predicting Troll Vulnerability', p.2.

[13]The term originated in Emma A. Jane, 'Flaming? What Flaming? The Pitfalls and Potentials of Researching Online Hostility', *Ethics and Information Technology*, vol. 17, no. 1, 2015, pp.65–87.

Though there's a bewildering array of misbehaviour on the internet these days, including serious criminal offences that involve sabotage, extortion, threats, stalking, and hate speech, not all of it is trolling. That's not to exculpate trolling in any way: as we'll see throughout this study, plenty of trolls have been prosecuted for their crimes, and rightly so. Trolling is emphatically *not* just harmless fun. But it seems to have taken on a range of meanings so broad as to verge on the incomprehensible. Even Jonathan Bishop struggles with how its meanings have changed over time. One of his papers, for example, states that '"trolling" once reflected the posting of provocative messages, whereas it has now been extended to cover the posting of offensive messages also',[14] while another has it that 'the term trolling has essentially gone from meaning provoking others for mutual enjoyment to meaning abusing others for only one's own enjoyment'.[15] Nevertheless, Bishop is right to argue that the reasons behind the massive upsurge in usages of the term are not (in the first instance) technologically driven:

> The term has been helpful for building the careers of politicians in search of causes to fight, as well as mass media organisations looking for a means to create a moral panic that provides both entertainment and interest to their audiences.... The way in which the word 'troll' has achieved the demon status of other transgressive terms like 'terrorist' shows the way in which the media manipulate and change the meanings of words for its own ends.[16]

Whitney Phillips agrees, adding that:

> the frequency with which aggressive online behaviors are *described* as trolling has only increased. According to the myriad reports on the issue, trolling is everywhere, and includes everything from harassing celebrities on Twitter to harassing people you know in real life to feminist political activism to child exploitation to being a 'total fucking dick' political pundit.[17]

One groundbreaking study expressed concern that '"trolling" has become a catch-all term for any number of negatively marked online behaviours' – and

---

[14]Bishop, 'The Effect of Deindividuation', p.28.

[15]Jonathan Bishop, 'Representations of "Trolls" in Mass Media Communication: A Review of Media-Texts and Moral Panics Relating to "Internet Trolling"', *International Journal of Web Based Communities*, vol. 10, no.1, 2014, pp.7–24, p.8.

[16]Ibid., p.7; p.11.

[17]Whitney Phillips, *This Is Why We Can't Have Nice Things: Mapping the Relationship Between Online Trolling and Mainstream Culture* (Cambridge, MA: MIT Press, 2015), p.154.

that was over a decade ago, before many of the moral panics described in Bishop's work had kicked off.[18] It's not surprising to read one self-confessed troll lamenting that 'now it's just an all-encompassing term for being an ass on the internet'.[19]

My problem with this line of argument isn't that it's wrong, exactly. It's rather that I'm sceptical whether there was ever a time when trolling implied a common purpose or *modus operandi*. This idea risks creating a bogus nostalgia for some phoney golden age when trolling supposedly 'meant something', whereas its most striking and disturbing characteristic is surely its sheer nihilism.[20] So it's likelier that what we're trying to define is actually a raft of dispersed, aimless actions. And evaluating this suggestion brings us round, eventually, to considering the key characteristics by which scholars have tried to define trolling.

Trolling defined by intention

To start with, there's the seemingly straightforward idea of intention. Long ago, a piece in the *New York Times* said that 'the word "troll" … denote[s] someone who *intentionally* disrupts online communities'.[21] Much academic research has concurred: 'Trolling in general is the posting of messages via a communications network that are *intended to* be provocative, offensive or menacing', claims one study.[22] Another defines it 'as the posting of incendiary comments *with the intent of* provoking others into conflict',[23] while the House of Lords Select Committee on Communications says trolling is '*intentional* disruption of an online forum, by causing offence or starting an argument'.[24] On these terms, then, the nature of trolling consists in the troll's frame of mind – in what they aim or plan to do when they set about trolling.

---

18 Claire Hardaker, 'Trolling in Asynchronous Computer-Mediated Communication: From User Discussions to Academic Definitions', *Journal of Politeness Research*, vol. 6, no. 2, 2010, pp.215–42, p.224.

19 Quoted in Phillips, *This Is Why …*, p.154.

20 See Nagle's excellent book *Kill All Normies*.

21 Mattathias Schwartz, 'The Trolls Among Us', *New York Times Magazine*, 3 August 2008. My emphasis.

22 Luis Gerardo Mojica, 'Modelling Trolling in Social Media Conversations', *arXiv*, 1612.05310, 2016. My emphasis.

23 Hardaker, 'Trolling in Asynchronous Computer-Mediated Communication', p.224. My emphasis.

24 House of Lords Select Committee on Communications, *Social Media and Criminal Offences*, 1st Report of Session 2014–15, p.7. My emphasis.

The trouble with all this is that it's seldom clear what trolls' intentions are, or whether they really have any in the first place. Recall the case of Sean Duffy. His macabre actions were so very odd – twisted, even – that it's hard to guess what he (thought he) was trying to do. Tellingly, at his trial, neither he nor his legal team offered any explanation or mitigation. Or consider the hacker who, under the Twitter handle @prom, took over the Cincinnati Zoo director's Twitter account in order to troll from it. Some context here: in May 2016, the Cincinnati Zoo was obliged to shoot dead a silverback gorilla named Harambe, to protect a three-year-old boy whose asinine parents didn't stop him from climbing into Harambe's enclosure. For some unknown reason, this rapidly became a *cause célèbre* amongst trolls. When the *New York Daily News* asked @prom why he had hacked the zoo director's account (some three months after the incident), and why he had simultaneously tweeted animal rights slogans from it alongside obscenities like #DicksOutForHarambe, he replied that he was 'not sure'.[25] So much for intentionality.

Any good literature student will tell you that the notion of the 'author's intention' is problematic to say the least. Certainly, if you wanted to define a literary genre, you wouldn't start by looking at authorial intentions. Take detective fiction, for instance. Detective fiction doesn't consist in the fact that people such as Sir Arthur Conan Doyle, Agatha Christie, or Raymond Chandler *intended* to write a certain kind of novel in which a sleuth decodes a series of clues to reveal whodunnit. Instead, it simply consists in the fact that the novels they wrote recognizably follow this pattern. That pattern is what makes it possible for a novelist to intend to write detective fiction in the first place – not the other way round. Wittgenstein once wrote that 'If the technique of the game of chess did not exist, I could not intend to play a game of chess'; similarly, if the techniques of detective fiction did not exist, we could not intend to write detective novels. And the same is true of trolling, since it too is a kind of writing. Explaining it through intentions is a non-starter: saying that trolling is defined by the intention to troll is saying nothing about what trolling really is.

One of the earliest definitions of trolling you'll find is in David Crystal's widely read book *Language and the Internet*, which came out back in 2001. He says trolling is:

> the sending of a message (a *troll*) specifically intended to cause irritation to others, such as the members of a chatgroup. It is an innocent-sounding

[25] Jason Silverstein, 'Harambe Hacker Takes Over Cincinnati Zoo Director's Twitter', *New York Daily News*, 21 August 2016. For more on the Harambe affair and its place in troll history, see Nagle, *Kill All Normies*, pp.5–7.

> question or statement, delivered deadpan, and usually short, though some trolls are verbose in their apparent cluelessness.[26]

This puts an interesting spin on the idea of intentionality: the troll is only innocent-*sounding* and only *apparently* clueless. Trolls, like wolves in sheep's clothing, conceal their true intentions. Thus, it's often claimed that the defining characteristic of trolling is deception.

Trolling defined by deception

Early definitions of trolling give a prominent place to the concept of deception. Its role seems slightly less pronounced in very recent research – which we might (with caution) interpret as corroborating Jonathan Bishop's point about the changing meanings of the word. Twenty-five years ago, in one of the trailblazing first academic studies of trolling, Judith Donath described it as 'a game about identity deception, albeit one that is played without the consent of most of the players'.[27] Trolls, for Donath, will first pose as genuine members of a community, in order to disrupt it from within. Another pioneering study by Claire Hardaker regards deception as one of four defining characteristics of trolling, and a more recent one by Marta Dynel goes further still, claiming it is one of 'two necessary conditions for trolling'.[28] She cites one of the arbiters of the contemporary online vernacular in support of her definition – the ever-helpful Urban Dictionary:

> Trolling does not mean just making rude remarks: Shouting swear words at someone doesn't count as trolling; it's just flaming, and isn't funny.… Trolling requires decieving [*sic*]; any trolling that doesn't involve decieving [*sic*] someone isn't trolling at all; it's just stupid. As such, your victim must not know that you are trolling; if he does, you are an unsuccesful [*sic*] troll.[29]

So, does this mean we have just defined trolling?

---

[26]David Crystal, *Language and the Internet*, 2nd edition (Cambridge: Cambridge University Press, 2006), p.56.

[27]Judith S. Donath, 'Identity and Deception in the Virtual Community', in *Communities in Cyberspace*, eds. Marc A. Smith and Peter Kollock (London: Routledge, 1998), pp.29–59, p.45.

[28]See Hardaker, 'Trolling in Asynchronous Computer-Mediated Communication', and Marta Dynel, '"Trolling Is Not Stupid": Internet Trolling as the Art of Deception Serving Entertainment', *Intercultural Pragmatics*, vol. 13, no. 3, 2016, pp.353–81, p.355.

[29]Urban Dictionary, s.v. 'Trolling', 3 January, 2014. Available at: https://www.urbandictionary.com/define.php?term=Trolling

Without a doubt, deception has played an important part in the history of trolling. Classically (if we can use this word of trolling without incongruity), a troll might, say, join the Facebook group of their local Green Party branch, and then, after 'liking' a few pro-environmental posts and signing a petition or two, post a question such as 'Could someone tell me if there is any actual proof for climate change?' To use a more literary example, imagine if, without mentioning that I teach English literature for a living, I wrote in a Royal Shakespeare Company forum: 'Hi. I've just read that Shakespeare wasn't who we think he is. Is this true?'. Time was when there'd be an explosion of replies within moments, some of them venting their frustration by SCREAMING THINGS AT ME IN CAPITAL LETTERS, others resorting to personal abuse out of sheer exasperation. More liberally minded forum users might then castigate these people, saying they should be educating and debating rather than ranting and swearing, and soon the initial question is buried under an avalanche of directionless argument – which, of course, the troll sits back and enjoys. But was I actually *deceiving* anyone by asking a (perfectly legitimate, after all) question about who Shakespeare was? Perhaps I was being disingenuous, but that's not quite the same thing. I didn't actively *pretend* to be clueless – I merely didn't reveal that I work in an English literature department and that, hence, I am well aware of how emotive and divisive this topic can be (which, as it happens, isn't something I'd normally mention in social settings, and so it's not as if I'd be exploiting the anonymous environment of the internet). Deception, then, is a strong word – perhaps too strong.[30]

To some extent, that's hair-splitting. The real problem with the idea of deception is that it calls into question the validity of a great deal of scholarly research into trolling. A sizeable proportion of academic studies of trolling base their findings, at least in part, on what trolls say about themselves – through interviews, questionnaires, and surveys. And yet trolls are said to be highly deceptive by their very nature. If they're deceptive, how can their questionnaires and interviews be credible? Just think for a moment about the psychologists who defined trolling as 'the practice of behaving in a deceptive, destructive, or disruptive manner ... on the Internet', and then (bizarrely) proceeded to use the internet to administer personality tests to over 1,200 people in order to build a psychological profile of the average troll.[31] Isn't this a bit like the (in)famous Cretan liar's paradox? Epimenides, an ancient Greek philosopher, reportedly observed that 'all Cretans are

[30]Dynel also comments that 'trolling is not the only manifestation of online deception facilitating the humorous entertainment of others on the Internet (e.g. films on YouTube which show some individuals being successfully deceived)' ('Trolling Is Not Stupid', p.374).

[31]See Erin E. Buckels, Paul D. Trapnell, and Delroy L. Paulhus, 'Trolls Just Want to Have Fun', *Personality and Individual Differences*, vol. 67, 2014, pp.97–102.

liars'. But Epimenides was himself from Crete. So if what he says is true, it must necessarily be false at the same time. Of course, the logical conundrum in play here isn't quite the same, but the point is that if we're saying trolls are deceptive, then we need to be cautious about how we interpret their behaviour – *including* the idea that they are deceptive. The better scholars in the field – Whitney Phillips, for instance – are well aware of this. It's a problem that verges on a paradox.

Trolling defined by its success

A similar sense of paradox surrounds another (so-called) defining characteristic of trolling. In Claire Hardaker's influential study from 2010, one of the main criteria for defining trolling is said to be its success. It might sound like a tautology to say that trolling has to succeed as trolling in order to count as trolling. But what's meant by this is usually one (or both) of two things. Trolling is considered successful when its targeted victims 'do not perceive an intent to troll and are provoked into responding as the troller desires'.[32] In other words, for my trolling to succeed, those hypothetical Shakespeare buffs need to think I really am that clueless and socially inept, and they need to be stung into an angry or exasperated response by my (apparent) clueless ineptitude. Pretty clearly, then, success consists in two separate things: firstly, trolling is 'deemed to be successful where it is not recognized by an online user as trolling',[33] while secondly, success in trolling also means 'to entice other online users into argument with success measured by the maximum number of responses received'.[34] Let's look at these notions of success in this order.

So, the key point about trolling, it's said, is that it succeeds only when and where trolls are 'assumed to be a genuine contributor of comments in the community whereas, in fact, [their] comments [are] a form of trolling transgression'.[35] This is helpful, to a degree. It helps flesh out why ideas of intention and deception are relevant, albeit in complicated ways, since 'successful trolls only very rarely reveal their goal'.[36] It also helps clarify how trolls can sometimes find themselves in the position of the laughed-at rather than the laugher-at, and hence explains some of the slipperiness of

---

[32]Hardaker, 'Trolling in Asynchronous Computer-Mediated Communication', p.224.

[33]Cruz, Seo, and Rex, 'Trolling in Online Communities', p.16.

[34]F. Vera-Grey, '"Talk About a Cunt with Too Much Idle Time": Trolling Feminist Research', *Feminist Review*, vol. 115, no. 1, 2017, pp.61–78, p.66.

[35]Cruz, Seo, and Rex, 'Trolling in Online Communities', p.22.

[36]Dynel, 'Trolling Is Not Stupid', p.360.

the concept of 'lulz', because if there is such a thing as successful trolling, then there must also be such a thing as failure, and for trolls, nothing is funnier than the so-called 'epic fail'. More precisely, failed trolls – trolls, that is, who are instantly recognized as such – are very quickly shown up as 'inept and incompetent, unable to properly rile the sophisticated members of the online community. They are not successful. As such, the troll is more amusing than aggravating'.[37] But once again, defining trolling in this way creates its problems.

To her credit, Claire Hardaker was wary of these problems from the outset. 'A strange irony of trolling research', she rightly notes, 'is that the most skilled, covert types of trollers will never be identified as such. They will always successfully evade or defend themselves against accusations of trolling, and will, therefore, appear to be just like any other sincere member' in any online community.[38] Rather like the ninjas of feudal Japan, the greatest trolls are those whose presence is never detected, or even suspected, in spite of the carnage they've wrought. Methodologically, this creates some pretty sizeable problems for scholars: imagine trying to study the invisible man when all you've got to analyse is his visible attributes.[39] Hardaker's research remains impressive nonetheless and is probably the most ambitious research into trolling to date. It's based on a vast corpus – 172 million words – of unmoderated discussion threads archived from Usenet, an early internet platform dating back to the 1980s, and its findings suggest that trolling online is almost as old as the internet itself. Yet the only way to try to identify trolling amidst this much data is to search through it for the characters TROLL* (the asterisk means the search will include variants like trolls, trolling, and trolled) – once you've found people complaining about trolling, you can start to look closer at what they're complaining about. Similar techniques are used by computer scientists developing algorithms to automatically detect instances of trolling: they, too, are triggered by the characters TROLL* (which, incidentally, could make it very hard for literary scholars to discuss the novels of Anthony Trollope online).[40] Hardaker sensibly sounds 'a cautionary note' about interpreting her results:

> Should a genuine troller successfully encourage many users to respond without anyone ever realising what she is about, then such an example will not have been captured by this search. This is because the search

[37]Bryn Alexander Coles and Melanie West, 'Trolling the Trolls: Online Forum Users Constructions of the Nature and Properties of Trolling', *Computers in Human Behavior*, vol. 60, 2016, pp.233–44, p.242.

[38]Hardaker, 'Trolling in Asynchronous Computer-Mediated Communication', p.205.

[39]H.G. Wells, let's not forget, shows us that this, though difficult, is not impossible.

[40]See, for example, Mojica, 'Modelling Trolling'.

looked purely for TROLL* and if this string or any of its variants did not occur in the thread, then the thread was not retrieved.[41]

But surely there's a more fundamental flaw than this: if trolls are defined by their success in avoiding detection as trolls, and if this methodology detects only those comments that have been called out as the work of trolls, then, by definition, the largest scale research into trolls yet carried out actually studies no trolls whatsoever. Though Hardaker's findings are fascinating, it seems pretty odd to argue that trolling isn't trolling if it's exposed as trolling whilst building an entire study on trolls who've been exposed – almost as if you wanted to study the behaviour of criminals who evade capture successfully and located their whereabouts using prison records. It's another methodological paradox: Schrödinger's troll, perhaps.

What about the other definition of successful trolling – the idea that it can be measured quantitatively, through the number of outraged replies provoked? At first blush, it seems quite commonsensical that 'If the responses to a post are few ... they are essentially a failed attempt at trolling since they did not generate any additional discussion'.[42] This explains why trolls are such desperate attention-seekers: if they don't get the attention they seek, they're not even proper trolls. Perhaps this is why 'Do Not Feed the Trolls' has become such a popular slogan: the only surefire way to thwart trolls is to ignore them.

But there are issues with this definition, too. No less commonsensically, pretty much everything we post on social media aims to get replies and responses. As Jonathan Bishop puts it:

> The term 'trolling' is now commonly used to describe the posting of any message designed to provoke a reaction. This has its difficulties. For instance, one might argue that most messages on Facebook, Twitter or Reddit are posted to get someone to respond to them or otherwise be provoked into reading them.[43]

There's also a problem in the opposite direction. If you're not a troll unless someone responds to your trolling, then someone who doesn't feed the trolls has, by definition, not actually been trolled. This doesn't seem right to me. For instance, one study mentioned in the last chapter describes how an academic set up a website to help recruit research subjects for a project investigating violence against women. The website was targeted by trolls, with sickening comments (some of which targeted vulnerable or abused women) such as

[41]Hardaker, 'Trolling in Asynchronous Computer-Mediated Communication', p.206.

[42]Tsantarliotis, Pitoura, and Tsaparas, 'Defining and Predicting Troll Vulnerability', p.6.

[43]Bishop, 'Representations of "Trolls"', p.45.

'What a cunt. Look, bitch, you can hate men all you want. I don't care, because you're obviously a sick cunt I wouldn't want anything to do with'.[44] It seems pretty clear that no reply is expected or desired here – the author of the comment 'wouldn't want anything to do with' the person he addressed it to. But it's trolling (of a sort) all the same. And even in the case of comments that are angling for a response, as in a taunt or goad, it doesn't seem right to say that their status as trolling depends on whether they get a reply. For instance: 'I see many narcistic [*sic*] and delusional womyn [*sic*] here who think that they are beautiful and entitled and should attract men "flies" [*sic*]'.[45] If you (very sensibly) decided not to dignify this pathetic outburst with a response, would that mean you hadn't been trolled? Would we want to say to the women who had received these appalling messages that, because they hadn't replied to them, they hadn't actually been subjected to trolling? To me, that sounds like invalidating their experience, or in layman's terms, fobbing them off. In sum: responding to trolling, though an important part of the dynamic of this kind of writing, doesn't simply define it.

Trolling defined by aggression

The bile directed at the research project just mentioned is a good example of another of the characteristics by which scholars have defined trolling: it's often said to be aggressive, malevolent, or malicious, by its very nature. Two of the earliest and most influential studies of trolling concurred on this point: Claire Hardaker argued that aggression is a defining feature of trolling and that it was essentially a malicious act; Judith Donath agrees it's malicious by nature and adds the claim that it's destructive, too. More recent researchers still operate under this assumption: the team of psychologists I mentioned earlier (Buckels, Trapnell, and Paulhus) describe trolling as destructive, while computer scientist Luis Gerardo Mojica describes it as malicious. Here, we seem to be getting a little closer to the heart of the matter.

It's not hard to see why these terms have been so important in trying to define trolling. Many of the trolls we'll meet in this book deal in death threats, racist abuse, and public humiliation as their stock in trade. When trolls team up to work together, the results can be even more terrifying, as the targeting of young Jessi Slaughter (just one of too many victims) showed. But they also show us that trolling is not as simple as aggression on the internet.

[44]Vera-Gray, '"Talk About ... "', p.71.

[45]Ibid.

Take the case of Bill O'Reilly, veteran right-wing Fox News broadcaster (until his dismissal in 2017, following revelations that he had paid tens of millions of dollars to settle multiple sexual harassment lawsuits quietly).[46] His website has been targeted more than once in any number of aggressive and malicious ways: it's been broken into, and the personal details of O'Reilly and many unfortunate visitors to his website were released publicly. This action is aggressive, malicious, malevolent, even threatening. But it's hacking, and doxing – *not* trolling. Late in 2009, however, his website was raided by trolls. This time, they bombarded the site with spam, consisting largely of cutesy pictures of cats, bunny rabbits, and ducks, as well as countless messages professing love and admiration for O'Reilly. The point was simply this: Fox News had labelled the trolling hotbed that is 4chan as an 'Internet Hate Machine' (quite accurately, let it be said), and O'Reilly had been especially vocal in calling for action against it. Realizing that to swamp O'Reilly with obscenities, threats, and abuse would only vindicate his position, the trolls took care to send him nothing that could be in any way construed as offensive or aggressive. They knew he would be made to look ridiculous for, as one troll put it, 'getting mad at kittens',[47] and they knew that the (perfectly true) allegations of hate speech made against them could most infuriatingly be countered by provocatively masquerading as the 'Internet Love Machine'. Denying O'Reilly the terms in which to frame his grievance was carefully calculated to inflame that grievance. Like previous hackers, they made use of O'Reilly's personal information – but this time, so as to have pizza delivered to his home address, as a gift.

The tactics are like those of many other trolling raids against many other hapless individuals. And some of these tactics are indeed aggressive: to make a targeted website crash under the weight of traffic; and to make your targets so angry they look ridiculous. And what, after all, is the purpose of pranking someone with pizza delivered to their home throughout the night? Is it really an innocuous gift ('Here, have a free dinner on me')? Or is it a threat (equivalent to saying 'We know where you live')? The conclusion to be drawn from this outlandish episode is that the *content* of trolling can be harmless and innocuous – and even though it seldom is, this strongly implies that it's something about the *act* of trolling rather than the subject matter that defines it.

Let's take another example. The iPhone 6 was released in September 2014. Within days, an advertisement went viral on social media – a pretty convincing-looking one, too, mocked up with Apple's logo and aping the 'look' of iPhone advertisements very closely. It explained that thanks to one of the innovative features of the latest iPhone iteration (the so-called 'wave-charge' function), the new iPhone 6 could be charged almost instantly

---

[46]For more on this, see Chapter 4 of Phillips's *This Is Why ...*

[47]Ibid., p.61.

by placing it in a microwave oven and giving it a few seconds at full blast. Years later, the internet is still awash with the carnage that followed – Apple users' chatrooms giving out stern warnings about this hoax, and threads responding to desperate pleas for help from people who had just fried an expensive, state-of-the-art piece of technology. The LAPD even tweeted a warning about it.

Yes, this was a destructive act: it certainly destroyed plenty of iPhones. But is it aggressive? Perhaps it's malevolent, but is it purely malicious? And if it is, are these things its primary characteristics? As an aside, a guilty confession: of all the instances of trolling described in this book, this is the only one I actually find genuinely funny. The new iPhone 6 retailed at around $649 on release, so a great deal of wanton destruction of expensive property was occasioned here. But if you were technologically clueless enough to think microwaving it a good idea, then why on earth shell out for such a costly piece of technology? (To draw an analogy: if someone struggled to read the flowing streams of consciousness in Joyce's *Ulysses*, why would they spend thousands on a rare first edition of it? Presumably, as nothing more than a vapid status symbol, like the latest iPhone.) Isn't there something ridiculous about being privileged enough to own something this costly, yet feckless enough to destroy it so unthinkingly? I'm not suggesting that the victims of this hoax deserved to lose their iPhones. But that's not to say they didn't perhaps deserve being made to look foolish. And in this respect, what we're dealing with might not be that different from a hoax or prank perpetrated in the 'real' – that is, the offline – world. So yes, trolling is aggressive, malevolent, malicious, destructive, but so are many of the practical jokes we play on one another. (Note that this doesn't make *either* practical jokes *or* trolling okay – it just shows the difficulty of trying to define what's unique to trolling.)

That there is an underlying aggression lurking beneath much of our everyday laughter is an uncomfortable truth, but it's one we've known for a long time: Freud made us confront it in his essay *Jokes and Their Relation to the Unconscious* in 1905. And it wasn't exactly news then. As long ago as the fourth-century BCE, in the dialogue *Philebus,* Plato's Socrates argued that laughter has a malicious heart at its centre, and that a 'curious mixture of pleasure and pain ... lies in the malice of amusement'.[48] The ancient Greeks, it seems, were no strangers to the idea of lulz. This moves us along, quite neatly, to another commonly diagnosed feature of trolling: apparently, it is 'aimed at amusing the individual partaking in it',[49] so that the word is 'generally used to describe online antagonism undertaken for amusement's sake'.[50]

[48]Plato, from 'Philebus', in *The Philosophy of Laughter and Humour*, ed. and trans. John Morreall (Albany: State University of New York Press, 1987), p.12.

[49]Cruz, Seo, and Rex, 'Trolling in Online Communities', p.17.

[50]Hardaker, "I Refuse to Respond ... ', p.202.

Trolling defined by amusement

There are obvious flaws to the idea of defining trolling in terms of amusement. Firstly, I receive jokes online from friends almost every day, and all of them are intended to amuse. A few of them even succeed. Secondly, we've already come across examples of trolling where it's hard to imagine what there is to laugh at, and I'm afraid there are more to come. Unlike trolling, the jokes I send and receive online are meant to amuse their targets. Trolling is different: 'Trolls may intend to amuse anybody but the targets'.[51] A joke that is funny to anyone except the person it's directed at seems like a curious concept, but once again, it shows a certain similarity between trolling and pranking. The aim is not so much to laugh at the joke as to laugh at the person targeted. Probably the classic trolling scenario involves a troll sending a message which they find somewhat amusing to a victim who, instead of finding it funny, is hoodwinked or (more commonly) offended by it and whose reaction the troll then finds highly amusing. 'Put simply', says Whitney Phillips, 'trolls laugh themselves into existence and sustain this existence through further laughter'.[52] So the idea of trolling as based on amusement or laughter makes a certain amount of sense, provided that it's clear we're talking about a sadistic, self-centred, lulzy kind of laughter, a laughter that is incomprehensible or even imperceptible to the mainstream internet user. 'This idea of self-entertainment seems to lie at the heart of the conceptualization of trolling', writes Marta Dynel.[53] But equally, of course, this makes it hard to use this concept as a yardstick for defining trolling, since doing so would involve understanding and accounting for the erratic and disturbing senses of humour that trolls seem to possess. Why it would be amusing to mock the untimely deaths of teenagers who died under tragic circumstances by defacing their photographs online is, I submit, beyond comprehension, but Sean Duffy seems to have found it so. Hence, if a definition of trolling has to wait on a definition of what is and isn't funny, then perhaps we had better move on.

Trolling defined by disruption or transgression

One last attempt at defining trolling, then. Many – but by no means all – of the scholars who study trolling have agreed that it 'can be seen as the broader term for attempts to wilfully disrupt online communities'.[54] The idea

[51]Dynel, 'Trolling Is Not Stupid', p.375.

[52]Phillips, *This Is Why ...*, p.31.

[53]Dynel, 'Trolling Is Not Stupid', p.372.

[54]Vera-Gray, '"Talk About ... "', p.66.

of trolling as a 'disruptive activity'[55] has been deemed important enough for Claire Hardaker to include it in her four defining characteristics of trolling; Buckels, Trapnell, and Paulhus included disruption in their top three. In a nutshell, 'a troll is a person who likes to disrupt stupid conversations on the Internet'.[56] The broad reach of this definition is broadened even further in some studies, by characterizing trolling as transgressive, that is, as 'transgressive messages designed to harm others for the sender's gratification and others' discomfort',[57] or, more concisely, as 'instances of transgression undertaken by antagonistic individuals'.[58] Cruz, Seo, and Rex go so far as to say: 'Given that transgression is the most obvious element of trolling, the definitions of trolling have centered on it'.[59] They also suggest that the notions of disruption and transgression are so similar that when describing trolling, these terms are interchangeable.[60]

Two of the best books you'll ever read about trolling are less than enthusiastic about the claims made for its transgressive nature. Whitney Phillips isn't convinced that trolling is as transgressive as we think, and more's the pity. She points out that the overt racism and misogyny of so much trolling isn't actually that far removed from the covert racism and misogyny of mainstream media outlets such as Fox News and the *Daily Mail*. The main differences she sees are that at least the overtness of trolling's bigotries has the virtue of honesty (if that's the right word for trolling), and that trolls aren't paid the multimillion dollar salaries drawn by some anchor men (and they usually are men) to peddle their no less reactionary views. Indeed, Phillips argues that the aggressive, devil-may-care individualism that underpins trolling, far from transgressing mainstream values, does the very opposite instead: 'trolling embodies precisely the values that are said to make America the greatest and most powerful nation on earth, with particular emphasis placed on the pursuit of life, liberty, and of course the freedom of expression'.[61] Her message is simple: if you don't like trolling, take a careful look at the culture that produces it. Angela Nagle has a similar viewpoint, and blames a culture of aggressive, brash individualism

---

[55]Dynel, 'Trolling Is Not Stupid', p.356.

[56]Phillips, *This Is Why …* p.1.

[57]Jonathan Bishop, 'The Art of Trolling Law Enforcement: a Review and Model for Implementing "Flame Trolling" Legislation Enacted in Great Britain (1981–2012)', *International Review of Law, Computers & Technology*, vol. 27, no. 3, 2013, pp.301–18, p.305.

[58]Cruz, Seo, and Rex, 'Trolling in Online Communities', p.15.

[59]Ibid., p.23.

[60]'Previous studies have largely focussed on trolling as discrete outbursts of disruption (i.e., transgression)'. Ibid., p.21.

[61]Phillips, *This Is Why …*, p.8.

too, but for her, this has to do with a tradition that unthinkingly celebrates transgression in the arts as an implicit challenge to social and moral norms. It's a tradition stretching from the Marquis de Sade through the Romantics to the avant-garde movements of the early twentieth century, before going mainstream in the sex, drugs, and rock-n-roll hedonism of the 1960s counterculture. She has harsh words to say about 'the utterly empty and fraudulent ideas of countercultural transgression that created the void into which anything can flow as long as it is contemptuous of mainstream values and tastes'. She argues, bitingly but not unreasonably, that 'When we've reached a point where the idea of being edgy/countercultural/transgressive can place fascists in a position of moral superiority to regular people, we may seriously want to rethink the value of these stale and outworn countercultural ideas'.[62]

Irrespective, though, of whether a carefree, transgressive attitude is a good thing or a bad thing, let's just ask: does it help us define trolling? To an extent, perhaps. But transgression isn't new, and it isn't unique to trolling – it's not as if we suddenly discovered the thrill of transgression when Sir Tim Berners-Lee invented the web. Angela Nagle is absolutely right to point out that writers have made their names by being transgressive for over two centuries. And the thing about transgression is that it seems to imply a set of norms or conventions or rules or laws that we can transgress. While this is certainly true of many online spaces (think of Wikipedia, with its clear guidelines for editors), the fact is there are plenty of others that are much less regulated, where etiquette and protocol are still in the emergent stage, and so there are many online contexts where we might need to ask: transgressive of what? Or, transgressive as opposed to what? A similar issue is raised with the notion of disruption. To my ear, the idea of disruption sounds as if something or someone came along and disrupted the state of affairs, which in turn seems to imply there was something like a 'normal' state – an equilibrium or a harmony, maybe – that existed beforehand. Does this normal, harmonious, undisrupted state of affairs really exist throughout most of the interactive spaces of today's online world, as the internet's default position? Plainly not.

What this means is that attempts to define trolling in terms of disruption or transgression lead to definitions so broad they verge on the useless. We end up saying things such as 'Trolling describes a range of antisocial online behaviors that aim at disrupting the normal operation of online social networks and media',[63] by which we really mean something like 'trolling behavior in discussion communities [is] defined ... as behavior that falls

---

[62]Nagle, *Kill All Normies*, p.105; p.108.

[63]Tsantarliotis, Pitoura, and Tsaparas, 'Defining and Predicting Troll Vulnerability', p.1.

outside acceptable bounds defined by those communities'.[64] Really, we might as well agree with that plaintive troll who grumbled that 'now it's just an all-encompassing term for being an ass on the internet'.[65]

But at least now we can figure out *why* we can't define trolling. If trolling is about breaking the rules and unsettling the norms of online communities, then, fairly obviously, it needs to be understood in relation to the rules and norms of those communities. More precisely, as Cruz, Seo, and Rex have argued, 'The ways in which trolling behavior is expressed and received is dependent on the dynamics of the specific community in which it is enacted'.[66] And that's the problem. Different online communities have different rules and norms, so 'what constitutes trolling may vary across different sites'.[67] On top of that, those rules and norms are changing all the time, so 'what constitutes trolling in online communities is not static. Instead, it evolves'.[68] And the biggest factor driving this evolution is probably the actions of trolls themselves: to continue trolling, they either need to find ever new, more creative means of deceiving their targets (remember Robert Nobbes's old fish, which grows wary of trolling after having been taken in by it), or ever more shocking ways of being offensive. It's not surprising, then, that one recent study of trolling concludes: 'From this analysis, it can be seen that neither the category "troll" nor the action of "trolling" has a single, fixed meaning'.[69]

Does it matter if we can't define trolling?

Where do we go from here? The direction Jonathan Bishop takes is to admit that trolling is a term with numerous meanings, in order to then try to enumerate them. He identifies, categorizes, and defines an array of different types of troll that is truly incredible in its breadth. There are, for example, Haters, E-vengers, SNERTs, Elders, Lolcows, Rippers, Bzzzzters, Lurkers, Flirts, Eyeballs, the Chatroom Bob, and the MHBFY Jenny (the acronym stands for My Heart Bleeds for You).[70] Much as I admire the linguistic

[64]Justin Cheng et al., 'Anyone Can Become a Troll: Causes of Trolling Behavior in Online Discussions', *Proceedings of the 2017 ACM Conference on Computer Supported Cooperative Work and Social Computing*, 2017, pp. 1217–230, p.1217.

[65]Quoted in Phillips, *This Is Why ...*, p.154.

[66]Cruz, Seo, and Rex, 'Trolling in Online Communities', p.17.

[67]Ibid., p.21.

[68]Ibid., p.18.

[69]Coles and West, 'Trolling the Trolls', p.243.

[70]For details, see Bishop, 'Representations of "Trolls"', pp.11–12.

exuberance here, and the sheer creative verve behind all this terminology, I can't help thinking the whole enterprise is misguided. Given what's just been said by Cruz, Seo, and Rex about 'the context dependency of trolling',[71] and how its meanings change over time, it seems likely that trying to define a dozen different types of troll will prove a dozen times harder than defining trolling. Take the SNERT: there are at least two different versions of what this acronym stands for. Depending on which source you consult (Wiktionary or Urban Dictionary, for instance), it could either mean 'Snot-Nosed Egotistical Rude Teen' or 'Sexually Nerdish Egotistically Repressed Troll'. This discrepancy doesn't inspire confidence in the categories Bishop is trying to define.

A more sensible approach, or so it seems to me, would be to accept and even embrace the fact that trolling is so hard to define. 'Trolling is' – and, I would add, ought to be – 'an inclusive term',[72] because trolling itself consists of 'a spectrum of behaviors',[73] and indeed 'there are multiple "grey areas"' between them as we move along the spectrum.[74] This needn't be a problem, provided we're clear that, as one researcher wisely put it, 'what has come to be called trolling should be taken as a starting point rather than a vague end point for understanding'.[75] In other words, surely it's better to leave open exactly what we mean by trolling, so that we don't shut ourselves off in advance to things that we've already decided, before we've even started to study them, can be safely ignored because they don't quite coincide with whatever strict sense of the term we've assigned to it. This way, maybe, in the course of studying trolling, we might end up broadening *as well as* sharpening our understanding of it, which is seldom a bad thing.

The more scientifically minded might object that, as Marta Dynel puts it, the term 'trolling' shouldn't 'be used as a capture-all term for a whole gamut of online behaviors'.[76] Leading the charge in favour of rigorous and precise definitions, she feels that 'academics must make clear distinctions' if they are to 'capture the underlying phenomena' they're studying, and this goes for trolling, too.[77] Accordingly, she is not best pleased that 'the label "trolling" tends to be (mis)used in reference to communicative practices

[71]Cruz, Seo, and Rex, 'Trolling in online communities', p.15.

[72]Tsantarliotis, Pitoura, and Tsaparas, 'Defining and Predicting Troll Vulnerability', p.1.

[73]Phillips, *This Is Why ...*, p.23.

[74]Cruz, Seo, and Rex, 'Trolling in Online Communities', p.17.

[75]Anthony McCosker, 'Trolling as Provocation: YouTube's Agonistic Publics', *Convergence: the International Journal of Research into New Media Technologies*, vol. 20, no. 2, 2014, pp.201–17, p.202.

[76]Dynel, 'Trolling Is Not Stupid', p.358.

[77]Ibid., p.354.

which are not trolling in the traditional sense'.[78] Convinced that trolling is defined by humour and deception – specifically, by humour arising from deception – she insists that anything that doesn't meet this definition is 'only being arbitrarily called "trolling" by individual Internet users'.[79] Basically, Dynel seems to think that if you don't accept her definition, you don't know what trolling is, and you're only muddying the waters by using the term inaccurately:

> the label 'trolling' is frequently overused and abused, because journalists, lay Internet users, and even researchers not preoccupied with trolling tend to base their understandings on their intuitions and/or isolated examples.... Also, Internet users tend to (mis)apply the term 'trolling' to ... all manner of aggressive and/or antisocial behaviors, some of which are properly termed flaming, e-bile, heckling or cyberbullying, among others.[80]

Up to a point, I can understand her frustration. Dynel, a linguist by trade, presumably thinks that words should mean what they say, and not whatever we think they mean, or want them to mean. But, of course, words mean what they mean because of the way that lay users use them, and that changes over time. It's widely held to be a good thing, a sign of the health of a language and a culture that's open to taking on new meanings. By contrast, Dynel's way of thinking is analogous to that of an art critic who insists that, in discussions of contemporary painting, 'gay' should retain its original meaning of brightly coloured, and 'black' shouldn't be used to designate people's race. Since the way we use words such as 'troll' and 'trolling' adapts to new contexts, the way we study and debate those words surely needs to adapt with it.

Dynel's position is roughly the opposite of mine. I hate to think what she'd make of this book: she thinks that 'offline interactions should not be (retroactively) termed "trolling"' – which is basically what I'm doing in each chapter – because, predictably, the term 'had better be reserved for the specific deceptive practices on the Internet'.[81] And yet we shouldn't dismiss her underlying desire to pin down a clear working definition of trolling. If for no other reason, we need to be able to say what trolling is as lucidly and tidily as possible because sometimes it can, does, and will lead to criminal proceedings against the offending troll. In these legal contexts, a clear idea of what trolling is becomes imperative, because we need to be able to say

---

[78]Ibid., p.353.

[79]Ibid., p.354.

[80]Ibid., pp.353–54.

[81]Ibid., p.374.

with exactitude which laws have or haven't been broken. And this points towards another flaw in Dynel's academic posturing: if the definition of what constitutes trolling parts company with the way the term is used in ordinary parlance, then how do lawmakers and law-enforcers go about tackling it?

And so, with all this in mind, let me spell out, at long last, a preliminary definition of what I take trolling to be in this book. I should stress that this definition is deliberately broad, open, and, above all, preliminary: perhaps it's more of a working hypothesis than a definition. Hopefully, we can improve upon it by tweaking it as we go along. Note also that this definition avoids any mention of the internet, or any other form of electronic communication: it is based on linguistic behaviours, and though they are common on the internet and on social media, they can also be found in writings penned centuries before these were invented. Here goes:

> *Trolling is to defame, insult, or humiliate an opponent in public, or else to make a public statement of views that are not sincerely held, but aim instead to cause controversy, or to be provocative and vexatious, sometimes with legal consequences.*

Each of the chapters that follows breaks my definition down into one of its constituent parts, so as to explore a different aspect of the literary ancestry of trolling in every chapter. So if you need to refer back to this definition later on, just turn back to the contents page.

Trolling through literature: Lord Byron as literary troll

Like so many things, then, trolling is easier to identify in practice than to define in theory. Sometimes it's tempting simply to echo what Saint Augustine famously said about the nature of time: *Si nemo ex me quaerat scio; si quaerenti explicare velim, nescio* – 'if no one asks it of me, I know what it is; if I want to explain it to someone who asks, I don't know'. This being so, it's high time we turned to some actual instances of literary trolling. Earlier, I drew a distinction between literature that represents or depicts acts of trolling (as in Evelyn Waugh) and literature that actually engages in trolling. As a perfect specimen of the latter, I now adduce a writer whose works tick, in one way or another, almost all the boxes in my preliminary definition of trolling: Lord Byron.

Byron's poetry is forever insulting, humiliating, and even defaming other people – real people, with reputations to bruise and feelings to hurt. He did so very publicly. Occasionally, he used his art to humiliate his ex-lovers – as in the celebrated short poem 'Remember Thee', which he wrote to Lady Caroline Lamb – although thankfully, unlike Archilochus, he abstained from 'slut'-shaming by not mentioning her by name. Top of his hit list, though, were fellow writers, especially those he saw as part of the literary establishment. Thus, he dealt in provocation and controversy. In terms of the foregoing discussions, it is plain to see that from the early stages of Byron's career, he set out to be aggressive towards the most prominent poets and publishers of his day; that he did so in order to be transgressive and disruptive; that his main aim was to amuse his readers at his targets' expense; that he did all this intentionally (as opposed, say, to his readers merely inferring it); and that those intentions were successfully carried into fruition.

In 1807, the 19-year-old Lord Byron was sent reeling by the *Edinburgh Review*'s hatchet-job criticisms of his first poetry collection, *Hours of Idleness*. His response – *English Bards and Scotch Reviewers* (1809) – was a poem lambasting writers whose works had found favour with the *Edinburgh Review*. In it, for example, Robert Southey (who would be appointed poet laureate just four years later) is derided as 'the ballad-monger Southey', and Byron basically tells him to shut up:[82]

Oh! Southey! Southey! cease they varied song!
A bard may chant too often and too long …
But if, in spite of all the world can say,
Thou still wilt verseward plod thy weary way …
The babe unborn thy dread intent may rue:
'God help thee', Southey, and thy readers too. (L.225–34)

Next on Byron's list is the literary titan of British romanticism, here dismissed as:

The simple Wordsworth …
Who, both by precept and example shows
That prose is verse, and verse is merely prose;
Convincing all, by demonstration plain,
Poetic souls delight in prose insane; …
Yet let them not to vulgar Wordsworth stoop,
The meanest object of the lowly group,
Whose verse, of all but childish prattle void,
Seems blessed harmony to Lamb and Lloyd. (L.237–43; 903–06)

---

[82]Quotations are from Lord Byron, *The Poetical Works of Lord Byron* (London: Oxford University Press, 1966).

This is followed by a swipe at Wordsworth's 'brother Coleridge':

Shall gentle Coleridge pass unnoticed here,
To turgid ode and tumid stanza dear? …
Yet none in lofty numbers can surpass
The bard who soars to elegise an ass.
So well the subject suits his noble mind,
He brays the laureat of the long-ear'd kind. (L.255–64)

Not content with slating all the major poets of his day, Byron turns his attention to novelists such as Matthew Lewis and Sir Walter Scott ('And think'st thou, Scott! By vain conceit perchance / On public taste to foist thy stale romance?' [L.171–72]), as well as a whole smorgasbord of other writers whose names are less well known today. 'Still must I hear? – shall hoarse Fitzgerald bawl / His creaking couplets in a tavern hall?' (L.1–2); 'Bowles! in thy memory let this precept dwell, / Stick to thy sonnets, man! – at least they sell' (L.361–62); 'No muse will cheer, with renovating smile, / The paralytic puling of Carlisle' (L.725–26). This acerbic tone still evokes winces from its readers today, but also, here and there, a smile or two. It's not just that Byron combines laughter and cruelty that makes him a troll, or even that he gets our laughter from his cruelty, as in lulz. Throughout the poem, Byron uses a range of strategies to position his voice that pre-empt those of trolling uncannily.

The first of these is to heap scorn on the mainstream and on public taste. Thus, like many a troll, Byron sets himself up as the voice of transgression:

What varied wonders … make the vulgar stare
Till the swoln bubble bursts – and all is air! …
O'er taste awhile these pseudo-bards prevail;
Each country book-club bows the knee to Baal,
And, hurling lawful genius from the throne,
Erects a shrine and idol of its own;
Some leaden calf – but whom it matters not,
From soaring Southey to grovelling Scott …
Sonnets on sonnets crowd, and ode on ode;
And tales of terror jostle on the road. (L.131–42)

It's an effective strategy: if you're taken with Byron's daring irreverence, you've given him license to hurl abuse and insult at his rivals, but if you're not, you've placed yourself on the side of the 'vulgar' and the 'crowd'. Byron then executes another manoeuvre from the classic troll's repertoire: he says that he's only stating what everyone else is thinking, but no one is courageous enough to say out loud: 'I've learn'd to think, and sternly speak the truth', he says (L.1058). Compare this with how some of today's trolls justify the abuse they mete out: having traduced refugees as terrorists or immigrants as rapists, for example, they'll claim that they're 'challenging political correctness' or such like, instead of admitting they've written baseless calumnies. Defending what's offensive by making a virtue out of defying orthodoxy is the very stuff of trolling, and Byron excels at it.

Furthermore, his preface also frames his poem in the terms trolls often use to frame their writings:

> An author's works are public property: he who purchases may judge, and publish his opinion if he pleases; and the authors I have endeavoured to commemorate may do by me as I have done by them. I dare say they will succeed better in condemning my scribblings, than in mending their own.[83]

This is the earliest literary airing I've come across of another familiar troll's defence: that those in the public realm should expect criticism, and that if they don't like these criticisms, they're free to exert their right to criticize in reply. Thus, Byron wields free speech as a carte blanche for abuse and insult, which presents the victim with the stark choice: respond in kind – thus dignifying the troll with a reply and lowering your tone to his level – or do not feed the trolls. Either way, the troll wins.

Byron's youth does not account for these brash outbursts: his fondness for insults and cheap gibes stayed with him throughout his career. The later *Don Juan* (1819–24) is suffused with the same scurrilous tone, and not even the dead are spared from it. Keats, whose early death from tuberculosis tragically cut short his brilliant career before his work had received public recognition, is subjected to treatment barely short of RIP trolling. Byron defames Keats by jibing that he had died because he lacked Byron's hard-nosed resilience to bad reviews: 'John Keats ... was killed off by one critique .../ 'Tis strange the mind, that very fiery particle, / Should let itself be snuffed out by an article'. Note how Byron briefly flirts with joining in the growing praise for Keats's work but instantly undermines the move (and the praise) with a snide dig – he says that Keats died 'Just as he really promised something great, / If not intelligible'. And all this from the man who wrote the line 'For noble spirits war not with the dead'. This was Byron's response to a right-wing newspaper's gloating poem that Charles James Fox, the great leader of the Whiggish faction, had passed away. Railing against the bias of mainstream media, he sent a reply admonishing this newspaper to 'let not canker'd Calumny assail' the memory of Fox with 'dastard tongues' – as if Byron was in a position to argue that poetry shouldn't speak ill of the dead.

---

[83]Ibid., p.113.

There's more to Byron's trolling than personal insults, though. His is the work of a thoroughgoing contrarian, whose writings were often calculated first and foremost to be controversial, provocative, even vexatious. Few anecdotes about him illustrate this more clearly than one that dates from his time studying at Cambridge, where the university's regulations prohibited students from keeping dogs in their rooms. Now Byron's love for his dog – a Newfoundland named Boatswain – was so great that later, while it was dying a horrific death from rabies, he nursed his dog himself, without any regard for his personal safety. Byron had a tomb built for Boatswain even larger than his own and composed a genuinely moving poem for the epitaph on it. So his reaction to being told he couldn't keep Boatswain in his rooms at Trinity College was to buy a pet bear and have that lodge with him instead. He took the bear for walks and treated it as much like a dog as possible. The college authorities were powerless to stop him. When a poem entitled 'Lord B – n to his Bear' appeared in the June 1808 edition of *The Satirist*, joking about the irony involved in a Lord so publicly opposed to slavery keeping a bear chained up in 'bondage' (which, like other lines in the poem, might also insinuate a bestial relationship), Byron's reply was even more contrarian: he showed he regarded the creature as an equal by declaring (in the postscript to *English Bards and Scotch Reviewers*) that this was 'a bear, kept by me at Cambridge to sit for a fellowship, and whom the jealousy of his Trinity contemporaries prevented from success'.[84] Maybe this isn't exactly trolling in its strictest sense. But it does at least demonstrate that Byron met all the criteria for trolling summarized earlier on: as well as being intentionally and successfully amusing in aggressive, transgressive, disruptive ways, he was also deceptive about it. Instead of admitting that his aim is to make the petty laws of Trinity College look ridiculous, he claims that his noble purpose is to educate the bear. Hence, Byron's words, far from dripping with heartfelt romantic sincerity, were instead aimed at provoking his readers. He had quite a gift for this.

The defining, epochal historical event of Byron's career was surely the Battle of Waterloo, fought on 18 June 1815. It put an end to the wars that had, for more than twenty years, shaken Europe from Madrid to Moscow. The victory jubilations throughout England that followed the news of victory were of a kind that would not be seen again until VE day in May 1945, some 130 years later. (Those that marked Armistice Day in November 1918 often had a muted, sombre character to them, probably owing to the unimaginable extent of the sacrifice it had taken to get there.) The Wordsworths and the Southeys celebrated, along with many local villagers, by climbing the mountain of Skiddaw, lighting a bonfire and dancing round it, roasting some beef, and hurling improvized fireworks down the mountainside while

[84]Ibid., p.127.

singing 'Rule Britannia' and 'God Save the King'. By contrast, Lord Byron greeted the news of Wellington's victory and Napoleon's defeat by saying out loud 'I am damned sorry for it'.

Writers joined hands across the political spectrum in lionizing the victorious British forces. For a dyed-in-the-wool Tory like Sir Walter Scott, it meant the rightful kings of Europe and their attendant aristocrats would be restored at last, and there would be no more carping about the Rights of Man. For first-generation romantics such as Wordsworth and Southey, who'd had to grow up and join the establishment, Napoleon was a convenient whipping boy: without losing any face, they could renounce the French revolution they'd embraced as idealistic young men by declaring that Napoleon had usurped the cause of liberty and gotten his due comeuppance. Thus, with a haste only slightly less indecent than that with which battlefield tourists swooped down on the trenches of Flanders a century later, writers of all stripes made a beeline for Waterloo, just weeks after the fighting ended.

Quickest off the mark was Sir Walter Scott, who began writing 'The Field of Waterloo' as early as August 1815. Though he sets out to praise the 'Heroes' who 'Fell thick as ripened grain' at 'Immortal WATERLOO!', the soldiers barely feature as a human presence in the poem at all. We know them by the parts Scott reduces them to: swords, bayonets, cannon, and horses. In defence they are 'ocean-rocks', in attack they are 'ocean's flood', but at no point are they individual human beings. Scott is more interested in gloating at Napoleon and berating him for retreating from the field, and in heaping praise that is little short of fawning on Wellington, 'his country's sword and shield'.

After Scott, Robert Southey, the poet laureate of the day, visited the site in October. In place of Scott's toadying, Southey's 'Poet's Pilgrimage to Waterloo' gives credit for the victory mostly to the soldiers, his 'brave countrymen' whom 'no fears could quail, no dangers could subdue'. More internationalist in his outlook than the flag-waving Scott, he also pays his fulsome respects to the soldiers of allied nations (such as 'The Portugals, in heart so near allied', and the 'True children of our sister Germany') for helping to defeat Napoleon over the long course of the wars. His highest tribute goes to Wellington, but where Scott praised him over many stanzas, Southey gives him a deft couplet, explaining 'how our great Commander's eagle eye / Which comprehended all, secured the victory'.

Plenty of other poets visited or wrote about Waterloo. Wordsworth penned two poems on the subject – one an 'Ode on the Morning of the Day Appointed for a General Thanksgiving: 18 January 1816', as his contribution to the national celebrations, and the other, 'After Visiting the Field of Waterloo', which he did five years later. Coleridge, Fitzgerald, and others also pitched in, and despite their many differences in approach and technique, all concurred that this was a great victory, born of valour, strength, and courage, and that Britain had safeguarded liberty from tyranny at the cost of no small sacrifice. The degree of consensus on the issue, and the strength of feeling behind it, are precisely what make for a perfect target for trolling.

Byron wrote about Waterloo in several places, paying tribute (controversially) to the dead of both sides. But in *Don Juan*, he's not so much writing as trolling:

That Briton must be bold who really durst
 Put to so much trial John Bull's partial patience,
As say that Wellington at Waterloo
Was beaten, – though the Prussians say so too; –

And that if Blücher, Bulow, and Gniesenau,
 And God knows who besides in 'au' and 'ow'
Had not come up in time to cast an awe
 Into the hearts of those who fought till now
As tigers combat with an empty craw,
 The Duke of Wellington had ceased to show
His orders, and also to receive his pensions;
Which are the heaviest that our history mentions.

But never mind; – 'God save the king!' and *kings*
 For if *he* don't, I doubt if *men* will longer –
I think I hear a little bird, who sings
 The people by and by will be the stronger.[85]

Everything Byron is claiming here – that Waterloo was no great victory, but instead a fiasco from which Wellington needed to be rescued by the Prussians; that the British Army's soldiers had no stomach for the fight until the battle had been won for them by Blücher; and that the whole thing was in vain since the unstoppable cause of revolution is still in the ascendancy – is said out of sheer contrarianism and is calculated to provoke and to inflame. That Byron knows he's being controversial to the point of vexatious is clear from the outset: you 'must be bold' to dare challenge the national(istic) consensus represented by 'John Bull'. Moreover, he contends that this consensus is biased ('partial'), and he presents himself as someone who's merely speaking a plain but unpalatable truth – a truth universally acknowledged in France and Prussia.

Hopefully I don't need to point out that these strategies anticipate what we now call trolling. So does the mocking tone, which, crucially, makes it impossible to tell whether Byron is joking or not. But does this tone come from his sneering derisively at the collective stupidity behind the myths of Waterloo (in which case he's being serious, despite the mocking tone) or

[85]Ibid., p.759.

does it rather suggest that Byron is merely, as we might say, having a laugh? It could be either. Thus, scornful mockery serves Byron as it serves most trolls: the key weapon in their armoury, but also their Get-Out-of-Jail-Free card – the claim that everything that's been said, however inflammatory, was said just for the fun.

It's worth looking more closely at how Byron's inflammatory humour works here. There are snide tauntings of his opponents (for example, the jibe that Wellington profited very nicely from his so-called victory). There are clever tactics that subtly wrongfoot his readers, even as they are drawn in (notice how to make the poem rhyme, you have to mispronounce 'Gniesenau', which looks at first like a cheap, xenophobic joke aimed at belittling the Prussians – until you realize that that is precisely how a 'John Bull' jingoist would likely pronounce it, so you can't tell if the joke is on the Little Englanders instead. Perhaps the ambiguity is the real joke, and it's at the reader's expense). And, after having shaken up a wasp's nest, there's a characteristically disingenuous shrugging of the shoulders at the end ('But never mind'), implying that anyway, the argument isn't worth pursuing. This is a move rhetorically designed to make his infuriated readers want to pursue it, and not least because the reasons he gives for walking away from the issue – that revolution is inexorable and monarchy doomed, so further debate is pointless – are practically guaranteed to incense them further.

Indeed, Byron has no intention of letting the issue drop: he is merely warming to his theme. The very next canto of *Don Juan* goes straight back to it. There, he once again positions himself as a writer whose 'unflattering Muse' is only speaking the uncomfortable truth, and adds that these are:

> Truths, that you will not read in the Gazettes,
> But which 'tis time to teach the hireling tribe
> Who fatten on their country's gore, and debts,
> Must be recited – and without a bribe.[86]

In another move that antedates trolling, Byron disparages the hacks in the pay of the mainstream media and sets himself apart from them by saying, 'I am no flatterer'. Like many a troll, then, he insists not only that he's being serious but also that it's the mainstream writers who are the phoneys, since they owe their livelihoods to the establishment. He also casts aspersions about his fellow poets, such as 'turncoat Southey', and their paeans to Wellington: 'Waterloo has made the world your debtor / I wish your bards would sing it rather better'. But if Byron's is the voice of truth, then mostly what he has to say about Wellington is snide inuendo ('some other things won't

[86]Ibid., p.770.

do to tell / Upon your tomb in Westminster's old abbey'), unsubstantiated insinuations of corruption and profiteering ('I shall be delighted to learn who, / Save you and yours, have gain'd from Waterloo?'), vituperative character assassination ('You *did great* things: but not being *great* in mind, / Have left *undone* the *greatest* – and mankind'), and more infantile jokes about unpronounceable surnames:

> Oh, Wellington! or 'Villainton' – for Fame
> Sounds the heroic syllables both ways;
> France could not even conquer your great name.[87]

Simply put, Byron isn't interested in actually making a case here, let alone debating one. His aims are simply to defame, insult, and humiliate the Duke of Wellington, and to cause controversy through the public statement of views that are provocative and vexatious. Yet the real target is not so much Wellington himself as the unthinking, blinkered consensus according to which, as he puts it in a couplet bowing under its load of irony, 'Glory such as yours should any dare gainsay, / Humanity would rise, and thunder "Nay!"'. But if you rise and thunder 'Nay' to his outrageous gainsaying, then you have risen to Byron's bait; and if you don't, his heretical views go unchallenged.

All in all, then, a more consummate past master at the art of trolling than Lord Byron would be hard to find. His poetry is plainly disruptive and transgressive; caustically aggressive towards his targets, while being genuinely amusing to readers who spot the humour and do not feel affronted by what he says; deceptive about his intentions (his stated aim is to tell the truth; his immediate aim is to belittle Wellington and the victory of Waterloo; his ultimate aim is to enrage and outrage the conservative, nationalistic groupthink of public opinion); and successful in carrying off all the above. Though Byron never laid hands on a computer – his daughter, Ada Lovelace, had not invented it yet – his writings bore all the characteristics of trolling in spades.

There is, however, a sensible objection to this conclusion: Byron wasn't trolling, so the argument would run, because he meant what he said. He was sincere in his admiration for Napoleon, and genuinely devastated that the *anciens regimes* of Europe were going to be restored. Thus, when he derides Wellington with couplets such as 'Call'd "Saviour of the Nations" – not yet saved, / And "Europe's Liberator" – still enslaved', he isn't trying to defame, insult, or humiliate, nor trying to be controversial, vexatious, or provocative: he really, honestly believes in what he says, and so Byron is no troll.

---

[87]Ibid., p.779.

There's no sense in trying to refute this, because, from what we know of Byron's views, this is as plausible a reading of *Don Juan* as any. Instead, it teaches us an important thing about trolling: you don't need to exhibit all of its characteristics all of the time in order to be classed as a troll. Trolling involves a diverse, complex range of strategies, and it's unlikely they could all fit into a short piece of text in one go. Some trolls, for example, pour insult and abuse upon their victims, without necessarily aiming to spark any controversy; others say outlandishly provocative and vexatious things, but in the service of an idea or cause they have a heartfelt commitment to, rather than just for lulz. This is an important point, at least as far as this book is concerned, because all the writings we will encounter in the chapters to follow exemplify only a certain specific aspect of trolling. Whether or not this is enough to label their authors as trolls is something to be debated on a case-by-case basis (Émile Zola probably wasn't; Oscar Wilde probably was; Lord Byron definitely was). But the overriding point has hopefully been made: however slippery a term trolling may be, it can indeed be found in the works of great authors of literary classics. Now, having demonstrated this, we're ready to embark on our Odyssey through Western literary history – and, having roamed from ancient Greece to the 1980s via the Battle of Waterloo, we should be feeling in pretty good shape about it. Time, then, to press on.

2

... to defame, insult, or humiliate an opponent in public ...

From flyting to flaming; from Beowulf to Shakespeare

Let's start at the very beginning, with *Beowulf*, the Ground Zero of English Literature. Our hero – the mighty Beowulf, son of Ecgtheow – has journeyed across the sea with fourteen followers to the court of Hrothgar, King of the Danes. Time was when Hrothgar's hall, Heorot, was widely renowned for its splendour and welcomed visitors from far and wide, but that's not why Beowulf and his warriors have come. Now, it's famous for all the wrong reasons: a monster named Grendel – a man-eater and descendant of Cain, no less – prowls through the night, dragging Hrothgar's best men off into the fens to their slaughter. Beowulf has come to Heorot to slay this monster, and upon arrival he announces to the whole court that he will tackle Grendel single-handed and unarmed (which, as it happens, works out for the best, since it transpires that Grendel can't be harmed by conventional weapons). Under these circumstances, you'd expect Beowulf to get, literally, a hero's welcome – so what happens next is likely to strike a modern-day, first-time reader as fairly odd.

A courtier named Unferth, who sits at Hrothgar's feet, 'spoke contrary words', as Seamus Heaney's much-loved translation has it.[1] (The sense of the original '*onband beadu-rūne*' is that he 'unbound secret contentious

[1] Seamus Heaney, *Beowulf* (London: Faber, 1999), p.17.

thoughts'.) In front of the king and the whole court, Unferth asks their visitor if he is the same Beowulf who couldn't even beat his own best friend Breca in a simple swimming race. He goes on to say that this seven-night-long contest was undertaken out of foolish pride and vanity, against everyone else's advice, and he concludes that if Beowulf is the kind of man who risks his life for mere bragging rights and can't even win, then he has no chance of lasting the night against Grendel, if he even dares to try.

Readers familiar with epic poetry will know that great warriors often trade insults as a warm-up to trading blows. In Homer's *Iliad*, for example, the Greek and Trojan heroes seem to give winning the war of words almost as much weight as their feats of arms. Typically, their squaring up to one another takes place amid plenty of graphic boasts and threats. Each taunts the other publicly, by insulting their country and culture, disparaging their lineage and ancestors, and above all, belittling their prowess and reputation. (Achilles and Aeneas baiting one another in Book XX is as good an example as any.) But the situation in *Beowulf* is surely something different. Beowulf and Unferth are – or are *supposed* to be – on the same side.

The narrator of the poem gives a simple explanation for Unferth's bizarre words: he's jealous of Beowulf's fame, and he can't abide 'that any other man under the heavens of middle-earth should win more glory than himself' ('*þæt ænig oðer man / æfre mærða þon ma middangeardes / gehedde under heofenum þonne he sylfa*'). But scholars of the literature of the Anglo-Saxons have long claimed there's more to it than that. It's been argued that this is an Old English example of an ancient genre of poetry known as *flyting*, which will be our focus in this chapter. Apparently, flyting was once a common form of poetic practice across northern Europe. It can be found in Old Norse poems and sagas, and it enjoyed huge popularity in Scottish verse a couple of centuries later. As we'll see in due course, it's even been suggested that the tradition of flyting survived on into the works of Shakespeare. Dictionaries of literary terms give rather pithy definitions of flyting, such as 'a verse contest in insults', or 'a slanging match in verse'.[2] More accurately, it's an interactive form of performance poetry, consisting of a duel between two warrior-bards, who take turns in trading progressively worse calumnies and insults, typically in front of an audience. The aim of the game is to outdo your opponent in both the heights to which your poetic inventiveness can soar and the depths to which your scurrilous taunts can sink – not unlike the rap battles of today. And there were winners and losers to this game: often, the audience would decide who got the better and who the worse of these outrageously vituperative exchanges of poems.

---

[2]Dinah Birch and Katy Hooper (eds), *The Concise Oxford Companion to English Literature*, 4th edition (Oxford: Oxford University Press, 2012); Chris Baldick (ed.), *The Oxford Dictionary of Literary Terms*, 4th edition (Oxford: Oxford University Press, 2012).

Based largely on a combination of abusive goading and deliberately offensive character assassination, flyting would appear to have a fair amount in common with trolling – or so this chapter will contend. But there is one fairly obvious difference. Strange as it may seem, given that flyting frequently descends to the crudest, coarsest language imaginable (and pretty quickly at that), it was once an art form, held in very high esteem, popular even in royal courts, with kings judging the victors and the vanquished. Trolling, on the other hand, seems to be met with nothing but opprobrium. But if we can understand why flyting once held so much appeal, perhaps we might understand why some people troll. In any case, I'm hoping that the strategies and dynamics of flyting, as we explore them in this chapter, will reveal a good deal about how trolling works as a kind of writing.

Let's get back to Unferth, whose calculated insults and snidely cast aspersions have seemed to some literary critics like the opening salvo in a flyting session. What's Beowulf to do here? He's a new arrival at a foreign court, standing in the presence of a powerful king. The stakes are high. If he ignores Unferth's slurs, he loses face, and if he doesn't give as good as he gets – that is, if his reply isn't a putdown as forthright, robust, and comprehensive as Unferth's – he suffers a humiliating defeat. And yet if Beowulf is to be certain of winning this war of words with a putdown like that, he has to put aside the gracious, courteous, well-spoken manners of a visitor to a royal court: he must descend to Unferth's level. And that is precisely the dilemma in which many victims of trolling find themselves. 'Do Not Feed the Trolls' isn't a great slogan if, like Beowulf, your reputation has been publicly insulted or defamed by them: naturally, you'd want to respond, to set the record straight. But doing so means engaging with the trolls, and the moment you've done that, you've played into their hands. Thus, though it was written well over a thousand years ago, *Beowulf* is alive to the dynamics of trolling.

Aptly, Heaney's Beowulf boasts he has 'raided a troll-nest'.[3] His reply to Unferth is indeed nothing less than a verbal assault. He says that Unferth is drunk, and it's the beer that's talking; he further says that he, Beowulf, won the swimming contest; that the reason it took so long was because he was swimming sword in hand, with heavy chainmail armour on; and that he needed this because he was being repeatedly attacked by sea monsters, of which he slew nine (he can prove this because their bodies washed up on shore), which he thinks has got to be a new record. He ends by saying that he wouldn't have had to come all the way to Heorot to fight Grendel if only Unferth had had the guts to stand up and defend his lord Hrothgar.

---

[3]Heaney, *Beowulf*, p.15. This involves a little poetic license on Heaney's part: the word '*eoten*' is normally translated as 'giant' or 'monster'; trolls come from Norse, not Anglo-Saxon, mythology.

Beowulf offers this as final proof that it's actually Unferth who's precisely the kind of spineless wonder he's declared Beowulf to be. Game Beowulf. Or is it? Though Beowulf's words dismiss Unferth's tirade as empty, beer-fuelled blather, his actions – dignifying those very words with a fulsome, comprehensive repudiation – treat him as a worthy adversary he must vanquish, that is, as an equal.

Fast-forward a millennium or so, to the year 2012, and a very different kind of swimming contest. At the Olympic Games held in London that year, British diver Tom Daley narrowly missed out on a medal, finishing in fourth place, agonizingly short of the podium. This was especially heartbreaking for Daley, and not just because he was in front of his home crowd. Barely a year before, while still in his mid-teenage years, he had lost his father to brain cancer. Speaking to the BBC shortly before competing, Daley described his late father as his 'inspiration', adding that winning a medal would make his struggles worthwhile: 'I'm doing it for myself and my dad. It was both our dreams from a very young age.... I always wanted to do it and Dad was so supportive of everything. It would make it extra special to do it for him.'[4]

Moments after Daley's final dive sealed the unfortunate result, a seventeen-year-old Twitter troll named Reece Messer tweeted him a short message: 'You let your dad down i hope you know that' [*sic*]. Shortly thereafter, another message twisted the knife: 'Hope your crying now you should be why cant you ever produce for your country your just a diver anyway a overhyped prick' [*sic*]. This, I take it, is as clear an example as you'll find of what is perhaps the simplest form of trolling: insulting, defaming, and/or humiliating someone. Let's leave to one side, for now, the issue of whether or not the insults and calumnies are sincerely meant or are purely contrarian, and whether or not they aim to provoke a reply or cause a controversy. The most basic, most visceral, and most disturbing aspect of trolling is surely the offence, pain, and indignity it heaps upon its targets. One can barely imagine, in this case, how Messer's dig about Daley's late father must have smarted, especially given the time and place.

If 'Do Not Feed the Trolls' means don't reply to them, then Tom Daley didn't feed the troll – not directly. Instead, he fed this troll to the public, by retweeting the message about his father to his 900,000 followers, and to whoever else might be reading. He prefaced it with a simple, dignified line: 'After giving it my all ... you get idiot's sending me this ...' [*sic*]. An international outcry ensued. Within hours, police announced they were aware of the tweet and were investigating it, and the following day, Messer was arrested and cautioned under the Malicious Communications Act. Meanwhile, messages of support for Daley flooded in from sports stars and

---

[4]'Police Investigating Twitter User Who Abused Tom Daley', *The Guardian*, 31 July 2012.

media celebrities, mostly reassuring him of the pride a grateful nation felt for him and how proud his father would have been, too. (And rightly so: Daley went on to become the most successful and decorated British diver in history, winning the European, Commonwealth, and World Championships multiple times each, and earning four Olympic medals, including a gold in 2020.)

Separated by an ocean of historical time, these two swimming contests nonetheless reveal much about the nature of trolling. Though Unferth stops short of calling Beowulf 'a overhyped prick', that's the gist of his words. Though his audience is smaller than the billions who use X/Twitter, it still includes practically everyone of any consequence in early medieval Denmark. Both verbal attacks were completely unprovoked, and both came from people you'd reasonably expect to be cheering the hero on instead of undermining them with jibes aimed at bruising their reputations. The main difference is that Beowulf is not in front of his home crowd and doesn't have access to a digital platform communicating with the rest of the world. Thus, he has no option but to defend his reputation with a direct reply to Unferth. Back home in Geatland, one assumes, there'd be no shortage of people shouting down Unferth's calumnies. What this suggests, then, is that the idea of a public or an audience is essential to trolling.

To put it another way: if Messer had typed the exact same words, placed them in a sealed envelope, and sent them anonymously to Daley as a poison pen letter, they would not be called trolling. They *would* still cause a great deal of pain and upset, and they would still breach the Malicious Communications Act on those grounds, but they would *not* be called trolling. Not because they're off-line – so is Unferth – but because without the idea of an implicit public or broader audience, before whom the target risks losing face, trolling ceases to be trolling. It becomes old-fashioned hate mail, or just plain insult. And this suggests that what's at stake in much trolling isn't just offending or insulting but public humiliation. Trolling, like flyting, has a triangular structure: yes, trolls take aim at their targets to belittle them, but more precisely, they aim to belittle their targets in the eyes of onlookers or third parties.

Note that it's the *idea* of a public or audience, rather than the actual readership, that's important here. You could troll someone with barely any followers on X/Twitter, or even if nobody actually reads what you've written, because your target has no way of knowing who has read what. Philosophers sometimes debate whether a tree falling in a forest makes a sound if no one's listening, but on the internet, most people have no way of knowing who is or isn't paying them attention. They therefore have no way of knowing if they've been publicly humiliated or not, but the *idea* that they might have been still persists and is all the more unsettling because it can't be verified. Conversely, the fact that millions of people were appalled by Messer's tweets and leapt to Daley's defence, with his reputation not being humiliated but instead enhanced for standing up to a bully, doesn't mean he hadn't been trolled.

Flyting as flaming?

These days, literature is mostly consumed in private. The paperback novel is there for individual enjoyment: mass produced in its thousands, its readers each have their own copy. Like a pair of blinkers, the physical form of the book shuts you off from the outside world, both flashing a 'do not disturb' badge and putting a physical barrier between you and everyone else. But things were not always this introverted. Before Gutenberg developed the technology of mass production, it wasn't possible for everyone to own their own books, so literature was consumed in public. It was recited. And this is why flyting is so important for our purposes: it was an *extremely* public literary genre.

One of very few scholars to have taken it seriously, Ward Parks, defines flyting as 'an exchange of insults and boasts between two heroes *in some public setting*'.[5] He points out that, like most forms of verbal contest in the Western tradition, it's based upon an adversarial relationship, and he likens it to a form of ritualized combat. Beyond that, defining its poetic structure is difficult because, as we'll see a bit later, success was partly judged by versatility, so poets had to deploy a variety of poetic forms and metres. Furthermore, Carole J. Clover adds that 'No single example stands as an epitome ... for the simple reason that the form is traditional and hence subject to the usual thematic and motival variation. Any individual flyting is thus a unique combination of clichés and only approximates the general definition'.[6] But there's no disputing that the most complete, most extensive, and most fully contextualized early example comes from a late thirteenth-century Icelandic saga about a legendary figure named Örvar-Oddr; in English, Arrow-Odd.

The protagonist, Odd, is everything you'd expect from a Viking hero: he travels far and wide, seeking glory and slaying his foes. His adventures bring him to Götaland – where Beowulf also hails from, aptly enough. Arriving at the court of King Herraud incognito, Odd comes into conflict with a pair of arrogant bullies named Sigurd and Sjolf, the king's top men, who take him for a lowborn itinerant, and mock him for being a beggar and a scrounger. After Odd defeats them in – what else? – a swimming contest, Sigurd and Sjolf demand a rematch, in the form of a drinking contest, which takes place before the king, his daughter, and the whole court. But it's a drinking contest with a difference: it also involves elements of a poetry slam. After drinking

[5]Ward Parks, 'Flyting, Sounding, Debate: Three Verbal Contest Genres', *Poetics Today*, vol. 7, no. 3, 1986, pp.439–58, p.441. My emphasis.

[6]Carol J. Clover, 'The Germanic Context of the Unferþ Episode', *Speculum: A Journal of Medieval Studies*, vol. 55, no. 3, 1986, pp.444–68, p.446.

down a horn of beer, each participant is required to compose and recite a piece of verse, presumably as a test of drunkenness or sobriety. Fuelled by the animosity between Odd and his tormentors, this is a fully fledged flyting session.

All the key elements of flyting are on show here, contextualized for us by the narrator: a basic structure of turn-taking; a mixture of boasts that vaunt the speaker's achievements with taunts that disparage his opponent's reputation; the steady escalation of insult, calumny, and defamation as the contest progresses; and the subject matter of these insults. Each stanza typically starts by asserting that the speaker's opponent was nowhere to be seen while the speaker was busy with the daring exploits aggrandized during the rest of the stanza, as in:

> Odd, you weren't there
> at the weapon-clash when
> we gave the king's troops
> a taste of death.
> Fourteen wounds
> I fared home with,
> while you were begging
> your bread from the farmers.[7]

But this structure is then embellished with further insult and slander. Common themes include allegations of weakness in battle (Odd calls Sigurd and Sjolf 'a pretty pair of milksops'); cowardice in the face of the enemy ('I conquered, / you sat quiet'); empty boastfulness ('you were lounging / at home ... the tall-story teller'); sponging off their liege-lord ('you seat-warmers'; 'beggars / taking titbits / from the table'); and preferring lascivious sex to fighting. Note how:

> Sjolf, you were gossiping
> with the girls, while we
> sent the fires raging through the fortress ...
> You, Sigurd, were lying
> enchambered with the ladies,
> while twice we clashed
> in combat with the Permians.
> Hawk-minded, we won
> our war like heroes,
> while you lay dozing under the linen.

[7]Hermann Pálsson and Paul Edwards (eds and trans.), 'Arrow-Odd', in *Seven Viking Romances* (London: Penguin, 1985), pp.25–137, p.102. Subsequent quotations are from this edition, pp.101–08.

spirals quickly downwards, degenerating in just a few stanzas to:

> You weren't around,
> Sjolf, when we reddened
> our steel on the earl …
> Mad for sex, you
> sat at home wondering
> whether to cuddle
> the calf or the kitchenmaid.

In other Norse flytings, similar taunts involve suggestions of adultery, cuckoldry, homosexuality, and incest. In fact, the flyting between Odd, Sigurd, and Sjolf is one of the least foul-mouthed, with 'scum' being about the worst insult hurled. As we'll see, this makes it atypical, at least when compared with later flytings. But in one respect, the saga of Arrow-Odd is very telling: the narrator informs us that 'There was loud cheering in the hall.... The king's men couldn't get enough of this entertainment'. Flyting, it seems, is very popular with its audience. As with trolling, then, it's not just about being abusive, offensive, or insulting, though these are the building blocks of both – it's about the audience. Public humiliation lies at its core.

There are other ways in which flyting is a prototypical form of trolling. The Old Norse root *flyta* is said to be related to the idea of 'egging', so provocation is an important component of it. We'll look at trolling as provocation in another chapter; for now, let's note that rising to your opponent's bait, or letting your opponent get under your skin, is as publicly humiliating in flyting as it is in trolling. *Flyta* also implies scatological insult, and, interestingly, is found in much Scandinavian *skaldic* poetry, which is where the mythological figure of the troll originates, too. (As it happens, Odd sometimes curses his enemies with the line 'may the trolls take you'.) The Old Norse root *skald* is where the English verb 'to scold' comes from.

So: flyting implies egging or provoking, through scolding or berating, using scatological insults. The troll who targeted the website of Fiona Vera-Grey's research project on violence against women with a hateful comment such as 'youre [*sic*] a perfect example of what happens when society pampers a cunt' seems to match this description – though, as we'll see, it's also more complicated than that.[8] Indeed, Vera-Grey herself points out that some might rather term such bile-filled outbursts 'flaming' instead of 'trolling'. The Urban Dictionary, for example, opines that 'Shouting swear words at someone doesn't count as trolling; it's just flaming'.[9] So, what is flaming, and how does it differ from trolling?

---

[8]See F. Vera-Grey, '"Talk About a Cunt with Too Much Idle Time": Trolling Feminist Research', *Feminist Review*, vol. 115, no. 1, 2017, pp.61–78, p.69.

[9]Urban Dictionary, s.v. 'Trolling', 3 January, 2014. Available at: https://www.urbandictionary.com/define.php?term=Trolling

'Flaming has been described as the communication of incessant profanity, insults, or expression of otherwise strong emotions'[10] and also as 'displaying hostility by insulting, swearing or using otherwise offensive language'.[11] This would appear to encompass most of the worst excesses of trolling: thuggish verbal abuse, hate speech, tirades of profanity, and so on. It would also include much of the Scottish flyting we're about to look at. Some scholars claim that 'trolling and flaming are markedly different phenomena, even if they show some affinity or overlap', in that while both can lead to extensive arguments, and/or emotional damage, 'trolling messages need not necessarily be aggressive', whereas flaming invariably is.[12] Others contend that 'the key difference between flaming and trolling is that the former is more profane and directly offensive, whereas the latter necessarily has an element of deception.'[13]

This distinction is so neat it's bound to be problematic. The idea that flaming is 'indicative of genuine expression of hostility and aggression',[14] whereas trolling is just a hoax or a prank, is simply not verifiable, and has been convincingly challenged in other studies.[15] Thus, 'while some scholars draw distinctions between trolling and the act of "flaming", others have categorized flaming as a type of trolling'.[16] This latter position will be the one we'll explore here. We'll see that the practice of flyting can sometimes 'suggest that flaming may be a distinct type of, rather than a separate category from, trolling'[17] – a position endorsed by a number of researchers including Jonathan Bishop; Coles and West; and Cruz, Seo, and Rex. But in order to do this, I'm afraid, we'll have to investigate flyting at its very worst.

Utter(ing) filth

The golden age of flyting, if we can call it that, took place in Scotland, some two hundred or three hundred years after Arrow-Odd's saga, and was very popular at the court of the Stuart kings, who would act as judges, and,

---

[10]Angela Gracia B. Cruz, Yuri Seo, and Mathew Rex, 'Trolling in online communities: A practice-based theoretical perspective', *The Information Society*, vol. 34, no. 1, 2018, pp.15–26, p.17.

[11]Peter J. Moor, Ard Heuvelman, and Ria Verleur, 'Flaming on YouTube', *Computers in Human Behavior*, vol. 26, pp.1536–546, p.1536.

[12]Marta Dynel, '"Trolling Is Not Stupid": Internet Trolling as the Art of Deception Serving Entertainment', *Intercultural Pragmatics*, vol. 13, no. 3, 2016, pp.353–81, p.358.

[13]Cruz, Seo, and Rex, 'Trolling in Online Communities', p.17.

[14]Dynel, 'Trolling Is Not Stupid', p.358.

[15]For example, Moor, Heuvelman, and Verleur, 'Flaming on YouTube', p.1539.

[16]Cruz, Seo, and Rex, 'Trolling in Online Communities', p.17.

[17]Ibid.

incredibly, even as occasional competitors. The earliest surviving example is the *Flyting of Dumbar and Kennedie* (1503), the most poetically complex probably is the *Flyting betwixt Montgomery and Polwart* (*c.* 1585), and Sir David Lyndsay's effort, dating from 1537, is remarkable for his opponent – none other than King James V. These flytings differ from our earlier Icelandic example in important ways. Firstly, they are not spontaneous, improvised, verbal barrages but rather carefully crafted, skilfully written verses – products of a highly literate, Renaissance-era culture. Secondly, the participants weren't warriors or heroes. As Robert Hughes points out, they were noted authors of some repute, and many were aristocrats. Take *Dumbar and Kennedie*: Dunbar was 'a Master of Arts, a Franciscan preaching friar, a priest in court service for a number of years, and the recipient of a royal pension from King James IV', while Kennedy 'had similar academic qualifications, was greatly admired as a poet and was of the blood royal'.[18] Thus, he says, Scottish flyting 'can be called, paradoxically, "the fine art of savage insult." ... It was evidently designed as an entertainment for a sophisticated, not a "common" audience'.[19] Thirdly, and quite bizarrely, given the first two points, its language was *much* filthier than Odd's 'milksops' and 'scum'.

There's probably a simple explanation for this: remember that Odd's was primarily a drinking contest. The poetry served as markers in a game, indicating whether or not contestants were still sober. The game ends when Sigurd and Sjolf keel over, and Odd stands victorious, 'having outdrunk, outrecited, and outinsulted his opponents'.[20] Scottish flytings, however, were judged *as* poetry. Their language, therefore, needs to go the whole hog. Thus, the *Flyting of Dumbar and Kennedie* gives us 'the earliest recorded instances of several current terms of insult', including a strong contender for the first written instance of the word 'shit' used as a noun to describe a person (as when Kennedy calls Dunbar a 'schit but wit', i.e. a witless shit, L.496), and the first attested use of the insult 'git' (which used to have the same double meaning as 'bastard', so when Dunbar calls Kennedy the 'feyindis gett', or fiend's git [L.244], he's really saying that Kennedy is the bastard son of the devil).[21] And I'm afraid that's just for starters.

Easily the most ribald and raucous of the three surviving flytings, *Dumbar and Kennedie* is full of graphic threats of physical violence. Each poet (or

---

[18]Geoffrey Hughes, *An Encyclopedia of Swearing: The Social History of Oaths, Profanity, Foul Language, and Ethnic Slurs in the English-Speaking World* (London: Routledge, 2015), p.175.

[19]Ibid.

[20]Clover, 'Germanic Context of Unferþ', p.449.

[21]See Hughes, *Encyclopedia of Swearing*, p.176. Quotations from *The Flyting of Dumbar and Kennedie* are from the Oxford scholarly edition, available at: http://www.oxfordscholarlyeditions.com/view/10.1093/actrade/9780198118886.book.1/actrade-9780198118886-div1-24

makar, to use the Scottish term) compares the other and his ancestors to devils, demons, and animals of various kinds; there are also accusations of treason against the king, and of betraying their country to the hated English. There are smutty schoolboy jibes about sexual depravity: Kennedy calls Dunbar an abominable buggerist and insatiable sodomite ('bugrist abhominabile /... sodomyte insatiable', L.526–27), while Dunbar says Kennedy mounts his mares for purposes non-equestrian (L.246). There are taunts about each makar's physical appearance: Dunbar, for instance, says that by the time winter comes around, Kennedy's breeches have been worn so thin they can no longer stop his 'bellokis gyngill', i.e. his bollocks [testicles] jingling (L.119). Kennedy, for his part, is prone to body-shaming, calling Dunbar, among many other things, a 'mandrag mymmerkin', or poison dwarf (L.19).

Much of the humour is woefully coarse and scatological: Dunbar claims that Kennedy has shat more worms than there is grass on the ground or life on the land ('ma wormis hes thow beschittin / Nor thair is gers on grund or leif on lind', L.195–96), to which Kennedy retaliates with a graphic three-stanza anecdote about Dunbar's incontinence during a sea voyage, the stains from which, he alleges, can still be seen on the ship's timbers twenty years on (L.452). Each insults the other's parentage: Kennedy calls Dunbar a son of a whore ('hursone', L.359), while according to Dunbar, not only is Kennedy a son of a bitch, he suckled her, too ('fed and bred of bichis syd', L.237). Kennedy even goes so far as to call Dunbar a 'wan fukkit funling' (L.38). Bearing in mind that 'wan' means weak, unenthusiastic, or lacking in energy, he's basically saying that Dunbar is a foundling who was feebly fucked into existence.

Thankfully, not all the insults are quite this crude: some involve cultural and classical allusions, as when Kennedy boasts that he drinks from the pure fountains of Mount Parnassus, inspired by the god Mercury, whereas Dunbar goes to a pool in a paddock each February or March to drink the frogspawn, then blabbers the noise he makes afterwards into men's ears, and calls it poetry (see L.337–44). Others involve elaborate puns, steeped in Renaissance culture. For instance, Kennedy describes Dunbar's coat of arms as featuring a gallows with a noose, and above it, written in poetry, the words 'Hang Dunbar' (L.413–15). Though outrageously funny in its own right, there's a complex pun involved here. Kennedy has just accused Dunbar's ancestors of selling out to the English king Edward Longshanks and said the Dunbars should thus be exiled from Scotland to live in England. Quartering and drawing are heraldic terms, and by adding 'hang' to them, Kennedy makes it clear what he thinks should be done to the traitorous Dunbars. Nevertheless, the fact that some jokes work on a sophisticated number of levels does not necessarily keep them from being revoltingly crude. The lowest of the low is surely when Dunbar calls Kennedy a 'cuntbitten crawdon' (L.50), which literally means a pox-afflicted coward. However, as

Robert Hughes points out, 'crawdon, an obsolete dialect term, contains a rich resonance of masculine contempt, since the sense of "coward" derives from a cock that will not fight. The remarkable adjective cuntbitten intensifies the insult by playing on the various meanings of cock'.[22] I apologize to readers who feel they didn't need to know this.

If Archilochus is the prototype for 'slut'-shaming, then surely Dunbar and Kennedy are the founding fathers of flaming. This vitriolic filth is disturbingly reminiscent of the bile and abuse that pollutes X/Twitter, YouTube, and other comment or gaming threads, and which is clearly both an affront and a threat to civilized debate. And yet, though we may deplore the content, we shouldn't simply write off the form. Unlike most flaming, flyting was exceptionally well-polished verse. It regularly deploys elaborate patterns of rhyme, internal rhyme, and, above all, alliteration. Victory consists in 'the demonstration of skill, not solely in personal execration'.[23] Rhythm and structure were clearly important too: 'Montgomerie and Polwart flyted one another in a variety of metres and forms which were designed to demonstrate their versatility'.[24] And so, as with certain vintages of hip-hop, I find myself admiring and enjoying its energetic verve and linguistic creativity, while deploring most of its content.

Above all, though: why would people write this way? Why did they get away with it? Why was it so popular? If anything, placing these questions in their historical context makes flyting seem more, not less, extraordinary. Firstly, as Hughes puts it, 'What makes the Scottish flytings the more striking is that they occur in a country with a vehement tradition against profanity'.[25] Historical records show that blasphemous or scurrilous talk was regularly punished in sixteenth-century Scotland, with penalties ranging from fines to pretty draconian corporal punishment. And secondly, let's not forget who was listening. In *The Flyting betwixt Montgomery and Polwart*, Montgomerie kicks off by telling the Baron of Polwarth to 'come kisse my Erse' (i.e. arse, L.12), who, in turn, ends by telling Montgomerie to go 'kisse the cunt of the Kow' (i.e. cow, L.817), having also called him 'turd fac'd' (L.785) and a 'shyte saddle' (L.778).[26] They were writing this stuff for James VI of Scotland – the same king for whom, just a few years later, as James I of England, Shakespeare would write *Macbeth*. Indeed, as it happens, there are plenty of similarities: Montgomerie narrates how some wandering

---

[22]Hughes, *Encyclopedia of Swearing*, pp.175–76.

[23]Ibid., p.175.

[24]R.D.S. Jack, *The History of Scottish Literature*, Vol. 1 (Aberdeen: Aberdeen University Press, 1988), p.51.

[25]Hughes, *Encyclopedia of Swearing*, p.175.

[26]Alexander Montgomerie and Patrick Hume, *The Flyting betwixt Montgomery and Polwart* (Edinburgh: Andro Hart, [*c*. 1585] 1621). Subsequent references to this edition.

'weird sisters' concocted gruesome spells and summoned Hecate while they officiated at Polwart's baptism. No doubt Shakespeare knew what played well at James's court. Certainly, he was adept at flyting scenes, as we'll see later. But, to put it mildly, it's a strange fact about British culture that these horrendously coarse contests were happening not just in a royal court but that they also lasted on into what most literary historians agree was the golden age of English literature.

It's quite clear that, as Hughes puts it, 'Flyting ... has an essential element of license, of wordplay, since otherwise the grievous insults would lead to duels and other extreme modes of exacting satisfaction'.[27] In other words, flyting is understood as a space apart, where 'language that would normally be taboo and extremely provocative does not lead to hostilities, but is tolerated in this particular conventional use'.[28] Nobody took it seriously; presumably it was 'just flyting', or harmless fun; no feelings were hurt. 'It can be safely assumed, for example, that Montgomerie does not expect anyone literally to believe him when he accuses Polwart of "peeping" like a mouse', writes Ward Parks.[29] Just as well for Sir David Lyndsay, who describes how his flyting opponent enjoys 'fukkand [i.e. fucking] lyke ane furious fornicatour' with low-born wenches.[30] Astonishingly, the man in question was none other than James V, his own king.

One can only imagine the frisson that the audience must have felt when these words were spoken, the nervous laughter at the flagrant breach of social and linguistic taboo. And if this accounts for the appeal of flyting, then it might be tempting to draw the simple conclusion that something similar accounts for flaming too. Recall how, in the last chapter, some scholars claimed that trolling was transgressive in nature. Perhaps, or so the argument might run, the reason why so much trolling, and flaming in particular, consists of the lowest obscenities, or of hate speech and rape threats, is that some people feel a certain thrill to the edginess involved in speaking the unspeakable. The trouble with this argument is that it is wrong, and not – or not only – because it legitimizes and apologizes for hate speech and rape threats. It's simply not comparing like with like.

It's one thing to say that, in an environment like a Renaissance-era court, with a culture constructed around pomp and pageantry, members of such a highly artificial community may well have felt the need to blow off some steam from time to time. Flyting, then, would be a kind of safety valve,

---

[27]Hughes, *Encyclopedia of Swearing*, p.177.

[28]Ibid., p.173.

[29]Parks, 'Flyting, Sounding, Debate', p.450.

[30]Sir David Lyndsay, 'The Answer to the Kingis Flyting', in *Selected Poems*, ed. Janet Hadley Williams (Glasgow: Association for Scottish Literary Studies, [1537] 2000), pp.98–100, p.99, L.49.

releasing pressure that might otherwise end either in actual combat, as in duelling, or in more malicious forms of back-biting and intriguing that were all too common amongst courtiers at the time. That's certainly the explanation given in a prefatory poem at the start of *The Flyting betwixt Montgomery and Polwart*. It tells us that 'by Ryme / *Anger* to asswage, make *Melancholy* lesse, / This flyting first was wrote', and compares the duelling makars to dogs who, 'Wak'd with the gingling of a courteour's spurres / Barke all the night, and neuer seeke to bite'. In other words, flyting disperses tension, so that no one ends up getting hurt.

The thing is that these days, hardly anyone lives in an environment that formal, stuffy, and stilted. So it's quite another thing to say that flaming and trolling are harmless fun that liberate us from convention. Breaking the law by inciting racial hatred or threatening sexual violence are not the same thing as calling your king a furiously fucking fornicator to his face. The former reasserts antiquated and deeply engrained privileges that can have no place in a modern society; the latter dismantles antiquated privileges in a spirit of healthy irreverence – provided the king in question has a sense of humour.

But there are other, more important, reasons why, foul-mouthed as they are, these flytings differ from flaming. These reasons are more structural. It's been said that trolling is a 'broader term for attempts to wilfully disrupt online communities, with flaming being a particular useful strategy for this purpose'.[31] But flyting doesn't disrupt the community: if anything, it strengthens it. Nothing Dunbar can say to Kennedy, however outrageous, can weaken the social bond between them: that's the whole point. And the flyting itself strengthens the community of the court, in roughly the same way jousting tournaments did, putting business on hold to enjoy some organized fun. This helps us explain why flyting and flaming are, in their basic structure, different things.

Flyting is a contest that one enters into. Though Lyndsay's flyting clearly expresses his grovelling reluctance, as a loyal subject, to hurl abuse at his king, he's a willing participant nonetheless. So are Dunbar, Kennedy, and all the others. Even King Herraud 'was told that Odd was willing to compete'. As Parks has it, flyting is underpinned by 'a process of explicit or implicit contractuation', whereby the protagonists 'have contracted for a fight'.[32] This explains why flyting is a space apart, as in a boxing match, where all the real talking is done in the ring, and when it's done, it all stays in the ring. But that is *not* the experience of Tom Daley, or Fiona Vera-Grey, or most other victims of flaming and trolling. They have been ambushed by a complete stranger who, out of the blue, lashes out with a verbal assault,

[31]Vera-Grey, 'Talk about ... ', p.66.

[32]Parks, 'Flyting, Sounding, Debate', p.451.

in front of an online reading public. It's the difference between a boxing match and the early 2000s wave of 'happy slap' attacks, in which you were suddenly punched in the face out of nowhere by some random passerby who's filming the incident on a phone to then post online 'for the lulz'. In a nutshell: flyting is symmetrical and reciprocal; flaming is asymmetrical. It is completely one-sided.

But before we conclude that flyting is a complete irrelevance for the study of flaming and trolling, let's pause to remind ourselves of something: Beowulf enters into no contract. He, too, is ambushed by a complete stranger who, out of the blue, lashes out with a verbal assault, in front of a very important audience. He is in Tom Daley's position. Interestingly, at the time of writing, there were no fewer than nine separate X/Twitter handles calling themselves Unferth. Their bios include 'I h8 Beowulf' and 'I will be the greatest warrior Heorot has ever seen ... I will make Heorot great again'. Here's a typical tweet from one:

> Literally I cannot stand when some people think they're better than everyone else. Bruh, you cannot defeat a monster that has killed thousands because, hate to break it to you, you're not that special. Fr some people just need to get over themselves. #hesgoingtodie[33]

There follows a whole thread of dialogue with a Beowulf avatar that reconstructs their flyting session in trollspeak. Taunts and digs such as 'Really Unferth? Why don't you @ me next time, too scared?', or '#swimmingisntevenhard', convey the verbal feel of the contest surprisingly well, and drag us from the Anglo-Saxon mead-hall into the digital age. Perhaps flyting has something to teach us about trolling after all.

From trolls to tricksters

Of all the flytings we know of, one in particular has a unique status. Its instigator, and most vocal participant, is neither a legendary hero nor a historic king, but a god. So are his multiple antagonists. In an episode of the Old Norse *Poetic Edda* known as the *Lokasenna*, believed to date from around the tenth century, the rogue figure of Loki decides to take on all the gods of Asgard at once, in an extraordinary flyting session.

Loki is a 'trickster' figure, best known for conniving to bring about the death of the god Baldur, and indirectly giving us the resulting custom of yuletide mistletoe. Understandably, he gets a frostier welcome at the feasts

---

[33]https://twitter.com/ayeitsunferth

of the gods after this incident, but Loki, who seems quite unable to grasp that actions have consequences, takes exception to being ostracized – even after he has killed Fimafeng, servant of his host, the sea-spirit Ægir. Loki does this for no other reason than that Fimafeng is being spoken highly of by the rest of the gods; they drive Loki out of their banquet by force in reprisal. Undeterred, he barges straight back in. Then, in a manner of speaking, Loki does an Unferth. That is, he disrupts the decorum and conviviality of the gods' banquet by hurling all manner of slander and abuse at them. This is *not* a contractual, reciprocal flyting: the gods are clearly very taken aback by Loki's onslaught. Structurally, this section of the poem resembles a flame war uncannily closely.

The language of the *Lokasenna* is much more tame than that of its later Scottish inheritors. Its structure is highly formulaic and is perhaps the most telling thing about it. As a rule, Loki hurls a stanza of abuse at one of the assembled deities, who then responds with a stanza spoken in their own defence. Loki dismisses this in a second abusive stanza, after which one of the other gods or goddesses comes to the defence of their wronged colleague by speaking another stanza. That deity will then become the target of Loki's next abusive stanza, defending themselves in turn, and so the cycle goes on. This structure is in and of itself instructive: generally, the gods and goddesses do not respond to Loki in kind, by lambasting him with insults of their own, *à la* Dunbar and Kennedy. Instead, they try to refute whatever Loki has said about them. This signals that they are taking his words seriously, rather than just in sport. They seem genuinely offended, hurt, and insulted. And well they might be.

Though fairly predictable, Loki's outbursts are no less outrageous for that. He rubbishes the valour and the prowess of the gods, and he 'slut'-shames the goddesses. Frey, the god of virility, is said to have sold his sword to pay a prostitute; Njörd, god of the sea, is accused of letting girls piss in his mouth; Bragi, god of poetry, is reproached for alleged cowardice. Even the regal Odin, mythological ancestor of the Nordic royal families, is said to be lacking impartiality, unfair and womanly in his judgements. The goddesses fare no better. Almost all are called whores. Frigg, goddess of wisdom and wife of Odin, is additionally called a lesbian. Gefjun, goddess of fertility, is said to have prostituted herself for jewellery, and Freya, the Nordic Venus, is accused of sleeping with her own brother, while Idun, goddess of youth and wife of Bragi, is accused of having sex with her brother's killer. Loki goes on to brag that he has slept with the wives of three major gods: Skadi, archer goddess and wife of Njörd; Sif, earth goddess and wife of the lightning god Thor; and the unnamed wife of Tyr, god of war, with whom Loki boasts to have fathered the son that passes as Tyr's. What's most curious about this incredible outpouring of insults is that many of them are not mentioned anywhere else in the entire corpus of extant Norse mythology. In other words, Loki seems to have made them up. They are almost certainly baseless slanders and calumnies.[34]

Defamation seems to be as important to Loki as filth and ribaldry were in the Stuart courts. It seems unimaginable that such a pack of scurrilous lies could be told about powerful deities – as if Judas Iscariot were to gatecrash the Last Supper to rant similar things about Christ and the other disciples. And yet, structurally, there is a certain familiarity about the poem. It's very formulaic, and something about its patterns ring true down the centuries. When a god or goddess joins the dispute, the first words of their stanza often tell Loki he's crazy. And, as a rule, Loki's stanza in reply begins with a short, stock phrase: '*þegi þu*', which basically means 'shut up'.

This pattern, virtually a call-and-response, is strikingly close to that of a typical flame war. If a malicious, hateful lie is told about you online, brimming with outlandish calumnies, a common response is to say the speaker must be crazy, and to dash off a quick riposte explaining why these absurd things can't possibly be true. The troll that wrote them will then find a reason for telling you to shut up. (If you have nine followers on X/Twitter, you should shut up because you're an insignificant nobody; if you have ninety thousand, you should shut up because you're an attention-seeking pseudo-celebrity. If you have no qualifications relevant to the topic under discussion, you should shut up because you don't know what you're talking about; if you are well qualified to speak on these matters, you should shut up because you're the voice of the establishment, a vested interest, part of the educated elite, and such like.) Chances are that, pretty soon, you'll end up telling the troll to shut up yourself, which is precisely what the troll wants, because at that point, the flaming proper begins, and insults start to fly. And this is more or less what happens in the *Lokasenna*. The great god Thor arrives, bursting in on a scene of linguistic carnage. He turns to Loki and each of his four stanzas begins by taking the very words out of Loki's mouth: '*þegi þu*'. At this point, Loki has done exactly what trolls like him set out to do: he has dragged the gods down to his level, reduced these powerful beings to yelping at him to shut up.

Unlike most trolls, Loki is completely open about his motivations. Before elbowing his way back into Ægir's hall, he declares: 'mockery and strife will I bring to the god's sons, / And mingle sorrow with their mead'; just before leaving it, he says 'I have said to gods and the sons of gods / What my mind was amused to say / But now I shall go'.[35] The trouble is that we're none

[34]Interestingly, this aspect of Norse flyting enters the digital world via the game *Assassin's Creed: Valhalla,* the 2020 iteration of Ubisoft's successful series.

[35]Olive Bray (ed. and trans.), *The Elder or Poetic Edda* (London: Viking Club, 1908), p.248; Paul B. Taylor and W.H. Auden (eds and trans.), *The Elder Edda: A Selection* (London: Faber, 1973), p.143.

the wiser for the explanation. Loki seems to enjoy breaking the rules and making a mess for its own sake – he is, as I've already mentioned, a trickster.

The trickster is a common and familiar figure across many of the world's diverse mythologies. Br'er Rabbit or Spider Anansi in some West African and Afro-Caribbean cultures, Coyote in some Native American mythologies, or Reynard the Fox in medieval Europe – all are tricksters to some degree. Tricksters are usually underdogs who live by their wits, regularly outsmarting characters who are stronger or more powerful. To do this, tricksters need a very thorough knowledge of the moral codes and social hierarchies operating within their culture, and they need to know when to follow the rules and when to flout them. (The mouse in Julia Donaldson's *Gruffalo* story is perhaps the best loved trickster in recent English literature.) Tricksters are playful and creative but also mischievous and amoral – simultaneously 'culture-hero and culture-villain'.[36] Their curious blend of savvy knowledge of, yet utter contempt for, cultural mores often goes right to the heart of the ideologies and mindsets that characterize that culture. For example, Loki knows that once he has seated at the banquet alongside the gods, their hospitality codes will give him license to behave however he chooses, and, in order to gain admittance, he reminds Odin that they are blood brothers, and that when their bloods mixed, Odin promised never to drink another ale without Loki. However, for his part, Loki has no concept that the obligations on a good host might imply a reciprocal responsibility for him to be a good guest, or that the bonds between blood brothers entail a respect that is mutual. Thus, he knows which rules to evoke in getting his way, and which ones to break. Like many tricksters, he is a slave to his whims and appetites, and these tend to be aimed low rather than high.

Since at least as far back as 2002, scholars have been pointing out similarities between the antics of the trickster and forms of online misbehaviour, with some going so far as to say that the troll is 'a modern variant of the Trickster archetype from ancient folklore'.[37] As Whitney Phillips puts it, 'trolls embody tricksters' amorality, impetuousness, and shameless desire to splash about in the muck'.[38] And indeed, in a 2010 interview with *Esquire* magazine, one self-confessed troll even invoked 'the trickster god Loki' as an aspirational

---

[36]Whitney Phillips, *This Is Why We Can't Have Nice Things: Mapping the Relationship Between Online Trolling and Mainstream Culture* (Cambridge, MA: MIT Press, 2015), p.9, see 'Trolls as Tricksters', pp.9–11.

[37]Erin E. Buckels, Paul D. Trapnell, and Delroy L. Paulhus, 'Trolls Just Want to Have Fun', *Personality and Individual Differences*, vol. 67, 2014, pp.97–102, p.97. The earliest argument I can find for a link between trolls and tricksters is in John Campbell, Gordon Fletcher, and Anita Greenhill 'Tribalism, Conflict and Shape-Shifting Identities in an Online Community', *Proceedings of the 13th Australasia Conference on Information Systems* (2002). However, they suggest the idea was in circulation as long ago as 1998.

[38]Phillips, *This Is Why …*, p.13.

role model.[39] Anthropologist Gabriella Coleman has spent considerable time and effort exploring the parallels between ancient trickster mythologies and modern online misbehaviour.[40] And, up to a point, it makes sense.[41]

Recall the case of Reece Messer, who Twitter-trolled Tom Daley back in 2012. Speaking to the *Daily Mail* just a few days later, Messer's view of the incident was pretty odd. On one hand, he insisted that he – not Daley – was the real victim of this sorry episode. It wasn't just that he'd been arrested and cautioned, or been subjected to opprobrium on a worldwide scale – it was the widespread calls to suspend him from Twitter. 'You can't do that', he protested. He was indignant that he had tweeted his apologies to Daley multiple times, and that they should simply have been accepted and the matter closed. 'It's Tom Daley's fault … I shouldn't be victimised – and I hope he loses the next competition that he is in', he was quoted as saying. On the other hand, though, he simultaneously gloated at emerging victorious from the debacle.

> Grinning broadly, Reece says he is delighted with the 'publicity'. He points out that the number of people 'following' him on Twitter has increased by 30,000 in a week. 'That tweet is the most notorious in Twitter history,' he adds. 'I was trending worldwide for two days and that's a hard feat. Only seven people can trend at one time and I'm quite proud because a lot of people don't trend and usually only celebrities trend worldwide. I think everyone is jealous and they wish they had all the attention that I do'.[42]

Like a true trickster, Messer invokes different sets of rules and justifications so he can claim to be *both* victim and victor, and he claims that others are jealous of his (risible) success when the more obvious explanation for his behaviour is that he is jealous of his target's success. Interestingly, this is precisely what the goddess Gefjun says of Loki in the *Lokasenna* – that he's sounding off only because he envies the gods their holy powers.

Yet there is, of course, a difference. Reece Messer wasn't living in a mythological world like Asgard. He was living in Dorset. His target wasn't a fictional, mythological, or divine entity, but a real person, with real feelings. But trolls seem not to realize this – or choose not to realize it. It's as if

---

[39]Quoted in Gabriella Coleman, 'Hacker and Troller as Trickster', 7 February 2010. Available at: https://gabriellacoleman.org/blog/?p=1902

[40]See 'Hacker and Troller as Trickster.' Available at https://gabriellacoleman.org/blog/?p=1902

[41]But perhaps only up to a point: there are benevolent tricksters who act out of noble motives and for the common good. See Ted Hughes's much-loved children's story *The Iron Man*, for instance.

[42]Tom Rawstorne, 'Inside the Twisted World of Tom Daley's Twitter Troll', *The Daily Mail*, 4 August 2012.

they (think they) are living in a world where their actions and words have no consequences. As the first team of researchers to make the connection between trolls and tricksters put it: 'they do not consider the consequences of their actions as the "trick" is performed for the sake of the trick itself'.[43] And this, I maintain, explains why the genre of flyting has so much to teach us about the nature of trolling. Recall what was said about the flytings in the Stuart courts: they were a space apart, in which no language, however foul or threatening, was taken seriously, but was instead viewed as part of a game – a game in which deliberately offensive words had no consequences. On the one hand, then, trolls such as Messer comport themselves as if they were sixteenth-century Scottish makars, as if they could say whatever they like without any ramifications, because it's only a game. On the other hand, and contradictorily, the 'fun' of the game is seemingly predicated on the fact that their opponents in this game inhabit a real world where words have real consequences. Like tricksters, trolls play one set of rules off against the other, invoking snippets of each as it suits them. Thus, though trolling isn't exactly the same thing as flyting, flyting can nonetheless reveal a large part of what trolls think they're about.

As Whitney Phillips puts it, trolls:

> don't have to mean the abusive things they say.... Targets of trolling, on the other hand, are expected to take trolls at their word.... What's more, [in a troll's eyes,] the fact that the target failed to realize and/or simply accept that the troll was 'just trolling' only justifies the attack. If the target hadn't been so oversensitive about 'harmless' words (words trolls use because they do indeed cause harm), he or she wouldn't have been trolled; therefore, it is the target's fault.[44]

A clearer example of the asymmetry of trolling you could hardly hope to find – and it seems to describe Messer and Loki equally well. Trolls choose their words and targets for maximum impact yet simultaneously refuse to own any of that impact whatsoever. They place the consequence-free world we find in flytings in a face-off with the world everyone else lives in from day to day. Thus, pioneering scholar of trolling Claire Hardaker has argued that 'sincerely engaging with a troller is akin to participating in a large, public game where one player is cheating'.[45] But perhaps we can put this point a

[43]John Campbell, Gordon Fletcher, and Anita Greenhill, 'Conflict and Identity Shape Shifting in an Online Financial Community', *Information Systems Journal*, vol. 19, no. 5, 2009, pp.461–78.

[44]Phillips, *This Is Why ...*, p.26; p.97.

[45]Claire Hardaker, '"I Refuse to Respond to This Obvious Troll": An Overview of Responses to (Perceived) Trolling', *Corpora*, vol. 10, no. 2, 2015, pp.201–29, p.212.

bit better. Certainly, trolling is necessarily public, as we established earlier, and in this respect, it's just like flyting. But it's not so much that trolls are cheating, rather that their victims don't realize there's a game in play. And so, unlike flyting, trolling is *not* just a game. 'The idea of playful provocation for the sake of mutual enjoyment and bond-building has been replaced by that of abusing others for only the troller's own sick entertainment'.[46]

This brings us to one final, and potentially controversial, problem. One of the more disturbing things that flyting has to teach us about trolling is that there have been times when many people of taste regarded flyting as entertaining and amusing. So could it show us what the incomprehensible appeal of trolling is? It was suggested earlier that a large part of flyting's appeal lay in its providing a form of release from the formality and pageantry of a courtier's life. We saw Robert Hughes opine that flyting 'was evidently designed as an entertainment for a sophisticated, not a "common" audience'.[47] And yet Hughes is wrong. Flyting was – albeit in a rather different form – an immensely popular spectacle among lay audiences in the sixteenth and seventeenth centuries. And to try to understand why, we'll turn to a name greater than that of all the gods, kings, heroes, and noblemen we've looked at so far – to a lowly glovemaker's son named William Shakespeare.

Shakespeare's trolls

Read any number of Shakespeare's plays, and you'll soon start to notice places where the dazzling cut and thrust of Shakespearean dialogue gives way to something altogether more vituperative. On-stage quarrels quickly descend to bouts of mutual name-calling, and characters resort to elaborate rhetorical strategies that seem to serve no purpose apart from winding one another up. Duelling lovers seem particularly prone to baiting each other in this way: Beatrice and Benedick in *Much Ado About Nothing*, Oberon and Titania in *A Midsummer Night's Dream*, and Kate and Petruchio in *The Taming of the Shrew* are among the best-known examples.

In 1935, a Shakespeare expert named Margaret Galway suggested that these scenes might best be understood in light of the tradition of flyting. Though her suggestion hasn't enjoyed much uptake, it stacks up in historical terms. Shakespeare's first plays were performed around 1592; the last of the known Scottish flytings dates from around 1585, and, as I've mentioned, might perhaps have furnished Shakespeare with material for *Macbeth*. Tentatively, I'd suggest that the incorporating of flyting scenes

---

[46]Dynel, 'Trolling Is Not Stupid', p.372.

[47]Hughes, *Encyclopedia of Swearing*, p.175.

into Renaissance drama might help account for the decline of the Scottish flyting tradition. A theatre audience is drawn from all strata of society, and so once anyone could go and watch it on the stage, flyting had ceased to be an aristocratic pastime, hence tarnishing its appeal in courtly circles. And yet it positively thrived on the stages of Southwark.

Galway's study identifies over fifty flyting scenes in the comedies alone. 'In one form or another', she determined, 'Shakspere [*sic*] employed flyting for comic purposes in the vast majority of his comedies'.[48] The most familiar kind is banter exchanged between aristocratic lovers as an ironic exercise in courtship. Such scenes, Galway notes, are 'almost invariably part of the dramatic fare wherever Shakspere's lords and ladies meet in playful mood, and they therefore constitute possibly the bulk of the flyting in his comedies'.[49] The blend of barbed taunt and bawdy innuendo found in this extract, which commences the hostilities in *The Taming of the Shrew*, is as good an example as any:

> KATE: I knew you at the first,
> You were a moveable [item of furniture].
> PETRUCHIO: Why, what's a moveable?
> KATE: A joint-stool.
> PETRUCHIO: Thou hast hit it. Come and sit on me.
> KATE: Asses are made to bear, and so are you.
> PETRUCHIO: Women are made to bear, and so are you. (II i 197–201)

However, Shakespeare's flytings are not confined to his comedies. 'There are also vestiges of flyting in some of the violent confrontations in Elizabethan tragedy, such as Hamlet's caustic repartee, the furious exchanges between Lear and Kent, and the berating of Oswald by Kent in *King Lear*,' adds Hughes.[50] You can also find at least some flyting in the plays set in the ancient world. 'Most terrific of all the flytings are those in *Troilus and Cressida*', Galway opines.[51] There, Shakespeare created a character named Thersites, whose sole dramatic purpose is to provide comic relief in flyting sessions with mighty Greek and Trojan heroes such as Ajax and Hector, and who describes himself, quite accurately, thus:

> HECTOR: What art thou, Greek? Art thou for Hector's match?
> Art thou of blood and honour?

---

[48]Margaret Galway, 'Flyting in Shakspere's Comedies', *Shakespeare Association Bulletin*, vol. 10, no. 4, 1935, pp.183–91, p.190.

[49]Ibid., p.184.

[50]Hughes, *Encyclopedia of Swearing*, p.176.

[51]Galway, 'Flyting in Shakspere's Comedies', p.186.

> THERSITES: No, no:—I am a rascal; a scurvy railing knave; a very filthy rogue. (V iv 25–8)

If this description reminds you of Falstaff, then I'd agree, adding that in my view, he provides, both qualitatively and quantitatively, the most remarkable flytings in Shakespeare's *oeuvre*, mostly in what are called the history plays. So: the main kinds of Shakespearean plays – comedies, tragedies, histories, and Roman (or more accurately, Greek) plays – all 'exhibit the art of vituperation, which unquestionably tickled the Elizabethan palate'.[52]

Not only can we find flyting scenes in all parts of the Complete Works, it's also something that stretches right across Shakespeare's career. *The Taming of the Shrew* is an early effort, from around 1592, but we can also find flyting scenes in his later works, such as *The Tempest*, when the drunken Stefano and Trinculo mock, berate, and body-shame Caliban. If anything, the flytings, rather than being injected by a young and green apprentice playwright from Warwickshire as a source of cheap humour, seem to have become more important, more frequent, and more central as Shakespeare evolved into a mature craftsman. They are deployed with increasing regularity and embedded with more skill:

> slanging matches ... are handled in a fashion which indicates that Shakspere [*sic*] regarded them as a particularly important part of the entertainment. For early in the comic proceedings, in each case, there is a brief flyting—just enough to whet the appetite of an Elizabethan audience; then the same fare, a little varied, is offered again; and continues to appear at intervals, with increasing spiciness, until at the end the biggest and best variety is produced. As theatre-goers well know, these are the tactics which a good playwright regularly employs when he has a special and repeatable treat in store for his audience.[53]

Galway points out that Shakespeare's use of flyting scenes in many ways parallels his use of songs: in the early plays, they are largely extrinsic, added in here and there at strategic intervals, partly for purposes of light relief, and partly perhaps because audiences simply expected to see them. Later on, songs become more integral to the plays, for example by commenting on the action or moving it along. The same, Galway argues, is true of flyting.

> Shakspere [*sic*], then, accepted flyting as a device that was valuable, not only because it was popular but because it was particularly helpful for purposes of comic satire, and he endeavoured, as his technical experience

---

[52]Ibid.

[53]Ibid., p.189.

> increased, to incorporate it wholly into the action of the play and to derive from it a maximum of dramatic effect.[54]

To get an idea of how this worked in practice, let's look at a character who engages in more flytings than any other, and who, almost uniquely, wins some whilst losing others – Falstaff.

'Do thou amend thy face, and I'll amend my life'

Shakespeare gives Falstaff some of the most outrageous insults and best put-downs in his whole flyting repertoire. Falstaff gets away with calling Prince Hal – the future Henry V, legendary victor of Agincourt and folk hero to the Elizabethan audience – everything from 'mad wag' to 'bull's pizzle' [i.e. penis]. When his friend Bardolph calls Falstaff fat, his devastating rejoinder is 'Do thou amend thy face, and I'll amend my life' (III iii 20). He routinely engages in slanging matches with his underlings – Bardolph, Poins, Mistress Quickly, and later his page boy – and he invariably gets the better of them. Interestingly, though, he wins not just through spurting out the crudest insults (though generally that is what he does), but by a range of other strategies well known to trolls.

Almost all attempts at landing an insult or an accusation on him fail to hit home, because he shrugs them off with barefaced lies. For instance, having accused Prince Hal and Poins of cowardice, when it was Falstaff that ran away from a fight, he makes up a story of having fought off two men, which he steadily inflates to four, then seven, then eleven – boasts that are obviously lies, because he claims to have fought in pitch darkness, whilst being able to describe his assailants' clothes. As in trolling, the obvious falsehood of his replies seems to matter less than coming up with a quick and forthright rejoinder. There is an intersection here between trolling and what is sometimes called 'spinning', perhaps. When he's unable to win through making up his own versions of events, he resorts to another common troll tactic: off-topic commenting. In *Henry IV Part Two*, he is accosted by the Chief Justice for failing to appear in court in connection with the robbery in which he claims to have fought off eleven men. Like many a troll, he is utterly brazen in talking provocatively about anything other than the matter at hand. He first tries to brush off the court attendant as if he were a beggar ('What! a young knave, and beg? Is there not wars? is there not employment? doth not the king lack subjects? do not the rebels want soldiers? Though it be a shame to be on any side but one, it is worse shame to beg than to be on

[54]Ibid., p.191.

the worst side' [I iii 73–7]). Then, confronted by the Chief Justice himself, he proceeds to ignore all questions, and instead to ask after the Chief Justice's health, imploring him to take better care of himself. Then he asks after the king's health, and proceeds, in answer to every question about the robbery, to answer about the king's illness instead, a 'perturbation of the brain. I have read the cause of his effects in Galen: it is a kind of deafness' (I iii 117–18) – and one that Falstaff has obviously made up. Well might the Chief Justice complain 'Sir John, I am well acquainted with your manner of wrenching the true cause the false way ... the throng of words that come with such more than impudent sauciness from you' (II i 112–15).

So, though Falstaff can trade ribald insults as low as the worst of them, his success at flyting is not down to vituperation alone but also to a range of rhetorical strategies that anticipate those of the twenty-first-century internet. At one point, when soliloquizing about how he's going to deceive his friend Master Shallow, he tellingly uses an angling metaphor reminiscent of trolling: 'If the young dace be a bait for the old pike, I see no reason in the law of nature, but I may snap at him' (III ii 325–27). He goes on to confess he's doing this for the lulz – he boasts he 'will devise matter enough out of this Shallow, to keep Prince Harry in continual laughter the wearing-out of six fashions ... and he shall laugh without *intervallums*' (V i 78–81). Plainly stated, Falstaff displays the key characteristics of the modern-day troll, and it might be worth reminding ourselves that, as we saw in the introduction, there's evidence to suggest that 'trolling' was already a current term in Tudor times.

Nonetheless, there are two people who can successfully troll Falstaff. One of these is Prince Hal, who, in *Henry IV Part One*, regularly out-insults Falstaff and exposes his lies with deft linguistic efficiency. This is probably down to Shakespeare's deference to rank: after all, it would hardly do to have the soon-to-be Henry V lose a war of words to a fat old drunkard. However, in *Part Two*, Prince Hal engages in little to no flyting. Presumably, Shakespeare needs him to grow up and show some of the decorum expected from a king in waiting. But clearly this created a problem: having one character who can humble the vainglorious Falstaff in a flyting session is structurally important to the play, because he is bound to need taking down a peg or two. Interestingly, Shakespeare got around this by introducing a brand new character, apparently for the sole purpose of flyting: the magnificently foul-mouthed Doll Tearsheet.

As Margaret Galway puts it:

> [Prince Hal's] loss as a comic character is in one respect well compensated by the gain of Mistress Tearsheet. The fact that she, like the Prince, has a genius for invective suggests that the flyting in the first part of the play

> had been popular, and that in the sequel Shakspere [*sic*] deliberately balanced the necessary suppression of Hal's vituperative gifts by an elaborate display of Doll's.[55]

Doll Tearsheet appears in just two scenes. The first includes long stretches of dialogue where she speaks barely a word; the second is easily cut altogether, since it's extremely short and contributes little to the storyline. And yet her small part includes among its lines a range of insults that make Montgomerie and Polwart's vocabulary seem genteel: 'Hang yourself, you muddy conger', 'you whoreson chops', 'thou damned tripe-visaged rascal', 'thou paper-faced villain', 'you blue-bottle rogue', 'you filthy bung', 'I scorn you, scurvy companion. What! you poor, base, rascally, cheating, lack-linen mate!'. Her terms of endearment are as ribald as her insults: 'Thou whoreson little tidy Bartholomew boar-pig', she calls Falstaff, affectionately chiding him to take better care of his body. She accuses Falstaff's friend, Ancient Pistol, of 'tearing a poor whore's ruff in a bawdy-house' and threatens him more gruffly than any male antagonist would dare: 'By this wine, I'll thrust my knife in your mouldy chaps, an you play the saucy cuttle with me. Away, you bottle-ale rascal! you basket-hilt stale juggler, you!'. And yet, with a hilarious irony, she complains that Pistol is 'the foul mouthed'st rogue in England'. Margaret Galway was quite right: 'there can be no doubt that Shakspere [*sic*] relied on ingenious vituperation as a high trump card'.[56]

'Ingenious vituperation', though, isn't quite the same thing as trolling: flaming may be vituperative by definition, but it is normally anything but ingenious. Furthermore, you could also argue, as Hughes does, that 'the great Shakespearean scenes of linguistic confrontation are essentially passionate expressions of character-conflict in which language is taken in deadly earnest, and lives are irrecoverably changed or even destroyed' – that is, they are about much more than just the lulz.[57] But let's remember that in many of the classic plays, the impact of Shakespearean drama is heightened when these deadly earnest scenes are inextricably juxtaposed with scenes consisting of profane slanging matches, baitings, and wind-ups, and not only that, but, crucially, all are played out before an audience. What's more, there are characters ranging from Falstaff to Hamlet sniping from the sidelines in soliloquy, letting the audience in on the joke. This mix of characteristics starts to make the situation in Shakespearean drama much closer to that in trolling.

In the Renaissance era, when literacy was the exception and books were still scarce, the stage was a mass medium, and by far and away the

---

[55]Ibid., p.185.

[56]Ibid., p.189.

[57]Hughes, *Encyclopedia of Swearing*, p.177.

best technology for reaching a large and diverse audience. As we've seen, there's strong evidencc that flyting scenes were immensely popular with Renaissance theatre-goers. The earliest printed edition of *The Flyting Betwixt Montgomery and Polwart* came out in 1621, not long after Shakespeare's death, and it opens with a short prefatory poem, which tells how 'in Playes / Best Actors flyte and raile, and thousand ways / Delight the itching Eare'. So it seems Shakespeare's audiences were itching to see flyting scenes, and found them delightful. The question is: why? And what light can this shed on trolling?

I would argue: quite a lot. Having a ringside seat while Doll and Falstaff or Kate and Petruchio berate one another is perhaps not that different from watching Dunbar and Kennedy laying into each other. But there is more to Shakespeare's flyting scenes than insults: as a rule, the audience of a play tends to know more about the storyline than an individual character, for whom the bigger picture is often incomplete. I mentioned in the introduction that the humour of trolling was in some ways similar to that of dramatic irony, whereby the audience laugh at the haplessness of a character who doesn't know what's going on around them. This is different from conventional flyting. It's much more like the situation of modern-day trolling, where victims often can't tell if they're being trolled or not. In other words, the audience of these scenes is placed in a position of knowledge superior to the victims of the insults on the stage: they are aware of something these characters are not. They know these characters are being trolled, which is something normally known only to those who are doing the trolling. In a manner of speaking, then, Shakespeare places his audiences in the sort of vantage point ordinarily occupied only by a troll.

We know that Falstaff is trolling Master Shadow: he tells us. We know that Petruchio is trolling Kate: straight after he 'rails and swears and rates, [so] that she, poor soul / Knows not which way to stand, to look, to speak', he tells us, in soliloquy, that 'she never looks upon her lure' – a telling metaphor that reveals he's trolling (IV i 120–21; 128). We know, from his many soliloquies, that Hamlet is baiting more or less everyone except Horatio. Note how, in each case, it's those most skilled at flyting who decide whether or not to let the audience in on the joke by breaking the fourth wall *à la* Brecht. A new level of public humiliation has thereby been added to the laughter, beyond that involved in simply trading insults and calumnies, because we now know that those insults and calumnies are just part of a bigger ruse (just as flaming is a useful strategy within trolling, not just an end in itself). Thus, the audience is placed in a privileged position, because the audience enters into the troll's confidence. So, though the media and the mix are structurally different, trolling in the theatre can show us what trolling in real life consists in. That's because Shakespeare's strategy is to let us occupy the vantage point of a troll, without us actually having to do any trolling. Thus, we get to share in Falstaff's lulz, but we don't have to take any of the guilt or responsibility for them. No doubt it is an ethically problematic position to be in.

It's a sad truth that plenty of people enjoy laughter at other human beings' expense. Both trolling and flyting deliver just that. Seventeenth-century philosopher Thomas Hobbes famously wrote that 'The passion of Laughter is nothyng else but a suddaine Glory arising from suddaine Conception of some Eminency in our selves by Comparison with the Infirmityes of others',[58] and though it's not a pleasant thought, most theorists, philosophers, and historians of laughter have conceded he has a point. Certainly, the idea of laughter as rooted in feelings of superiority explains why many jokes, like many trolls, are eyewateringly sexist, racist, or ethnocentric. No doubt it also accounts for the popularity of flyting, and for the fact that plenty of literary and poetic cultures around the world have similar genres involving (often quite elaborately) ritualized altercation or insult: the Welsh *ymryson*; the Provençal *tenso* debate-poem of the medieval troubadours; verse contests in the Japanese *Haikai* tradition; Malian *Sanankuya,* or social bonding through mutual insults; a form of intertribal flyting called *naqā'iḍ* from pre-Islamic Arabia; the West African *Ikocha Nkocha,* another verbal game based on trading insults; its possible descendant in African American culture, 'playing the dozens', in which participants take turns insulting their opponent's mother; and, latterly, rap battles. Like it or not, it seems there's a transhistorical, global penchant for getting a safe laugh from a low-punching joke at your opponent's expense.

Claire Hardaker draws a similarly depressing conclusion in her research into trolling: 'part of the human condition is to find a degree of entertainment in conflict, whether in the form of high-risk sports, action films, violent computer games, or linguistic aggression in television programs'.[59] But though this is a view you could reasonably take, it isn't mine. Granted, Hardaker's comments might account for the appeal of flyting – but that's not what she's talking about. She's trying to make a point about trolling. And with trolling, I'd argue we're dealing with a slightly different kettle of fish. Once more, it comes down to the role of the audience.

As we saw with Loki, trolling is not straightforwardly a contest. It's asymmetrical and one-sided, as if you could somehow cross flyting with blind man's buff. The lulz trolls laugh may well accord with the smug, gloating kind of laughter Hobbes described in his philosophy. Shakespeare's trolls invite us to share in this laughter – they show us what it consists

[58]Thomas Hobbes, *The Elements of Law, Natural and Politic*, ed. Ferdinand Tönnies (London: Cass, [1640] 1969), p.42.

[59]Claire Hardaker, 'Trolling in Asynchronous Computer-Mediated Communication: From User Discussions to Academic Definitions', *Journal of Politeness Research*, vol. 6, no. 2, 2010, pp.215–42, p.238.

in. But, unlike Shakespeare's audiences, the modern-day troll's readership is seldom let in on the joke with a nod and a wink and a soliloquy. So for most people, the laughter and enjoyment are *not* the same as those which accompany a well-played humorous game, because the game is so one-sided it isn't recognizably a game. Hence, I'd turn to a different philosopher, Ludwig Wittgenstein, for a description of what's involved:

> What is it like for people not to have the same sense of humour? They do not react properly to each other. It's as though there were a custom amongst certain people for one person to throw another a ball which he is supposed to catch and throw back; but some people, instead of throwing it back, put it in their pocket.[60]

Those people would, of course, be trolls. This description evokes the kind of childish brats who, as soon as they start losing, pick up their ball and take it home – bending the rules in whichever way it suits them, as in the unwinnable, one-sided games that Unferth, Loki, and their trollish descendants play.

So hopefully the flyting contest, in its various guises, has led us at last to understand what trolling is, and what it isn't. Unlike flyting, trolling isn't a competition, and it has no level playing field. It's a game only when one player decides to call it such, and they change the rules while this game is in play. We might even ask: who wouldn't want to be a troll, since it's a game you can't possibly lose?

Conclusion

Or can't you? Surely we can come up with a better conclusion than that. Let me end with what the *Huffington Post* described as 'A Twitter Masterclass on Dealing with a Racist Troll'.[61] On 19 January 2015 – the public holiday commemorating the work of Dr Martin Luther King Jr – the American writer Ijeoma Oluo was subjected to a protracted barrage of the vilest racist abuse by a Twitter troll using the alias Dildo Baggins, and the handle @mrscrotum21. The torrent of racial slurs, profanities, and scatological jibes was eyewatering even by the standards of many trolls, and there is no need or desire to repeat them here. Oluo, quite rightly, wasn't about to let this go unchallenged, and her response was truly inspired – an admirably

[60] Ludwig Wittgenstein, *Culture and Value*, trans. Peter Winch (Oxford: Blackwell, 1980), p.82.

[61] See Andreas Krebs, 'A Twitter Masterclass on Dealing with a Racist Troll', *Huffpost,* 3 February 2015. Available at: https://www.huffpost.com/archive/ca/entry/racism-on-twitter_b_6598134

fitting tribute to King's legacy. Not responding would be letting the troll get away with it; rational debate with a foul-mouthed bigot was clearly not a live option. Under these circumstances, most people would probably rise to the bait and engage in a flame war. But Oluo responded to each taunt, insult, and racial slur with calm dignity, replying to each abusive tweet with a short, simple, uplifting quote from Martin Luther King Jr.

'Let no man pull you so low as to hate him'; 'Hate destroys the hater'; 'I believe that unarmed truth and unconditional love will have the final word in reality'; 'We must either learn to live together as brothers, or we are going to die together as fools'; and so on. The goads, taunts, and jibes that were stymied so effectively with quotations such as these became progressively more abusive, more explicitly racist, and more crude. Presumably, the troll was trying harder to wind Oluo up, or getting exasperated at his lack of impact, or both. But Oluo's straight-faced response in the face of extreme provocation recalled King's noble tradition of dignified passive resistance. The insults and quotes went back-and-forth for hours, before the troll began mocking Oluo's strategy, tweeting spoof MLK quotes like '"I hope I get shot soon" – Martin Luther King Jr' and '"I only say this shit for the RTs" [i.e. re-tweets] – Martin Luther King Jr'. Oluo then changed her strategy:

> IJEOMA OLUO: @mrscrotum21 I wish you peace and love and freedom from the hatred that hurts your heart
>
> DILDO BAGGINS: @IjeomaOluo who's that a quote from
>
> IJEOMA OLUO: @mrscrotum21 that's me. Sending love and hope to you
>
> DILDO BAGGINS: @IjeomaOluo I have plenty of that
>
> IJEOMA OLUO: @mrscrotum21 not enough to displace the hate in your heart
>
> DILDO BAGGINS: @IjeomaOluo no I'm just trolling. This isn't an account to be taken seriously.

Were this a simple game – like a flyting session – the victory would at this point be Oluo's. As soon as any troll is forced to own up to their trolling, they have basically lost. But for Oluo, this was no game, and she made sure the troll knew it. She tweeted historic photographs of police brutality against African Americans, along with the question 'you mock this?', and, as the troll tried to worm a way out of the mess, she added comments such as 'you mock every dead child, you mock every burned home, you mock every lynched father', and 'I would never laugh at your murder. I would never taunt your grieving. I would never mock your fight for equality'. Eventually, the rarest of things happened: the troll apologized. Publicly. Online. He tweeted: 'you are so nice and I'm so sorry'.

Oluo was successful precisely because she didn't allow herself to get drawn into a digital flyting session. To do so would have been demeaning to the day and to the subject matter, gifting an easy victory to the troll.

But the use of quotations was also nothing short of ingenious. By engaging with the troll through the words of King, Oluo achieves so much: she reminds her readers (and the troll) of the importance of the day and the struggle it commemorates, and she gives her replies the resonances of King's legendary eloquence, plus the gravitas of his reputation. In short, she meets low blows with high rejoinders. But, more infuriatingly for the troll, she keeps her own thoughts and her own persona close to her chest. Both remain hidden until she is ready to reveal them, leaving the troll no public face or public statements of her own to attack. Whitney Phillips has remarked that 'the mask worn by trolls precludes reciprocity; only the troll can wear the mask'.[62] Certainly, I wouldn't want to suggest that Oluo was somehow using King as a mere mask or mouthpiece, but nevertheless, she found a way to use his words to shatter the asymmetry that trolling depends on, defeating its one-sided structure by ventriloquizing her replies through King, and leaving her own thoughts and feelings unexposed to the troll until the time was right.

In the next chapter, we'll be looking more closely at the question of public face and public personae, and instead of Martin Luther King Jr, we'll be looking at his namesake, the German theologian Martin Luther. But before we travel back in time to 1517, let me end with the suggestion that Oluo's is a strategy we'd all do well to consider. By responding to crass taunts with highbrow quotes, we can deprive trolls of the very personal feelings they delight in hurting, and leave them with nothing to get their claws into. And I'd add that the body of texts we call literature, from Homer to Toni Morrison, is a resource replete with one-liners for tackling trolls on pretty much any occasion. After all, why engage in a flame war when you can simply quote Shakespeare – even if it's nothing more than an uncomplicated putdown such as 'Do thou amend thy face and I'll amend my life'?

---

[62]Phillips, *This Is Why* …, p.33.

3

... or to make a public statement ...

Trolling the pope: Martin Luther goes viral

Schoolchildren of my generation were routinely taught that the history of the world had its course changed forever on 31 October 1517, when a German monk named Martin Luther nailed his ninety-five theses to the door of the Castle Church in Wittenberg. This document, we were told, contained a merciless onslaught on the authority of the Catholic Church and triggered the Reformation. It was a deft debunking of the fraud and extortion authorized by the pope in the selling of church-sanctioned pieces of paper – called indulgences – which purported to grant time off for good behaviour to any soul languishing in purgatory. Such a chord did Luther strike with his German readership that within just a few years, the church had been split in two, Protestantism had emerged as a faith able to inspire millions of zealous followers throughout central and northern Europe, and wars were being fought to suppress it. All told, very few documents can claim to have had the huge impact on world history that Martin Luther's *Ninety-Five Theses* did.

This wasn't just a revolution in religion or in theology. Historians have argued for at least fifty years that it was a revolution in communications technology. In other words, Martin Luther would have lived and died as an obscure academic in one of Germany's new universities if he hadn't stood on the shoulders of Johannes Gutenberg, pioneer of the printing press. 'Strong claims have been made for the importance of printing as a major causal factor of the German Reformation', notes one leading historian of the period, with another going so far as to assert bluntly 'No printing, no reformation'.[1] And behind this train of thought is some sound reasoning:

> [Printing] broadcast subversive messages with a rapidity that had been impossible before its invention. More than that, it allowed the central ideological leader, Martin Luther, to reach the 'opinion leaders' of the movement quickly, kept them all in touch with each other and with each other's experience and ideas, and allowed them to 'broadcast' their (relatively coordinated) program to a much larger and more geographically diverse audience than had ever been possible before.[2]

When put in these terms, it's easy to see that anyone with a serious interest in how our digitally networked culture has developed needs to take the figure of Martin Luther very seriously.

Let me be clear from the outset: Martin Luther was *not* a troll. When summoned to the Diet of Worms in 1521, and effectively placed on trial for his life, he was given the opportunity to recant and retract his writings and teachings. At this point, a troll, exulting in the pleasure of having duped and infuriated the best minds in the Catholic Church and the Holy Roman Empire, might have uttered something along the lines of '@hisholinessthepope hahahaha yeah fam I only wrote that shit for the lulz:D'. Instead, Luther's response had all the dignity of a Gandhi or a Mandela: '*Hier stehe ich. Ich kann nicht anders. Gott helfe mir. Amen*' – 'Here I stand. I can do nothing else. God help me. Amen'.[3] This is not the reply of a troll. Whether you see a troll as an angler – someone who 'attempt[s] to waste time through provoking futile argument whilst appearing outwardly sincere'[4] – or as more like Scandinavian monsters 'sending antagonistic, inflammatory messages with the intent of provoking others into conflict',[5] the simple fact is that Martin Luther was neither. Nevertheless, Luther was *accused* of trolling, or at least of trolling-type behaviours, on multiple occasions at that – and, as we'll see, these accusations were not entirely

---

[1]Mark U. Edwards Jr, *Printing, Propaganda, and Martin Luther* (Minneapolis, MN: Fortress Press, 2005), p.2; Bernd Moeller, 'Stadt und Buch: Bemerkungen zur Struktur der Reformatorischen Bewegung in Deutschland', in *Stadtbürgertum und Adel in der Reformation: Studien zur Sozialgeschichte der Reformation in England und Deutschland*, ed. Wolfgang J. Momsen (Stuttgart: Klett-Cotta, 1979), pp.25–39, p.30.

[2]Edwards, *Printing, Propaganda, and Martin Luther*, p.7.

[3]These words neither appear in the transcripts of the proceedings nor in the accounts of any eyewitnesses. As with so much about Luther's story, the best-known facts could well be folklore.

[4]F. Vera-Grey, '"Talk About a Cunt with Too Much Idle Time": Trolling Feminist Research', *Feminist Review*, vol. 115, no. 1, 2017, pp.61–78, p.72.

[5]Marta Dynel, '"Trolling Is Not Stupid": Internet Trolling as the Art of Deception Serving Entertainment', *Intercultural Pragmatics*, vol. 13, no. 3, 2016, pp.353–81, p.358.

groundless. Perhaps, then, Luther might exemplify the distinction discussed earlier between *trolling* and *being a troll.*

But that is not the main reason why Luther deserves a chapter in this book. We saw, in the previous chapter, that trolling needs to be public in order to count as trolling. Luther stands at a pivotally historic moment in this respect: 'Most historians would accept today that a public opinion emerged during the Reformation period'.[6] The historians are backed up on this point by Marshall McLuhan himself, the original media guru: 'Printing from movable types created a quite unexpected new environment – it created the *public*. Manuscript technology did not have the intensity or power of extension necessary to create publics on a national scale'.[7] But the printing press didn't do all this by itself. In fact, before Luther, it had been in existence for a good seventy-five years, churning out printed material with no wider sense of who or what this output was for than a scribe in a medieval scriptorium had. Its power was only realized when it was finally wielded by writers and publishers genuinely committed to reaching as many readers – especially ordinary, everyday people – as possible. And they only did this because of the religious zeal of Martin Luther. This is not to suggest that Luther knew what he was doing: he seems to have been as oblivious as everyone else to the potential of the printing press at first, and no less astonished at the scale of his readership and his impact than anyone else.[8] Yet the point remains that 'the coincidence of the spread of Reformation ideas with the availability of the new technology of printing led to the emergence for the first time in European culture of a genuine public opinion'.[9] And, as we'll see throughout this chapter, that public reacted in ways that tell us much about trolling today.

We should not underestimate the size or scope of this public reaction. Martin Luther was a public figure in a way that no one had been before. He was, in essence, the world's first bestselling author, as well as the prototype for a new kind of crusading public intellectual. And he was arguably the most divisive figure in European history before the French Revolution. But this wasn't (just) because of his controversial theological views. It was because he was so effective at spreading them. As we'll see, he grasped clearly enough that there was little interest in abstruse scholastic tomes written in Latin, no matter how many copies of them were printed.

---

[6]Peter Matheson, *The Rhetoric of the Reformation* (Edinburgh: T&T Clark, 1998), p.30.

[7]Marshall McLuhan, *The Gutenberg Galaxy: The Making of Typographic Man* (Toronto: University of Toronto Press, 1962), np.

[8]'In letters from early 1518, Luther seemed rather surprised at how widely the *Theses* had been disseminated.' Timothy J. Wengert, *Martin Luther's Ninety-Five Theses, with Introduction, Commentary, and Study Guide* (Minneapolis, MN: Fortress Press, 2015), p.5.

[9]Matheson, *Rhetoric of the Reformation*, p.56.

So he turned to a new format: 'Luther compounded his enormity when he disseminated his program through thousands of vernacular pamphlets spread among the common people'.[10] This, as we'll see, was a form custom-designed to reach a mass readership. And he wrote in their language – German.

Most people would agree that, as one expert put it, 'Luther had a great capacity to communicate with ordinary readers'.[11] It wasn't just that *what* he was saying was so provocative and controversial, it was rather that, as some have claimed, he 'had a singular power with language', to the point that 'Luther is considered to hold the same position in the German language that Shakespeare and the King James Bible have in English'.[12] Probably only Goethe could claim to have shaped German letters to a greater extent than Luther. Indeed, theologian Gerhard Ebeling once described Luther as a *Sprachereignis* – a 'language-event'[13] – and it's hard to disagree. Luther's literary impact was felt throughout the German-speaking lands, even where his religious message fell on deaf ears. It's worth belabouring that point in case anyone was wondering what Martin Luther is doing in a book about literature. Though he didn't write novels or plays, he is nevertheless one of the most influential authors in European literary history.

Although his famous words to the Diet of Worms oozed sincerity, straightforward openness, and honesty beyond the point of bravery, the fact is that Luther's public face was very carefully constructed – a persona calculated to maximize the impact on his audience. The extent of that impact was truly unprecedented anywhere in history, and it seems to have taken everyone, including Luther himself, by surprise. Such was the runaway success of his combined use of the printing press and the vernacular German language that his most authoritative biographer refers to the fallout as the 'unexpected reformation'.[14] So, if he was the first to use the latest technology to reach a mass audience, with a message that went far beyond anything its author might have envisioned, and spinning way beyond his control, then surely Luther was the first person in history to see something he wrote 'go viral'.

---

[10]Edwards, *Printing, Propaganda, and Martin Luther*, p.7.

[11]Timothy F. Lull, 'Luther's Writings', in *The Cambridge Companion to Martin Luther*, ed. Donald K. McKim (Cambridge: Cambridge University Press, 2003), pp.39–61; p.39.

[12]James Arne Nestingen, 'Approaching Luther', in *The Cambridge Companion to Martin Luther*, pp.240–56, pp.241–42.

[13]Gerhard Ebeling, *Luther: Einführung in sein Denken* (Tübingen: Mohr Siebeck, [1964] 2006), p.1.

[14]Heiko A. Oberman, *Luther: Man Between God and the Devil*, trans. Eileen Walliser-Schwarzbart (New Haven, CT: Yale University Press, 1989), pp.111–206.

When something goes viral, the origins of the outbreak are often hard to trace; the facts behind it become difficult to establish. Such, we will now see, is the case with Luther. But nonetheless, one thing ought to strike any historian of trolling as clear from the outset: it is *very* instructive that probably the first thing in world history to go viral was a statement of heresy, posted publicly on a community chatroom-type platform, and couched as a bid to provoke discussion and debate.

Who posted what? (Some myth-busting)

'Martin Luther the historical figure assigned to teach biblical studies at an obscure university in the eastern part of what is now Germany and Martin Luther, cultural symbol, parted company on or about 31 October 1517, and have had an unpredictable relationship ever since', wrote another of Luther's modern-day biographers – and with good reason.[15] To understand why, let's go back to what was taught to my generation of schoolchildren in Religious Education lessons. I remember being told that Luther was a gifted biblical scholar who felt that the church was swindling its flock. The idea of putting the forgiveness of sins on sale, he realized, had no basis anywhere in Holy Scripture, so the selling of indulgences was a scam. The mass of ordinary people, being uneducated, would be easily taken in by this scam, and, being poor, could least afford it. So, he wrote a document of ninety-five arguments (*theses*) debunking indulgences and nailed them to the door of the Castle Church in Wittenberg on 31 October 1517. He chose Hallowe'en for maximum publicity because the following day – All Saints' Day – would see the church packed with worshippers. He used the German language and the printing press to reach as many ordinary people as possible. In response, the pope and his followers used both reason and force to try to contain Luther's message but couldn't. Because he knew the Bible so well, Luther was able to quote it time and again to back up his views. He even translated it into German so the ordinary people could follow his arguments. Eventually, the church split, and he formed a new faith – Protestantism.

Almost everything in this summary is questionable. Much of it is false. Let's start with those indulgences. Yes, they were sold; yes, their theological basis was dubious; yes, the sales tactics often made yesteryear's PPI brokers seem principled. The transactions involved seem hard to comprehend. Take the Castle Church, Wittenberg, where Luther preached. Twice a year, the local ruler, Elector Frederick III, displayed his collection of holy relics there. Paying to view them would get you no less than 100,000 years

[15]Nestingen, 'Approaching Luther', p.240.

off of purgatory.[16] Attending the mass on these occasions would get you another 200 days off, so it was time well spent. And one of these two annual opportunities to get fast-tracked to heaven was All Saints' Day. So, in effect, Luther had put a poster on the door of the church where he preached telling his congregation that their coming to church that day was a complete waste of time. Perhaps this is an early indication of his trollish temperament.

What about the *Ninety-Five Theses* themselves? What exactly did they say? Well, in an important sense, they *said* nothing at all. They merely offered up propositions for debate – or at least, that's what they claimed to do. In this respect, again, Luther could be said to resemble a troll: someone who posts incendiary, heretical comments, only to deny that they ever actually *said* or *meant* any of them – they were only trying to start a debate, trolls will say, and they can't see what all the fuss is about. Here is how the *Ninety-Five Theses* begins:

> Out of love and zeal for bringing the truth to light, what is written below will be debated in Wittenberg with the Reverend Father Martin Luther, Master of Arts and Sacred Theology and regularly appointed lecturer on these subjects at that place, presiding. Therefore, he requests that those who cannot be present to discuss orally with us will in their absence do so by letter. In the name of our Lord Jesus Christ. Amen.[17]

The practice of publicly posting theses for debate was not uncommon in university towns at the time, because it was an essential part of the academic process. Students were examined on their defence of a set of theses, drafted by their supervisor, at a public debate. Just two months earlier, Luther, as a doctor of the church, had written a (very different) set of ninety-seven theses on scholastic theology for his student Franz Günther to defend – Günther did so successfully, and was awarded a bachelor's degree. Historians agree that 'The theses for such debates, according to the University of Wittenberg statutes, were to be posted on the doors of the churches in town'.[18] So perhaps there was nothing unusual about what Luther did; perhaps he was only doing his job. Some scholars maintain that 'far from seeing the *Ninety-Five Theses* as programmatic, Luther regarded them as opening up a necessary debate'.[19]

---

[16]The figure of 100,000 years comes from Wengert, *Martin Luther's Ninety-Five Theses*, p.xix. Some earlier scholars put the figure at nearly two million years. See Ernst Borkowsky, *Das Leben Friedrichs des Weisen* (Jena: Eugen Diederichs, 1929), pp.56–7.

[17]Wengert, *Ninety-Five Theses*, p.13.

[18]Wengert, *Ninety-Five Theses*, p.xxxvi.

[19]Matheson, *Rhetoric of the Reformation*, p.46.

Or did he? The problem is that no such debate, discussion, or disputation seems to have occurred. Though some of the church authorities assumed that it must have done – as per standard procedure – Luther himself admitted it didn't. Moreover, it seems unlikely that he ever intended to: it's hard to believe he had a student lined up to defend these theses, partly because they were so incendiary, and partly because they were written in a none too scholarly style. As Timothy Wengert puts it:

> Luther's theses had a very different character from others that he wrote at the same time, and the invitation to people unable to attend the disputation to answer by letter is unique. Moreover, there is no indication that the disputation was ever held. Thus, it would seem that Luther's intent was not so much holding a run-of-the-mill disputation in Wittenberg but rather to begin a discussion of a church practice that he found particularly disturbing.[20]

Looked at from this perspective, Luther's behaviour starts to look more and more like trolling: he bends, or even flouts, the norms and conventions of a discussion forum to air contentious views. That there was no obvious intention of actually holding a public debate suggests that Luther was hijacking the platform rather than making proper use of it, while the unprecedented request for letters in response to his theses sounds like an attempt to draw as many people as possible into posting replies to his controversial writings – writings he could always disown as only harmless debate if those replies got too heated.

This portrait of Luther as a troll, however, overlooks one important obstacle. Astonishingly, there is no evidence that he ever attached his *Ninety-Five Theses* to the Wittenberg church door in the first place. Certainly, he never mentioned it – not once, anywhere in the thousands upon thousands of pages he wrote (published or unpublished), including his surviving letters and conversations as well as scholarly treatises and demagogic pamphlets. Furthermore, there are no eyewitness accounts of it, either. In fact, there is no record of it *at all* that dates from Luther's lifetime. For such an earthshattering event, this is pretty remarkable. Its very first mention is in the preface to an edition of Luther's Latin works, written by his second-in-command Philip Melanchthon, four months after Luther died. But Melanchthon first arrived in Wittenberg only in August 1518 – nine months after the event. Could it be, then, that the reason why no public debate ever took place is that the theses were never actually made public for debate? Since they were written in non-standard style, and requested discussion by private correspondence,

[20]Wengert, *Ninety-Five Theses*, p.xxxix.

maybe they were never intended for display to begin with. Rather than being a forerunner of the troll, then, perhaps Luther went viral without ever wanting to.

Indeed, there's little to no evidence that, in October 1517, Luther had his sights on a large public. It's often assumed that, because the printing press was so pivotal to the story of Luther's success, the *Ninety-Five Theses* must have been a printed document, written for mass circulation. But this is highly doubtful. There are no records or surviving copies of any Wittenberg printing. It's certainly possible that there was one: a couple of months earlier, the printers had run off copies of the ninety-seven theses Luther wrote for Franz Günther, and these, too, had vanished from history until one was rediscovered quite recently. It would have been simple enough for Luther to get his *Ninety-Five Theses* printed if he was indeed aiming at a large-scale readership: 'The only printing press in Wittenberg in those days, run by Johann Grunenberg, was housed in the basement of the Augustinian friary (along with the kitchen and the toilet), right under Luther's study'.[21] But then again, if he only intended the document for private circulation, with no plans for public debate, why have it printed?

There is, in fact, evidence to suggest that Luther did *not* want the *Ninety-Five Theses* to reach a broad public. This evidence is related to another misunderstanding about Luther's theses. As a schoolboy, I was taught that a large part of what made Luther such a revolutionary was that he wrote in German, the language of the people, instead of Latin, the language of the church – and so I always assumed that the *Ninety-Five Theses* must have been written in German. They weren't: they were written in Latin. Less than three months after he wrote them, Luther's colleague Christoph Scheurl offered to translate the *Ninety-Five Theses* into German for him. Luther refused, replying that his scholarly discussion document 'was not fitting for educating the common folk'.[22] (He wrote a German-language executive summary instead, called the *Sermon on Indulgences and Grace*, of which more later.) He actually spurned these early opportunities for self-publicity. Nevertheless, by then, Latin editions had already been printed in Nuremberg, Leipzig, and Basel, to the extent that 'in letters from early 1518, Luther seemed rather surprised at how widely the *Theses* had been disseminated'.[23]

To sum up: the closer we look at the evidence for what actually happened in 1517, the harder it becomes to gauge whether Luther was or wasn't a publicity-grabbing troll. Even if they were attached to the Wittenberg Castle Church door, much of the mythology that attached to the *Ninety-Five Theses*

---

[21]Ibid., p.xxxvii.

[22]See ibid, p.xli, p.38.

[23]Ibid., p.5.

is demonstrably false. Though the image of Luther nailing his writings to the church door resonates so perfectly with traditional Christian iconography, which associates nails and carpentry with redemption, it wouldn't have been like that. The doors of Wittenberg's churches were effectively university noticeboards and would have needed replacing pretty frequently if a hole had been hammered into them every time the students had exams coming up, so wax was the adhesive of choice.

One thing we know for sure: in one sense of the word, Martin Luther did indeed post his *Ninety-Five Theses* on 31 October 1517. That is, he sent them, by post, to Albrecht von Brandenburg, Archbishop of Mainz – the highest-ranking clergyman in the German-speaking parts of the Holy Roman Empire. Though perhaps not exactly trolling, this was certainly provocative: for example, the eleventh of the *Ninety-Five Theses* basically accuses bishops who tolerate the sale of indulgences of malpractice. Yet it was Albrecht himself who had authorized a set of hard-sell tactics for indulgence preachers. These required city dignitaries to lay on a lavish procession to escort the indulgence preacher, under the papal banner, from the town gates to the church, while local churches rang their bells and suspended all sermons so as to yield their pulpits to the indulgence preachers. Luther knew Albrecht had done this. His *Ninety-Five Theses* contains many a swingeing attack on Albrecht's guidelines.[24] But, in the cover letter he sent, he wrote that this document of Albrecht's must have been printed 'surely without the consent or knowledge of your Reverend Father' – a wilfully disingenuous dig.[25]

Digs like this abound throughout the *Ninety-Five Theses*. Thesis 73 notes that the pope has 'thundered against' those who obstruct the sale of indulgences; Luther follows it, in Thesis 74, with a deft piece of trolling: 'much more so does he intend to thunder against those who, under the pretext of indulgences, contrive to harm holy love and the truth'.[26] It doesn't actually *state* that the pope is wrong; it doesn't quite *claim* to correct him; it doesn't exactly *say* that the pope has parted company with the truth, or that Luther presumes to know what the pope really ought to be doing instead – but all the same, it's not hard to see how his readers would have seen in this striking sentence a lot of juicy bait to rise to. And it isn't an isolated example. Thesis 54 openly defies Albrecht's instructions on the sale of

[24]Albrecht was a young man, still in his mid-twenties, and still fairly new to his job. He had, in fact, bought his position, for an obscene amount of money, running into tens of thousands of ducats. He'd borrowed the cash from a banking family in Augsburg and had a simple plan for paying it back: he was going to take a cut from the proceeds of the sale of indulgences across Germany. Luther didn't know this at the time. Perhaps it might have been more interesting if he did.

[25]Martin Luther, 'Letter to Albrecht', in *Ninety-Five Theses*, ed. Wengert, pp.31–6, p.34.

[26]Wengert, *Ninety-Five Theses*, p.23.

indulgences: 'An injustice is done to the Word of God when, in the very same sermon, equal or more time is spent on indulgences than on the Word'.[27] It's a fairly bold statement, even brash, but not without a certain grounding in common sense. Next, having established this as a vague truism that's hard to disagree with, Luther's fifty-fifth thesis ups the ante by flying to an extreme conclusion:

> It is necessarily the pope's intent that if indulgences, which are a completely insignificant thing, are celebrated with one bell, one procession, and one ceremony, then the gospel, which is the greatest thing of all, should be preached with a hundred bells, a hundred processions, and a hundred ceremonies.[28]

The hyperinflated rhetoric, the bald, unembellished style, the simplistic reasoning behind it, which leads to the drawing of provocatively bogus inferences, and the obviously inflammatory claim to reveal what the target really thinks in spite of everything he says – all this is the very stuff of trolling. In fact, the *Ninety-Five Theses* have proven to translate surprisingly readily into ninety-five brusque yet barbed tweets.[29]

Whatever consequences Luther may or may not have intended his biting document to provoke, what really happened next quickly mushroomed far beyond his control. 'Luther's *Ninety-Five Theses* burst onto the European scene like wildfire', and not because of their content, but because 'pamphleteers saw gold. They recognized early that Luther's *Theses* touched a raw nerve'.[30] It's important now to understand the sheer magnitude and vastness of the Luther phenomenon – the unparalleled extent to which his writings went viral.

From Wittenberg to viral

Let's pause here to take note of an important fact: there was no such thing as copyright in the sixteenth century. Even if there had been, it would have been unenforceable in the German-speaking parts of the Holy Roman Empire, which were a veritable mosaic of dukedoms and principalities, each beyond the jurisdiction of the others. Moreover, copyright made no sense at the

---

[27]Ibid., p.21.

[28]Ibid., p.21.

[29]See https://twitter.com/luther95theses?lang=en

[30]David M. Whitford, 'Luther's Political Encounters', in *The Cambridge Companion to Martin Luther*, pp.179–91, pp.181–82.

time. After all, printed papers were heavy to carry, transportation networks (whether packhorse, river barge, or wagon) were slow, levies and tolls on trade passing through many small sovereign territories would soon mount up, and any one of these states *en route* could simply seize and burn the papers if suspicious or hostile towards their contents. Individual publishers weren't yet established enough to have large-scale distribution networks that tackled such problems. So, if a printer in, say, Wittenberg or Leipzig had a hit on their hands, there was nothing to stop a printer four hundred miles away in, say, Strasbourg or Basel from simply reprinting it. On the contrary: this was quite normal. Thus, printed works could be duplicated and circulated at a speed and on a scale never before seen in history. The moral rights of authors over their works, and the power of sovereign states to enforce their authority over how printers traded, simply did not operate as constraints. In a sense, then, the distribution network disseminating Martin Luther's writings had more in common with the internet age than it did with the heyday of print in the late-nineteenth to late-twentieth centuries. Hence, before he could say 'Johannes Gutenberg', Luther found his *Ninety-Five Theses* had been printed and distributed in three major imperial cities at different corners of the Holy Roman Empire, without his knowledge or consent. In today's terms, he was going viral.

It would be wrong, though, to paint too vivid a picture of Luther as an unwitting victim. If he ever was – and we've just seen that the 'if' is genuine – this stopped at an early stage. Luther's main objection to disseminating the *Ninety-Five Theses* was that they weren't suited to popular consumption; so, he intended to write something that was. He called it the *Sermon on Indulgences and Grace*, and it came out in March 1518. It was 'Luther's earliest attempt in German to explain to the non-scholarly world what he was trying to say' and it 'turned him into a best-selling author overnight' – indeed, into 'the first living bestselling author the world had ever seen'.[31] Across Germany, it was reprinted an astounding twenty-five times in just over two years. No written document had ever before attracted such a big readership so quickly. Besides showcasing 'Luther's remarkable ability to take complicated, scholarly debates and turn them into simple, direct words',[32] it also gives us, I will later suggest, an early insight into his talent for trolling. The two are not unrelated: in those days, writing about theology in plain German was itself a provocation of sorts. In fact, that Luther was writing simple prose in the vernacular language instead of Latin was perhaps the main reason for this success. Scholars mostly agree that '*The Ninety-Five Theses* ... had relatively limited circulation in vernacular

[31]Wengert, *Ninety-Five Theses,* p.x, p.xli.

[32]Ibid., p.xi. Wengert continues: 'This talent will reveal itself over and over again in Luther's career – from *Freedom of a Christian* in 1520 to the *Catechisms* of 1529.'

editions and was, in any case, difficult to understand. Instead, it was his *Sermon on Indulgences and Grace* that first introduced Luther to a truly broad public' and that 'this tract more than any other catapulted Luther into the public eye'.[33]

Though Luther was reportedly 'as surprised as anyone', and rather taken aback, at having come up with a hit of such unprecedented size, he quickly learned from it. It would be hard to argue that, within a year or two of the *Ninety-Five Theses*, Luther was still standing haplessly by while the reach of his writings ballooned, or that he was anything other than a savvy, canny media operator. He was, on the contrary, 'far and away the most published author in all Europe well into the next decade'.[34] To get a sense of the scale, let's look at some numbers.

It's been reckoned that 'if we assume conservatively that each printing of a work by Luther numbered one thousand copies, we are talking about an output for Luther of 3.1 million copies during the period 1516 to 1546'. That equates to approximately one printed copy of a work by Martin Luther per four people in the German-speaking Holy Roman Empire at the time.[35] Not, I hasten to add, one in four literate people, or one in four Protestant-sympathizing people – just per head of population. That is a remarkable level of exposure, which few writers in history or in the present, in print or online, have ever achieved. Furthermore, these numbers do *not* include the flyaway success of Luther's translation of the New Testament into German. Even if we confine ourselves to the form of the pamphlet – a cheap, small, and simple form of printing that had a huge impact on everyday people – Luther still accounts for a full one-fifth of all known pamphleteering between 1500 and 1530, and that despite the fact that he wrote and printed little to nothing for the first half of this period.[36]

In the years 1518 to 1544, his total output of German language works (2,551 printings and reprintings, excluding his translations of the Bible) was about five times greater than the total output, within the same time frame, of all his Catholic opponents put together.[37] Furthermore, it was

---

[33]Edwards, *Printing, Propaganda, and Martin Luther*, p.169; Wengert, *Ninety-Five Theses*, p.38.

[34]Wengert, *Ninety-Five Theses*, p.xli; p.xii.

[35]See Edwards, *Printing, Propaganda, and Martin Luther*, p.39. Edwards argues here that six million pamphlets were printed during this time, equating to one for every two people, so, by the same maths, I calculate that three million copies of Luther's works comes out at one for every four.

[36]See Hans-Joachim Köhler, 'The *Flugschriften* and Their Importance in Religious Debate: A Quantitative Approach', in '*Astrologi Hallucinati*': *Stars and the End of the World in Luther's Time*, ed. Paola Zambelli (New York: de Gruyter, 1986), pp.153–75.

[37]Edwards, *Printing, Propaganda, and Martin Luther*, p.29.

nearly double the productivity of the seventeen next most prolific of his Protestant allies combined.[38] Neither Thomas Jefferson nor Lenin nor Mao Tse-Tung could claim that their respective revolutions were spearheaded by their actual writings to anything like the extent that Luther could.[39] If we were to factor in his biblical translations, the numbers would show him to be more dominant still. It wasn't just that Luther wrote so much (though he did) – it was that his writings were reprinted and reprinted time and again across many different German-speaking countries. It was a phenomenon on a scale never known before, dwarfing the feebly short-lived twitterstorms we call 'viral' today.

But we shouldn't deduce from all this that Luther's prescient eye had somehow seen in the printing press a power that others had yet to grasp and that he planned to seize on its potential. Firstly, it seems likely that he only discovered this after (and because) his *Sermon on Indulgences and Grace* became a smash hit. Secondly, and more importantly, we shouldn't forget how new the technology was. Yes, it's undeniably true that 'the reformation saw the first major, self-conscious attempt to use the recently invented printing press to shape and channel a mass movement', and that 'printing was used to reach an audience far larger than any previous movement reached and one that could not have been reached as quickly and as effectively before printing's invention'.[40] But it's no less feasible to argue it the other way around: the technology of printing, and the uses to which it was put, were themselves perfected by the Reformation. As an example of what I mean, consider the literary form we call the pamphlet.

In 1517, the year of the *Ninety-Five Theses*, a huge boom in pamphleteering began. By the end of 1518, there had been a 530 per cent increase in the production of pamphlets. By 1526, printings and reprintings of pamphlets were at a level around 55 times higher than before the *Ninety-Five Theses*.[41] In the seven-year period from 1520 to 1526 – the formative years of the Reformation – over six thousand different pamphlet titles were printed, 'representing conservatively over 6.6 million copies ... which works out to one exemplar for every two people in the empire', and enough for every literate person in Germany to have owned about twenty.[42] Though printing had been around for seventy-five years, the pamphlet had been largely

38Mark U. Edwards Jr, 'Luther's Polemical Controversies', in *The Cambridge Companion to Martin Luther*, pp.192–205; p.194.

39Edwards, *Printing, Propaganda, and Martin Luther*, p.xii.

40Ibid., p.1, p.xi.

41See Köhler, 'The *Flugschriften* and Their Importance'.

42Edwards, *Printing, Propaganda, and Martin Luther*, p.21, p.172; Matheson, *Rhetoric of the Reformation*, p.60.

peripheral to its early history. Why did this format undergo a sudden and unprecedented surge of popularity at the start of the Reformation? By way of an answer, let me quote at some length:

> The Reformation perfected the use of the small booklet or pamphlet as a tool of propaganda and agitation. Frequently in quarto format – that is, made up of sheets folded twice to make four leaves or eight pages – and without a hard cover, these pamphlets were handy, relatively cheap, readily concealed and transported, and accordingly well suited for delivering their message to a large popular audience. They could be easily transported by itinerant peddlers, hawked on street corners and in taverns, advertised with jingles and intriguing title pages, and swiftly hidden in a pack or under clothing when the authorities made an appearance. They were ideal for circulating a subversive message right under the noses of the opponents of reform.... The handy quarto size, perfect for cheap but still legible type, the small number of sheets, and the modest decoration (if any) meant that these works could be turned out quickly and cheaply by printers. They did not demand the same heavy investment in paper and multiple sets of type that conventional books did. They also took less time to produce and could therefore be sandwiched between larger print jobs and whipped out quickly to respond to changing events. The small size and ease of production also allowed for relatively inexpensive prices.[43]

In short, the format was perfect for the needs of people like Luther, and it was this format more than any other that enabled his writings to go viral. (Around a fifth of all pamphlets printed in these years were by Luther, though, for reasons we've discussed, the credit for this lies more with Germany's printers than with him.)

The cheapness, speediness, and portability of the pamphlet form allowed for dissemination on a thitherto inconceivable scale. It was a revolution in communications technology directly comparable to the burgeoning of Web 2.0, in that it involved a similarly serendipitous intersection between the new technology and the needs of its end users – both writers *and* readers. More importantly, this trend for pamphleteering was unlike any form of literature ever before produced. Since this book deals in literary history, let's pause to take stock of something truly groundbreaking: the pamphlets of the early Reformation were probably the first time ever – at least in European history – when literature was produced with the common people as its intended readership. As evidence for this, consider the 'drastic turn to

[43]Edwards, *Printing, Propaganda, and Martin Luther*, pp.15–16.

the vernacular'[44] – that is, the fact that most of them were written not in Latin but in German.

This trend was no less pronounced or remarkable than the unexpected flooding of the market with a sudden outpouring of pamphlets. Once again, consider the numbers involved:

> the number of pamphlets written in German rose seven-fold from 1519 to 1521, and the proportion of German to Latin pamphlets completely reversed itself, going from about three Latin pamphlets published for every German one to three German pamphlets for every Latin one. In the following year the presses of the empire put out nine German pamphlets for every one Latin pamphlet.[45]

There was a 72 per cent decline in the use of Latin for pamphleteering in just three years. By any standards, that's a revolution in print culture. Once again, Luther led the charge:

> In 1518, 47 percent of the printings of Luther's works are in German. This rises to 63 percent in 1519, 85 percent in 1520, 78 percent in 1521, 95 percent in 1522, and then hovers in the high eighties and low nineties for the rest of the decade.[46]

The two trends seemingly went hand in hand: the demographic that was educated enough to read German but not Latin clearly overlapped the demographic that had enough disposable income to buy a pamphlet but not a book.

Luther's target readership, then, were everyday people. Both the topics he dealt with and the tone in which he dealt with them indicate he was addressing not scholars and clergymen but layfolk:

> Luther was, for the most part, not arguing with or even addressing other theologians.... He explained technical issues in simple terms, undergirded with citations of Scripture, and without benefit of the learned distinctions that graced scholastic sermons and treatises of his age. He largely avoided the vocabulary of theological scholarship or, in the few cases where the technical distinction was important, he patiently defined the term for the laity's benefit.[47]

---

[44]Ibid., p.21.

[45]Ibid.

[46]Ibid., pp.181–82.

[47]Ibid., p.44.

More precisely, Luther was deliberately rejecting this distinction between scholars, theologians, and clergymen, on one hand, and laymen, on the other. According to his teachings, *all* baptized Christians were priests – he promoted the idea of a 'priesthood of all believers' – and so his writings tend to deal not with abstruse points of theology but rather with practical issues uppermost in his readers' minds: how to pray; how (and whether) to confess; the proper functions of sacraments such as marriage, the Eucharist, baptism, and the last rites; and the religious dimensions of secular topics such as usury. In other words, his writings aim to overcome the distinction between the church elite and the everyday people by empowering the people to take charge of religious matters for themselves.

This is why it's been argued that Martin Luther invented the idea of the reading public in the sense we understand today, that is, the abstract idea of a collective of readers, each of whom has an individual opinion that matters equally, yet whose importance derives not from their personal views but from their critical mass as a collective, the size of which in turn indicates the importance of the writer. And if this is so, then surely it was also Luther who created the conditions necessary for trolling to thrive. After all, we saw in a previous chapter that trolling by definition requires a public. But it is amplified when that public is large – and amplified exponentially when that public is unquantifiably large. Moreover, when that public is faceless and anonymous, it becomes frustratingly impossible to gauge the extent of the harm a troll has done, which in turn makes it hard to know how to respond. That, certainly, was the experience of Pope Leo X, who reportedly both dismissed Luther as a stereotypical drunken German and praised him as an acutely minded theologian. Irrespective, then, of whether Luther was a troll or not, he blazed the trail to the comments sections and chatrooms where they congregate.

At the same time, though, the phrase 'reading public' doesn't do justice to the scale of Luther's reach. According to historians, 'Only a small fraction of the population in sixteenth-century Germany could read German – perhaps 30 percent in the cities and 5 percent overall. An even smaller fraction could read Latin'.[48] But this doesn't mean that Luther was writing only to them and for them. Quite the contrary: precisely because literacy rates were low and books were scarce, sixteenth-century writers knew their works would be read out loud, often to gatherings of people in homes or in public places such as inns, market squares, or churches. Writers of the time – including Luther – anticipated this. 'They crafted their writing for oral transmission using colourful expressions, rhyme, engaging stories, and the like. They explicitly urged their readers to share their reading with others'.[49]

[48]Ibid., p.193.

[49]Ibid.

Huge indeed though Luther's reading public was, it exploded even further thanks to 'the multiplier effect of the semi-public reading of pamphlets'.[50] Take this as a concrete example:

> A treatise such as Luther's 1520 *On the Freedom of a Christian* might see twelve reprintings within a year or two of its publication, representing, say, thirteen thousand copies. But one preacher, such as Mattheus Zell, who read this treatise and incorporated its message into his sermons, could multiply its influence many times over.[51]

Sixteenth-century culture was still very much driven by word of mouth: hence, the news that a monk named Martin Luther had spoken out against indulgences would likely have been spread by the rumour mill sooner, faster, and further even than by the *Sermon on Indulgences and Grace*. But the key point is that the spoken word and the printed word weren't entirely separate categories. Indeed, Marshall McLuhan argued that 'prose remained oral for centuries after printing'.[52]

McLuhan would probably have gone so far as to say that literacy rates in sixteenth-century Germany are a red herring when discussing the extent of Luther's public impact. The emergence of a reading public, he writes,

> has usually been confused with ideas about 'the extent of literacy'. But even if literacy were universal, under manuscript conditions an author would still have no public. An advanced scientist today has no public. He has a few friends and colleagues with whom he talks about his work.[53]

Conversely, Luther had a huge public, even though most of them could not read. As historian Mark Edwards has written:

> we should not make the mistake of thinking that a printed message could reach only those who were able to read. It may be a conceit or at least a naïveté of our modern, literate culture to fail to recognise how well the illiterate could get access to the printed page. One reader could share the fruits of his or her reading with hundreds and even thousands of other people.[54]

[50]Matheson, *Rhetoric of the Reformation*, p.36.

[51]Edwards, *Printing, Propaganda, and Martin Luther*, p.39.

[52]McLuhan, *Gutenberg Galaxy*, p.136.

[53]Ibid., p.132.

[54]Edwards, *Printing, Propaganda, and Martin Luther*, p.38.

As an example of the intermeshing of the printed word with the spoken word, consider the form of the sermon. On the face of it, it's the epitome of oral culture, declaimed from the pulpit to a congregation, many of whom could not read. Many preachers, therefore, incorporated readings from printed works into their sermons for the benefit of the illiterate. Conversely, many sermons found their way into print: they often served as the basis for a pamphlet, since they were roughly the same length. And here again, Luther was at the very forefront of this curve: he is reckoned to have preached around 4,000 sermons in his lifetime, of which about 2,300 have come down to us in some form.[55] Furthermore, the years when his fame and his public mushroomed were precisely the years when he used the spoken and the printed word in tandem: by 1525, Luther's sermons counted for two in every five printings of his works, falling slightly to one in three by 1530.[56] Recall those figures about his dominance of the marketplace for pamphlets in the early years of the reformation, and it's hard to separate his success in the pulpit from his success in the pamphlet.

The reformation, then, wasn't just a revolution driven by printing: it was, if you like, a multimedia revolution. One historian, indeed, has drawn up a diagram of the various flows of information at the time – from sermons in the pulpit; from pamphlets read in private or out loud; from official debates in town halls, courtrooms, or universities; from non-official debates in taverns and marketplaces; even from things like the singing of hymns or ballads – and tabulated how these flows overlap one another. Tellingly, he describes it as a 'web' of public opinion, in which information flows in all directions from multiple sources.[57] Not for the first time, we're impelled to the conclusion that while digital technology may be new, digital culture is not.

Given all this, it's not surprising that historians like Edwards have argued that Luther spearheaded 'the West's first large-scale media campaign'.[58] Edwards writes: 'It may strike some as anachronistic to speak of a media campaign in the early sixteenth century. But in means, method, and scope, the Evangelical publishing blitz of the early 1520s has all the earmarks [*sic*] of a modern campaign'.[59] In many respects, he's absolutely right: not only was Luther using a sophisticated mix of the latest technology with the word of mouth to cross international boundaries and to target the biggest public possible, he might even have invented the very idea of doing so. And he

[55]Fred W. Meuser, 'Luther as Preacher of the Word of God', in *The Cambridge Companion to Martin Luther*, pp.136–48, p.136.

[56]Edwards, 'Luther's Polemical Controversies', p.193.

[57]See Matheson, *Rhetoric of the Reformation,* pp.38–41.

[58]Edwards, *Printing, Propaganda, and Martin Luther,* p.21.

[59]Ibid., p.15

seems to have been pleased at the results, writing in a high-spirited pamphlet from as early as January 1521: 'That I began in God's name and [that] my teaching is the true word of God has no stronger proof than that it has spread so quickly throughout the world'.[60] In other words, he used the same criteria for success as any modern media campaign. My misgivings about Edwards's use of the term have nothing to do with the anachronism involved in foisting modern terms on the early sixteenth century. On the contrary, I'm not sure that describing what Luther unleashed as a 'media campaign' presents him as modern enough.

In the first place, the term seems to cast Luther as someone who had the panache of a Saatchi and the reach of Charles Foster Kane. Perhaps he did; perhaps he didn't. But either way, unlike them, he didn't have a premeditated media strategy. He didn't first sense the potential in the new printing technology and then formulate a strategy for exploiting it, as a media entrepreneur would. Instead, he discovered it along the way, making up his tactics (very cannily and astutely) as he went along. Interestingly, the 1521 pamphlet I just quoted exults not in his message being universally embraced and accepted but in the way it 'caused disunity'. This sounds less like a twentieth-century marketing executive and more like a twenty-first-century troll.

Secondly, though, and more importantly, Luther differed from today's well-groomed media strategists in his singular failure to keep control over the message he was spreading. What began as an earnest debate about whether forgiveness could be bought and sold very quickly became a seriously heated disagreement about something else altogether – about who had the right to interpret Scripture. Some background here: Luther's *Ninety-Five Theses* and his early arguments with his Catholic opponents quoted liberally from the Bible as backup for his views – he demonstrated a gift for this throughout his career. But his opponents' riposte was generally that the passages Luther quoted couldn't mean what he thought they meant, because the pope thought otherwise. Luther's position was that the Bible meant what it said; the church's position was that the final say over what the Bible meant belonged to the pope.

What incensed the Catholic Church, then, wasn't the finer points of Luther's views about indulgences but rather the threat to papal authority implied in his insistence that the words of Holy Scripture trumped the views of the pope. As for Luther, his earliest writings don't so much as mention the issue of the pope's final authority over biblical interpretation – it doesn't seem to have even occurred to him in the *Ninety-Five Theses* or the *Sermon on Indulgences and Grace* that other people might refute his readings of the Bible. Some historians have even maintained (implausibly, I feel) that Luther

[60]See Luther, *Answer to the Goat Emser at Leipzig*, 1521.

seriously expected the pope to agree with the biblically backed arguments in his *Ninety-Five Theses*.[61] Thus, 'whatever Luther may have expected to result from the *Theses* had taken an unexpected (and, perhaps, unwanted) turn, one that was light years from the original debate'.[62] Moreover, his teachings were then picked up and forwarded by supporters who claimed to be promoting his views, even though many of them were not entirely on message. And that, I maintain, is simultaneously why it makes sense to claim that Luther had gone viral, *and* that this was not a media campaign in the current sense of that term.

Luther lost control of his central message at a fairly early stage, and the wider it circulated and the more contexts it entered, the less recognizable it became. No well-oiled media campaign would ever allow the public image of its brand to be hijacked to this extent. But that is what it means to go viral. It's not just the scale or reach of a message's circulation but also the loss of control over its meaning and its increasing detachment from its originating context – all of which are the perfect nightmare for a choreographed media campaign, yet a dream come true for a troll.

Luther's public persona – the mask of a troll?

Martin Luther, then, was unable to control the extent to which his message spread, and only partially able to control how his message was spun. Yet he seems to have been extremely adept at crafting and controlling his public persona, no matter how big or how varied his public grew. This, too, was crucial to his success. Luther had another rare gift: he could come across as profoundly serious and morally earnest, with a godliness verging on the angelic; *and* he could come across as a scurrilous rabble-rouser, bullying his allies and publicly humiliating his enemies, while spewing foul-mouthed hate speech. He was, perhaps, both saint and troll.

What makes him so interesting is that these perceptions of him weren't down to whose side his readers took: it wasn't that Protestants thought he was a saint and Catholics thought he was a troll. Sometimes even his closest allies thought he'd gone too far in baiting and abusing his opponents – further than befitted a man of God. Yet Luther's example suggests that scant reputational damage arises from trolling in the name of the Lord. Or, put another way: that Luther was able, in spite of it all, to retain his public image as the most holy, god-fearing, pious man of his age seems to bear out the deep-seated difference between trolling and being a troll. The difference

[61]See, for example, Wengert, *Ninety-Five Theses*, p.39.

[62]Ibid., p.11.

is surely in the maintenance of a public persona. Someone who trolls may be 'just trolling', but they're not 'just a troll' if they can successfully portray themselves as trolling in the service of a noble cause.

In the last chapter, we came across Whitney Phillips's idea that trolling is a bit like wearing a mask. Typically, only the troll gets to decide the extent to which their public face coincides with their private self behind that mask. Often, that extent will be not at all, but even where there is overlap, it's up to the troll how that is presented. Notice, for example, how the troll we met at the end of the last chapter readily positions himself as such with the handle Dildo Baggins @mrscrotum21 and compare that with the connotations of a handle like @realDonaldTrump, with 'real' presumably opposing itself to the 'fake' news of traditional media. It's fairly clear from this that the online profiles and personas used by trolls are part of the literary and rhetorical strategies they use in trolling, not far removed from creating a fictional character.

Luther was a key innovator in this respect. Indeed, 'Martin Luther' is, like so many public profiles and personas, a pseudonym. Martin Luther was actually born Martin Luder (sometimes spelt Ludher). The surname by which he is known to history was a carefully crafted mask: 'he changed his name, shifting the spelling of the family name to give it a more ancient but radical ring – Lu*th*er is a pun on the Greek word for freedom, *Eleutherius*'.[63] Lu*th*er hints or nods at, but doesn't exactly say, 'the free one'. Tellingly, Luther took on this pseudonym at exactly the same time that he unleashed his *Ninety-Five Theses*: among its earliest recorded written instances is a letter he wrote to Johannes Lang on 11 November 1517, less than a fortnight after sending his theses to Archbishop Albrecht.[64] The moment he decided to go public was the very moment he decided he needed a decent profile. This profile was effective because it didn't just resonate with those scholarly enough to pick up on the echoes of ancient Greek. Later, when he was writing for a German-speaking public, it took on an additional level of meaning, because in the German of those days, *Lauter* meant 'the pure one'.[65] It's also interesting that Luther's pseudonym retained a close association with the very institution he decried – the Catholic Church: he would regularly publish as Martin Luther, Augustinian. As he grew famous, this was abbreviated to M.L.A., retaining the association without spelling it out.[66] This is just one example of how 'Luther's public persona could stretch to fit a variety of specifics'.[67]

---

[63]Nestingen, 'Approaching Luther', p.241.

[64]Wengert, *Ninety-Five Theses*, p.13.

[65]Matheson, *Rhetoric of the Reformation*, p.103.

[66]Edwards, *Printing, Propaganda, and Martin Luther*, p.184.

[67]Ibid., p.89.

These days, we tend to take it for granted that an online persona requires a good profile photograph. We tend to roll our eyes at this, as if it signalled the vanity of our age. Trolls exploit this vanity, whether by manipulating their judge-by-appearance readers' expectations with a fake profile picture, or (contradictorily) by excoriating their targets' appearance as portrayed in their profile picture. Whilst Luther didn't quite go this far, he, too, understood the importance of a good profile picture. Rather than a twenty-first-century foible, this was arguably more important in the sixteenth century, when large-scale illiteracy meant a majority of people had no choice but to judge a book by its cover. Hence, one in-depth study into the iconography of Luther's works shows how visual representations of him were common – usually in woodcuts – and invariably stressed three key factors of his public persona.[68] Firstly, that he was a monk: Luther is always depicted in the habit of an Augustinian; secondly, that he was a learned scholar and teacher: he is constantly portrayed wearing his doctoral hat or beret; thirdly, that he was a man of the Bible: he is always shown with one ready to hand, usually holding it and sometimes reading it. In addition to these three ubiquitous signs, a fourth is very common, but with some variation: a dove indicating the presence of the Holy Spirit, and/or a saintly halo, representing his superhuman godliness. As Edwards has pointed out, the advantage of this pictorial iconography is that it doesn't have to specify, for example, what Luther's godliness consists in, or what made him such a great teacher, or why a Bible in his hands is any different from one in yours or mine.[69] To this observation, I would add that Luther's choice of symbols is manipulative to the point of trolling: after all, his teachings dispensed with the institutions of sainthood and of monastic orders, on the grounds that no Christian, however monkish or saintly, was theologically superior to any other Christian – except, apparently, for Luther, whose profile picture clung to the trappings of a monk and a saint. All Christians are equal, but the Christian who points this out is more equal than others.

There's no doubt that these self-publicizing strategies reached unprecedented levels of success. Pamphleteers and writers of the time would regularly refer to him as 'the pious Luther', or 'pious and right'.[70] One of his contemporaries, Hartmuth von Cronberg, summed up the popular mood when he wrote that 'there has undoubtedly not been a truer more Christian teacher living in a thousand or more years than this doctor Luther'. Others went further still: as the reformation went on, Luther was compared to the prophet Elias, sent to reveal the antichrist, or to the angel of the apocalypse,

---

[68]R.W. Scribner, *For the Sake of Simple Folk: Popular Propaganda for the German Reformation* (Oxford: Clarendon, 1994).

[69]Edwards, *Printing, Propaganda, and Martin Luther*, pp.83–4.

[70]Ibid., p.85.

foretold in the Book of Revelation. Luther, though, was always careful to stop short of making such claims about himself.

Perhaps it will be asked: so what? Many writers take pseudonyms with advantageous connotations; many put carefully posed portraits on the covers of their books; many have reaped popular acclaim and bestseller status as a result. This doesn't make them trolls, and it doesn't make Luther one, either. It merely underscores his status as the first celebrity author in history. It's true, indeed, that while the manipulative construction of one's public persona is practically a precondition for trolling, it isn't unique to trolls, and it isn't sufficient reason to diagnose trolling. So let's turn now to sketching out some of the rhetorical strategies Luther pioneered for today's trolls and how they evolved over time.

A portrait of Luther as a troll

As with almost any writer worth the reading, Luther's writings developed across his career, as he experimented with different styles, tones, and forms. It's been claimed that 'during Luther's lifetime the Reformation went through two phases that shaped the character of Luther's controversial writings and their audience'.[71] I'd argue, though, that Luther's writings underwent at least three clearly distinguishable periods. We'll look at them in chronological order:

> In the first phase Luther defined a movement. He addressed most of his polemics to an empire-wide audience of readers and auditors. He pointed out the failings within the papally controlled Catholic Church and advocated reforms based on his understanding of the gospel. He attacked, but he also sought to persuade, to educate, and to inform.[72]

The writings of this first phase were those that made Luther's reputation, principally the *Ninety-Five Theses* and the *Sermon on Indulgences and Grace*. Their emphasis is very much on theological debate and on its practical implications for everyday life. What they have to say is immensely provocative in itself: Luther has no need to resort to rhetoric to make it any more so.[73] That is not, however, to say that Luther is ever above needling or point-scoring at this stage, but he does so to underscore the exposition and explanation of his views.

---

[71]Edwards, 'Luther's Polemical Controversies', p.192.

[72]Ibid.

[73]See Matheson, *Rhetoric of the Reformation*, p.46.

As an indication of the (fairly limited) kinds of trolling that Luther practices in this first phase, let's consider the ending of the *Sermon on Indulgences and Grace*:

> Although some (for whom such truth really damages their treasure chests) now want to call me a heretic, nevertheless I consider such blathering no big deal, especially since the only ones doing this are some darkened minds, who have never even smelled a Bible, who have never read a Christian teacher, and who do not even understand their own teachers but instead remain stuck with their shaky and close-minded opinions. For if they had understood them, they would have known that they should not defame anyone without a hearing and without refuting them. Still, may God give them and us a right understanding! Amen.[74]

Note that even at this early stage, Luther is trying to set up an adversarial 'them and us' opposition, even as he disingenuously appeals to God to defuse any antagonism. The passage accuses 'them' of ignorance, stupidity, godlessness, narrow-mindedness, and 'blathering', and implies a mercenary motive behind all these faults. And yet, at the same time, it also says that throwing baseless insults around is unchristian – though not, apparently, when Luther does it. Heads Luther wins, tails they lose. It is notable that Luther does absolutely nothing whatever to defend himself against the charge of heresy – he just flings counteraccusations against 'them' instead, impugning their intelligence and integrity. And yet he does so while clearly saying that 'refuting them' in scriptural discussion would be the more proper thing to do. This, once again, is a case of the asymmetry of trolling. Finally, note that Luther positions himself here as the wronged victim, and that in spite of this piece of writing doing everything that 'they' have wronged him by doing.

Luther was a master at this deft polemical footwork so familiar to trolls and used it throughout his career – not just in the first stage. Paradoxically, the fact that he is remembered today as a victim of religious persecution might, ironically, be down to his rhetorical aggression. Consider the advice he gave a few years later to his friend and follower Johannes Agricola – who might have been the man who lit the fire on which Luther famously burnt the papal bull of excommunication. Agricola had once written disapprovingly of the Catholic loyalist Duke Ulrich of Württemberg. But, once Ulrich converted to Protestantism, Agricola's censorious remarks were very much out of place, and offended not just Ulrich but also other influential Protestant rulers including Philip, Landgrave of Hesse and Albrecht, Count of Mansfeld. Having alienated these powerful allies,

[74]Luther, *Sermon on Indulgences and Grace,* in Wengert, *Ninety-Five Theses,* pp.47–8.

Agricola could not apologize profusely enough. Luther, though, was having none of it, and told Agricola:

> I hear you just caved in to Philip of Hesse, [and] gave him too humble an answer, which I was sorry about. You should now publish an Introduction where you answer the *Graf*, and include that you earlier humbly sought peace, but because they rage and do not want peace you are forced not to be humble but to fight for the matter according to justice, and you are sorry about your humility.[75]

This masterclass on how to be the aggressor whilst appearing to be the victim, crafting a public face out of righteous indignation that lacks any real sincerity, sheds a good deal of light on the passage we have just read from the *Sermon on Indulgences and Grace*: Luther was certainly good at this kind of trolling.

Indeed, he was also remarkably successful. These early pamphlets did not just set forth the theological basis for the reformation. They constructed Luther's public face so successfully that nothing he did thereafter really tarnished it. As Edwards puts it, they

> laid the foundation for the special charisma that Luther later enjoyed, establishing him in the public eye first as an earnest and constructive pastor and man of the Bible concerned above all for the religious well-being of the laity. Luther made his appearance in the vernacular press as the angry critic of the papacy only after this first impression had been well established.[76]

To an extent, the rhetorical strategies of the second phase of Luther's writings were enabled by his successful construction of a public persona in the first phase:

> In the second phase Luther was engaged in building and defending an institution. He addressed most of his polemics to readers and auditors who were already Lutherans. He continued to explain and educate but spent proportionally more effort exhorting his co-religionists. He continued to appeal to Scripture but supplemented these appeals with claims to personal authority.[77]

---

[75]Luther (9 September 1529), in *D. Martin Luthers Werke: Kritische Gesamtausgabe – Briefwechsel*, Weimar: H. Böhlau, vol. 5, p.151, quoted and translated in Lyndal Roper, *Martin Luther: Renegade and Prophet* (London: Vintage, 2016), p.370.

[76]Edwards, *Printing, Propaganda, and Martin Luther*, p.11.

[77]Edwards, 'Luther's Polemical Controversies', p.192.

In other words, the second phase drew heavily on the reputation he had built as a godly man of the Bible and an innocent victim of 'the establishment'.

Strangely, given that Luther was at this time engaged in no less a task than the founding of the first major new religion in Europe for over four centuries, it was during this second phase that Luther gave freest reign to his sense of humour. Taking his cue from the success of Erasmus's *Praise of Folly*, Luther 'loved to describe himself as a fool'[78] and drew on Saint Paul's epistles to back him up: 'Because the foolishness of God is wiser than men; and ... the wisdom of this world is foolishness with God'.[79] His preaching began to employ flamboyant humorous gestures: 'Maybe I owe the world and my God just one more act of folly', he once quipped.[80] The use of humorous buffoonery makes good sense, because it contrasts so starkly with the pompous, sanctimonious aura that surrounded the papacy. One of his preferred techniques is satire – a literary strategy which, as the next chapter shows, can sometimes verge on trolling. 'At the early stage of his reforming career, he used little satire',[81] writes Matheson, but as he sought to define and defend his movement, he found it an excellent tactic, exaggerating the faults of 'them' to make them look ridiculous in contrast to 'us'. For example: 'they' – the Catholic Church – think that the secret of getting into heaven is to do good works, but if that was true, says Luther, then surely donkeys would get into heaven, since even an ass does plenty of good works while the pope does none.[82]

Though historians and biographers have not yet dubbed Luther a troll, at least one of them has described his writings using the same metaphor from which one sense of the term 'trolling' derives:

> He treats feeble opponents, such as Alfeld at the beginning of the *Babylonian Captivity* of 1520, much as an angler plays a fish on a line. He offers a mock recantation of his previous writings, but only to move on to still more radical positions about Indulgences and the Papacy.[83]

This kind of trolling shares with satire a tendency to fly to extremes, to polarize. Its humour, where it has any, lies in the extent to which it strings along its hapless target. Luther first thanks Alfeld profusely for prompting

---

[78]Matheson, *Rhetoric of the Reformation,* p.126.

[79]1 Corinthians 1:25; 3:19.

[80]Luther, in *D. Martin Luthers Werke: Kritische Gesamtausgabe – Schriften*, Weimar: H. Böhlau, vol. 6, p.404, quoted and translated in Matheson, *Rhetoric of the Reformation,* p.118.

[81]Matheson, *Rhetoric of the Reformation,* p.126.

[82]See Meuser, 'Luther as Preacher', p.144.

[83]Matheson, *Rhetoric of the Reformation,* p.126.

him into rethinking and reformulating his ill-considered heretical views, only to then explain he hadn't taken them far enough. Luther's comic wrongfooting of his opponents was often successfully calculated to expose them to ridicule. But none of his trolling was as vicious or as earnest as his polemical destruction of his erstwhile ally turned rival, Andreas Rudolph Bodenstein von Karlstadt.

After Luther, Karlstadt was the next most prolific writer of the German Reformation – albeit a very distant second. He'd written a swingeing denunciation of corruption in the Catholic Church a full year before Luther's *Ninety-Five Theses*. On Christmas Day 1521, with Luther under protective custody in the Wartburg Castle, Karlstadt officiated at the first ever Protestant communion service. He was deemed important enough and dangerous enough by the Catholic Church to be summoned to debates alongside Luther, and he was excommunicated in the same papal bull as him. For a while at least, he and Luther regarded one another as fellow travellers. But they crossed swords, partly over the nature of the Eucharist, and partly over how far to support the popular discontent that culminated in the Peasants War of 1525. Karlstadt then fell between two stools: the more radical brand of Protestantism he favoured was discredited and crushed along with the peasant uprisings it was alleged to have fomented. Karlstadt had no choice but to make his peace with Luther, who, for his part, took him in and sheltered him in Wittenberg. But there was a price: Karlstadt had to recant any of his writings that were at odds with Luther's. That Luther was thus putting Karlstadt in the same position the pope put Luther in does not seem to have occurred to him. Not content with bringing Karlstadt to heel, Luther then set about humiliating him, through what can only be classed as trolling. Above all, Luther's feud with Karlstadt is replete with his 'snorts of disbelief and derision' and his 'harsh language and personal attacks on his opponents'.[84] But there was far more to it than that.

Karlstadt presented himself as a humbled Lutheran, using all of Luther's rhetorical moves. Karlstadt claimed he was putting forth ideas for debate – it didn't follow that he actually held such views. He also pointed out, in true Lutheran fashion, that what counted wasn't what he thought, but what the Holy Scriptures said:

> He had asked in his writings to be instructed if he erred.... He had written according to the best of his abilities and understanding, but he conceded that many others might well have been given by God greater perception and understanding of Scripture than he. The readers of his books should have considered this and not held anything to be

[84]Matheson, *Rhetoric of the Reformation*, p.126; Lull, 'Luther's Writings', p.55.

> proven and godly without first assuring themselves from Holy Scripture. Until this was done, his readers should consider his teachings as no more than opinion.[85]

All this rhetorical positioning is familiar from the first stage of Luther's earlier career. Perhaps that's why Luther knew how to destroy it so effectively.

Though we've seen how Luther had initially presented himself as someone who knew he could be wrong and who was open to debate and to instruction, he demolishes Karlstadt for such posturing:

> Luther ... interpreted Karlstadt's concessions as not merely an admission that his teachings should not be considered as certain, but as proof that they were false. True instruction by the Holy Scripture ... Luther explained ... [meant] a person so instructed is certain and sure of his position, and he will confess to this position 'courageously, freely, and confidently' in the face of death and the devil.[86]

First Luther insisted Karlstadt recant; then he used Karlstadt's recantation to destroy his reputation. Even some of Luther's allies, such as Wolfgang Capito, noted his double standards – by the same rationale, Luther's own *Ninety-Five Theses* could not have found favour with God. So Luther went one further.

Karlstadt had emulated Luther's polemical strategy of saying that he knew of no passage in the Bible that disproved his views and asking his opponents to produce a scriptural basis for refuting him. This was one of Luther's most effective rhetorical moves when trolling his Catholic opponents. However, when used as a move against him, he dismisses it outright:

> all this trading of accusations, Luther maintained, was the devil's trick, diverting men from the proper study of the gospel. They should ask their 'Evangelists' to point them 'away from Luther and Karlstadt' and towards Christ but not, as Karlstadt did, only to his work.[87]

Apparently, when Luther demands what scriptural grounding there is to his opponents' arguments, he is referring them to the fount of Christianity, the Bible; but when his opponents demand it of him, they are distracting us from the fount of Christianity in favour of their own vainglorious and erroneous writings. Heads Luther wins; tails Karlstadt loses.

---

[85]Edwards, *Printing, Propaganda, and Martin Luther,* p.133.

[86]Ibid., p.134.

[87]Ibid., p.142.

Like many trolls, Luther was quick to interpret the moral outrage that followed some of his comments as a sure sign that he'd struck a nerve. He even began joking about it: 'My very greatest fear and anxiety', he wrote, 'is that my case might fail to be condemned by Rome, because then I would definitely know that it is not pleasing to God'.[88] This strategy drove him to make ever more extreme pronouncements, which he in turn defended as being merely simple, down-to-earth, heartfelt statements of the truth: 'What can we theologians do, when we have to see and hear such great lies, all dressed up in God's words?'[89] In this, perhaps, lay the roots of his downward rhetorical spiral: making increasingly radical and provocative statements propelled him to dress them up as homespun truths, propelling him in turn to come up with yet more outrageously radical and provocative statements, and so on and on. It's a dynamic familiar to us in today's trolling. And eventually, it took Luther to the same destination trolls make for: personal abuse and hate speech.

A particularly unpleasant example of this third and final phase of Luther's career would be his 1545 work *Against the Papacy at Rome, Founded by the Devil*. This work has been described by fairly sympathetic historians as 'extraordinarily nasty even for Luther', and as so 'unreadable' and 'offensive' as to 'stretch and strain our categories to breaking point'.[90] In it, he knows no restraint whatsoever. It gives free vent to 'Luther's old obsessions with sex, sodomy and extravagance'.[91] Its misogyny and homophobia exceed the standards of its day by some margin and would count as hate speech in any culture that recognized the concept. This 'virulent, rambling treatise lambasts Pope Paul III as a sodomite and transvestite',[92] feminizing the pope by addressing 'Her Sodomitical Hellishness Paula III', and blending an 'anti-feminine bias' with 'barrow-loads of references to sodomy and bisexuality'.[93] The pope, whose family name was Farnese, becomes *Fartz Esel* – fart ass. Indeed, according to Luther, 'the Pope and his entourage are born from the devil's anus; the Papalists are encouraged to foul their pants, to hang the chain of turds around their necks and sniff them appreciatively'.[94] What's more, Luther 'threw around words for excrement

---

[88]Luther, in *D. Martin Luthers Werke: Kritische Gesamtausgabe – Schriften*, Weimar: H. Böhlau, vol. 6, p.469, quoted and translated in Matheson, *Rhetoric of the Reformation,* p.129.

[89]Luther, in *D. Martin Luthers Werke: Kritische Gesamtausgabe – Schriften*, Weimar: H. Böhlau, vol. 54, p.242, quoted and translated in Matheson, *Rhetoric of the Reformation,* p.205.

[90]Edwards, 'Luther's Polemical Controversies', p.203; Matheson, *Rhetoric of the Reformation,* p.199.

[91]Roper, *Martin Luther,* p.388.

[92]Ibid., p.381.

[93]Matheson, *Rhetoric of the Reformation,* p.212.

[94]Ibid., p.207.

with great abandon' throughout the entire work.[95] This blend of the lowest toilet humour with an androcentric discourse based on domination and hate are prototypical of today's flame wars.

Another obvious feature that Luther's later writings share with trolling and flaming is their sheer verbal violence. Death threats, incitements and exhortations to violence, and glorifying of murder, torture, and mutilation are common to both. This is enabled in both cases by a rhetorical strategy of total dehumanization:

> Luther bestialized his opponents, most frequently likening them to pigs and asses, or called them liars, murderers, and hypocrites.... The targets of his ire become under his pen the vilest of hypocrites, totally wicked and insincere, willing minions of the devil, deserving the most horrible fate.[96]

The 'black ecstasy of the language' behind Luther's later 'polemical excesses',[97] however, is no mere troll's quest for lulz at his targets' expense. 'Often', Edwards explains, 'Luther directed his attacks not at his human opponents but at the devil whom he saw as their master, and, of course, no language was too harsh when attacking the devil'.[98] This is conducive to the slipperiness of trolling – consider the title, *Against the Papacy at Rome, Founded by the Devil*: Luther needn't disclose the extent to which he distinguishes (or not) between the two targets named therein. For example:

> Luther contrasts Jesus's refusal of the Devil's offer of all the kingdoms of the world with the Pope's lust for power: 'Come here, Satan!' he has the Pope say. 'And if you had more worlds than this, I would accept them all, and not only worship you, but also lick your behind'. Luther concluded that 'All of this is sealed with the Devil's own [excrement], and written with the ass-pope's farts'.[99]

It's impossible to differentiate the pope from the devil himself here – to the point where they even seem to share a digestive system in common – which shows just how far Luther is prepared to go in dehumanizing his opponents.

Unsurprisingly, historians and biographers have often been stumped as to what to make of the sheer malice shown here, let alone of 'the stream of anal

---

[95]Edwards, 'Luther's Polemical Controversies', p.202.

[96]Ibid., pp.202–04.

[97]Matheson, *Rhetoric of the Reformation,* p.202; p.200.

[98]Edwards, 'Luther's Polemical Controversies', p.195.

[99]Roper, *Martin Luther,* p.381.

and obscene references in Luther's later writings', which have been rather diplomatically described as 'most puzzling'.[100] Confusingly, he seems to have been in deadly earnest: 'at his creative best Luther had once gloried in his own "clowning", but no longer'.[101] There has been abundant speculation that the virulence of these later writings is 'the product of a psychologically sick man', attributable to Luther's putative senility, or perhaps to his finally succumbing to the strain of his long, momentous career.[102] However, thanks to what the twenty-first century has taught us of the dynamics of trolling, I think we can venture an alternative explanation: this kind of hate-filled ranting is simply what comes of debasing the public sphere.

Although, incredibly, '*Against the Papacy at Rome* also contained reasoned exposition of Scripture, history, and doctrine',[103] Luther must surely have known by now that the Reformation he had unleashed had gone beyond the bounds of any rational argument. It's been rightly observed that 'such works preached only to the converted – no Catholic would have been persuaded by these words and images of such violence'.[104] Edwards opines that the reason why 'his always pungent language became more coarse and scatological' derives from this fact – from the final evaporation of any pretence at sensible discussion:

> The self-righteousness, the vulgarity, and the violence owe much to Luther's intense conviction that he was engaged in the climactic battle between the true and false church, that the real opponents were not men but devils, and the stakes were salvation and eternal life.[105]

Of course, the profundity of Luther's faith differentiates him from a troll trolling 'for the lulz', but however different his motives, the workings of cause and effect are the same:

> The battle had taken on apocalyptic proportions, and in the war between light and darkness the supporters of darkness deserved all the abuse that could be heaped upon them. The dynamics of polarization were at work.[106]

---

[100]Matheson, *Rhetoric of the Reformation,* p.149; p.207.

[101]Ibid., p.207.

[102]Edwards, 'Luther's Polemical Controversies', p.204. See also p.205.

[103]Ibid., p.203.

[104]Roper, *Martin Luther,* p.382.

[105]Edwards, 'Luther's Polemical Controversies', p.204; p.195.

[106]Edwards, *Printing, Propaganda, and Martin Luther,* p.93.

This kind of polemic abrogates the very possibility of dialogue and replaces it with rift and schism. And that's precisely what trolling is said to do to our public discourse in the twenty-first century.

So the journey Luther travelled to reach this destination – basically, a foul-mouthed, ranting, bigoted, bullying old man – was no different from the route taken by countless trolls. He began by making a knowingly contentious and divisive statement and played the victim when he was denounced for doing so. His polemical footwork deftly ensured his opponents would always appear in the wrong, however duplicitous his arguments eventually became. Lastly, the pretence of any possibility of level-headed, reasoned discussion having been abandoned, the floodgates were finally opened to mud-slinging and verbal thuggery of the lowest kind. Yet Luther still maintained the public face of a virtuous man of God and an innocent victim of the devil's minions. At least we can say of Luther that it took him a quarter of a century to complete this journey. Today's trolls are slack-paced if it takes them a quarter of an hour.

Once a troll, always a troll?

This chronological account of how Luther's trolling took different guises and used different strategies at different times is, perhaps, only half the picture. It could just as easily be argued that there were constants to his career, and that the different forms his trolling took were all derived from those underlying constants. For example, Luther must have known all along that his views would prove deeply – perhaps uniquely – controversial. He must have known they would make him enemies from the start, and he likely sensed the possibility of these enemies accusing him of heresy. It's interesting to note how much of his public positioning of those views follows from this one fact, because it's here that a strong and clear relationship exists between his writings and those of twenty-first-century trolls: 'The unthinkable is being paraded in public; moreover it is driving for support'.[107] Though that statement is a description of Luther's works, it's also true of trolls who spew hate speech, or who deny climate change, or who insinuate that Covid-19 was spread by telecommunications equipment. All know in advance they will be denounced and vilified, and for a troll, that's the whole point. Luther shows us that trolling strategies accrue directly from the public packaging of heresy.

The first of these strategies we've already mentioned: Luther began by positioning his ideas not as *his* views but as views *one might* take up, if only

[107]Matheson, *Rhetoric of the Reformation,* p.32.

for the sake of debate. Trolls exploit this move shamelessly: it enables them to deny they're heretics and to berate their opponents for being too dense or too inattentive to understand the difference. Luther, however, soon took full ownership of his views, surprisingly early on. In doing so, he pioneered another common trolling strategy: he set himself up as an advocate not exactly of free speech but of something that sounds very much like it – as someone who's saying what he feels is right, because 'the establishment' is blind to it. Hence the importance of his pseudonym *Eleutherius*: 'the free one'. In point of fact, though, Luther, like any troll, was manifestly opposed to free speech, because his writings seek to quash by any means necessary (including death threats)[108] the views of anyone who dares to disagree with him. Instead of a universal right to freedom of speech, Luther insisted instead on the right to do and say whatever *he* felt, in his conscience, was right. This became a central plank in his theology: to oversimplify, Luther was arrogating to himself the right to vent spleen and upset people if he felt moved in his heart by the Holy Spirit to do so.

Relatedly, Luther learnt the appeal of posing as an anti-establishment figure very early on. Trolls understand this all too well. By airing heretical views that 'the establishment' was hostile to, Luther got to claim he was only 'saying publicly what at least some of his contemporaries may very well have been thinking and sharing privately: that the bases for ... the sale of indulgences were theologically shaky'.[109] His *Ninety-Five Theses* used this strategy effectively: theses 81 to 89 contain the very cheapest point-scoring anywhere to be found in the *Theses*, but none of it apparently comes from Luther himself – all are described as 'sharp questions of the laity' and conveniently placed in the mouths of everyone else, of 'the people'.[110] In just this way, today's trolls position themselves as fearless individuals who are only (they claim) saying what everyone else is thinking but are too cowed to say out loud. As a heretic's defence, it's an excellent strategy precisely

[108]'Simon Lemnius, one of Melanchthon's most gifted students, was next to attract Luther's wrath.... Taking a student prank too far, he published a volume of Latin epigrams which mocked many of the prominent citizens of Wittenberg.... Some argued that the verses were relatively innocuous: after all, penning gently mocking poems in Latin and Greek was a hobby in which Luther and Melanchthon had often indulged. Luther, however, was enraged; he had a poster printed and attached to the church doors, a format used to offer bounties for criminals. It roundly condemned the young man, saying he deserved the death penalty. This was not quite the same thing as advocating his execution, although according to Lemnius himself, Luther had said in public that he would not preach in the town until Lemnius had been executed.' Roper, *Martin Luther,* p.373.

[109]Wengert, *Ninety-Five Theses,* p.39.

[110]Thesis 82, for example, says that people are asking why, if the pope has the power to free any soul from purgatory, does he not just release every soul immediately out of Christian love, instead of demanding filthy lucre, which he intends to put to worldly use in building the lavish Saint Peter's Basilica.

because (paradoxically) no evidence could ever be cited for it. It also sets up a straw target as *them*, as *the enemy* – basically, 'the establishment' or 'the mainstream' – to which a *we* is implicitly opposed – the writer and, by extension, the reader. This enemy needs to be demonized, so it's not surprising that an abusive tone enters into the discourse at this point (if not sooner). It did with Luther; it does with trolls. It's been said that Luther's 'edgy style, in which he repeatedly attacked scholastic theologians and their "opinions", made a splash with the German reading public',[111] but whether you find the style 'edgy' or just plain abusive is largely down to whether you see the writer as a heroic figure taking on the establishment and telling it like it is, or as a troll.

We've seen that, from the very start, Luther chose to avoid abstruse scholarly styles in setting out his ideas and preferred instead to present them in a down-to-earth, homespun tone that regularly descended to the level of the coarse. When it did so, though, Luther instantly resorted to defences familiar to trolls: extolling the virtues of the plain-speaking man as against the lies of 'the establishment'; insisting that his opponents' arguments are so bogus they call for strong words to expose it; and excusing himself by saying that his heated language is merely a sign of how strongly he feels about the topic:

> Luther himself is aware of the coarseness of the writing. He knows it is unseemly for a minister of the Gospel to curse, instead of blessing. 'But I have to talk ... with unfitting words'. He is a 'rough customer', and has jumped in like a peasant, with heavy boots. But when he has been stirring around in the papal stink for a while he just cannot take any more and has to stop and yell. 'Look, look, how my blood is thumping in my body, how it longs to see the Papacy punished'.[112]

It's been said that 'there was always something splendidly uncalculating and direct about the good pamphlet',[113] but it might be truer to say that, as with so much trolling, Luther excelled at pamphleteering because he gave the *appearance* of being uncalculating.

This claim to directness has to do with the fact that 'pamphlets were very close to oral culture.... Effective pamphlets reflected the lively discussion of home, tavern, bathhouse and street, and in turn provoked it', and it's certainly true that 'much of Luther's most effective writing evokes the patterns of oral

---

[111]Wengert, *Ninety-Five Theses*, p.39.

[112]Matheson, *Rhetoric of the Reformation*, p.210, quoting Luther, in *D. Martin Luthers Werke: Kritische Gesamtausgabe – Schriften*, Weimar: H. Böhlau, vol. 54, p.277; p.263; p.292.

[113]Matheson, *Rhetoric of the Reformation*, p.61.

discourse'.[114] Let's note that similar claims have been made for the internet, where trolls have made 'live chat' and 'discussion' forums their habitat of choice. The spontaneity and directness associated with the pseudo-orality of chatrooms provide trolls with a range of loopholes they can exploit in attack and in defence. The directness of the second person – comments aimed rhetorically at 'you' – proves a particular flashpoint when carried from the register of the face-to-face spoken word to depersonalized written text. Here again, Luther showed the way: 'the reader is drawn in by being addressed in the second-person singular: "You see!" "Look at this!" "Work it out for yourself!" Such vocatives or imperatives make for interactive reading'.[115] Whether historian Peter Matheson means the word 'interactive' in the same way that digital technology is said to be 'interactive', the point is that Luther is apt to appear as a plain-speaking man or as a badgering troll to more or less the extent that the reader is polemically manipulated into identifying with his 'you', or feeling subjected to personal attack by it.

This in turn reveals, through Luther's example, an intrinsic link between certain trolling strategies and an implicit right-wing populism, that certain professional trolls – in the vein of controversial bloggers such as Milo Yiannopoulos or Katie Hopkins – exploit only too well. Heretical statements are necessarily divisive, and the successful heretic is the one who knows how to manipulate that divisiveness so as to create a following, a 'you' which feels part of a 'we' because it is defined in opposition to 'them'. Luther also set himself up as an underdog – indeed, as a champion of underdogs. Notice, however, that this does *not* make him a democrat, any more than his insistence on speaking his mind made him a champion of free speech. Though Luther wrote rabble-rousing tracts aimed at the peasantry, his real politics came to the forefront as soon as they began taking up arms and organizing themselves: at that point, he wrote a pamphlet entitled *Against the Murderous, Thieving Hordes of Peasants*. It's been argued that Luther's politics were 'from today's perspective, largely conservative; but that makes them no less revolutionary in their own time'.[116] I'd argue that there's no need to explain away this tension between the conservative and the outspoken revolutionary once we start to see Luther as akin to a right-wing populist with a knack for trolling.

That knack for trolling manifested itself most clearly whenever Luther went on the offensive against 'the establishment'. The strategies he used to do so are well known to any troll. Though few could match his gifts of

---

[114]Ibid., p.61, p.121.

[115]Ibid., p.207. Interestingly, Matheson is quite insistent about the 'interactive' nature of these writings: 'the sixteenth-century pamphlet was written for an interactive situation' and, in particular, 'Luther's pamphlets are interactive' (p.20; p.129).

[116]Whitford, 'Luther's Political Encounters', p.190.

scholarly argument or incisive scriptural interpretation, Luther was more preoccupied with public lambasting of theologians and clerics than with actually debating their differing viewpoints. As we saw earlier, his *Sermon on Indulgences and Grace* ends with a snide parenthetical comment that the church authorities refuted his arguments only because 'for [them] truth really damages their treasure chests'[117] – just as trolls regularly besmirched (for example) economists opposed to Brexit as being in the pay of the European Union. Luther regularly challenged the church authorities to defend their position on the basis of the Holy Scriptures – well aware that, as far as the church was concerned, they had already done so several times over, and that if Luther didn't accept the church's interpretation of the Holy Scriptures then further discussion was fruitless. Yet this, too, was turned against them: Luther complained, and his followers believed, 'that it was his opponents who had refused to enter into proper measured debate on the basis of Scripture'.[118] This non-debate epitomizes the structure of trolling: for example, demanding proof of climate change from a climate activist, then proof that the proof is proof, then proof that the proof of the proof proves the proof, and so on, until the climate activist loses patience, at which point, the troll triumphantly declares climate change a hoax, because the climate activist has offered no proof and has admitted defeat by walking away from the discussion. (It's a common trolling strategy colloquially known for some reason as 'sea-lioning'.)

Every good troll knows when (and how) to play the victim – how to feign righteous indignation at having their words so horribly misunderstood, or how to appear genuinely hurt that their target has stopped replying to them. In this, they are once again descendants of Martin Luther. The Lutheran narrative went like this: Luther had tried to reach a quick and amicable resolution to his disagreements with the church in Rome. Rome had blanked him. Then, Rome 'had taken to the press and smeared his name and lied about his teachings. He had been forced to respond to defend the truth and expose error', or, as his supporter Michael Stifel wrote, 'no pious Christian could have tolerated such sacrilegious falsifying of the holy word of God'.[119] Luther had always stated publicly that he was open to instruction, but instead of showing him the errors of his ways, Rome had resorted to force, declaring him an outlaw, burning his books, and threatening his life. Under these conditions, Luther surely had the right to defend his reputation, his teachings, and above all his life, by whatever means necessary. Of course, this is a grossly one-sided narrative, but for us in the twenty-first century to ask how much truth is in it is to miss the point altogether: it's a masterclass

---

[117]Luther, *Sermon on Indulgences and Grace*, p.47.

[118]Edwards, *Printing, Propaganda, and Martin Luther*, p.96.

[119]See ibid., pp.96–8.

in rhetorical positioning before a mass public. Luther was perhaps the first person ever to (have to) do it, and his life depended on his success; trolls do this every day, for fun.

As we saw in his duel with Karlstadt, the idea of Luther using the latest media technology to claim victim status seems laughable when compared with his use of that same technology to heap insult, scorn, and violent abuse on his victims. To say, as Edwards does, that 'Luther found it polemically effective ... [to] denigrate the authority of his opponents with *ad hominem* attacks' is to understate the point in a way that is overly generous to Luther.[120] One of Luther's preferred strategies for playing the man instead of the ball was to find a quibble with his target's interpretation of the Bible, and then 'to attribute [his] opponents' misreading to a lack of the Holy Spirit, which guaranteed a proper understanding. The fault must lie in the man, not in the text'.[121] Simply put, Luther's enemies were godless because they misunderstood the Bible, and they misunderstood the Bible because Luther said so. That this was the very same treatment he bridled against when it was visited upon him by the pope neither stopped him from resorting to it regularly nor from airing his plaintive grievances when it happened to him. Heads Luther wins, tails his opponent loses – again, Luther's polemical strategies exploited the asymmetry of trolling.

With increasing frequency, though, he would expose his opponents to the torrent of 'violent, sharp, abusive, slanderous, and foolish words that Luther employed in his writings'. Some of the politer terms he coined for the pope included neologisms such as 'soul-murderer', 'monastery-muncher', or 'key-thief'; some of his more colourful ones include 'the Farting Donkey at Rome' or the 'donkeypopefart'.[122] Many of his supporters, including the erudite scholar of Greek Philip Melanchthon and the down-to-earth soldier-turned-pamphleteer Haug Marschalck, found themselves in the embarrassing position of having to defend Luther from his own verbal excesses, which seemed incompatible with his public persona, so wedded to the trope of godliness. Melanchthon even felt moved to refer to this when delivering the oration at Luther's funeral: 'I will not quarrel with those good-hearted men who tell us that Dr Luther was a bit too rough', he said.[123] Luther himself came close to offering his excuses (without actually retracting any of his insults or demonstrating any contrition whatsoever) as early as 1520: 'In an illuminating passage towards the end of the *Appeal to the German Nobility* Luther admits that his attacks may have been too swingeing and that they

[120]Ibid., p.207n38.

[121]Ibid., p.110.

[122]Matheson, *Rhetoric of the Reformation,* p.206.

[123]Hans J. Hillerbrand, 'The Legacy of Luther', in *The Cambridge Companion to Martin Luther*, pp.227–39, p.228.

will alienate many. He would prefer, however, to bear the world's anger than God's'.[124] Melanchthon and Marschalck opted for a more measured defence: the direness of the situation had driven Luther to strong words. But the verbal thuggery at which Luther excelled made it easier for his opponents to dismiss him: according to the Catholic Duke Georg of Saxony, Luther 'does nothing but scold, curse, rave, and rage'.[125]

Perhaps it's inevitable that a heretical statement will eventually culminate in a slanging match: as philosopher Ludwig Wittgenstein once said, 'Where two principles really do meet which cannot be reconciled with one another, then each man declares the other a fool and a heretic'.[126] Reasoned argument is not a live option by this point: the populist construction of a supposedly heroic 'I' who speaks for 'us' against a hateful 'them' is a rhetorical strategy that has run its course. Luther's supporters will be as roused by his tirades as his opponents will be appalled at them, and the only card left to play as things descend into entrenched uproar is to claim, as trolls so frequently do, that 'They started it'. Puerile though that card is, Lutheran pamphleteers played it as often as twenty-first-century trolls:

> But who started this in the first place? Indeed, you Romans! For when Luther first wrote against you in Latin and warned you in a friendly fashion, you would not tolerate any criticism from him. Instead you insulted him so badly [by calling him] a heretic and [attacked him] with such inappropriate treatises that you gave him great cause to write in German.[127]

Though this particularly sanctimonious extract didn't come from Luther's own pen, he said and wrote similar things often enough.

It's not hard to see, then, that however far a public persona may be predicated on laudable-sounding aims such as speaking uncomfortable truths to power, there is a very slippery slope curving steeply downward from this lofty posturing to the textual gutter fight. If there's a difference between Luther and today's trolls, it is that trolls have the benefit of Luther's example and understand how to propel any conversation towards this downward slope. Luther can at least be given the benefit of some doubt – that he reaped the unintended consequences of his high-risk and very public rhetorical strategies. Yet even this is no defence against some of his later excesses.

---

[124]Matheson, *Rhetoric of the Reformation*, p.183.

[125]See Edwards, *Printing, Propaganda, and Martin Luther*, p.159.

[126]Ludwig Wittgenstein, *On Certainty*, ed. G.E.M. Anscombe and G. H. von Wright, trans. Denis Paul and G.E.M. Anscombe (Oxford: Basil Blackwell, 1975), §611.

[127]The words are from an anonymous pamphlet printed in Strasbourg in 1522. See Edwards, *Printing, Propaganda, and Martin Luther*, p.96.

By the end of his life, Luther, like so many trolls, ended up falling back on hate speech. His targets were those of many trolls: establishment figures, principally the pope, and ethnic minorities, principally the Jews. His vitriol became misogynistic, homophobic, and anti-Semitic, even by the standards of his age, and perhaps even by the standards of today's trolls. His most recent biographer opines that 'Luther was a grand hater', and it's hard to fault this verdict.[128] His later, anti-Semitic writings are too upsetting to quote at any length, but equally, given that Luther is still remembered to this day as a principled man of God, it's important not to pass them by. Here's just one by no means isolated example, summarized by Lyndal Roper to spare the reader from too much direct quotation of hate speech:

> He imagined Jews kissing and praying to the Devil's excrement: 'the Devil has ... emptied his stomach again and again. That is a true relic, which the Jews, and those who want to be a Jew, kiss, eat, drink and worship'. In a kind of inverted baptismal exorcism, the Devil fills the mouth, nose and ears of the Jews with filth: 'He stuffs and squirts them so full, that it overflows and swims out of every place, pure Devil's filth, yes, it tastes so good to their hearts, and they guzzle it like sows.'[129]

Historians who object to reading Luther in light of his later appropriation by the Nazis would do well to remember that Luther himself called for all governments of the day to burn synagogues to the ground, and for all good Christians to chase Jewish people away by pelting them with pigs' excrement. We shouldn't mistake this for a twisted form of populism gone wrong – an extreme rhetorical setting up of an 'us' by demonizing a 'them'. As Roper rightly observes, 'this is no longer rational argument.... Rhetoric like this stops thought: it overwhelms through the torrent of violent imagery'.[130] Written in the same era as the last of the Scottish flytings, it shares their viciousness but lacks their playfulness: it's simply no different from the flaming practiced by internet trolls.

In spite of all this, Luther's reputation as a heroic figure – part saint, part intellectual, part revolutionary – has remained intact for around five centuries, and he is still taught under this guise to schoolchildren today. This is probably down to his phenomenal success at manipulating his public persona and at presenting an acceptable public face. 'On the whole', writes Edwards, 'the impression Luther gave was of a morally earnest critic of

---

[128]Roper, *Martin Luther,* p.383.

[129]Ibid., pp. 393–94, quoting Luther, in *D. Martin Luthers Werke: Kritische Gesamtausgabe – Schriften*, Weimar: H. Böhlau, vol. 53, p.587.

[130]Ibid., p.394.

scholastic theology',[131] and it is true: Luther *gave this impression*, but he did so as trolls do – through a range of sly rhetorical practices.

As we've seen, the outcome of Luther's rhetorical strategy was a divided, polarized, irreconcilable public sphere. It's time to look at what else his example can teach us about the effects of trolling.

Do Not Feed the Protestants

How did the authorities in the Catholic Church respond to Luther's troll-like methods? The simplest and most accurate answer is that, for the most part, they didn't. In this, they were no different from those of us in the twenty-first century who can think of no better strategy for dealing with trolls than ignoring them. And they shunned Luther for the same reasons we avoid trolls: to refrain from dignifying them with a response.

> Not to reply was to surrender much of the vernacular reading public to Luther and his friends. To reply was to further by both message and medium the position of the Evangelicals [i.e. Protestants]. This was the Catholic dilemma.[132]

Thus, Luther's example can help us evaluate the strengths and drawbacks of the 'Do Not Feed the Trolls' strategy that is so familiar to us today.

'One of the most striking characteristics of the Evangelical media campaign in the early years of the Reformation', observes Edwards, 'is the extent to which the Evangelical publicists operated almost unopposed'.[133] To get a sense of what he means by this, let's turn again to some numbers. As we saw earlier, the sensational volume of Luther's output from the *Ninety-Five Theses* onwards totalled a colossal 2,551 printings of his various writings, excluding the bestselling figures of his German translation of the Bible. During the same time frame, the combined total output of all Catholic writers arguing against him totalled just 514 printings. Since a small number of these publications bore no date, it's possible that the number could have been anywhere up to 542, but the difference remains stark and the point remains clear: Luther published five times more than the combined forces of the opposition put together. Nor was he a lone operator: there were plenty more Protestant writers, such as Karlstadt, Agricola, and Melanchthon,

---

[131]Edwards, *Printing, Propaganda, and Martin Luther*, p.163.

[132]Ibid., p.58.

[133]Ibid., pp.28–9.

wading in against the Catholics. This is what Edwards means when he says that 'the polemical contest was massively one-sided'.[134]

To compare like with like, we should factor in the language used in Catholic writings and in Lutheran writings. Throughout the years 1518 to 1555, just 40 per cent of pro-Catholic writings were in German; almost two-thirds were in Latin.[135] Compare that to Luther: over 80 per cent of the printings of his works were in German during the formative years of the Reformation. So, for the German-speaking readership, the numbers are more in the region of around two thousand readable publications by Luther answered by around two hundred pro-Catholic works.[136] One-sided indeed.

An illustrative anecdote: the most charismatic and successful indulgence salesman in Germany was a man named Johann Tetzel. His preaching made use of some catchy advertising jingles, which Luther derided in the *Ninety-Five Theses* and the *Sermon on Indulgences and Grace.* In reply, Tetzel wrote a German-language rebuttal, entitled *Vorlegung*, and, in Latin, fifty theses of his own, which spoofed some of the catchphrases in Luther's theses. Almost overnight, Luther's *Sermon* was reprinted two dozen times – an unprecedented level of circulation. By contrast, neither of Tetzel's documents, Latin or German, was ever republished. Very roughly, this reflects the kind of numbers involved on each side throughout the first three decades of the Reformation. How to account for such a dramatic asymmetry?

In the simplest terms, responding to Luther was counterproductive at almost every level. 'Inadvertently and ironically, the Catholic counterattack necessarily helped propagate the very message it wished to expunge'.[137] It's easy enough to see why: 'To refute Luther, first Catholic publicists had to explain what Luther was about. In doing so, they conveyed information that might actually attract readers rather than repel them'.[138] Indeed, 'even in the most damning of presentations, readers would learn of Luther's radical reformulation of Christian teaching'.[139] Pro-Catholic authors soon found they couldn't win: 'By refuting Luther's views they actually propagated them'.[140] Unsurprisingly, then, they preferred not to feed the Protestants. But this by itself isn't new: it's an inherent risk in addressing almost any

---

[134]Ibid., p.196.

[135]This figure fluctuates somewhat over time: towards the start, less than a sixth of pro-Catholic writings were in German, rising to almost half in the pivotal years of 1525 to 1529, and then declining again. During the 1530s, the Catholic diocese of Cologne still published around 85 per cent of its output in Latin.

[136]For more on these numbers, see ibid., pp.29–40.

[137]Ibid., p.58.

[138]Ibid., p.63.

[139]Ibid., p.58.

[140]Ibid., p.165.

subversive argument. (Ancient Greeks who found themselves on the wrong end of a Socratic dialogue clearly preferred to stop responding, or to confine their answers to bland platitudes such as 'It must surely be so', than to give the Athenian gadfly more rope to hang them with.) What makes the Reformation different from previous debates is the communications technology involved, which, by its nature, did away with any possibility of a level playing field. 'Printing not only spread the dispute to the far corners of the Holy Roman Empire of the German Nation and beyond, it inherently favoured Luther's side of the argument. In a crucial way, it not only conveyed Luther's message but also embodied it'.[141]

Earlier, we saw how printing, and in particular the pamphlet – quick and cheap to produce and distribute – made it possible for Luther's message to go viral on a historic scale. But it did more than this. Seldom has McLuhan's dictum that the medium is the message proven more true than in the Reformation:

> By their very nature as objects, vernacular pamphlets were the physical embodiment of a message. Multiplied by the art of printing into hundreds of exact copies, cheap to buy and handy to pass around, these pamphlets were in some sense what they contained: an address to the laity to become involved in an unprecedented way in their own religious destiny. Anyone could buy a pamphlet. And anyone who could read it, or have it read, became a participant in the debate and was asked to take sides. A pamphlet was not privileged communication. It ... opened to scrutiny papal fiat, conciliar decrees, city council rulings, and princely mandates – and asked the public to make up its own mind. Even if it urged ultimate deference toward hierarchy and authority, as most of these pamphlets in fact did, by ... their very nature as an address to a large (and largely lay) audience, they were subversive of the hierarchical views of many contemporaries. And their message reinforced that potential, for it urged ... subversion of traditional views of authority.[142]

The democratizing potential of the pamphlet format recalls the optimism of the early days of the internet, which claimed to give everyone with a computer a mouthpiece through which to address the world, independently of government control or traditional media channels – recall, for example, the utopian vision of John Perry Barlow's 1996 *Declaration of the Independence of Cyberspace*. But, of course, neither the printed pamphlet nor the internet is inherently democratic, and neither is particularly well-suited to level-headed, even-handed, detailed, and nuanced debate: both

[141]Ibid., p.7.

[142]Ibid., pp.57–8.

are arguably better suited to populist agendas, or can, at the very least, be hijacked to serve such ends with discomfiting ease.

One of the best-known and most successful of Luther's Catholic opponents was a Franciscan doctor of theology named Thomas Murner. He penned a diatribe entitled *Concerning Doctor Martin Luther's Teaching and Preaching*, and it dedicated an entire chapter to the argument that 'matters of faith should not be disputed before the ignorant common folk'. It doesn't seem to have occurred to him that this was an almost entirely self-defeating exercise. As Edwards puts it: 'We may wonder what the "common people" thought of this argument when they read or heard it in the vernacular. Even if they agreed with Murner in principle, in the very reading or hearing they were violating this principle. The medium subverted the message'.[143] The combination of printing technology and the German language that was so advantageous to Luther was no less disastrous when deployed by those defending the Catholic establishment. Even something as straightforward as writing in German was likely to backfire. It undercut the Catholic insistence on a distinction between clergy and lay people, and it pandered to Luther's notion of a priesthood of all believers. More starkly: how was a Catholic apologist to meet the Lutheran demand that they ground their arguments in Scripture? If they wanted to quote the Bible in German, the only German translation available was, of course, the bestselling translation by Martin Luther.

On Luther's side, any response to his writings whatsoever was grist to his mill. In this respect, he was positioned just as the trolls of today: if the reply to his works came in a tone of shrill outrage, Luther's riposte was that 'the true preaching of the Word of God always causes "uproar" (*uffrur*)'.[144] If it took the form of a well-argued rebuttal, then his supposedly heretical views benefited from 'the acknowledgement that the message was serious enough to warrant refutation'.[145] If the rebuttal struck home, and scored a point or two against Luther's views, he could simply reformulate them. We've seen how, when the Franciscan professor Augustin von Alveldt wrote a pamphlet explaining to Luther the error of his ways, Luther replied (in *On the Babylonian Captivity of the Church*) by giving Alveldt a fulsome and warm set of thanks for bringing these issues to his attention – only to go on to say how Alveldt's criticisms had spurred him on to rethink his position in ways that were more radically heretical still. By the time word got round that Luther had been officially designated a heretic, in the early 1520s, the very act of replying to him played into his hands: 'Further debate only

[143]Ibid., p.63.

[144]Matheson, *Rhetoric of the Reformation*, p.3.

[145]Edwards, *Printing, Propaganda, and Martin Luther*, p.72.

gave apparent legitimacy to the Evangelical claim that there was something to debate ... [and] gave at least the impression that papal decisions were not final'.[146]

It's not surprising, then, that Luther's writings met with little to no sustained opposition from the Catholic Church. But it's important to note that their silence was rooted in two very different sets of reasons, each of which seems to have a different lesson for us in the twenty-first century. On the one hand, disengaging with Luther was a lofty point of principle:

> The Roman Catholic church saw itself as the only legal institution of religion. It represented the status quo, and its opponents were rebels, heretics, and outlaws.... For the Roman church to engage in organized, 'official' polemics with the Evangelicals, it would have to acknowledge that there was something to debate. Normally one does not even argue with outlaws.[147]

The fairly obvious disadvantage to this strategy of disengagement is that refusing discussion simply results in an unopposed opponent. This left Luther free to found a new religious movement that has endured for over five hundred years, with hundreds of millions of followers around the world.

On the other hand, withdrawing from the debate was also a practical move, necessitated by technologically related concerns:

> From the outset the Catholic apologist was at a serious disadvantage in this battle, for both the medium and the message favored the Evangelical position.... By a subtle irony, the very means chosen to rebut Luther – vernacular pamphlets attacking him and his message – undercut the message the authors intended to convey.... By their very existence Catholic pamphlets did what they argued should not be done.[148]

Here, there is a salutary lesson for us to learn. We should choose our media with the same care with which we choose our battlegrounds, for they are one and the same thing. Take Twitter (also known as X): like the pamphlets of the 1500s, which were quicker to produce and shorter to read than books, X/Twitter's unique selling points are its brevity and its instantaneity. Its very form therefore lends itself to vapid soundbites and hampers thoughtful debate or discussion of detail. Why should we be surprised when it's used for bullish grandstanding, crass bombast, and thuggish belligerence? And why take to X/Twitter to decry this, let alone to try to formulate an

---

[146]Ibid., p.79.

[147]Ibid., pp.78–9.

[148]Ibid., p. 58.

alternative to it? As if the very idea of a short, sharp, punchy message did not in itself evoke verbal violence. Surely we would do better to pick other battlegrounds.

The Reformation, then, teaches us the dangers both of ignoring the trolls, and of trying to play at their own games. Its aftermath tells a grim story – the years that followed saw the complete breakdown of the public sphere, resulting from and in an increasingly polarized society, in which religious hatred and violence became legitimized. Since these, too, are said to be the effects of trolling, or at least its dangers, we should, once again, take the time to see if there's anything we can learn from literary history.

The sixteenth-century echo chamber

The historical context from which Luther emerged was the culture of the Renaissance, in which humanists such as Erasmus had encouraged a climate of questioning and debate. Erasmus had a term for discussion of this sort: he called it 'colloquy'. 'Colloquy implies respect, openness to the good sides of the other, awareness of one's own shortcomings, a sense of balance and equilibrium'.[149] It also implies mutual good faith, along with a readiness to accept one's own view as flawed, and a recognition that however much you disagree with the views propounded, the alternatives to colloquy are usually far worse: rift, schism, division, and so forth. Sadly, Lutherans and Catholics alike swung their wrecking balls at this culture of colloquy. Yet some of the blame for this has to be placed on the technologies they were using.

Colloquy was rooted in a model of face-to-face debate, even though it often took place through letters and correspondence. Angry exchanges, however heated, could be retracted, and hurt feelings or bruised reputations could be massaged with winning words, halfway houses, apologies, and mutual laughter. Public reconciliations were easy to arrange in face-to-face discussions, and the antagonists of both sides got kudos for compromise and forgiveness. (Colloquy was contemporary with Renaissance-era flyting and might be called its opposite.) This culture simply could not be replicated in the format of the new technology: 'Committing differences to writing hardened the conflict into permanent form, while launching it into a much wider public arena, through the medium of print, took it a step farther still'.[150] Discussion had to be condensed into new formats, with less wiggle room for finding the middle ground, while things became so public

---

[149]Matheson, *Rhetoric of the Reformation*, p.218.

[150]Ibid., pp.185–86.

that neither side could back down. Opponents were no longer real human beings but disembodied words on a page.

In essence, then, the openness of Renaissance-era colloquy was subjected to the same technological transformation that is said to have given rise to trolling in our own time. The results were no different:

> Printing brought a new power to wound. The thousand duplicates of each printed tract meant that the 'game' was fought out time and time again, in the market, the parish, the home, the court. Old rivals and enemies would be sniggering at one; family and friends would be embarrassed. At stake was no winner's crown, but one's dignity and self-respect. Nor was there any outside instance to which to appeal for mediation. Pope, Council, Emperor were distant abstractions. The city magistrates might eventually come down hard on abusive ditties or tracts, but by then the damage would be done. There were no grounds for confidence that a proper 'debate' could be facilitated, that an impartial mediator existed, that one's response would be respected, that the questions and anxieties of one's parishioners, followers, dependents would be attended to. Frequently, therefore, it seemed that the only way to deal with personal or group hurt was to respond in kind, to channel one's indignation into rage, and fire off a reply. Thus the vicious circle continued.[151]

Sadly, it's all too plain to see in the sixteenth century a prophecy of the twenty-first: the deeply personal yet simultaneously depersonalizing impact of technological mediation, intensified by its hitherto inconceivably broad public reach, and compounded by the apparent powerlessness of traditional law enforcement in the face of the new communications technology. Then as now, the effect of the technology on public debate was to push it to extremes.

In fairness, the tendency towards polarization wasn't restricted to print technology: it could be found in low-tech outlets too, as in Luther's sermons. For Luther in particular, 'every sermon was a battle for the souls of the people, an apocalyptic event that set the doors of heaven and hell in motion, part of the continuing conflict between the Lord and Satan'.[152] But the audience for a sermon was limited to the capacity of the church; its duration was short, and it ended when it ended. When the same sermon was printed, its impact became unquantifiable, in terms of both the size of its readership and its longevity. Print polarized because it couldn't be retracted or unsaid; it raised the stakes precisely because it was inherently public.

---

[151]Ibid., p.191.

[152]Meuser, 'Luther as Preacher', p.137.

Luther himself seems to have enjoyed carrying his rhetoric to extremes. In his writings, 'whenever God's word appears, so does the devil.... Whenever Christ appears, Herod surfaces too'.[153] And yet he regularly accuses his opponents – would you believe it? – of carrying things to extremes, so as to stir the pot, which Luther says is a sure sign they are doing the devil's work. Of course, diagnosing devilry in his opponents is nothing if not carrying things to extremes, yet it gives Luther an excuse to polarize further, as there can be no possibility of reaching a compromise with Satan himself. If the Catholic strategy was 'Do Not Feed the Protestants', Luther soon devised a counterstrategy of 'Do Not Feed the Devils':

> At times he drew the logical enough conclusion that his opponents were so devilish that there was no point in arguing with them at all.... It was not necessary to reply to the devil. He would leave it in the hands of God, who was the true judge. 'For who can stop the mouths of everyone, yes, of every devil'.[154]

Once you have (quite literally) demonized your opponent, then not only has any middle ground vanished but so too has any prospect of dialogue. You end up in an echo chamber, talking to yourself and, at best, followers who find common cause not with your reasoning but with your lambasting.

This polarization was not one-sided. It was all too easy for Catholics to paint a picture of Luther as 'a religious demagogue whose writings challenged traditional authority and threatened to overturn the established order' through 'explicit incitements to rebellion'.[155] Luther himself gave them plenty of ammunition, as in this passage from his *On the Babylonian Captivity of the Church*, 'I tell you truly that no law can justly be imposed on Christians, neither by human beings nor by angels, no matter how much they wish to do so, since we are free from them all'.[156] Indeed, to give a sense of just how polarized the debate had got, quoting Luther eventually became a way of snubbing him:

> It is a fascinating characteristic of a significant number of the Catholic pamphlets against Luther that in proving a point they often contented themselves with listing excerpts from Luther's works.... Sometimes commentary or exposition followed the list of excerpts, but often not.[157]

[153]Matheson, *Rhetoric of the Reformation*, p.193.

[154]Matheson, ibid., quoting Luther, in *D. Martin Luthers Werke: Kritische Gesamtausgabe – Schriften*, Weimar: H. Böhlau, vol. 26, p.145.

[155]Edwards, *Printing, Propaganda, and Martin Luther*, p.154; p 61.

[156]Luther, *On the Babylonian Captivity of the Church*. See ibid., p.161.

[157]Ibid., p.161.

The very words that Luther used to convey his message were paraded in public by his opponents as proof of his self-evident foolishness and heresy. No debate was needed.

So the technology of the pamphlet, which seemed so ideally suited to disseminating a message to a mass readership across all boundaries, actually ended up speaking only to specific, niche, sectarian readerships, on each side. Instead of facilitating communication and understanding, it divided readerships into echo chambers and set them against one another. Hence, 'most of Luther's polemics after 1527 or 1528 were addressed to his own supporters. The time for proselytizing had largely passed'.[158] From then on, he knows that 'he cannot convince the Papalists, but he hopes to destroy their credibility … to shock people into a new decisiveness. There can be no middle ground'.[159]

How far is this situation really to be blamed on the technology? Further than we might have thought. Historians often characterize the writings of both Catholics and Protestants at this time as 'propaganda', which is to say, one-sided publicity of their viewpoint, instead of theological discussion. Edwards, we have seen, extrapolates from this that the Lutheran publishing phenomenon was a 'modern media campaign'. Matheson disagrees, for reasons that are compelling. He thinks 'it is a category mistake to see the literature of this period as propaganda'[160] and not just because it makes the Lutherans 'appear as slightly disguised marketing executives'.[161] Rather, argues Matheson, 'although the sixteenth century had almost nothing corresponding to today's mass-media, it did boast an intricate, complementary, and remarkably effective variety of what we might call "mini-media".'[162] Since each printing shop had its own sympathies and allegiances, and catered to their clientele, it was easy to surround oneself with likeminded publications that only reinforced and radicalized one's views, and, since print runs were small and the reach of any given printer's distribution would be correspondingly narrow, it was easier still to unplug oneself from other opinions.

The dynamics of the echo chamber, in which we retreat from the rancour of public debate into smaller arenas where we are spared the trouble of encountering views other than our own, and where we thereby become more rancorous, more one-sided, and more prejudiced without even noticing it, were as well known to the sixteenth century as they are to us. In both cases,

[158]Edwards, 'Luther's Polemical Controversies', p.200.

[159]Matheson, *Rhetoric of the Reformation,* pp.203–05.

[160]Ibid., p.248.

[161]Ibid., p.46.

[162]Ibid., p.43.

they are seemingly driven by a flight from aggression in the public sphere, and in both cases, they end up becoming drivers of that very aggression.

There were, indeed, voices who spoke in moderation. Theologian Johann Eberlin von Günzburg, for example, started out as a pamphleteer who wrote trenchant, biting critiques of the Catholic Church in terms that were broadly sympathetic to Luther. He left the Franciscan order and travelled to Wittenberg in 1522 to study under Luther. Within less than two years, his pamphlets began warning against the dangers of lack of respect for those with whom we argue, of unthinkingly disregarding custom and tradition, of the tendency towards using the words of the Bible as a means for self-aggrandizing posturing, and of polarizing arguments so far as to make them irresolvable.[163] But the problem that such moderates faced, then as now, was that the public sphere had become so divided that consensus-building was much harder than mutual entrenchment and mud-slinging:

> Who had the right to say definitively what Scripture taught when church Fathers could be cited on both sides of an issue, when university theological faculties divided into opposing camps, and when academics could not convince each other of the correctness of their reading?[164]

It became harder to identify – let alone to discuss sensibly – the issues involved because of the personalizing rhetoric that equated important issues with a vilified and discredited individual, whether Luther or the pope. Indeed, things degenerated to the point where it's questionable whether the word 'debate' can be applied to them at all.

It seems that 'books and pamphlets were, in fact, "read" in this period with explosive indignation and a highly selective focus'.[165] The scare quotes that Matheson puts around 'read' here rightly call our attention to the fact that writers of both sides disengaging from one another went hand in hand with readers disengaging from writers of the other side. Oftentimes, when a Protestant 'read' a pro-Catholic work or conversely, 'the reader never got beyond the first page, either because of boredom or fury'.[166] Some of the handwritten scrawl in the margins of these pamphlets gives fascinating testimony to this. One of the most revealing can be found on a copy of one of the few pamphlets written by a woman, Argula von Grumbach. In a splutter of rage, its anti-Protestant owner has written across it: 'née von Stauff, née the hellish brothel of Luther'.[167] There is no attempt at argument here.

[163]See ibid., p.191.

[164]Edwards, *Printing, Propaganda, and Martin Luther,* p.109.

[165]Matheson, *Rhetoric of the Reformation,* p.91.

[166]Ibid., p.50.

[167]See ibid., p.54.

Nothing indicates that the owner has read anything more than the author's name, which, by itself, was enough to provoke such fury that the need was felt to deprive her of that identity by reverting to her maiden name (thus spuriously casting her as an unmarried mother, hence spuriously casting her as a whore). The author's gender is used as a pretext for baseless aspersions about her sex life, which in turn form the pretext for the baseless dismissal of her views, which in turn becomes the pretext for the baseless dismissal of Luther's. This is not argument but synecdoche, bordering on free association. Rage and hate have crowded out any attempt at logic or comprehension. It's the same luridly sexualized, hate-filled misogyny that characterizes so much of today's trolling, especially of female targets, and it's interesting to note that, already in the sixteenth century, certain individuals felt compelled to write instantaneous, inarticulate, incandescent little replies at the merest thought of views they probably hadn't read and knew little about. Twitter did not invent this need – it merely filled it.

Was impatient rage the default position of the sixteenth-century reader? If so, was this a cause, effect, or symptom of the rhetorical aggression expressed in the writings of the authors they were reading? Or was it the natural way in which to consume a form of communications technology that thrived on speed and brevity and, in so doing, discouraged thoughtfulness and deliberation? I don't suppose we'll ever be able to answer these questions – but I do claim that, notwithstanding, there are lessons and warnings we can take from the consequences and effects of Luther's troll-type rhetoric.

Conclusion

On the face of it, the lessons we have to learn from Luther's example seem pretty dire. It didn't take long for the verbal warfare to erupt into open warfare, and it took well over a century to restore a semblance of peace to Europe. Religiously motivated violence was the norm rather than the exception in Europe from the mid-1520s to the late 1640s. During the last three decades of this time alone, one-third of the population of the Holy Roman Empire died in battle, slaughter, and famine. It would take another three hundred years and the invention of modern mechanized warfare to surpass this kind of destruction. Its deadly consequences still flare up today (for example, in Northern Ireland). Such was the human cost of the breakdown of dialogue and debate with those whose views seem heretical. We would do well to remember that.

If nothing else, this should remind us that trolling has real-world consequences. In other chapters, I've tried to draw analogies between the actions of real-life trolls and those of their literary counterparts – between Sean Duffy and Dennis Barlow in Evelyn Waugh's *The Loved*

One, or between Reece Messer and Unferth in *Beowulf*. In this chapter, the analogies to be drawn are of a larger, weightier scale. Thanks to a new communications technology – one which favoured short, sharp messages and delivered them with unprecedented speed to unprecedented numbers – Luther was able to present his agenda as a challenge to 'the establishment' and was careful to speak the language of 'the people' in doing so, to set up an 'us' versus 'them'. 'They' were addressed only under a facile pretence of debate, in which any strategy, however hypocritical, was used to ensure Luther always came out on top, and when this wore thin, 'they' became the targets of trolling tactics so vicious they crossed the line into hate speech. These are precisely the tactics that the world's most-followed Twitter troll, Donald Trump, used to take the White House in 2016, and they served him as well as they served Luther in building a zealous following and setting himself up as its figurehead. Trolling works. That is the lesson that Luther teaches us. And one of the reasons it works is because its targets and their supporters are so wrongfooted by it that they don't know how to respond to it, and so often choose not to.

On a more positive note, Luther's example reveals that trolling can be a means to an end, and the end itself can sometimes, in spite of everything, be a worthy one. This is important. That Luther had scored some valid points was pretty clear from the fact that the Catholic Church very quickly reigned in the selling of indulgences (without, needless to say, admitting any wrongdoing). It's a fair conclusion, then, that his trolling resulted in calling out corruption and, if nothing else, putting a stop to a financial investment scheme that verged on extortion. If trolling produces real-world effects, then Luther shows us that some of these can be positive and for the common good. We ought to reflect on that, precisely because so many people in the sixteenth century didn't. For Catholics, Luther's trolling meant he was nothing more than a dangerous heretic and populist demagogue; for Protestants, no blow was too low against those whose corruption had turned the Christian Church into a protection racket. Neither side paused often enough or long enough to separate the argument from the rhetoric. The lesson I would urge we draw is the need to ask whether the end can justify the means of trolling. Perhaps it can't. But if it can, we need to reflect that the reprehensible and offensive strategies of trolling can be used in the service of a worthy cause before we make decisions about whether to legislate and regulate against trolling. 'Attempt to smoke out the trolls', warns Phillips, 'and you simultaneously smoke out the activists'.[168]

But (you may well ask) can we really compare the sixteenth century with the twenty-first and expect to learn anything meaningful from it? There

---

[168]Whitney Phillips, *This Is Why We Can't Have Nice Things: Mapping the Relationship Between Online Trolling and Mainstream Culture* (Cambridge, MA: MIT Press, 2015), p.155.

are good grounds for doubt. Foremost among them would be the wise observation that our cultures are so different. 'One of our difficulties in dealing with sixteenth-century polemics may be that the distinction between elite and popular culture, high and low, which we tend to presuppose was by no means cemented at this time', writes Matheson.[169] Thus, at the time Luther was calling the pope a devilish fart-arse, Scottish noblemen were calling one another far worse things in the formal setting of a royal court, for the entertainment of the highest echelons of society. It's been rightly said that Luther would often 'use a truly Rabelaisian flood of terms to extol or to ridicule something',[170] and the comparison should remind us that Luther's and Rabelais's dates overlapped: the founding of the European novel was getting underway at this time, carrying with it from the start regular torrents of lurid, sexualized, scatological, misogynistic profanities. It could even be pointed out that William Shakespeare and Christopher Marlowe weren't above pandering to their audiences with grotesque anti-Semitism. Renaissance culture had not yet been sanitized by the reserve of the Enlightenment or the prudery of the Victorians. For some, that is its charm.

But there's a flaw to this argument. If Luther's rhetoric was merely par for the course by the standards of his day, then why did so many of his supporters – even his closest friends and confidants – regularly feel the need either to apologize on his behalf for going too far (as did the erudite scholar Melanchthon and the popular pamphleteer Marschalk) or to remonstrate with him for his verbal excesses (as did humanist Petrus Mosellanus and theologian Johann Eberlin von Günzburg)? Surely the fact that Luther attracted condemnation even from his own sympathizers for his reprehensible vocabulary and rhetoric indicates that his words were felt to be gratuitous even by the ribald standards of the Renaissance. Furthermore, the fact that in spite of this Luther himself seldom, if ever, felt the need to retract or apologize says something about his temperament that needs no historical contextualizing.

Luther was as much a great writer as a great theologian: his craftsmanship with the pen makes him second only to Goethe in shaping the history of German literature. Nevertheless, I find it helpful, reassuring even, to picture Luther as operating under conditions much closer to those of the twenty-first century than to those of, say, the nineteenth or early twentieth. In his day, for example, there were no libel laws or copyright laws; in our day, the global reach and anonymity of the internet makes them less enforceable than at any other time in history. This has its implications for what gets said in the public sphere. He, like so many of us, was working with a brand

169Matheson, *Rhetoric of the Reformation*, p.158.

170Ibid., p.122.

new form of communication technology, which, like so many of us, he often allowed to get the better of him, and later regretted it:

> Luther wrote far too much and far too quickly, some portions of his writings often being at the printer while he completed the rest. He seems seldom to have revised what he wrote.... He loses control over his own emotions, and loses sight of his audience.... Luther himself frequently admitted that he had been carried away by outbursts of rage; sometimes during angry and sleepless nights he would dash down some all too human thoughts which after cooler reflection he would have withdrawn. Sometimes, however, it was already too late, for they had already been spirited away by someone and appeared in print. At other times the rage and fury of his opponents spurred him on; he glowed inwardly with satisfaction at the thought that he had stirred the devil and his minions to such mad contortions.[171]

After 1517, it would be around 470 years before writers would again find themselves so caught up in, and caught out by, the speed of the technology they were using. Was Luther, perhaps, as close to the hapless, overzealous, self-obsessed blogger as he was to a troll? In one respect, perhaps he was. To return to a point I made at the beginning: Luther meant what he said. He stood by it. He may have been trolling, but he wasn't 'just a troll', and if he used the tactics of one, it was to achieve ends he held most deeply and profoundly to be right.

This brings us to the issue of 'meaning it', or, more precisely, of saying things known to be tasteless or potentially offensive *without* actually meaning them. Why would sane, rational people ever do this? Actually, deliberately insincere speech has quite a venerable literary history, as we are about to see. It's time, having explored the consequences of the public nature of trolling, to turn to another issue and to start a new chapter.

---

[171]Ibid., p.120, p.192.

4

... of views that are not sincerely held ...

U Can Has Babeez! – Jonathan Swift's *A Modest Proposal*

I first came across Jonathan Swift's *A Modest Proposal* as a sixteen year old about to embark on my A-levels. The teacher (the same one who suggested I read Evelyn Waugh's *The Loved One* – evidently she had a taste for bleak and caustic satire) made us read it as homework, without offering a word of context or explanation. Many of us didn't get it. Accordingly, the 'modest proposal' of Swift's title – ostensibly a well-meant, carefully reasoned, economically costed scheme to reduce poverty, begging, and starvation in Ireland by encouraging the Catholic peasantry to sell their freshly weaned one-year-old children for slaughter, as delicacies for the tables of their landlords – aroused precisely the kind of horror and disgust that Swift hoped it would, only without any trace of the ironic laughter he was aiming at. The class that followed began in uproar.

If you've read *A Modest Proposal*, you'll understand why. If not, here's a bit of context. Ever since it first came out in 1729, it's been hailed as probably the finest piece of satire the English language has ever produced. It looked and sounded like one of the countless ephemeral pamphlets churned out by the printing presses during the Enlightenment, all canvasing support for some well-meant and public-spirited (yet all too often hare-brained) scheme for improving the lot of humanity. Like those pamphlets, it's essayistic in its format and blends lofty appeals to the greater good, to religion, and to patriotism, with a hard-headed facts-and-figures approach grounded in the faith the so-called age of reason placed in science. Unlike those other pamphlets, though, the idea for which Swift offers a straight-faced, blow-by-blow justification is that famine and poverty in Ireland could be averted if only the rich could indulge themselves in eating the children of the starving poor as a luxurious snack.

Quite a few of my fellow students had taken all this at face value, and the teacher was faced with a barrage of moral outrage and sickened indignation. I remember one girl seemed to be choking back tears as she sobbed, 'I don't know how anyone could be so cruel'. Pressure began to mount on the teacher to explain herself: why had she set us the task of reading something so upsetting, so barbaric? Eventually, a hand went up, and someone finally ventured the comment 'But Miss, he's not actually being serious, is he?' I am sorry to say this hand wasn't mine: I was so taken aback by all the strongly, deeply felt revulsion that I no longer knew what to make of Swift's text. Had I been wrong to laugh at it? I remember noticing at the time that the hand-raiser's comment was half-observation, half-question, and this probably showed just how far the moral backlash against Swift had disconcerted the rest of the class.

The teacher handled the situation perfectly. Of course Swift isn't being serious, she told us – this is *satire*, so he doesn't mean what he says. But those who hadn't picked up on it shouldn't feel bad, she said: she was quite convinced there would have been plenty of appalled landlords in eighteenth-century Dublin who thought Jonathan Swift was a terribly hard-hearted man.[1] Pennies dropped and the class got underway. That day, we learnt the textbook definitions both of 'satire' – writing in which flaws are exposed to ridicule, usually by means of comic exaggeration – and of 'irony' – when the meaning an author intends to convey is at variance with the literal meaning of their writing. We were taught that the former typically depends upon the latter. We learnt that when Swift writes something such as 'I grant this food will be ſomewhat dear, and therefore very *proper for Landlords*, who, as they have already devoured most of the Parents, ſeem to have the beſt Title to the Children',[2] he is not to be taken literally; he's making the point that the economic system of his day was so inhumane, so little short of cannibalistic, that it might as well have gone the whole hog. Not only did we learn all this, but we had also seen at first-hand how powerful, how

[1]Much as it pains me to contradict a teacher who was such a formative influence on me, her hunch is not born out by recent research. Swift's pamphlet was advertised widely in newspapers right from its first publication and was marketed for its wit and irony. This 'spoils any claim that the *Proposal* might have over all but the most obtuse reader's credibility'. See James Ward, 'Bodies for Sale: Marketing *A Modest Proposal*', *Irish Studies Review*, vol. 15, no. 3, 2007, pp.283–94, p.285.

[2]Jonathan Swift, *A Modest Proposal For preventing the Children of Poor People From being a Burthen to their Parents or the Country, And For making them Beneficial to the Publick* (Dublin: S. Harding, 1729), p.7.

effective, and yet how slippery satire and irony can be. Thirty years on, the class is one of just a handful that still stand out clearly in my memory.

It's because Swift made an art out of saying grotesque, despicable things without actually meaning any of them that he is an important figure in the literary ancestry of trolling. The terms 'satire' and 'irony' are often invoked by trolls in defence of trolling and also by scholars who study it. Since these are literary terms for literary techniques, it follows straightforwardly that the study of trolling necessitates a grounding in the study of this kind of literature. Let's start, then, by evaluating the similarities and differences between satire and trolling.

Satire as trolling

Some years ago, an article in *Esquire* magazine featured an interview with a self-confessed troll who described trolling as 'satirical performance art'.[3] This is a common justification of trolling. Think back three chapters, to the numerous scholarly attempts to define what trolling is, and it's easy enough to see some striking resemblances between satire and trolling. Let's recap some of trolling's characteristics, so we can evaluate whether or how they are shared by satire.

Trolling was described in one of the earliest studies of the phenomenon as 'a game about identity deception';[4] *A Modest Proposal* is exactly the same thing. It was published anonymously, and nothing gives away its status as a piece of satire until long after the reader has been drawn in. Swift couches his proposal first in the vocabulary of a humanitarian ('It is a melancholly Object to thofe, who walk thro' this great Town, or travel in the Country, when they fee the *Streets*, the *Roads*, and *Cabbin-Doors*, crowded with *Beggars* of the female Sex, folowed by three, four, or six children, *all in Rags*, and importuning every Paffenger for an Alms. Thefe *Mothers*, inftead of being able to work for their honeft Lively-hood, are forced to ... beg Sustenance for their *helplefs Infants*'). He poses as a moralist ('my Scheme ... will prevent thofe *voluntary Abortions*, and that horrid practice of *Women murdering their Bastard Children*, alas! too frequent among us; sacrificing the *poor innocent Babes*, I doubt, more to avoid the Expence than the Shame, which would move Tears and Pity in the moft Savage and inhuman Breaft'). He claims to be a patriot ('[This] is *in the prefent deplorable ftate of the Kingdom*, a very great additional grievance; and therefore whoever

[3]Sanjiv Battacharya, 'The Battle for the Internet's Future', *Esquire*, 25 January 2014.

[4]Judith S. Donath, 'Identity and Deception in the Virtual Community', in *Communities in Cyberspace*, ed. Marc Smith and Peter Kollock (London: Routledge, 1998), pp.29–59, p.45.

could find out a fair, cheap and eaſy method of making theſe Children ſound and uſeful Members of the common-wealth would deſerve ſo well of the publick, as to have his Statue ſet up for a preſerver of the Nation').[5] Most famously, he assumes the guise of a mathematically minded political economist, whose arguments are backed up by carefully calculated sums – all in order to propose the many benefits (not just financial) of eating one-year-old children. Thus, *A Modest Proposal*, from the very words of its title onwards, plays a game of identity deception. As one critic puts it: 'Swift is a sort of guerrilla warrior, camouflaged by irony and hiding in the jungles of the Proposer's misapprehensions and indirections'.[6]

Earlier we saw that, in addition, trolling is defined as aggressive in its orientation. So too, in a way, is satire. Satire, like trolling, has a target. Satire, like trolling, is adversarial. However, unlike trolling, which often tends towards pure nihilism and misanthropy, satire generally implies that, since its target is in the wrong, there must be a right position:

> the satirist takes sides, represents problems in terms of the wrong side being taken, the right being opposed to it.... For the satirist tacitly assumes that a right side exists and that his or her readers can perhaps be 'cured' of wrong tendencies and brought onboard. Either/or prevails, not neither/nor, even less both/and. In other words, 'A Modest Proposal' works by being pointed, its satire sharp rather than blunt.[7]

Having said this, satirists such as Swift seldom trouble themselves to set out what the right answer might be. Clearly eating babies is not the best solution to Ireland's economic woes, but it is no more incumbent upon Swift as a satirist to show what the real solution might be than it is upon a troll.[8] Satire and trolling not only are both adversarial and aggressive, then, but also both are primarily negative in orientation. Making positive formulations is equally alien to the spirit of both.

Trolling was furthermore described as 'online antagonism undertaken for amusement's sake'.[9] Having just established that satire is necessarily antagonistic, it should be fairly uncontentious to add that satire aims to

---

[5]Swift, *A Modest Proposal*, p.3; p.5; pp.3–4.

[6]Robert Phiddian, 'Have You Eaten Yet? The Reader in *A Modest Proposal*', *Studies in English Literature, 1500–1900*, vol. 36, no. 3, 1996, pp.603–21, p.611.

[7]G. Douglas Atkins, 'It's Not an Essay: Jonathan Swift's "A Modest Proposal" and the Immodesty of Satire', in *Reading Essays: An Invitation* (Atlanta: University of Georgia Press, 2008), pp.55–61, p.57.

[8]We'll see, later on, that Swift suggests plenty of practical solutions to the problem: the point is that these are inessential to satire as a genre.

[9]Claire Hardaker, '"I Refuse to Respond to This Obvious Troll": An Overview of Responses to (Perceived) Trolling', *Corpora* vol. 10, no. 2, 2015, pp.201–29, p.202.

amuse, and it aims to amuse people at the expense of a targeted object. Swift certainly did: witness his dig that the costlier the price of children in a meat market, the more fitting they are for a landlord's table. So this is another clear overlap: both satire and trolling are undertaken for amusement at someone else's expense.

Among the other definitions of trolling we explored earlier was the claim that 'transgression is the most obvious element of trolling'.[10] Few sentences in English literature can be more transgressive than Swift's mock-assertion 'that a young healthy Child well Nurſed, is at a year Old a moſt delicious, nourishing, and wholeſome Food, whether *Stewed, Roaſted, Baked,* or *Boyled*; and I make no doubt, that it will equally ſerve in a *Fricaſsee*, or a *Ragoust*'.[11] Not content with this masterpiece of grotesquery, he goes on to lampoon the two best-known manifestations of the spirit of the age he lived in. He heaps scorn equally on the age of reason and on the cult of sentiment that was setting itself up as a counterweight to it. Hence, nobody is spared.

On one hand, that is to say, this Modest Proposer deals in hard-nosed statistics and computations, thereby 'mimicking the practice of rationalizing offensive acts through reference to superficially connected cost-benefit calculations', in modern parlance.[12] Take, for example, Swift's offhand market research behind his proposal:

> Suppoſing that one thouſand Families in this City, would be conſtant Cuſtomers for Infants Fleſh, beſides others who might have it at *Merry-meetings*, particularly *Weddings* and *Chriſtenings*; I compute that *Dublin* would take off Annually about twenty thouſand Carcaſes; and the reſt of the Kingdom (where probably they will be Sold ſomewhat Cheaper) … eighty thouſand.[13]

The incongruity of turning the merriment of a wedding breakfast into a cannibalistic feast, let alone dining on the flesh of one child to celebrate the baptism of another, is hilarious, but what makes the joke cut is the point that economic rationalization flattens all human values to financial ones.

On the other hand, though, that is not to say that the modest proposer is a flint-hearted pen-pusher. Unlike, for example, Dickens's satire on

---

[10]Angela Gracia B. Cruz, Yuri Seo, and Mathew Rex, 'Trolling in Online Communities: A Practice-based Theoretical Perspective', *The Information Society*, vol. 34, no. 1, 2018, pp.15–26. p.23.

[11]Swift, *A Modest Proposal,* p.6.

[12]Shane Herron, 'Dark Humour and Moral Sense Theory: Or, How Swift Learned to Stop Worrying and Love Evil', *Eighteenth-Century Fiction*, vol. 28, no. 3, 2016, pp.417–46, p.428.

[13]Swift, *A Modest Proposal*, p.13.

utilitarianism in *Hard Times*, Swift is careful to give his political economist plenty of human feelings, especially the kind of effusive sympathy with his fellow creatures that was becoming fashionable at a time when literary sentimentalism, a precursor to Romanticism, was in the ascendancy. Thus:

> Despite the proposer's reputation as a cold calculator, he actually makes frequent reference to moral feelings to justify his decisions, as when ... the very first words of the satire relay an emotion: 'It is a melancholy Object'. What is troubling here is not so much the lack of feeling, or even the wrong type of feeling, but rather the response *to* feeling.... We agree with him that the situation in Ireland is melancholy. We agree with him in lauding attempts to alleviate suffering. However, we intuitively feel that his plan to alleviate such misery is not just unaccountably grotesque, but also misleading, disingenuous, and unreasonable.[14]

Not only, then, is Swift's humour transgressive even by today's standards – unsurprising, perhaps, given that we place a far stronger taboo against cruelty to children than did the eighteenth century – but Swift went out of his way to set himself gloriously at odds with the driving principles of his own day.

Scholars of trolling have suggested a couple more distinguishing features by which to define it, but these needn't detain us long. One of them is success: trolling needs to actually succeed in deceiving and antagonizing its targets, and in amusing its readers, who laugh at its transgressive nature. I sometimes find myself wondering whether this criterion is tautologous,[15] but *A Modest Proposal* meets it nevertheless: if the example of my A-level English class is anything to go by, it is still taking people in, it is still shockingly transgressive, it is still outrageously funny, and it is some marker of its success that it has been doing all this continuously for nearly three hundred years. Finally, the last characteristic of trolling is said to be the intention behind it: trolls deliberately set out to troll others, even though they hide their intent to do so. We'll be looking at this issue of intention for much of the rest of this chapter.

All told, then, Jonathan Swift seems to tick all the boxes for trollhood. In fact, it's surprising how few people have commented on this. The first to make the connection was the barometer of popular culture that is MTV: its website once ran a short feature entitled 'The World's Greatest Trolls in

[14]Herron, 'Dark Humour', pp.426–27.

[15]What I mean is that success isn't something separable from deceiving or amusing people – it is built into those activities. Put more simply: either you deceived someone, or you didn't; either they were amused, or they weren't. It seems odd and contrived to talk about whether or not you deceived or amused someone *successfully*. Queen Victoria never said, 'We are unsuccessfully amused'.

the Days Before the Internet', and Jonathan Swift topped the bill (followed by Friedrich Nietzsche, Marcel Duchamp, Orson Welles, Muhammad Ali, and Andy Kaufman).[16] Since then, only one blogger (of whom more later) and one brief scholarly paper have elaborated on the idea. This seems strange, since some of the tactics Swift uses are the everyday stock-in-trade of many trolls.

For example, Swift is a master of the technique known as the humblebrag: the disingenuous, ostensibly self-deprecating but actually self-serving move whereby one calls attention to one's virtues by disowning them.[17] It's a move frequently resorted to by trolls: past masters range from Martin Luther to Donald Trump, via Jonathan Swift. Swift's is a *modest* proposal, after all. It both draws upon and lays bare the manipulative nature of the humblebrag from an early stage, as when the modest proposer announces: 'I ſhall now therefore humbly propoſe my own thoughts, which I hope will not be lyable to the least Objection' – if his suggestion was truly humble it wouldn't hope to quash all dissent from the outset.[18] Critics have long been alert to this, calling attention to 'when the modest proposer nonchalantly claims that he has "no other Motive than the *Publick Good of my Country, by advancing our Trade, providing for Infants, relieving the Poor, and giving some Pleasure to the Rich*"',[19] or rightly pointing out that 'the humility of "AFTER all, I am not so violently bent upon my own Opinion, as to reject any Offer proposed by wise Men", is mock humility bordering on sarcasm and arrogance. We will all recognize this aggressive trope'.[20] But only recently has Jim Salvucci taken the step of making a link between Swift's use of such tactics and trolling.

Salvucci's discussion is brief yet suggestive. He calls attention to some of Swift's more trollish tactics, including the humblebrag, but draws particular attention to the trolling dynamics that unfold in *A Modest Proposal*:

> The Proposer trolls the hapless reader by launching with an ostensible reasonableness before slipping subtly into increasingly outlandish claims and suggestions and culminating in a lengthy list of apparently serious-minded schemes.[21]

---

[16]Aaron Goldfarb, 'The World's Greatest Trolls in the Days Before the Internet', *MTV News*, 28 November 2014. Available at: http://www.mtv.com/news/2007569/pre-internet-trolls/

[17]For more on the humblebrag, see Harris Wittels, *Humblebrag: the Art of False Modesty* (New York: Grand Central Publishing, 2012).

[18]Swift, *A Modest Proposal*, p.6.

[19]Herron, 'Dark Humour', p.427.

[20]Phiddian, 'Have You Eaten Yet?', p.615.

[21]Jim Salvucci, 'Jonathan Swift: Troll Level – Expert'. Paper presented at *Jonathan Swift in the 21st Century*, Jay I. Kislak Symposium, University of Pennsylvania, 23 February 2017. Available at: https://www.youtube.com/watch?v=gKQzdycmmqk

For Salvucci, the issue is clearcut: 'Swift was, in fact, a troll of the highest order', and, conversely, 'much of today's trolling has plenty in common with Swift's satiric efforts'.[22] But though I would agree with him that there's ample evidence to convict Swift of trolling, it doesn't follow from this that Swift was *just* a troll, any more than it followed that Luther was. Like Luther, Swift (who was, coincidentally, a Protestant clergyman) was trolling in the service of a cause; few would disagree that Swift's was a worthy one. More significantly, though, I differ with Salvucci's view that trolling is a modern equivalent to Swiftian satire. Swift may have been trolling, but the converse does not hold: it doesn't follow and it's simply not true to claim that trolls are only doing what Swift did. It's important to look into this and to take the time to clarify the issues at stake.

Trolling as satire

In February 2015, a blog post containing a strikingly immodest proposal went viral and quickly provoked an international torrent of outrage and condemnation. It was written by a men's rights activist named Roosh V. Entitled 'How to Stop Rape', it argued that non-consensual sexual intercourse taking place on private property should be decriminalized. Here is an extract from it:

> If rape becomes legal under my proposal, a girl will protect her body in the same manner that she protects her purse and smartphone. If rape becomes legal, a girl will not enter an impaired state of mind where she can't resist being dragged off to a bedroom with a man who she is unsure of – she'll scream, yell, or kick at his attempt while bystanders are still around. If rape becomes legal, she will never be unchaperoned with a man she doesn't want to sleep with. After several months of advertising this law throughout the land, rape would be virtually eliminated on the first day it is applied.[23]

The outcry that followed was on a global scale: 38,000 people signed a petition demanding Roosh V be banned from entering Canada; 50,000 people signed a petition asking the Scottish parliament to ban an event he was organizing there, even though he had no plans to attend it in person.

---

[22]Ibid.

[23]The original blog post is long since unavailable. It is quoted by Angela Nagle, *Kill All Normies: Online Culture Wars from 4chan and Tumblr to Trump and the Alt-Right* (Winchester: Zero Books, 2017), p.90.

There were calls to take down his website and ban his books (in which he brags about his sexual conquests and gives tips on how to pick up women). In response, Roosh V claimed that the blog post had been satire.

'Let's just say it was not quite Swift', quipped Angela Nagle.[24] But why wasn't it? The very first sentence of the above extract flags up the text's status as a proposal, in which legalizing a horrific crime is argued to be beneficial to the public good. So far, so Swiftian. What, then, makes Roosh V a troll instead of a satirist? Nagle's answer is admirably clear:

> How it would work as satire remains unclear, but it is not altogether implausible that it was some kind of attempt at a satirical or knowing tone that just didn't quite work. It didn't work primarily because his own views are too close to those being described satirically, so there is no level of knowing absurdity to them. A typical example of his style would be quotes like: 'My default opinion of any girl I meet is worthless dirty whore until proven otherwise'.[25]

That is the first, most obvious difference between *A Modest Proposal* and 'How to Stop Rape'. In the former, 'in order to negotiate the ironies of the piece, the reader must learn to distinguish between Swift's voice and the Proposer's'.[26] This is not possible in the latter.

Swift, for example, orchestrates a jarring mismatch between the tone of the proposal and the subject matter being proposed. Roosh V does not. Swift's proposal suggests, for instance, that eating children will have an additional benefit of reducing domestic violence:

> Men would become as fond of their *Wives*, during the Time of their Pregnancy, as they are now of their *Mares* in Foal, their *Cows* in Calf, or *Sows* when they are ready to Farrow; nor offer to Beat or Kick them (as is too frequent a practice) for fear of a Miſcarriage.[27]

Thus, 'in *A Modest Proposal* ... it is not the violence or brutality of the proposer's plan that creates the satire's notorious power, but the perverse detachment and dark inventiveness he employs to embellish garden-variety brutality and violence, veiling it with the robes of mock morality'.[28] You could, perhaps, argue that Roosh V does something similar, juxtaposing the violence of a screaming, yelling, kicking girl with a conceit that commodifies

---

[24]Ibid.

[25]Ibid.

[26]Phiddian, 'Have You Eaten Yet?', p.608.

[27]Swift, *A Modest Proposal*, p.13.

[28]Herron, 'Dark Humour', p.425.

the female body by likening it not to a cow or a mare but to a purse or a smartphone. And you might have a point, were it not for the fact that if we are to read this conceit ironically, as a piece of satire, then the most obvious butt of the joke is its victim: if a girl will fight to protect her smartphone, Roosh V seems to be insinuating, then why won't she fight to protect her body? The implication is that we're meant to laugh at the rape victim, not at the rapist, whereas in Swift, we laugh at the man who is more tender towards his livestock than he is towards his pregnant wife. That is why Swift provokes laughter and Roosh V provokes outrage.

Authors' intentions and readers' perceptions

What is perceptible in satire that is unclear in trolling is an *implied authorial intention*. This is a key point. Satire is necessarily ironic, but the point the satirist is trying to make is nonetheless clear, whereas trolling typically uses irony to conceal any such intended meaning from its readers. In other words, for satire to work as satire, it has to be perceptible to its readers as such. For trolling to work as trolling, though, it often remains imperceptible, to at least some of its readers. Recall Whitney Phillips's point about the asymmetry of trolling:

> the power dynamic between the troll and his or her target is, and can only ever be, fundamentally asymmetrical. Trolls don't mean, or don't *have* to mean, the abusive things they say. They get to choose the extent to which their statements match their personal beliefs; they get to establish that they're just trolling. Targets of trolling, on the other hand, are expected to take trolls at their word, and are only trolled harder if they resist. Consequently, trolls exercise what can only be described as pure privilege—they refuse to treat others as they insist on being treated. Instead, they do what they want, when they want, to whomever they want, with almost perfect impunity.[29]

The analogy between trolling and the prank or hoax springs to mind once again. Perhaps that's why I found my classmates' perspective so instructive all those years ago: for them, Swift was *not* writing satire, or at least not on a first reading. They had been set up, taken in – just as in a hoax.

Does this suggest, then, that some part of trolling resides in the eye of the beholder? That if you detect the joke, it's satire, but if you don't, you've

[29]Whitney Phillips, *This Is Why We Can't Have Nice Things: Mapping the Relationship Between Online Trolling and Mainstream Culture* (Cambridge, MA: MIT Press, 2015), p.26.

been trolled? Things aren't quite as simple as that – and fortunately so, since, if trolling was purely subjective, it would be impossible to call it out. Trolls, indeed, often disown their trollhood by finding fault with their targets' readings and perceptions of them as such – online gaslighting, if you will. So, if the difference between satire and trolling isn't determined by readers' perceptions, does it come from the opposite direction – from authors' intentions? Let's consider the case of Swift.

Besides Jim Salvucci, the only other person to evaluate Jonathan Swift's writings as trolling is blogger, scholar, and author Robin Bates, who surmises:

> Swift is not a troll because he is more interested in exploring his issues than in riling up the enemy. He genuinely thought that ... social engineers were dehumanizing the people they were supposed to be helping. He wrote about these subjects in dramatic ways that attracted wide readership, but he never got lost in his irony or his audience's responses. To use today's language, he never focused primarily on more clicks.[30]

The idea here is that since Swift sincerely cared about the condition of the poor in Ireland, and was genuine about the need for economic change, there is a human face behind the mask of his irony, whereas the troll's mask has no such humanity behind it. On this account, the difference between Swift's satire and trolling does indeed lie in authorial intention: it's the difference between saying something you don't sincerely mean to make a point and never sincerely meaning anything you say.

However, this, too, is overly simplistic. If what counts as trolling is the troll's frame of mind, then trolls can all too easily disown their trolling as inadvertences – just as Roosh V claimed that 'How to Stop Rape' was failed satire. Since only he knows whether he is truthfully in favour of decriminalizing rape or not, this idea of authorial intention effectively places the diagnosis of trolling in the hands of the trolls themselves; clearly a methodological absurdity. Does that mean, then, that the issues of intention and sincerity are red herrings?

Not quite. As Swift's *Modest Proposal* shows us, the key difference between trolling and satire lies not exactly in whether the intentions behind the irony are sincere and genuine, nor in the response of individual readers, but in the way that an implied authorial intention is reconstructed from the words on the page (or screen) by readers. It's important to note that this needn't mean all readers: just because some of them miss the joke, as

---

[30]Robin Bates, 'Reflections on Internet Trolling', *Better Living through Beowulf*, 30 May 2018. Available at: https://betterlivingthroughbeowulf.com/reflections-on-internet-trolling/

my classmates did, it doesn't follow that the joke is in fact a hoax.[31] It's no less important to note that the authorial intention is an *implied* authorial intention: later, we'll see evidence that Swift might in fact have hated the Irish, blamed the poor for being the authors of their own misfortunes, and penned his satires with a view to amusing a small circle of his friends, while vexing the rest of the world. All this ought to make him a troll. The reason it doesn't is because *A Modest Proposal* gives us good grounds for inferring from the text that Swift was morally opposed to eating the children of beggars. Conversely, 'How to Stop Rape' gives us no good grounds for supposing that its author is morally opposed to decriminalizing rape.

So far, then, we've seen that whilst trolling resembles satire, there's more to satire than can be reduced to trolling. The upshot, as Salvucci puts it, is that:

> irony in both trolling and satirizing are used as covers for all manner of excess and insult. If one were to conceive a Venn diagram of trolling in juxtaposition with satire, the overlap would be significant.[32]

The overlap, as I see it, goes something like this: neither trolls nor satirists are sincere in their words; both use irony for comic effect; both seek to provoke laughter, and even outrage. But satire gets us to see that something is wrong with the world, and from this realization, readers diagnose the writer's irony and laugh at it. Trolling doesn't, so its targets miss the irony and diagnose that something is wrong with the troll. Satire unites our outrage and our laughter; trolling splits its readers into those who are outraged, and those who aren't, but laugh at those who are. Perhaps it is facile to say that satire unites us whilst trolling divides us. But it's closer to the truth than the idea that trolls are just satirists who need to work on their material a bit more. The distinction turns on whether the irony is detectable to the many or to the few. We're about to see a worked example of how important this distinction is.

Are you trying to be funny?

The reason we need to be clear about where satire stops and something more dangerous starts is that, in England at least, satire amounts to a legal defence against prosecution for trolling-related offences. So whether something is

[31]As Robert Phiddian observes: 'The *Modest Proposal* is simply too aggressively alienating to be successful as a hoax, and I would suggest that we should not try to read it that way.... According to legend, some readers went to their maps in search of Lilliput, but most did not; and I suspect that a similarly small percentage of the *Proposal*'s readers has been slow enough to take it seriously.' Phiddian, 'Have You Eaten Yet?', p.605; p.607.

[32]Salvucci, 'Jonathan Swift: Troll Level – Expert', np.

classed as satire or not can literally mean the difference between freedom and imprisonment. Let's start by exploring a case study.

In the spring of 2016, the United Kingdom was tearing itself apart over the most bitter and acrimonious political debate for around thirty years – the question of whether to leave the European Union, which was to be decided in a referendum. The pro-Brexit faction breached electoral spending rules and was later found to have acted dishonestly to cover it up; it had also enlisted the services of the now-disgraced political consultancy firm Cambridge Analytica, which was later found to have made use of illegally obtained social media data; furthermore, one pro-Brexit fanatic murdered a pro-Remain MP, Jo Cox, in cold blood and broad daylight. Nevertheless, the referendum went ahead regardless and returned a narrow margin of victory for the Leave camp. Although its grass-roots level activists had routinely played the immigration card all along, the official line of the pro-Brexit campaign had been that leaving the EU was primarily about restoring sovereignty over the United Kingdom to the British parliament. So it came as something of a surprise when the Brexiteers in government then showed their true colours and sought to bypass parliament altogether, circumventing the normal legislative process, and withdrawing Britain's EU membership by invoking the government's prerogative powers instead of holding a debate in parliament. Irrespective of the question of Brexit, something was out of joint constitutionally. You cannot restore sovereignty to parliament by taking away rights granted by parliament without consulting parliament.

Cometh the hour, cometh the woman. The British government was taken to the highest court in the land by a successful businesswoman named Gina Miller, who, almost instantly, became a lightning rod for all the hate and bile that had lurked beneath the pro-Brexit faction all along. She received death threats, rape threats, acid attack threats, and abuse on a level that few people have ever had to endure. Much of it was racially and/or sexually motivated: seemingly, there is something about a woman of colour being successful, empowered, altruistic, wealthy, conventionally attractive, and in the public eye that is irresistibly magnetic to hate-filled trolls.[33] Among her many tormentors was a fifty-year-old aristocrat named Rhodri Colwyn Philipps, 4th Viscount St Davids. A few days after her legal challenge succeeded in bringing the government to book, he posted comments on Facebook describing Miller (who was born in what is now Guyana) as a 'boat jumper' and offered '£5,000 for the first

[33]For details, see Amy Binns, 'The Remoaner Queen Under Attack: the Trolling of Gina Miller', in *Anti-Social Media: the Impact on Journalism and Society*, ed. John Mair, Tor Clark, Neil Fowler, Raymond Snoddy, and Richard Tait (Bury St Edmunds: Abramis, 2018), pp.10–16.

person to "accidentally" run over this bloody troublesome first generation immigrant'. He added: 'If this is what we should expect from immigrants, send them back to their stinking jungles'. He was duly prosecuted for making racially aggravated malicious communications. At his trial, he represented himself, and said in his defence that his Facebook posts were 'meant to be a form of satire, a literary technique, iterated in my personal style, which may not be to everyone's taste, but is understood and accepted by everyone who knows me'.[34]

Philipps's resorting to the literary technique of satire as his defence could have been a shrewd move. The Crown Prosecution Service's document *Social Media – Guidelines on Prosecuting Cases Involving Communications Sent via Social Media* (authored by the then director of public prosecutions, Sir Keir Starmer) states in plainest legalese that:

> Prosecutors should only proceed if they are satisfied there is sufficient evidence that the communication in question is more than (i.e. crosses the high threshold necessary to protect freedom of expression, even unwelcome freedom of expression):
>
> **a** Offensive, shocking or disturbing; or
>
> **b** Satirical, iconoclastic or rude comment; or
>
> **c** The expression of unpopular or unfashionable opinion about serious or trivial matters, or banter or humour, even if distasteful to some or painful to those subjected to it; or
>
> **d** An uninhibited and ill thought out contribution to a casual conversation where participants expect a certain amount of repartee or 'give and take'.[35]

The key term here appears under item b, which is tantamount to saying that satire is a legal defence against accusations of harassment and hate speech. That's why defining satire and differentiating it from trolling is so important. It is, in fact, a fine point of law.

Perhaps it seems strange that literary techniques can amount to legal defences. But it turns out that literature is in fact surprisingly important. In America, the landmark ruling of the Supreme Court in the 2015 case of *Elonis v. United States* – the first time the Court had ruled on the limits of free speech on social media – hinged on Anthony Douglas Elonis's contention

---

[34]See 'Aristocrat Guilty Over "Menacing" Gina Miller Facebook Post', BBC News, 11 July 2017. Available at: https://www.bbc.co.uk/news/uk-40574754

[35]Keir Starmer QC, *Social Media – Guidelines on Prosecuting Cases Involving Communications Sent via Social Media* (London: Crown Prosecution Service, 2013, updated 2018), p.7.

that, during his acrimonious divorce, he had been writing rap lyrics rather than making death threats when he posted the following lines on Facebook:

> If I only knew then what I know now ...
> I would have smothered your ass with a pillow.
> Dumped your body in the back seat.
> Dropped you off in Toad Creek and made it look like a rape and murder ...
> Took all the strength I had not to turn the bitch ghost.
> Pull my knife, flick my wrist, and slit her throat.
> Leave her bleedin' from her jugular in the arms of her partner.[36]

Though this defence had failed him in the District Court, the Supreme Court found in his favour, and Elonis's conviction was overturned. The issue hinged on the nature of intention: at first, the District Court had found it was unimportant whether Elonis had actually intended to carry out his threats or not; what mattered was whether a reasonable person would feel threatened by his words. However, the Supreme Court overturned this position, and found that the prosecution had failed to prove that Elonis had intended to communicate a true threat. Had Rhodri Philipps been writing in America, then, he might well have been acquitted. Under British law, however, things are different. A statement from Gina Miller was read out in court, and the impact of Philipps's words on his victim was a key piece of evidence. So the fundamental question of whether what counts is the writer's intention or the reader's interpretation isn't an abstract methodological debate for literary critics – your freedom can depend upon it.

If satire is to be invoked as a successful defence, the writer presumably needs to demonstrate that their words are ironic rather than sincere, joking instead of serious. Perhaps that's where Philipps went wrong. When pressed by the judge on the question of whether his posts had been racially aggravated, Philipps responded that phrases such as 'boat jumper' and 'send them back to their stinking jungles' were 'statements of fact, not a racist comment at all'.[37] It's hard to see how invoking satire as a defence can be reconciled with making statements you believe to be literally, factually true and accurate, since it's not satire if you mean everything you say. Whether or not it was in consequence of this, Philipps was found guilty and sentenced to twelve weeks. Yet if he'd stuck to his guns about irony and satire, he might have walked free.

---

[36] *United States v. Elonis*, 135 S. Ct. 2001, 2006-16 (2014).

[37] See 'Aristocrat Guilty Over "Menacing" Gina Miller Facebook Post'.

The dangers of irony

This case remains interesting precisely because of the way Philipps's defence sought to legitimize his words through a curious combination that appealed to irony and satire, on the one hand, whilst insisting on being taken literally, on the other. This is not unusual. It's a common tactic amongst trolls, especially those on the alt-right. A 2017 report from the Data and Society Research Institute found that an internet culture of irony and in-jokes was facilitating the spread of white supremacist thought, Islamophobia, anti-Semitism, misogyny, and homophobia online.[38] In fact, perhaps the most surprising thing about Philipps's shrugging off his words as banter was that it was an aristocrat in his fifties resorting to this feeble defence, and not a brat in his teens, called out for using racial slurs and circulating Pepe the Frog memes. The ubiquitous use of irony and humour as defences for saying the unsayable range from Richard Spencer dismissing the notorious 'Hail Trump' Nazi salutes as irony, to Milo Yiannopoulos backpedalling on his disturbing view that thirteen-year-old children could give meaningful consent to sex by characterizing his remarks as humour, to Donald Trump clarifying that his asinine suggestion that Covid-19 could perhaps be cured by drinking bleach was sarcastic. Whether or not these flimsy post-hoc justifications are believed and accepted isn't the point. 'Whether undertaken sincerely or ironically, the outcome is the same', the report observes.[39]

Irony, once the crowning aesthetic virtue of postmodernism, has been appropriated. It is now used by boys who cry wolf for the lulz – and some of these boys are actively trying to bring about a world in which we can no longer tell the difference when a (real, non-ironic) pro-fascist movement shows up. At the risk of oversimplification, 'troll culture became a way for fascism to hide in plain sight'.[40] Trolling has enabled the alt-right to weaponize irony, as a way of espousing and fuelling hate with impunity.

Of course, that's not to claim that every troll is a fascist or a fascist sympathizer. It's theoretically possible that some of those who spit out bile and hate online do it because they (think they) are being funny. And, for some people, perhaps there is indeed something funny about the thought of provoking outrage from a crowd of riled-up liberals. But it's hard to see what's funny about hate speech and threats of violence. The late, great

---

[38]Alice Marwick and Rebecca Lewis, *Media Manipulation and Disinformation Online* (New York: Data and Society Research Institute, 2017).

[39]Ibid., p.12.

[40]Jason Wilson, 'Hiding In Plain Sight: How the "Alt-Right" is Weaponizing Irony to Spread Fascism', *The Guardian*, 23 May 2017. See also Alexander Reid Ross, *Against the Fascist Creep* (Chico, CA: AK Press, 2017).

philosopher Stanley Cavell once wrote a magnificently entitled essay called 'Must We Mean What We Say?'.[41] His argument is neat and simple: it focuses not on the philosophical implications of the 'mean' but rather on those of the 'must'. Words mean what they say regardless of what we mean when we say them; therefore, we must mean what they say.

This returns us to the issue we have never really left: the thorny nature of authorial intention. When we first came across this topic three chapters ago, we looked briefly at the case of a troll who called himself @prom: he said he was 'not sure' why he had hacked the Cincinnati Zoo director's Twitter account and posted a mixture of offensive obscenities from it alongside animal rights slogans. Alt-right trolls saw to it that this incident went viral, because it allowed them to riff on the long-standing racial slur 'ape'. Commenting on this incident, Angela Nagle asks:

> Given the Harambe meme became a favorite of alt-right abusers, was it then just old-fashioned racism dressed up as Internet-savvy satire, as it appealed most to those seeking to mock liberal sensitivities? Or was it a clever parody of the inane hysteria and faux-politics of liberal Internet-culture? Do those involved in such memes any longer know what motivated them and if they themselves are being ironic or not? Is it possible that they are both ironic parodists and earnest actors in a media phenomenon at the same time?[42]

For Nagle, the only sensible way of proceeding is to foreground intention and disregard claims of irony altogether – to stand up to trolls by demanding of them exactly what point they are trying to make, what it is they really stand for, and how far they are prepared to go in pursuing it.[43] The *Guardian*'s Jason Wilson concurs: 'In future, the best step may be to meet irony with sincerity'.[44]

We seem to have come a long way from Jonathan Swift. What would he make of this idea? What if *A Modest Proposal*'s first publication had been greeted with the kind of po-faced indignation it met with in my English class all those years ago? Perhaps it might seem, on the face of it, as if meeting irony with sincerity would necessarily spell the death of the great literary genre that is satire. But I'm not sure that Swift would have jumped to this conclusion.

---

[41]See Stanley Cavell, *Must We Mean What We Say? A Book of Essays* (Cambridge: Cambridge University Press, 2001).

[42]Nagle, *Kill All Normies*, p.7.

[43]See her comments in Wilson, 'Hiding in Plain Sight'.

[44]Ibid.

In fact, *A Modest Proposal* makes it quite plain what it stands for: it points out plenty of easy and implementable solutions to the problems of Ireland's poor other than cannibalizing their babies. Towards the end of the pamphlet, the modest proposer says (ironically, of course) that it is no good talking of taxing absentee landlords five shillings in the pound; or stimulating the Irish economy by buying only Irish-made clothes, furniture, and household articles; or boycotting the consumption of foreign luxury goods; or demanding landlords be merciful towards their tenants; or teaching shopkeepers honesty instead of how to cheat the poor on the quality, quantity, and price of what they sell; or encouraging '*Parcimony, Prudence and Temperance*' instead of '*Pride, Vanity,* [and] *Idleneſs*'; or of the Irish learning the values of patriotism and unity instead of factional divisiveness. 'I repeat', he says, 'let no Man talk to me of theſe and the like Expedients, till he hath at leaſt ſome Glimpſe of Hope, that there will ever be ſome hearty and ſincere Attempt to put them in Practice'.[45] If challenged, then, Swift could have listed any number of positive steps that could be taken instead of eating the children of the poor. Far from just trying to be funny, therefore, Swift's *A Modest Proposal* invites its readers to look beyond his irony and see that simple, effective solutions could well be ready at hand.[46] More than anything else, this is what differentiates him from a troll.

When irony isn't ironic

What makes satire satire, I have argued so far, is that its irony generally gives its readers a clear line of sight through the literal meaning to the intended meaning. Since trolling doesn't, it falls to the reader to push back against the irony. The purpose of this section is to scrutinize this idea more carefully. At bottom, there is surely a problem with this idea of confronting irony: it passes the onus from writer to reader. This could well be a difficult position to put readers in. As an extreme example: is it reasonable to ask Gina Miller to check whether someone she has never met has actually put a price on her head?

---

[45]Swift, *A Modest Proposal*, pp.14–15.

[46]Indeed, evidence suggests that Swift was saddened and disappointed when a rich English aristocrat wrote to him after the publication of *A Modest Proposal* to trade jokes and banter about killing and eating babies – because this response lacked any glimmer of recognition of Swift's real target: namely, the conditions of poverty in Ireland, as created and perpetuated by people just like the author of the letter himself, that is, rich English and Anglo-Irish aristocrats. See David M. Palumbo, 'From "Laughing" to "Rayl[ing]" with a "Few Friends": *A Modest Proposal* as Private Satire', *The Eighteenth Century*, vol. 59, no. 3, 2018, pp.259–78, esp. p.267.

Reasonable or not, Miller has not just followed Nagle's suggestion but also taken it a step further, by meeting in person with one of the men who trolled her. In a discussion arranged and filmed by the BBC, Miller came face to face with a man named Alan who had sent her a barrage of hate and abuse. When pressed on his motivations for sending Miller racist and sexist bile, what was striking about Alan's comments was that they revealed not a trace of any irony whatsoever: he professed an apparently sincere commitment to the cause of Brexit and an apparently sincere sense of disenfranchisement and grievance as a white single father.[47] In fairness to him, Alan did express his remorse and contrition, pledging not just to desist from online hate speech but also to call it out in the future when others do it. Yet this, too, underscores the impression that Alan wasn't just joking. Since it's often said that trolls do not sincerely mean what they say, the question is then raised as to whether people such as Alan, or Rhodri Colwyn Philipps, can really be said to be *trolling* at all. What makes them trolls and not plain and simple racists? We'll return to this question in just a moment.

For now, let's stay with the question of confronting trolls over the meaning of their words. As a counterpoint to the case of Gina Miller, take an incident that befell congresswoman Alexandria Ocasio-Cortez, better known as AOC. Like Miller, AOC seems to have become a target for large-scale trolling because she is a woman from an ethnic minority in the public eye, as well as being altruistic, successful, conventionally attractive, and empowered – the youngest US congresswoman in history to date. The incident I have in mind is in some respects the opposite of what happened to Miller: Miller's began with online trolling and ended in a face-to-face meeting; Ocasio-Cortez's began face to face, in a public meeting, which spilled over into online trolling. It's relevant here primarily as a moment of what I can only call neo-Swiftianism.

At a town hall meeting convened in Queens Public Library by Ocasio-Cortez to discuss proposals for a Green New Deal, a member of the public rose to her feet during the discussion, and proceeded to deliver a rambling, erratic, but apparently emotional and heartfelt rant, that went something like this:

> We're not gonna be here for much long [*sic*] because of the climate crisis. We only have a few months left. I love that you support the Green Deal but it's not, you know, getting rid of fossil fuel is not gonna solve the problem fast enough. A Swedish professor's saying we can eat dead people

[47]See 'Activist Gina Miller Meets Troll Who Sent Her Abusive Messages – What Happens Next?', BBC News, 11 May 2020. Available at: https://www.bbc.co.uk/news/av/stories-52488074/activist-gina-miller-meets-troll-who-sent-her-abusive-messages-what-happened-next

> but [*removes her jacket to reveal a T-shirt bearing the slogan 'SAVE THE PLANET. EAT THE CHILDREN'*] that's not fast enough. So I think your next campaign slogan has to be this: We got to start eating babies. We don't have enough time. There's too much CO_2. All of you, you, you know, you're pollutants. Too much CO_2. We have to start now. Please. You are so great. I'm so happy that you're really supporting New Green Deal, but it's not enough. You know, even if we would bomb Russia, we still have too many people, too much pollution. So we have to get rid of the babies. That's a big problem. Just stopping having babies, that's not enough. We need to eat the babies, and this is very serious. Please give a response.[48]

The response Ocasio-Cortez gave was calm, polite, and dignified. She welcomed the speaker's sense of urgency but reassured her there was still enough time to fix the climate crisis, plenty of options left to explore, and plenty of hope for the future.

What happened next was instructive. A film of the incident went viral. Ocasio-Cortez was pilloried in the right-wing media for not confronting, condemning, or even ruling out the eating of children. (Presumably she'd have faced the same roasting if she had simply refused to dignify the outburst with a reply.) Donald Trump Jr, the then-president's son, jibed on Twitter that the ranting woman in the audience 'seems like a normal AOC supporter to me', to which his father responded that AOC (*not* the woman advocating the eating of babies) 'is a Wack [*sic*] Job'.[49] Amid an outburst of memes about baby-eating that lowered the tone to the downright puerile, Ocasio-Cortez herself took to Twitter to remark: 'This person may have been suffering from a mental condition and it's not okay that the right-wing is mocking her and potentially make [*sic*] her condition or crisis worse. Be a decent human being and knock it off'[50] – which, of course, only produced further sneering digs about the mental health of climate change activists and Ocasio-Cortez supporters. Eventually, a little-known right-wing conspiracy theorists' organization claimed responsibility for the stunt on Twitter, saying they had planted the woman in the audience to 'troll AOC', and adding that 'Malthusianism isn't new, Jonathan Swift knew that. Sometimes, only satire works'.[51]

---

[48]The video of the incident from which this speech is transcribed has been circulated on the internet so many times that finding the original source for citation purposes has proven to be impossible.

[49]Tweets by Donald Trump Jr, @DonaldJTrumpJr, and by Donald J. Trump, @realdonaldtrump, both 4 October 2019.

[50]Tweet by Alexandria Ocasio-Cortez, @AOC, 4 October 2019.

[51]Tweet by Lyndon LaRouche Political Action Committee, @larouchepac, 4 October 2019.

What are we to make of this bizarre episode? If nothing else, I think it underscores the suggestion in the previous chapter that not feeding the trolls is seldom the best strategy. True, Ocasio-Cortez got credit in some quarters for the respectful and compassionate way in which she handled an apparently deranged member of the public, and admittedly, the same people who ridiculed her for not responding to the issue of cannibalism might well have ridiculed her all the more for lacking a sense of humour had she taken this suggestion seriously and literally. Perhaps, as is so often the case with trolling, there simply was no right way of handling it. The point of the contrast with Gina Miller's approach is to point out what happens if we don't follow Nagle's strategy of holding trolls to their words. Miller revealed a troll's racism that was apparently sincere, and confronted it head-on. Ocasio-Cortez missed the opportunity to unmask the contempt for democracy that underpins climate change conspiracy theorists, in that they have become desperate enough to resort to disrupting town hall meetings with bizarre pranks. The contrast between the two incidents suggests that Nagle's advice is the right approach: when in doubt, call it out. (As it happens, though, Ocasio-Cortez got the last laugh, with a shoulder-shrugging tweet that read 'Turns out the woman yelling was a Trump supporter'.)

The spectre of Swift in the Ocasio-Cortez incident raises questions of its own. Was this satire, or trolling, or somehow both? What does it tell us about the relationship between the two? What makes a woman who stands up and proposes we tackle climate change by eating babies different from what Swift did in *A Modest Proposal*? In this case, I'd suggest the woman in question differs both from Swift, on one hand, and from Alan and Philipps, on the other. It should have been clear enough that she wasn't sincerely in favour of eating babies: if we were in any doubt, her absurd suggestion that climate change might be ameliorated by bombing Russia to reduce the population ought to have signalled that she couldn't and didn't mean what she said. But she gives no clue as to what point she is actually trying to make: she doesn't reveal that she thinks climate change is an elaborate hoax, because that would expose her to reasoned debate, which she would lose. She dons the mask of a troll, and that is indeed the term that describes her best. Swift was a satirist, because readers can see through his irony to the point he is making; this woman is a troll, because readers are in principle able to deduce that she can't be sincere about what she is saying, but they are given no glimpse of the point behind the irony. Under close examination, it turns out that Alan and Rhodri Colwyn Philipps are probably neither satirists nor trolls: since readers have no basis from which to diagnose any irony, the only safe assumption is that what they wrote was sincerely meant and, hence, neither satire nor trolling but just plain racist abuse. And that's why it's important to confront it whenever and wherever we can.

There are, I realize, obvious objections to taking this line. The encounter between Miller and Alan, as heartwarming as it was awkward, conveyed a reassuring message that beneath a gruff or brutish exterior, trolls are only human. But not all of us have the BBC to facilitate a meet-up in a safe space, and even if we did, it's asking a lot of the victims of trolls to confront their aggressors. Can we seriously expect the estranged wife of Anthony Elonis to get in touch with her ex to ask if he's really being threatening and abusive, or if he's exercising his talent for rapping instead? Obviously not. That is why the decision of the United States Supreme Court in the Elonis case is problematic, to say nothing of disappointing. We can put the matter more plainly with a simple thought experiment. Imagine a world in which (God forbid) a contract killer had taken Rhodri Colwyn Philipps at his word when he plainly and literally offered £5,000 for the contract on Gina Miller's life, and that, in consequence, Miller had been assassinated. Why should the burden of proof fall on the prosecution to demonstrate Philipps's sincerity rather than on Philipps to demonstrate his irony?

Sadly, this is no mere hypothetical question. In December 2016, a man walked into a pizzeria in Washington, D.C., with an AR-15 assault rifle, a.38 revolver, and a 12-gauge shotgun, and opened fire. His motivation, he wrote online, was 'Standing up against a corrupt system that kidnaps, tortures, and rapes babies and children in our own back yard'.[52] Trolls had created and promoted a conspiracy theory according to which the Comet Ping Pong pizza restaurant was the centre of an elaborate satanist paedophile ring involving senior Democrats, including members of Hillary Clinton's team. The death threats with which the restaurant was then inundated may or may not have been meant ironically. But the bullets fired by the man who took them at face value were real bullets, not ironic bullets. It's a miracle that no one was hurt.

Back in the 1980s, another great American philosopher named Richard Rorty hailed irony as one of the three supreme virtues of our open, democratic, pluralistic, postmodern society. In those days, his work was touted as one of the keenest commentaries on the intellectual culture of his times. But perhaps those times have changed. Perhaps the time has come for us to recognize the wisdom behind Stanley Cavell's simple and disarming question: 'must we mean what we say?' That isn't to say we should routinely expect those who have been targeted to demand answers of those who trolled them. But it is, perhaps, a best-case scenario.

[52]For discussion of this unfortunate incident, see, *inter alia*, Carrie Goldberg, *Nobody's Victim: Fighting Psychos, Stalkers, Pervs and Trolls* (London: Virago, 2019); Bert Spector, *Constructing Crisis: Leaders, Crises, and Claims of Urgency* (Cambridge: Cambridge University Press, 2019), pp.97–8; and chapter 3 of Anna Merlan, *Republic of Lies: American Conspiracy Theorists and Their Surprising Rise to Power* (London: Cornerstone, 2019).

Disaster trolling

This section changes tack a bit. It returns to the question of whether Swift was trolling. That's because there's something troubling about the fact that Swift's *A Modest Proposal* apparently inspires half-baked conspiracy theorists for whom there's something laughable about the idea of climate change. The uneasiness arises not just, I think, from the prospect of Swift's humanitarian concerns being hijacked by the far right to lampoon a global crisis that is already resulting in the very kinds of famine, misery, and poverty Swift was crusading against. Nor is it quite right to say that there's nothing funny about climate change: it has inspired plenty of good satire over the years. Perhaps the source of the anxiety is that if we disapprove of using the trope of baby-eating to mock the biggest challenge humanity faces today, then why shouldn't we disapprove of Swift using this trope to mock the biggest challenges of his? Was Swift's a very specific kind of trolling – what is sometimes called (and I'll define the term presently) disaster trolling?

Let's first take a moment to contextualize Swift historically. At the time he wrote *A Modest Proposal*, the situation in Ireland was truly dire. Three successive harvests had failed, and, in a precursor to the later horrors of the years 1845 to 1849, the country was staring famine in the face. The land was owned by Anglo-Irish gentry, who, over the years, had been turning peasants out of their small farms, and replacing unprofitable subsistence farming with shepherding, a much less labour-intensive kind of agriculture. This had resulted in unemployment and rural depopulation on a massive scale. But things got worse yet. When the cheap Irish wool coming onto the market began to undercut the price of English wool and thereby hurt the pockets of the landowning ruling classes, the British parliament simply banned imports of wool from Ireland. Ireland's entire economy had been destroyed for nothing, since its chief cash crop was suddenly worthless. The impact on the Anglo-Irish landowning classes responsible for making the country destitute was slender: most were absentee landlords who lived in London, thus extracting wealth from Ireland and the Irish in order to spend it in England. Even on their visits to Ireland, they preferred to consume luxurious foreign imports than goods that might support the local economy. In fact, it's been reliably estimated that at the time *A Modest Proposal* was written, about half the people in Ireland depended for their survival on the meagre and unreliable welfare system known as Poor Relief. Under these dire circumstances, perhaps it's not surprising that some of Swift's more privileged readers preferred to focus on the jokes about eating babies than on the underlying plight of the Irish poor, since the latter was clearly no laughing matter.

In short, the situation in Ireland was so grim it would have been an easy target for what's known today as disaster trolling. In essence, disaster trolling consists of taking advantage of tragedies such as natural disasters to gloat over the misfortunes of others, as offensively and publicly as possible. It usually involves leaving jeering, hateful comments about innocent victims on news and media websites' coverage of the incident, though blogs, YouTube videos, and sometimes the social media accounts of NGOs providing humanitarian aid have been targeted too. Note that attempts at humour in these comments are very rare, unless you happen to find something amusing about heaping scorn and abuse on other people's suffering. Presumably, the laughter derives from the moral indignation these comments provoke.

Disaster trolling as a phenomenon is poorly understood, because few scholars have taken the trouble to study it seriously. Among those who have, the works of Whitney Phillips and of Anthony McCosker stand out as particularly interesting.[53] Startlingly, both of them argue that disaster trolling has its positives. For Phillips, disaster trolling can be understood as a reaction against, and perhaps even an antidote to, the catastrophe-obsessed mainstream media, whose self-appointed role as tragedy merchants means they profit from the misery of others. Accurate though this characterization of certain 'news' outlets may be, it's unclear how a justification for disaster trolling can be derived from it. For McCosker, on the other hand, the incendiary and savage nature of the disaster troll's comments are provocations which have the salutary effect of stimulating and reaffirming our sense of 'digital citizenship'. In other words, disaster trolling provokes us into rallying around to defend our shared values from distasteful and malicious verbal sadism. McCosker therefore regards the offending comments as 'productive intensifiers' and as 'active, resistant, and creative' attempts 'to intensify and sustain engagement, affect attention and contest forms of participation'.[54] To be fair, I would have no objection to describing Swift's *A Modest Proposal* in roughly these terms. But as claims made for disaster trolling, they seem less convincing. To see why, let's consider one of McCosker's own examples.

Around lunchtime on 22 February 2011, a major earthquake, registering a magnitude of 6.3, struck the second-most populous city of New Zealand – Christchurch. A total of 185 people lost their lives, and the number of injured casualties ran well into four figures. Later the same day, an unedited, unvoiced film was uploaded to YouTube, comprising six minutes of raw footage of the immediate aftermath of the tremor in the city centre of Christchurch. The scenes are graphic and visceral. They include shots of apparently lifeless bodies; of severe and disfiguring injuries, including flesh hanging

[53]See chapter 5 of Phillips, *This Is Why …*, and Anthony McCosker, 'Trolling as Provocation: YouTube's Agonistic Publics', *Convergence: The International Journal of Research into New Media Technologies*, vol. 20, no. 2, 2014, pp.201–17.

[54]Ibid., p.213, p.215.

off a woman's face; of masonry falling into the streets, presumably from aftershocks; of bystanders frantically trying to lift heavy wreckage from on top of injured people trapped beneath it; of survivors succumbing to hysteria as they give vent to their shock, grief, and fear. Entitled 'Major earthquake hits Christchurch, New Zealand', the film quickly went viral. By the end of the year, it had attracted around three million views and over eighteen thousand comments.

Here is one of those comments, made about two months after the earthquake by someone who went by the username of Annieberkowitz8. It's as inflammatory and upsetting an instance of disaster trolling as any you will have the misfortune to read:

> TO THE FAMILIES OF THE EARTHQUAKE VICTIMS: You can rest assured I and the rest of the world are pleased your piece of shit family member is dead and rotting in the ground, we laugh at your suffering and think it's pathetic you are upset because your family member was an insignificant worm who was shit while they were alive and now they are dead squashed filthy shit rotting in the ground. Especially those two filthy babies that were squashed REST IN PISS YOU FUCKING RODENT PIECES OF SHIT.[55]

I'm afraid I can't bring myself to agree with McCosker that this comment is a 'provocation that instigate[s] and help[s] to sustain interaction and attention to place, personal experience and the tragedy of the event'.[56]

Certainly, McCosker is right that posts of this nature provoke responses. Surveying a sample of 1,639 comments, he found that 62 per cent of them were @replies – that is, comments responding to comments by other commenters. Interestingly, the proportion grows as time goes by: in the first month of the video's life, 42 per cent of 865 comments are @replies, whereas between September and mid-December, 88 per cent of 239 comments were @replies, 'indicating that as time passes commenters tend to engage less with the event and more with each other', as McCosker puts it.[57] Perhaps it may be true, then, that the provocations of disaster trolls 'sustain interaction'. But if, in McClosker's view, such provocations sustain our attention to the tragedy of the event, then why is it that commenters engage less with the event and more with each other? Can these two things be simultaneously true? Not only, then, does disaster trolling sneer at the misery of others, it also obfuscates and smothers that misery behind a smokescreen of self-centred chatter and babble.

---

[55]Cited in ibid., p.211.

[56]Ibid.

[57]Ibid., p.213.

Whitney Phillips doesn't cover the Christchurch earthquake in her work, but her general approach to this incident might go something like this: little over a month before this disaster, Haiti, one of the poorest countries in the world, was shaken by an earthquake of biblical proportions – substantially more powerful than the one in New Zealand. The casualties were literally innumerable. The dead could have totalled anywhere from 100,000 to 316,000, the homeless perhaps a million, and the millions of lives severely disrupted by loss of life, limb, livelihood, home, family, or education were far beyond tally. The international response was often little better than shambolic: US air traffic controllers assumed command of Haitian airports and repeatedly turned away a flight carrying a Médecins Sans Frontières field hospital, to give just one isolated example. The scale of the devastation dwarfed that at Christchurch: the two events are so disproportionate to one another that they aren't meaningfully comparable in any way. And yet the latter knocked the former out of Western news schedules, which managed to treat the Christchurch victims as human beings just like us – where 'us' is taken in contradistinction to a 'they' who are dehumanized as faceless, helpless, powerless, countless, and, crucially, black, revealing in turn the implicit whiteness of the 'us'. Though Phillips does not say this, the thrust of her argument would likely be that the contempt of Annieberkowitz8 for the Christchurch victims isn't that different from the contempt of Western media for the Haitian victims. And that is indeed a view you could take. But surely there are better ways of calling out media-peddled racism than comparing dead babies to 'fucking rodent pieces of shit'.

How are Jonathan Swift's jokes about dead babies any different? How can they help us understand disaster trolling? In an important sense, they're *not* that different. After all, in the midst of a humanitarian catastrophe, Swift is laughing at the misfortunes of others. Defending him by saying that his purpose is ultimately benevolent won't quite do, because Phillips and McCosker would make the same claims for disaster trolling. Misguided though I think those claims are, I have already suggested that *A Modest Proposal* does more or less what McCosker claims disaster trolling does, so the question is begged: why isn't Swift a disaster troll? Defending Swift with the argument that he obviously didn't mean what he was saying won't do either, because it is far from clear *what* Annieberkowitz8 actually means these words to say and hence how (let alone why) we would take them literally. That, plus the fact that there seem to be at least some people who take Swift literally, too.

Earlier, when contrasting Swift with Roosh V, I pointed out that the targets of Swift's humour are generally the landlords, that is, those at fault for creating the situation and not the innocent victims of it. True though this may be, there is nevertheless the odd occasion when *A Modest Proposal* makes fun of dead babies. It laments 'the great deftruction of *Pigs*' and argues that pork is in 'no way comparable in Tafte, or Magnificence to a well grown, fat Yearling Child, which Roaſted whole will make a considerable Figure at a *Lord Mayor's Feaſt*, or any other Publick Entertainment'. It argues that this will in turn lead to 'Improvement in the Art of making good *Bacon*' and in 'Propagation of *Swines Fleſh*'.[58] This is not (primarily) a joke about the ruthless English colonial masters, the heartless Anglo-Irish landlords, or the feckless Irish peasantry. It's *prima facie* a jibe about babies being worth less than pigs, that preventing a pig's death with a baby's death is a good trade-off. To be fair, such jokes are rare in Swift. But they aren't altogether absent. So what's the difference?

The difference is that the disaster that Swift is trolling was a man-made disaster; the disaster that Annieberkowitz8 is trolling was not. Therefore, the deaths of the babies in Ireland were preventable; the deaths of the babies in Christchurch were not. There were people who were responsible, directly and indirectly, for the deaths of the babies in Ireland, and those people seem indeed to have been more preoccupied with feeding pigs than with feeding children. Though Swift's jokes are about dead babies, then, the butt of his jokes remains the society that let this happen. The butt of Annieberkowitz8's jokes are instead apparently the dead babies and their grieving families. That, I maintain, is what differentiates Swift from a disaster troll. But it is a fine distinction. Note that it hinges on the nature of the disaster and *not* on the nature of the writing. Consequently, since we're exonerating Swift on the basis of his target rather than his writings, it follows that perhaps his writings aren't that different from disaster trolling. And this in turn suggests that perhaps Swift might have been trolling after all.

Private satire, or, could Swift have been trolling?

The crux of this chapter has been the issue of authorial intention and how it is complicated by the use of irony. Trolling may well be ironic, but it does not generally reveal itself as such. Consequently, it's hard to diagnose where trolling ends and abuse or hate speech starts. The only safe working assumption, I have argued, is that words should be taken to mean what they say unless they give the reader clear signals to the contrary. Satire gives us these clear signals: it signals its irony loud and clear, thereby getting readers to see the point or criticism it's really trying to make. But having said all this, we would be wrong – and, I think, somewhat naïve – to assume that the satirist sincerely and wholeheartedly believes in the point they are making or intends their criticisms to be taken seriously. Satire is about the construction of an *implied* authorial intention: the author may very well have beliefs or

[58] Swift, *A Modest Proposal*, p.13.

aims seemingly incompatible with the message of the satire. But this lack of commitment needn't and doesn't demote a satirist to the level of a troll.

Such, I maintain, is the case with Jonathan Swift. Swift's stated aims and intentions behind his satirical writings were not focussed on improving the lot of his fellow humans – far from it. In fact, he wrote in a letter to his friend, the poet Alexander Pope, that 'the chief end I propose to my self in all my labors is to vex the world rather then divert it'.[59] In a famous declaration of intent, penned shortly before he wrote *A Modest Proposal*, Swift sets up a dichotomy of purpose behind the genre of satire:

> There are two ends that Men propose in Writing Satyr, one of them less Noble than the other, as regarding nothing further than the private Satisfaction, and pleasure of the Writer; but without any View towards *Personal Malice*; The other is a *Publick Spirit*, prompting Men of Genius and Virtue, to mend the World.[60]

Swift makes it perfectly clear that his motivation is primarily the former: 'if my Design be to make Mankind better', then, he wryly observes, he ought to be paid for it. 'I am sure it is [in] the Interest of those very Courts and Ministers, whose Follies or Vices I Ridicule, to reward me for my good Intentions', he quips. Instead, Swift states plainly that his writings are intended for private consumption, not for the public good: 'I expect and desire no other Reward, than that of Laughing with a few Friends in a Corner'.[61]

True, a certain amount of irony is detectable in this mission statement: as if Ministers of the Crown could seriously be expected to pay writers to ridicule them. Nevertheless, critic David M. Palumbo argues on the basis of this passage that Swift is best understood as writing a kind of 'private satire'. Instead of wanting to change the world for the better, Palumbo argues, 'Swift values satire in terms of its ability to elevate him above his enemies'.[62] Private satire is less a political intervention and more an in-joke among those who regard the stupidity of the world and its problems as rather beneath them. 'The laughter of Swift's 1728 theory of satire is, therefore, an assertion of power', says Palumbo,[63] but it's not a tangible kind of power: it consists largely in a feeling of superiority and self-satisfaction. And, Palumbo notes, it was a mode of writing that seems to have failed Swift: by

[59]Dated 29 September 1725.

[60]Jonathan Swift (1728), *The Intelligencer*, No. 3. See Jonathan Swift and Thomas Sheridan, *The Intelligencer*, ed. James Wooley (Oxford: Clarendon, 1992), p.61.

[61]Ibid.

[62]Palumbo, 'From "Laughing" to "Rayl[ing]" … ', p.264.

[63]Ibid., p.259.

August 1734, he was writing to Edward Harley, second Earl of Oxford and son of Swift's friend and political ally Robert Harley, as follows: 'You see my old murmurings are not yet ceased, but it is the same thing, as if they were; because I am now grown desperate; and have nothing to do but rayl with a very few friends in a safe corner of the house'. Note the difference, which is small but significant. For Palumbo, 'the changes – from "Laughing" to "rayl[ing]" and from "few Friends" to "very few friends" – register more than a general sense of disenfranchisement derived from Swift's … political life in Ireland. Rather, this subtle but important change signals a more personal dimension of Swift's … disempowerment'.[64] In effect, Palumbo's argument casts *A Modest Proposal* as a damp squib: beforehand, Swift poked fun at the idea that satire could 'mend the World' or 'make Mankind better'; afterward, he seems to have abandoned the very idea altogether.

This being so, it's worth asking: what's the difference between what Palumbo calls 'private satire' and trolling? If private satire is about trying to vex the rest of the world through raillery with a very few friends, for the smug self-satisfaction of laughing at other people's problems, then well may we ask. Swift's own description of his aims and intentions makes him sound just like a troll in search of lulz. Indeed, trading in-jokes from 'a safe corner of the house' recalls the stereotype of the troll as someone who writes things from the security of his mother's basement that he would never dare breathe to anyone's face. And, if we do what this chapter has been suggesting, and set aside what Swift claims his intentions are in order to ask instead what he's actually saying and doing in his writings, then the image of Swift as a troll comes into rather sharper focus.

For instance, there are places in *A Modest Proposal* where Swift is not above resorting to anti-Catholic hate speech to raise a laugh. One of the useful by-products of eating Irish children, he observes, is that 'it would greatly leſſen the *Number of Papiſts*, with whom we are Yearly over-run, being the principal Breeders of the Nation, as well as our moſt dangerous Enemies, … with a deſign to *deliver the Kingdom to the Pretender*'.[65] In a piece of public-spirited satire, perhaps one might laugh this off: religious bigotry isn't the joke's *modus operandi* but its intended target, since it's precisely this kind of sectarian division that prevents Ireland from uniting in the face of its challenges. However, as a piece of banter written by an Anglican clergyman for the private amusement of his circle of friends, it starts to look like an all-too-familiar Protestant slur about where the loyalties of Catholic citizens lie.

The best argument against reading *A Modest Proposal* as trolling would seem to be that it's clearly a well-meaning intervention on behalf of the Irish

---

[64]Ibid., p.259, p.273.

[65]Swift, *A Modest Proposal*, p.11.

Catholic peasantry. But the grounds for this argument are questionable. We would do well to resist the temptation to construct an image of Swift as an enlightened, progressive, liberal humanitarian. He was no such thing. In a sermon called 'On the Poor Man's Contentment', which he preached as Dean of Saint Patrick's Cathedral in Dublin, he addressed his congregation thus:

> Among the number of thoſe who beg in our ſtreets, or are half-ſtarved at home, or languiſh in priſon for debt, there is hardly one in a hundred who doth not owe his misfortunes to his own laziness or drunkenneſs, or worſe vices.
>
> To theſe he owes thoſe very diſeaſes which often diſable him from getting his bread. Such wretches are deſervedly unhappy; they can only blame themſelves; and when we are commanded to have pity on the poor, theſe are not underſtood to be of the number.[66]

It is, furthermore, questionable whether Swift, in spite of *A Modest Proposal's* appeal to Irish patriotism, held Ireland and the Irish in anything short of contempt. He is purported to have remarked, 'I count no man truly unfortunate that has not been condemned to live in Ireland', and his writings are littered with disparaging references to the 'savage old Irish', as he calls them in a letter to his friend Alexander Pope.[67] I hope the point I'm trying to make here is clear enough: there's evidence to suggest that Swift was as motivated by bigotry and misanthropy as he was by philanthropy, and, if intentions are to count for anything, this would surely make him a troll, not a satirist.

Perhaps, then, my classmates of all those years ago weren't so far off the mark. As one critic puts it: 'Perhaps the speaker is *not* ironic after all. Perhaps he gives voice to Swift's anger and despair. In such a world, Swift thinks the unthinkable: maybe it *is* better to kill them young'.[68] 'Indeed', observes another, perhaps 'one comfortable, well-fed year followed by an easeful oblivion has a lot to recommend it'.[69] But in an important sense, these remarks are beside the point. The problem with an argument along the lines of 'In reality, Swift despised the Irish, hence *A Modest Proposal* can't be ironic' is that the cart cannot be put before the horse in this way. What's at issue isn't what Swift 'really' thought or believed or meant or was trying

[66]Jonathan Swift, *The Sermons of the Reverend Dr Jonathan Swift, Dean of St Patrick's, Dublin*, carefully corrected (Glasgow: Robert Urie, 1763), pp.237–38.

[67]Dated 23 July 1737.

[68]Dustin Griffin, *Satire: A Critical Reintroduction* (Lexington: University Press of Kentucky, 1994), p.165.

[69]Phiddian, 'Have You Eaten Yet?', p.618.

to do (as if any of that were knowable – hence the scare quotes). At issue is rather his strategy of couching all of that behind thoughts and beliefs that *nobody* could sensibly and seriously hold. Or, to put it another way, the reason it doesn't matter whether Swift pitied Irish beggars or despised them, or whether he was bigoted or tolerant in his views towards Catholicism, is that neither set of beliefs could yield a justification for rationalizing infanticide and cannibalism. Thus, Swift remains an ironist and a satirist either way.

Nevertheless, it remains true that, as Salvucci puts it, 'viewing Swift through the lens of contemporary trolling can re-intensify the perceived acrimony that pervades his satiric work'.[70] The notion of private satire brings it further to the fore. The traditional moral justification for Swift's laughing at the misfortunes of others is that he aims at a greater public good – raising awareness of the plight of the starving poor, highlighting the injustice of the situation, agitating for change, and so on. But if he's not aiming at a greater public good – if, instead, he only wishes to rail and laugh at other people's miseries with a small circle of friends – then the gap between his satire and trolling narrows considerably. But this itself is strange because, as the last two chapters argued, trolling is necessarily public, whereas here, we seem to be suggesting that Swift was trolling precisely because he preferred a private to a public readership. How to account for this apparent contradiction?

We shouldn't assume that our ideas and concepts translate readily and without distortion into those of the eighteenth century. Let us remember that the idea of aiming at a greater public good didn't necessarily entail addressing oneself towards a greater public. In an age before democracy meant universal franchise, when only the elite could vote, and effective power lay in the hands of an oligarchy, then laughing with a very small circle of well-connected friends might actually be a more effective course of action than (for example) large-scale pamphleteering for the masses. In this climate, satire meant something rather different from what it means today. For Swift's friend Pope, the chief poet of the age, satire was a genre to be employed and valued precisely because it was an elitist art form: to oversimplify, it consisted of looking down on the foolish, the ignorant, the hoi-polloi, and the rabble, jeering at them from lofty poetic heights.

Obviously, too, the line between trolling and satire was not drawn as we might draw it, because our concept of trolling was lacking as such. More importantly, the familiar distinction between 'laughing with' and 'laughing at' was also a differently drawn line. Indeed, laughing probably had a very different place in the culture of the Age of Enlightenment from the role it plays

[70]Salvucci, 'Jonathan Swift: Troll Level – Expert', np.

in our own time. We've already come across the views of the philosopher Thomas Hobbes, who argued in his influential work *Leviathan*:

> *Sudden Glory*, is the passion which maketh those *Grimaces* called LAUGHTER.... The passion of laughter is nothing else but sudden glory arising from some sudden conception of some eminency in ourselves, by comparison with the infirmity of others.[71]

In those days, then, it was thought that laughing came about through feeling superior to others, hence all laughter was laughter at another's misfortunes, or at another's expense. We can surmise from this that the sense of humour was likely crueller than the twenty-first century might appreciate.

All in all, then, Salvucci is quite right to say that 'it takes some effort to discern a fundamental difference between the operation of some of Swift's work and much present-day trolling'.[72] But the effort is worth making, and it does eventually yield results. Swift was not exactly, and in any case, not *just* a troll. Indeed, what's objectionable about the strange, seemingly oxymoronic notion of Swift's private satire has helped reveal what's so objectionable about trolling. It isn't just the cruelty of the laughter in trolling. It's that the sharing of in-jokes at the expense of others is an intrinsically elitist, anti-democratic, divisive practice. Swift's private satire overlaps with trolling not so much in the derision that sometimes borders hate speech as in the bare fact that it's based fundamentally on exclusion, on a refusal to treat others as equals.

Conclusion

I began this chapter with one brief anecdote about my schooldays; let me end it with another. This one is a guilty confession. As a ten-year-old boy, I recall being told off in class by the teacher for laughing at a joke my friend had told me about the famine then devastating Ethiopia. I do not remember the joke itself – all that I remember was that I found it very funny. I didn't need the teacher to tell me that laughing at the joke was wrong. I knew that all too well. I didn't need her to tell me that what was happening in Ethiopia wasn't funny. I knew that too. But somehow that didn't seem to mean that the *joke* wasn't funny. It was – or at least it seemed so to a privileged, well-fed, ten-year-old white boy in a wealthy democracy five thousand miles

[71]Thomas Hobbes, *Leviathan: Or the Matter, Forme and Power of a Commonwealth, Ecclesiasticall and Civill* (Harmondsworth: Penguin, [1651] 1981) p.125.

[72]Salvucci, 'Jonathan Swift: Troll Level – Expert', np.

away from the famine. Nowadays, I very much doubt that I would laugh at any such joke: by the time of the famine in neighbouring Somalia, in 1992, my sense of humour had grown up a bit, so, when I heard jokes about Ethiopians being recycled into jokes about Somalians, I did my best to challenge them. By that time, too, I had done my A-levels and read *A Modest Proposal*, and hence I also found myself wishing I could go back for just a moment to being that ten-year-old boy again, so I could put my hand up and ask the teacher who told me off: 'But Miss, what about Jonathan Swift?'

Let's be frank about it: *A Modest Proposal* is and remains uproariously funny. It is funny not in spite of its cruelty but because of it. It should serve as a helpful reminder that decrying the excesses of trolls need not mean advocating bland humourlessness. To quote from the 2012 judgement of the Lord Chief Justice for England and Wales in a case involving an appeal against a conviction for tweeting a mock bomb threat: 'Satirical, or iconoclastic, or rude comment, the expression of unpopular or unfashionable opinion about serious or trivial matters, banter or humour, even if distasteful to some or painful to those subjected to it should and no doubt will continue at their customary level, quite undiminished'.[73] Swift, I have no doubt, would concur.

There have always been those who have felt uncomfortable with the cruelty of Swift's humour. *A Modest Proposal* cannot fully extricate itself from the charge that it is, as one critic puts it, 'entertaining to everybody but the starving poor for whom it claimed to be advocating'.[74] Perhaps the best way of shrugging this off (which is not the same thing as refuting it) is to point out that the reader becomes the object of Swift's humour and ridicule to an even greater extent than do the starving Irish beggars. 'At the heart of the *Proposal's* abiding power to unsettle readers lies Swift's positioning of the readers among the eaters', remarks Robert Phiddian, quite correctly.[75] Since 'those who could read such a pamphlet almost by definition had sufficient wealth and social power to be implicated in the oppression',[76] he argues that the real target of Swift's laughter is neither the heartless landowning classes nor the helpless starving peasants but Swift's middle-class readers, who are complicit in the situation. This leads him to observe that 'Swift has always been there ahead of the reader, not to prepare the way but, rather, to lay mines in it'.[77] And that, of course, makes Swift sound once more rather like a troll – deviously wrongfooting his reader's every move.

---

[73]*Chambers v DPP* [2012] EWHC 2157(Admin), LCJ.

[74]Sean D. Moore, *Swift, the Book, and the Irish Financial Revolution: Satire and Sovereignty in Colonial Ireland* (Baltimore, MD: Johns Hopkins University Press, 2010), p.174.

[75]Phiddian, 'Have You Eaten Yet?', p.618.

[76]Ibid.

[77]Ibid., p.609.

It should be clear by now that though Swift was never *just* a troll, the inference that he might sometimes have been doing what would today be called trolling is not without some merit. Rather than going over all this ground again, let's instead leave the last word to Swift himself. He wrote his own epitaph – which has rightly been called 'an exquisitely bleak *apologia pro vita sua*'[78] – and since the recurring theme in this chapter has involved confronting writers about the intentions behind their words, it's only fair to end with these lines of poetry called 'Verses on the Death of Dr Swift', in which Swift explained once and for all what his motivations were, and what he was about:

PERHAPS I may allow, the Dean
Had too much Satyr in his Vein;
And seem'd determin'd not to starve it,
Because no Age could more deserve it.
Yet Malice never was his Aim;
He lash'd the Vice but spar'd the Name.
No Individual could resent,
Where Thousands equally were meant.
His Satyr points at no Defect,
But what all Mortals may correct;
For he abhorr'd that senseless Tribe,
Who call it Humour when they jibe.[79]

---

[78]Simon Critchley, *On Humour* (London: Routledge, 2002), p.14.

[79]Jonathan Swift, *Poetical Works*, ed. Herbert Davis (Oxford: Oxford University Press, 1967), p.512, L.459–70.

5

… but instead aim to court controversy …

Oscar Wilde as a contrarian troll, or, How to put the 'wit' into 'Twitter'

'Work is the curse of the drinking classes'; 'Fathers should neither be seen nor heard'; 'Perhaps, after all, America never has been discovered. I myself would say that it had merely been detected'. These celebrated one-liners are over a century old, yet they gleam with a wit that shines brighter than most of the jokes we receive through today's social media. Shakespeare may have penned the maxim that 'brevity is the soul of wit', but it was Oscar Wilde who showed us its truth. So: what do the much-loved witticisms of Oscar Wilde have in common with the vilified writings of trolls?

Take a closer look at those quotes and you'll notice they share a few features in common. Firstly, their effect is partly down to their deftness and punchiness. Not only are they all very short, they're concise enough to fit comfortably into the length of a tweet. Secondly, they work by flipping conventional bourgeois Victorian morality on its head. They take well-worn expressions of familiar ideas and repurpose them, turning upside down and inside out the orthodox values they'd normally express. This was Wilde's trademark *modus operandi*.[1]

---

[1]So much so that Wilde was derided as a one-trick pony by Wyndham Lewis – a literary troll of the modernist era whom we'll meet in the next chapter. Lewis is said to have quipped that Wilde's entire *oeuvre* and reputation were built on 'exercising his one trick of reversing

Perhaps it's too obvious to need pointing out that trolling isn't trolling if you're saying things that everyone agrees with. As we saw in the first chapter, trolling is often said to be transgressive – and indeed the examples we've come across so far are often wilfully defiant of whatever is deemed acceptable by convention. Wilde was certainly that, but then again, which genuinely innovative writer or artist is not? The property of transgressive, convention-defying humour doesn't by itself distinguish Jane Austen's *Northanger Abbey* from the Sex Pistols' *God Save the Queen*. Rather than accusing Wilde of breaking the rules of common taste and decency – which sounds suspiciously like the charges brought against him in court, which charges he always denied – perhaps a better way of looking at the characteristics Wilde shared with trolls would be to draw attention to his insatiable appetite for controversy.

Trolling often looks downright contrarian, and Wilde was one of the most thoroughgoing contrarians of all. His contrarianism was the defining characteristic of his great sense of humour; the engine-room driving his lightning-fast wit. That's what this chapter aims to establish first and foremost. But it then goes further than that. In the previous chapter, the focus was on investigating authorial intention. This chapter is different. Contrarians rejoice in going against the flow, swimming against the tide, and setting themselves at odds with the mainstream. To understand contrarianism, then, we have to keep the writer in the same frame as their public.

Contrarianism is rooted in a relationship to one's culture and community, albeit an outwardly adversarial one. A contrarian's sense of humour, though it may seem outrageous to the community at large (and Wilde's sense of humour usually did), is nevertheless based on an underlying set of shared values which the contrarian must presuppose, if only in order to deride it. We saw, in the previous chapter, that the laughter involved in trolling is typically divisive because it is exclusionary. This chapter will try to show that Wilde's writings can offer us an alternative, which, though exclusionary in some ways, nevertheless appeals to a broad public, even while it purports to despise them.

Wilde's arch tone and barbed wit have made him one of the best-loved writers in the English language. Yet, at the same time, there is at the very least an overlap between the way his writings work, and the way trolling does. I want to suggest that Wilde's example reveals that there might be a more positive cultural precedent for some of the antics we call trolling, and that his legendary wit could offer a better model of good practice for

conventional morality without saying anything very interesting about it.' Clearly, though, this is itself a glaring example of the very fault Lewis decried in Wilde, and probably self-consciously so. It wouldn't surprise me if Lewis even learnt the art of trolling from Wilde – but that would be a digression.

those contrarians who wish to press society's buttons than the strategies and tactics of today's trolls. Having established, in previous chapters, that there is such a thing as trolling in a good cause, the aim of this chapter is to explore whether there are (relatively) good ways of trolling – which is to say, trolling in ways that do not stoop to verbal brutality, hate speech, public humiliation, and bullying. In other words, Wilde shows us all how to raise the tone. Simply put: if you want to troll, or if troll you must, then troll like Wilde.

Wilde the Great Contrarian

Whatever else he was or wasn't, Oscar Wilde was, in the words of poet Yahia Lababidi, a 'great contrarian'.[2] It's been claimed that 'the contrarian dogma is simple and easy to understand: "Whatever is popular is wrong", as Oscar Wilde proclaimed at London's Royal Academy of Arts'.[3] But, as we'll discover, it turns out to be less simple on closer examination. So, what do we mean when we call Wilde a contrarian?

Wilde scholar Jerusha Hull McCormack, author of *The Man Who Was Dorian Gray,* explains things as follows. 'In the broadest terms', she writes, people like Wilde

> are what we might call 'contrarians'. This is a useful term for describing those who think against prevailing conventions in a way that appears to be systematically perverse, hence 'contrary' to the dominant discourse. Thus Wilde is often accused of merely inverting common epigrams in his own philosophical sayings, such as: 'Education is an admirable thing, but it is well to remember from time to time that nothing that is worth knowing can be taught'.[4]

There are countless other apt examples she might have cited too: 'The world is a stage, but the play is badly cast';[5] 'Wicked women bother one. Good women bore one. That is the only difference between them';[6] 'Prayer must never be answered; if it is, it ceases to be prayer and becomes

[2]See Yahia Lababidi, 'Great Contrarians', *The Wildean*, 32, 2008, pp.29–42.

[3]Windsor Mann (ed.), *The Quotable Hitchens* (Cambridge, MA: Da Capo, 2011), p.xv.

[4]Jerusha Hull McCormack, 'Oscar Wilde as Daoist Sage', in *Philosophy and Oscar Wilde*, ed. Michael Y. Bennett (New York: Palgrave Macmillan, 2017), pp. 73–104, p.77.

[5]Oscar Wilde, 'Lord Arthur Savile's Crime', in *Complete Short Stories*, ed. John Sloan (Oxford: Oxford World's Classics, 2010), pp.3–21, p.10.

[6]Oscar Wilde, *Lady Windermere's Fan,* in *The Complete Plays* (London: Methuen, 1999), pp.29–104, p.81.

correspondence'.[7] Their humour and wit are one thing, but their impact also depends on their shattering of traditional folk wisdom.

In calling Wilde a 'great contrarian', Lababidi goes further still: 'Being [a] great contrarian meant standing everything on its head, and taking unconscionable positions'.[8] A contrarian, then, is somebody who, for whatever reason, is in disagreement with popular wisdom or popular taste; but a great contrarian is someone who speaks out against popular wisdom or popular taste, enjoys speaking out against them, and even grounds their identity on regularly and consistently speaking out against them. In other words, great contrarians invariably court controversy.

Wilde's appetite for scandal is well-known, not least because it backfired on him so spectacularly. His appetite for controversy is easily obscured by it, because it was less sensational. Yet it was thanks to the contrarian style in which he framed his controversial views that he became established as a writer in the first place. Take a turn of phrase from one of his essays, like 'The ancient historians gave us delightful fiction in the form of fact; the modern novelist presents us with dull facts under the guise of fiction'.[9] What seems like a neat comparison between fact and fiction, as represented (or not) by historians and novelists respectively, is actually a backhanded way of comparing the ancients with the moderns, whereby the modern is found to be dull by comparison with the delights of the ancients. Had Wilde simply stated that Thucydides's *History of the Peloponnesian War* had a better plot than Emily Brontë's *Wuthering Heights*, or that he found Charles Dickens's books boring in comparison to those of Herodotus, it would be easy to write him and his views off as trolling, pure and simple. But the polish of his wit, in playing four contrasting sets of opposing ideas deftly off against each other (ancient/modern, delightful/dull, fact/fiction, which, controversially, is said *not* to correspond to the distinction between novels and history books), makes that same view seem intriguingly paradoxical, cleverly amusing, idiosyncratically distinctive, and therefore attractive to hold, even if that view is not altogether in accordance with the truth. Would-be trolls might do well to take note of this: they will probably get further with a well-crafted controversial witticism than they will with abuse, bile, and hate speech.

It should be clear enough from this that Wilde had a gift for intricate argumentation and that his gift was to couch it in prose so neat and nimble that the argument itself is half-hidden behind the glitter and polish of the wit. Wilde's prose is of such a smoothly streamlined design that it leaves those who

---

[7] Oscar Wilde, *The Epigrams of Oscar Wilde*, ed. Alvin Redman (London: Senate, 1996), p.106.

[8] Lababidi, 'Great Contrarians', p.40.

[9] Oscar Wilde, 'The Decay of Lying', in *The Complete Works of Oscar Wilde*, vol. 4, ed. Josephine M. Guy (Oxford: Oxford University Press, 2007), pp.71–103, pp.75–6.

disagree with him nothing to latch their claws onto, and it makes those who try look ridiculous. Put another way, to want to argue rationally with a turn of phrase like this is to miss the point. Rational argument isn't the correct mode of responding to delightful prose like this, because it would come across as humourless, pedantic, and unable to appreciate Wilde's trademark wit. But that itself is the strategy behind Wilde's argumentation: the wit ends up precluding further discussion. To understand Wilde's mastery of controversy, then, we have to keep his wit rooted within its polemical stratagems, *even while* his aphoristic style forestalls this. One-liners are not supposed to get mired in debate, after all.

This is how Wilde got away with his contrarianism. Take a simple example: 'My duty is a thing I never do, on principle'.[10] What this line says is both morally wrong (and shockingly so to a Victorian ear) and a logical fallacy (someone who habitually neglects their duties can hardly appeal to their principles). To raise such objections, though, is to reveal oneself to be obtuse (the logical fallacy undercuts the immorality, so the line can hardly be taken seriously) and humourless (this self-contradiction is funny). And that's how Wilde repeatedly gets away with saying things that still stand out today for their stark contrariness to common sense and/or traditional values. Look and learn, trolls.

Wilde's contrarianism may also have owed its success to his frank and open disregard for the usual norms and conventions of sensible argument and debate. His works are full of characters who engage in discussion only in order to snub it. Consider the following: 'I can stand brute force, but brute reason is quite unbearable. There is something unfair about its use. It is hitting below the intellect';[11] 'Arguments are extremely vulgar, for everybody in good society holds exactly the same opinions';[12] 'I dislike arguments of any kind. They are always vulgar, and often convincing';[13] 'A man who allows himself to be convinced by an argument is a thoroughly unreasonable person'.[14] All this meant that Wilde's position was designed to be rhetorically unassailable from the outset.

As a result of this flair for controversy, Oscar Wilde 'conquered literary London one dinner table at a time'.[15] He became a celebrity whose fame (or, more accurately, notoriety) rested less on his literary works than on his contrarian pronouncements. 'Philanthropy seems to me to have become

[10]Oscar Wilde, *An Ideal Husband*, in *Complete Plays*, pp.105–212, p.197.

[11]Oscar Wilde, *The Picture of Dorian Gray*, in *The Complete Works of Oscar Wilde*, vol. 3, ed. Joseph Bristow (Oxford: Oxford University Press, 2005), p.202.

[12]Oscar Wilde, 'The Remarkable Rocket', in *Complete Short Stories*, pp.100–110, p.107.

[13]Oscar Wilde, *The Importance of Being Earnest*, in *Complete Plays*, pp.213–99, p.285.

[14]Wilde, *An Ideal Husband*, p.121.

[15]Lababidi, 'Great Contrarians', p.32.

simply the refuge of people who wish to annoy their fellow creatures';[16] 'I have met hundreds of good women. I never seem to meet any but good women. To know them is a middle-class education';[17] 'I am always thinking about myself, and I expect everybody else to do the same. That is what is called sympathy'.[18] As with any of Wilde's best lines, their wit is inseparable from their contrarianism. And the relationship is symbiotic: though the deftness of the wit by no means excuses some of Wilde's more controversial pronouncements, it nevertheless ensures they go unchallenged. Again, there is much for trolls to learn from his example.

Some Wilde scholars have been understandably wary of drawing such conclusions: perhaps there's a danger that labelling Wilde a contrarian downplays his creativity, by casting his writings as mere reactions and responses to generally accepted viewpoints, of a predictably wilful and perverse nature. One of them – Ilona Urquhart – rightly observes that 'His stylised public persona and witticisms based on reversals of Victorian standards means that his work has often been read as a contrarian rejection of moral values for aesthetic values, simply intended to shock and provoke'.[19] She's quite right to object that Wilde was never 'simply' or just or only a contrarian – but this doesn't mean he was no contrarian. Other Wilde scholars rightly point out that his contrarianism was in essence a pose, and that he went to great lengths 'to construct his contrarian identity'.[20] This is indisputable. But it also makes Wilde's contrarianism harder to differentiate from trolling. Take a line like 'If one could teach the English how to talk, and the Irish how to listen, society here would be quite civilised'.[21] Because he put it into the mouth of one of the characters in his plays, there's no telling whether Wilde means a word of it, or whether he is just trying to be provocative. That contrived ambiguity makes him closer to a troll and less like a bloody-minded contrarian grumpily berating the public.

And yet berating the public was Wilde's forte. In one of his essays, he wrote 'England has done one thing: it has invented and established Public Opinion, which is an attempt to organise the ignorance of the community, and to elevate it to the dignity of physical force'.[22] Enlarging upon this point

---

[16]Wilde, *An Ideal Husband*, p.116.

[17]Wilde, *Lady Windermere's Fan*, p.84.

[18]Wilde, 'The Remarkable Rocket', p.103.

[19]Ilona Urquhart, 'Devils, Souls, and the Spectre of Matthew Arnold in Oscar *Wilde's The Picture of Dorian Gray*', *Australasian Journal of Victorian Studies*, vol. 20, no. 2, 2015, pp.14–27, p.18.

[20]Joseph McQueen, 'Oscar Wilde's Catholic Aesthetics in a Secular Age', *SEL Studies in English Literature, 1500–1900*, vol. 57; no. 4, 2017, pp.865–86, p.872.

[21]Wilde, *An Ideal Husband*, p.185.

[22]Oscar Wilde, 'The Critic as Artist', in *Complete Works*, vol. 4, pp.123–206, p.201.

in conversation, he declaimed: 'To disagree with three-fourths of the British public on all points is one of the first elements of sanity, one of the deepest consolations in all moments of spiritual doubt'.[23] As regards matters of literature and art, he went so far as to say (in what was perhaps his finest essay, 'The Soul of Man under Socialism') that 'the public ... degrades the classics'.[24] Warming to his theme, he went on: 'A true artist takes no notice whatsoever of the public. The public to him are non-existent. He leaves that to the popular novelist'.[25] Still, when it came to writing a popular novel, *The Picture of Dorian Gray*, he made sure he included the line 'To be popular one must be a mediocrity'[26] – whether ironically or not who can say?

Such a disregard for public opinion – even an antagonistic contempt for it – is a built-in feature of contrarianism. It might seem, then, that contrarianism has much in common with trolling. But there are nevertheless important differences. Both contrarians and trolls fly in the face of public opinion and taste. But whereas contrarians hold views that are opposed to public opinion, trolls needn't hold any views of their own at all. Contrarianism is predicated on the importance of individualism; trolling is all too often reducible to nihilism. Wilde was never *just* a troll because he believed in positive values: he believed in art, in beauty, and, perhaps above all, in individualism. Or, as he once put it, and rather more elegantly: 'To be good is to be in harmony with oneself. Discord is to be forced to be in harmony with others'.[27] It would serve well as a mantra for contrarians. Trolls simply prefer the discord.

Contrarian or troll? (and how to tell the difference)

As epithets go, is 'contrarian' a praiseworthy or a blameworthy one? Is seeking controversy a good thing or a bad thing? Before going any further, let's clarify the nature of contrarianism further, to see how it resembles and differs from trolling. In exploring these matters, this section will step back momentarily from Oscar Wilde.

It's not difficult to talk up the positives of contrarianism. Claims can be made for it as anything from a marker of personal integrity to an

---

[23]Wilde, *Epigrams*, p.120.

[24]Oscar Wilde, 'The Soul of Man under Socialism', in *Complete Works*, vol. 4, pp.229–68, p.251.

[25]Ibid., p.259.

[26]Wilde, *Dorian Gray*, p.336.

[27]Wilde, *Epigrams*, p.112.

undervalued civic virtue. Here, for example, is Jemima Kelly extolling the virtues of contrarianism in the *Financial Times*:

> contrarians bring value because they encourage those who disagree with them to think about their own positions, to question why they are so sure about them in the first place (or at least those who are open-minded enough to manage this), and then either to adapt their position or to feel more confident in the truthfulness of their original stance. Thus, they are helpful in widening out the scope of public debate and improving its quality, even when it turns out that they are wrong.
>
> At a time when free speech is under attack across the world and groupthink is on the rise, those who question and poke at assumptions behind the status quo are more important than ever. We should recognise the value of such challengers, not punish them, even if they turn out to be wrong. In the end, it's not about being right. It's about making sure we have the conditions – such as a willingness to scrutinise our own positions and to seek out those who might disagree – that are needed for democratic society to function.[28]

Tolerating contrarianism is perhaps the simplest way to nurture diversity of thought. In the UK there is, in fact, an annual Contrarian Prize, awarded to the contrarian of the year: the prize cites 'Nelson Mandela, Mary Wollstonecraft, Millicent Fawcett, Abraham Lincoln, Mahatma Gandhi, Rosa Parks and Galileo' as 'good examples' of contrarians – people who demonstrated independent thinking, boldness, honesty, courage, and sacrifice.[29]

Most contrarians, needless to say, fall rather short of these ideals. Some might merely enjoy the frisson that goes with playing the devil's advocate. Some might have a dogmatic and spectacularly unthinking suspicion or disdain for whatever they are told by governments and authorities. (Conspiracy theorists and contrarians are *not* the same thing, though both reject public opinion.) Some instinctively enjoy gainsaying other people, and so they take up contrary positions almost automatically, as in the following sketch from *Monty Python* that Kelly rightly points to as a splendid example of what true contrarianism is *not*:

> MICHAEL PALIN'S CHARACTER: I came here for a good argument.
> JOHN CLEESE'S CHARACTER: No you didn't; you came here for an argument.

---

[28]Jemima Kelly, 'How Not to Be a Contrarian', *Financial Times*, 29 January 2021.

[29]See http://contrarianprize.com/about-the-prize/

MICHAEL PALIN'S CHARACTER: Well an argument's not the same as contradiction.
JOHN CLEESE'S CHARACTER: It can be.
MICHAEL PALIN'S CHARACTER: No it can't. An argument's a connected series of statements to establish a definite proposition.
JOHN CLEESE'S CHARACTER: No it isn't.
MICHAEL PALIN'S CHARACTER: Yes it is! It isn't just contradiction.
JOHN CLEESE'S CHARACTER: Look, if I argue with you, I must take up a contrary position.
MICHAEL PALIN'S CHARACTER: But that isn't just saying 'No it isn't'.
JOHN CLEESE'S CHARACTER: Yes it is!
MICHAEL PALIN'S CHARACTER: No it isn't! Argument is an intellectual process. Contradiction is just the automatic gainsaying of anything the other person says.
JOHN CLEESE'S CHARACTER: No it isn't.

As this sketch so aptly puts it, the 'automatic gainsaying of anything the other person says' is a poor substitute for the more intellectually committed values of contrarianism. But it also helps us see what the more superficial forms of contrarianism have in common with trolling. Trolling, as we saw in Chapter 1, typically involves disrupting a conversation, by disrupting the community's conventions for discussion. That's exactly what John Cleese is doing here – covertly disrupting the common conventions for argumentation, while overtly denying that he is doing any such thing.

Many of the scholarly forays into research around trolling flag up communication strategies that sound suspiciously like Cleese and Palin's Pythonesque to-ings and fro-ings. Gabriella Coleman observed that the term 'troll' began as a label attached to 'people who did not contribute positively to discussions, who argued for the sake of arguing',[30] while Fiona Vera-Gray similarly diagnoses certain forms of trolling as 'messages that waste a group's time by provoking futile argument'.[31] Such kinds of trolling are often more sophisticated than the 'Yes it is', 'No it isn't', which recall children's pantomimes – but often not *that* much more sophisticated. At its least toxic, trolling might (for instance) involve asking for sources to substantiate facts that are well-known or self-evident (so-called 'sea-lioning'), posting facile or off-topic questions, or agreeing strongly with the most clueless contribution to a discussion thitherto. There may be something contrarian about this, but it certainly isn't the kind of contrarianism that Jemima Kelly has in mind.

[30] Gabriella Coleman, *Hacker, Hoaxer, Whistleblower, Spy: the Many Faces of Anonymous* (London: Verso, 2014), p.132.

[31] F. Vera-Grey, '"Talk About a Cunt with Too Much Idle Time": Trolling Feminist Research', *Feminist Review*, vol. 115, no. 1, 2017, pp.61–78, p.66.

Much of what we call trolling is less innocent than this, and less harmless, too. Rather than simply stymying or derailing argument, the more disturbing forms of trolling involve 'inciting and escalating arguments',[32] often through 'the posting of deliberately objectionable materials in a given context, with the hope that other individuals will be deceived into providing an indignant reply'.[33] At best, 'their aim is to trick their target into devoting time and energy responding to an outrageous position that no serious participant in the debate actually holds'.[34] At worst, 'they promote viewpoints defying decency or facticity'.[35] This is how trolling opens up a space in which all manner of aberrations ranging from rape jokes to Holocaust denial get bandied about.

One team of researchers hit the nail on the head when they commented that: 'Such users engage in discussions without the intention of constructively contributing to the dialog, but rather to disrupt it. They act as agents of chaos on the Internet, and they are commonly referred to as *trolls*'.[36] Clearly, then, trolling involves confronting public taste and opinion. So how is it different from contrarianism? It would be easy enough, perhaps, to latch onto the idea of 'constructive contributions' mentioned here, and to differentiate between constructive contrarianism and destructive trolling. But the aforementioned team of researchers reject any such distinction. They try to make the case that trolls bring 'a range of trolling benefits for community engagement, such as eliciting alternative viewpoints by generating dynamic disruptions'.[37] Through interviews with self-confessed trolls, they found that some trolls claim virtues that sound just like the virtues Kelly attributes to contrarianism.

Here, for example, is what a troll who goes by the alias of Huldrefolk had to say about trolling:

> I like to disrupt things because ... I think it's productive ... to be confronted with different perspectives ... it would be bringing something to a post that is not ... being covered already.... It is like a game, whether or not

---

[32]Paraskevas Tsantarliotis, Evaggelia Pitoura, and Panayiotis Tsaparas, 'Defining and Predicting Troll Vulnerability in Online Social Media', *Social Network Analysis and Mining*, vol. 7, no. 1, 2017, pp.1–15, p.1.

[33]Angela Cruz, Yuri Seo, and Mathew Rex, 'Trolling in Online Communities: A Practice-based Theoretical Perspective', *The Information Society*, vol. 34, no. 1, 2018, pp.15–26, p.16.

[34]Ralph DiFranco, 'I Wrote This Paper for the Lulz: the Ethics of Internet Trolling', *Ethic Theory and Moral Practice*, vol. 23, 2020, pp.931–45, p.936.

[35]Benjamin Aspray, 'On Trolling as Comedic Method', *JCMS: Journal of Cinema and Media Studies,* vol. 58, no. 3, 2019, pp.154–60, p.156.

[36]Tsantarliotis, Pitoura, and Tsaparas, 'Defining and Predicting Troll Vulnerability', p.1.

[37]Cruz, Seo, and Rex, 'Trolling in Online Communities', p.23.

> people see it is as a game, it is a virtual arena where you are exchanging opinions and competing to a certain extent.... The thing about trolls is that they disrupt the game and make it more dynamic.... When it [trolling] is productive it contributes to ... the momentum and ultimately strengthens the community – like it adds more building blocks.[38]

The researchers took this as straightforward evidence that trolling has, or at least can have, the values and virtues we earlier ascribed to contrarianism:

> Here we see that trolling transgressions can at times serve as a mechanism for mitigating in-group biases and insular thinking, which we are increasingly seeing in online communities on the Internet ... [Hence] we challenge the dominant view of trolling as merely a value-destroying anti-social practice. In some instances, trolling practices can be viewed as a social mechanism for community interaction and engagement. They often prompt responses that reinforce the community ethos, fuel humor, and enable the expression of minority opinions.[39]

If Cruz, Seo, and Rex are right, then maybe there simply is no fundamental distinction between trolling and contrarianism. No doubt many trolls would agree: after all, however hateful their outpourings might be, there is no expression so vile that some troll or other will not defend it as challenging political correctness, defying the establishment, or (in the last resort) exercising the right to free speech. Like Huldrefolk, then, they are claiming the virtues of contrarianism as their own. This seems rather wide of the mark to me.

Let's leave aside the fairly obvious methodological problems with taking at face value the words of those who regularly say provocative and deliberately controversial things they don't actually mean. If what trolls like Huldrefolk say were true, then the internet would be a more open-minded, tolerant space thanks to trolling. More often than not, though, trolling closes down conversation, leading to frustration, anger, hate, and fear. So something is out of joint.

We can turn for guidance to one of Aristotle's long-lost treatises – his profoundly insightful diatribe 'On Trolling', rediscovered and translated from the ancient Greek in 2016 by philosopher Rachel Barney (or maybe, just maybe, she wrote one of the finest pieces of philosophical parody you'll ever read). Aristotle/Barney maintains that a troll is *not* the same thing as a contrarian or 'lover of controversy', though the two resemble one another outwardly. In the Aristotelian view, 'one who disagrees loudly on the blog on

---

[38]Ibid. Ellipses in original.

[39]Ibid., pp.23–4.

each occasion is a lover of controversy', as opposed to a troll, whose aim is 'not … controversy in general, but confusion and strife among a community who really agree'.[40] Thus, the two pursue similar strategies, but to different ends. A troll, says Aristotle/Barney, aims to divide the community against one another: he 'destroys the thread by disputing what is known to be true, or abusing what is recognized as admirable; or he creates fear about a small problem, as if it were large, or treats a necessary matter as small'.[41] Obviously, contrarianism may, at times, necessitate doing such things too. But the contrarian has an alternative viewpoint to convert others to. Not so the troll.

So: how do we root out the trolls from the ranks of the contrarians? In the previous chapter, I made the case for confronting trolls on whether they actually mean what they say. It's only a small step from there to confronting trolls about their real aims and objectives. If well timed, these interventions can quickly sort the contrarian wheat from the troll chaff. Here's a good example of how to do it, from a discussion board aimed at Western expats. A new user going by the name of 'exit strategy' started a new thread under the title 'Hong Kong Chinese or British', by posting the following thread:

> Not sure if this belongs here or in politics forum, and it probably has been discussed, but periodic updates of the topic have a value. Do the Chinese in HK feel that H[ong] K[ong] was better under the British? Or just the same. Or is it better now under the Communists, with S[pecial] A[dministrative] R[egion], and all that. The decade now passed allows us to see what the difference really is. A lot of HK Chinese might not have been old enough to know, but those 20 and over in 1997 might have an opinion.[42]

Note how 'exit strategy' takes great care to position the question, disclaiming any controversy in advance by admitting that the question might be better placed in a different chat, and admitting (disingenuously?) that such a controversial and divisive question might perhaps have been covered before, but nevertheless deserves revisiting. This *could* be a genuine invitation to free-thinking and exchange of opinions by someone who likes a good bit of controversy. But it could *also* be exactly how a troll might insinuate division into a community chat. The first response it got, by a user named 'jimbo',

---

[40]Rachel Barney, '[Aristotle], On Trolling', *Journal of the American Philosophical Association*, vol. 2, no. 2, 2016, pp.193–95, p.194, p.193.

[41]Ibid., p.193.

[42]For details see Christopher J. Jenks, 'Talking Trolls into Existence: On the Floor Management of Trolling in Online Forums', *Journal of Pragmatics*, vol. 143, 2019, pp.54–64, p.61.

was downright exemplary: 'Before we start, what are your actual thoughts on this? Or are you just trolling? ☺'.[43]

Thus, with a little bit of effort and skill, we can learn to tell a troll from a contrarian. (Michael Palin could, at any point, have just asked John Cleese 'So what exactly do you think an argument consists of, then?'). Put simply: a contrarian will be able to articulate views at odds with the rest of the community and give reasons for holding them that, though not perhaps what the community might call 'good' reasons, are nevertheless consistent on their own terms. Not so the troll.

In distinguishing between the contrarian and the troll, however, we have solved one problem only to pose another. Because as often as not, it would be quite impossible to apply any such test to Oscar Wilde. He perfected elusiveness. On the one hand, his plays, essays, and fiction contain much intellectual and conceptual debate which seek to rationalize the upside-down views they espouse – so he passes the test as a contrarian, defending controversial views. On the other hand, he also passes the test as a troll, on several counts. For one thing, as we've seen, he often renounces or repudiates the value of any such rationalizing of his ideas. The conclusion to one of his better-known essays reads, 'Not that I agree with everything that I have said in this essay. There is much with which I entirely disagree. The essay simply represents an artistic standpoint, and ... in art there is no such thing as a universal truth'.[44] And for another thing, we've also seen that his aphoristic style is designed precisely to preclude any confrontation, challenge, or discussion. Faced with inflammatory lines like 'As long as a woman can look ten years younger than her own daughter, she is perfectly satisfied',[45] all you can really do is take them or leave them.

This, I maintain, is why would-be trolls have much to learn from Oscar Wilde. He earned his stripes as a contrarian, but he avoided getting his views pinned down in overmuch debate, to the extent that to this day the jury is out on whether and how far to take his views seriously. He averted such pinnings-down not through verbal thuggery and rhetorical deviousness but through verbal elegance and rhetorical finesse. The result is that he remains a loved and admired author, despite the fact that for all we know, he might have been trolling us for much of the time. And that is why I repeat: if you want to troll, or if troll you must, then troll like Wilde. The rest of this chapter will show you how.

---

[43]Ibid.

[44]Oscar Wilde, 'The Truth of Masks', in *Complete Works*, vol. 4, pp.207–28, p.228.

[45]Wilde, *Dorian Gray*, p.211.

How to troll like Wilde #1: Mainstream contrarianism

Paradoxically, contrarian humour is surprisingly mainstream. It always has been. Or, to put it another way, we've known since classical times that humour shares certain core features with contrarianism: it often consists in breaking with convention, in taking popular wisdom and inverting it, in shattering the normal patterns of everyday life, and so on. As Cicero observed in *De Oratore*, the most common kinds of jokes are those where 'we are expecting to hear a particular phrase, and something different is uttered'.[46] This was Wilde's great gift – as in 'It is perfectly brutal the way most women nowadays behave to men who are not their husbands'.[47] So, whilst a comedian and a contrarian are not the same thing, there is often considerable overlap between them. In the words of philosopher Simon Critchley, 'jokes are a play upon form, where what is played with are the accepted practices of a given society'.[48]

In previous chapters, we've come across a theory of laughter predicated on laughing *at*. That is, a form of laughter that derives from feeling superior to the victims of our laughter, the butts of our jokes. Or, as the seventeenth-century thinker Hobbes put it, laughter is a 'suddaine Glory' exalting ourselves at the expense of the 'Infirmityes of others'.[49] This kind of laughter, sometimes called lulz, underpins trolling. But there are other theories of laughter, and they can help us understand Wilde's success better.

By the mid-eighteenth century, Hobbes's ideas were losing ground to a different theory, which, by the time Wilde was writing, had come to be accepted as the most convincing intellectual explanation for laughter. The basis for this concept of laughter is the idea of incongruity. As German philosopher Arthur Schopenhauer put it: '*laughter* results from ... the suddenly perceived incongruity between a concept and the real objects that had been thought through it in some relation; and laughter itself is just the expression of this incongruity'.[50]

Probably the earliest articulation of this idea can be found in a book called *Reflections upon Laughter*, published in 1750 by Francis Hutcheson,

[46]Cicero, Quintus Tullius, *On the Orator*, Book II, trans. E. W. Sutton and H. Rackham (Cambridge, MA: Harvard University Press, 1967), p.389.

[47]Wilde, *Lady Windermere's Fan,* p.82.

[48]Simon Critchley, *On Humour* (London: Routledge, 2002), p.10.

[49]Thomas Hobbes, *The Elements of Law, Natural and Politic,* ed. Ferdinand Tönnies (London: Cass, [1640] 1969), p.42.

[50]Arthur Schopenhauer, *The World as Will and Representation*, trans. E.F.J. Payne, vol. 1 (New York: Dover, [1818] 1969), p.59.

a key figure in the early years of the Scottish Enlightenment. It was elaborated and refined by Immanuel Kant in his *Critique of Judgement*, then by Schopenhauer, then by British romantic-era essayist William Hazlitt, who went so far as to argue that the link between incongruity and laughter distinguished men from beasts: 'Man is the only animal that laughs ... for he is the only animal that is struck with the difference between what things are, and what they ought to be'.[51] By the mid-nineteenth century, Søren Kierkegaard had made laughter at the incongruities of this world into a crucial plank in his outlook and thought, thereby inventing existentialist philosophy. Nietzsche then famously took this idea to its extremes.

So, by the time Wilde came along, it was widely accepted that the cause of laughter was incongruity. In 1870, a year before the young Wilde went off to university, American poet James Russell Lowell summed things up thus: 'Humour in its first analysis is a perception of the incongruous'.[52] Perhaps this helps explain why so many of Wilde's jokes take the form they do: 'When her third husband died, her hair turned quite gold from grief';[53] 'She is a peacock in everything but beauty';[54] 'I never travel without my diary. One should always have something sensational to read in the train'.[55] All these wonderful lines work in a similar way: they breathe life back into stale, hackneyed clichés by giving them new meanings that are glaringly incongruous with the familiar meanings of those clichés *and* strikingly defiant of Victorian social decorum, too. In other words, contrarianism and incongruity walk hand in hand here.

This kind of contrarian incongruity could well change the way we go about trolling for the better – better, certainly, than the destructive nihilism of lulz, though admittedly that's not setting the bar very high. Consider the following example. A paper by philosopher Ralph DiFranco cites 'an actual exchange on the dating app Tinder in which a user named Maddy was asked "Do you prefer lace or cotton underwear?" and responded with "I prefer corgis".'[56] The wit of this withering put-down works much like the cut-and-thrust ripostes of the dialogue in Wilde's plays. It's cutting, even cruel. Its humour derives from incongruity, and its own insouciance towards that incongruity recalls Wilde at his most contrarian. (For a gender-reversed counterexample, compare Wilde's 'What on earth should we men do going

[51]William Hazlitt, *Lectures on the English Comic Writers* (London: John Templeman, 1841), p.1.

[52]James Russell Lowell, *My Study Windows* (Boston: James Osgood, 1871), p.132.

[53]Wilde, *Dorian Gray*, p.317.

[54]Ibid., p.174.

[55]Wilde, *Importance of Being Earnest*, p.264.

[56]See DiFranco, 'I Wrote This Paper ....', p.940.

about with purity and innocence? A carefully thought-out buttonhole is much more effective'.[57])

Maddy's words meet most definitions of trolling. It's an off-topic response; it flouts the conventional forms of expression we associate with dating apps; it's rude, provocative, vexatious, and so on. And yet it's perfectly praiseworthy under the circumstances, as a response to an unwanted advance from a creepy, predatory male. As DiFranco observes: 'Ordinarily, being unresponsive and disregarding the interests and goals of one's interlocutor are considered wrong, however in the case under consideration these behaviors seem unobjectionable'.[58] In fact, it's a response that was applauded for its wit on Buzzfeed, as one of '19 Times Women Gave the Best Damn Responses to Men on Tinder'.[59] This implies that wit and a sense of humour, far from being alien to the practice of trolling, can actually make it successful and bring it acclaim.

Wilde found himself living in a time of po-faced moral earnestness.[60] He had to find a way to tackle head-on the humourless self-righteousness of late Victorian culture. He found it: by harnessing incongruity as a laughter-generating force, he could give voice to all sorts of contrarian ideas that challenged the Victorian moral majority. He grasped the contradictory ways in which humour both depends upon and defies social convention with such dexterity that he enchanted the establishment by ridiculing it, and grew in popularity by decrying the popular. Paradoxically, Wilde's was a mainstream contrarianism.

If that sounds like a contradiction in terms, that's because there's something inherently paradoxical in the incongruity theory of laughter. On one hand, there's clearly something contrarian about this kind of humour. But then again, how can it be called 'contrarian' if pretty much everyone finds it funny? Critchley pinpoints this problem when he says: 'no social congruity, no comic incongruity'.[61] That is, in order for us to laugh at the incongruous, we must share a certain outlook, including a standard of taste that directs us in our understanding of what is laughable, and what isn't. In a nutshell, we must share a sense of humour – and this is a culturally constructed, culturally relative, culturally variable thing (as anyone can attest who has ever had

[57]Wilde, *Lady Windermere's Fan*, p.84.

[58]DiFranco, 'I Wrote This Paper ....', p.940.

[59]See Remee Petel, "19 Times Women Gave the Best Damn Responses to Men on Tinder," *BuzzFeed*, 9 June 2015. Available at: https://www.buzzfeed.com/remeepatel/tinderellas-slaying-tinderfellas

[60]Analogously, it may be significant that, as Angela Nagle observes, trolling has emerged during what she calls a 'strange period of ultra puritanism', in which once-acceptable jokes were suddenly taken all too literally by a morally impassioned and vocal minority. See *Kill All Normies: Online Culture Wars from 4chan and Tumblr to Trump and the Alt-Right* (Winchester: Zero Books, 2017), p.8.

[61]Critchley, *On Humour*, p.4.

to explain how Shakespeare's jokes might once have been found funny). Somehow, then, laughter depends on everyday shared conventions *and* laughter shatters everyday shared conventions. Critchley puts it like this: 'The incongruities of humour both speak out of a massive congruence between joke structure and social structure, and speak against those structures by showing that they have no necessity'.[62] Wilde's wit thrived on this conflict: its contrarianism spoke out against Victorian values; yet this is precisely what made it appeal to the Victorians, who loved its controversial subversiveness.

Trolling is different – and so much the worse for trolling. Trolling is typically hostile towards these underlying social congruences and everyday shared conventions. That is, the prevailing sense of humour, which determines what is and isn't an appropriate topic for joking, is precisely what a troll's sense of humour sets out to destroy. This explains why trolls regard anything such as dead babies, teenage suicide, and racist abuse as quality material for joking with: the aim of the laughter is to break the taboos and defile the decorums that delimit what society thinks is funny. Thus, trolls are trying to demolish one of the most precious things shared by members of a society or culture – their sense of humour. Yet the examples of Wilde and of Maddy suggest that trolls who resort to outrageous content and verbal thuggery are shooting themselves in the foot. If their aim is to challenge or transform our sense of humour, the first thing they need is a powerful sense of humour.

This isn't to suggest that trolls never make use of incongruity. They can and they do. But there's an important difference between *laughter* based on incongruity and *humour* based on incongruity. Recall the case we came across near the start of this book, when a troll superimposed the face of a young girl who had tragically killed herself under a train onto the face of Thomas the Tank Engine. This is nothing if not incongruous. Someone I once described this to did actually laugh at it. But that laughter was, they said, a way of dealing with shock at the completely unexpected – that is, the incongruous. As essayist William Hazlitt wrote: 'laughter may be defined to be ... convulsive and involuntary movement, occasioned by mere surprise or contrast (in the absence of any more serious emotion), before [the mind] has time to reconcile its belief to contrary appearances'.[63] Trolling may well get us to laugh out of shock in this way – perhaps an unintentional nervous giggle at the frisson of the outrageous. But this is a profoundly different kind of laughter from the laughs we laugh at the contrarian wit of Maddy or Wilde, for whom laughter is grounded in a sense of humour rather than in some kind of psychological reflex action.

We've already seen that trolling is defined in terms of transgressive or disruptive laughter. Yet the wit of Oscar Wilde was as subversive as that of any troll. It was also more effective and (though these things are no doubt

[62]Ibid., p.10.

[63]Hazlitt, *English Comic Writers*, p.3.

partly subjective) more funny. So, why do trolls prefer the smug arrogance of lulz, the 'suddaine Glory' of laughing at another's expense, to the undeniably subversive power of contrarian laughter at the incongruities of the world around us?[64] Probably most hardcore trolls shun Wilde's example on grounds that his mainstream contrarianism was so mainstream as to outweigh its contrarianism. They are wrong. Common sense might suggest that you can't transfigure mainstream humour with jokes that everyone gets. But actually, Wilde's celebrated wit was surprisingly successful in shifting the ground of the Victorians' sense of humour.

However, we shouldn't think, for a moment, that the difference between Wilde's methods and those of the trolls is clear-cut. Indeed, that is the point of the Maddy example: its use of incongruity cuts across all efforts to differentiate humour from lulz, or wit from trolling. The riposte 'I prefer corgis' is at once a cutting, withering rejoinder and a stinging put-down, on the one hand, and a brilliantly crafted witticism, on the other. It meets all the criteria for trolling I've ever come across, yet its shining wit wouldn't be out of place in the script of a play by one of Wilde's most illustrious successors (Tom Stoppard, say, or Caryl Churchill). And what conclusions are to be drawn from all this? That whilst Maddy's wit, like Wilde's, might not always be clearly distinguishable at root from the forms of laughter that trolls typically use, nevertheless its mainstream contrarian humour is completely different in one obvious and important respect: it works. To sum up: Wilde's coupling of a contrarian disposition with a sense of humour based on incongruity yielded a wit that was pointedly barbed and invariably controversial. Therein was its appeal. The excesses of trolls, bypassing the mainstream standards of humour and taste with more outlandish contrarianism and incongruity, doom themselves to oblivion precisely by their wanton outlandishness.

How not to troll like Wilde #1: Beware the in-joke

Trolls' contempt for the mainstream is their weak spot. Because of this disdain, the impact of most trolls is localized instead of far-reaching, and short term instead of long term. Wilde demonstrates this for us clearly, if in a roundabout way. While on a lecturing tour of America, he reflected on the uproar that he and his friends had instigated in their youthful days at

[64]Contrasting Wilde's wit with trolling's lulz isn't to suggest that Wilde's humour was cruelty-free. Look back, for example, at the case of the woman who 'is a peacock in all but beauty'. What qualities does a peacock traditionally have besides beauty? Pride, and without the beauty, there are no grounds for the pride. Here, the misogynistic lulz at the woman's expense are barely concealed behind the wit of the incongruous wordplay.

Oxford. By adopting the pose of the aesthete, they had affected a worship of art that placed beauty above morality, pleasure above restraint, and the work of art next to God Almighty. But, reminisced Wilde, they had scarcely meant a word of it: 'We were delighted and amused at the typical English way in which our ideas were misunderstood. They took our epigrams as earnest, and our parodies as prose', he recalled.[65] Perhaps the most notorious incident of this kind involves a quip that Wilde made whilst still an undergraduate at Magdalen College: 'I find it harder and harder every day to live up to my blue china'.[66] This remark attracted the attention, not to mention the ire, of vicar John Burgon, who preached the following in a sermon from the pulpit of the University Church of St Mary the Virgin:

> When a young man says, not in polished banter but in sober earnestness, that he finds it difficult to live up to the level of his blue china, there has crept into these cloistered shades a form of heathenism which it is our bounden duty to fight against and crush out if possible.[67]

This, Wilde later remembered, was 'the first time that the absolute stupidity of the English people was ever revealed to me'.[68]

On the face of it, this seems to be a classic example of trolling: it begins with a public statement of views that are not sincerely held, but instead aim to court controversy, or to be provocative and vexatious. Moreover, it succeeded in riling up the moral guardians of the day. In this example, Wilde and his friends seem to pre-empt the 'ironic in-jokey trolls'[69] found on today's internet. Their humour is aimed not at mainstream tastes but against them, and is so thoroughly contrarian that the prevailing sense of humour can't recognize it as humour. Thus, a typical form that trolling takes is the in-joke: a joke that needn't be that funny in and of itself, because it has a secondary source of laughter, namely, at the oblivious ignorance of those who aren't in on the joke.

Though the blue china example might seem to suggest that such in-jokes work, Wilde's example actually suggests the opposite. In-jokes work best when they're recognizable as jokes beyond their small immediate closed circle – in other words, when they're not exactly in-jokes. For an example of one that fell flat, let's turn to one of the biggest controversies in Wilde studies – namely, the debate over whether Wilde embedded an in-joke into the title of his best-known play, *The Importance of Being Earnest*.

---

[65]Wilde, *Epigrams*, p.120.

[66]See Richard Ellmann, *Oscar Wilde* (London: Hamish Hamilton, 1987), p.43.

[67]Wilde, *Epigrams*, p.120.

[68]Ibid.

[69]Nagle, *Kill All Normies*, p.8.

By the late twentieth century, when it was possible to discuss the topic of homosexuality more openly and more frankly than in Wilde's time, critics began to suggest that the word 'earnest' was a late-Victorian euphemism, used only by those in the know, for 'homosexual'. Where this story originated is unclear, since it can be traced to two different origin myths. One is that it alludes to a book of poems called *Love in Earnest* by Wilde's contemporary John Gambril Nicholson – the poems in question are pederastic lovesongs to young boys, of whom the loveliest is named Ernest. (Whether Wilde knew of Nicholson's work has never been proven, though they did once publish poems in the same magazine.) The other is that 'earnest' involves a pun on its near-homonym *uraniste*, a term proposed in the 1860s by pioneering sexologist Karl Heinrich Ulrichs for men with desires for young boys. The two aren't mutually exclusive, since Nicholson's choice of the name Ernest may itself have derived from Ulrichs's coinage. However, there is as little evidence that Wilde knew Ulrichs's work as there is that he knew Nicholson's. In short, we just don't know whether Wilde meant 'homosexual' by the word 'earnest', or not.

If intended, such a pun would have had perforce to have been an in-joke, given that it alluded to a criminal activity that was utterly taboo. Only the tiniest handful of people – a few participants in the underground homosexual subculture of London at the time – would have been able to detect it. Consequently, there's never been a clear critical consensus as to whether Wilde was indeed punning in entitling his play *The Importance of Being Earnest*, or not. But if he was, then this is precisely how trolls use in-jokes today: a massively controversial, hugely incongruous, downright contrarian statement (in praise of paedophilia, no less) is hidden in plain sight, visible only to the troll and a small circle of like-minded initiates. That mainstream society and taste not only remained oblivious to the joke, and took the title at face value, but fell in love with the play bearing said title, elevating it into the echelons of canonical English literature, is even funnier to those initiated than the actual (rather feeble) joke itself.

When the joke, if such it was, finally came to light almost a century later, its reception was predictably divisive. Some admired Wilde for his wit, and for going (and staying) under the radar of Victorian propriety. Others, including titans of the British stage knighted for their services to theatre, were fizzing with rage at the thought that there might have been things in Wilde's script they didn't know about – let alone at the idea that they might unwittingly have played a part in a play intended as a comic paean to homosexuality. The venerable Sir Donald Sinden wrote the following in a letter to the *Times* dated 6 February 2001:

> Sir, In the 1940s I was privileged to talk, at considerable length, about the first production in 1895 of Oscar Wilde's *The Importance of Being*

Earnest with three of the original participants: Irene Vanbrugh, the first Gwendolen; Allan Aynesworth, the first Algy; and Lord Alfred Douglas, who was in Worthing with Wilde when he wrote the play and was present at the first night at the St James's Theatre.

Although they had ample opportunity, at no time did any of them even hint that Earnest was a synonym for homosexual. The first time I heard it mentioned was in the 1980s and I immediately consulted Sir John Gielgud whose own performance as John Worthing in the same play was legendary and whose knowledge of theatrical lore was encyclopaedic. He replied in his ringing tones: 'No – no! Nonsense, absolute nonsense: I would have known'....

I am emboldened to write this because only last week a theatre critic (not your own), in reviewing the latest production of *The Importance*, stated that 'the word "earnest" was Victorian slang for homosexual'.

The rot is setting in and, if unchecked, will doubtless be regurgitated in countless PhD theses.

Yours faithfully,
DONALD SINDEN[70]

Provoking outrage as high-pitched as this is the stuff most trolls can only dream of. But what caused such a shrill reaction? Homophobia, perhaps? Or just traditionalism bridling at newfangledness? There could be any number of explanations. But such indignant responses to in-jokes generally share one feature: they are infuriated by the idea of knowledge from which they have been excluded. From this, we can infer the characteristic of the in-joke that makes it so appealing to trolls: its divisiveness.

The anatomy of an in-joke might go something like this. A very small number of people are in on the joke. Of the rest, some will see through the joke, while the others are hoodwinked by it. Of those who are hoodwinked, some will remain oblivious to the fact, while others eventually catch on to it. Of those who catch on, some will see the funny side of being hoodwinked, while others won't. Of those who don't, some will respond by denying they were ever hoodwinked in the first place, perhaps (like Sinden) by refuting the existence of the joke itself. Note how, at every step, in-jokes divide and fragment our sense of humour, by using exclusion to insinuate division. That's why Whitney Phillips's history of internet trolling is dominated by a string of examples of in-jokes, such as the 2007 Jenkem Hoax.[71] The repurposing of Pepe the Frog is a better-known, more sinister example.

[70]Sir Donald Sinden, 'Important to Stop Rot about Earnest', *The Times*, 6 February 2001, p.19.

[71]Whitney Phillips, *This Is Why We Can't Have Nice Things: Mapping the Relationship Between Online Trolling and Mainstream Culture* (Cambridge, MA: MIT Press, 2015), pp.3–6.

If Wilde's use of the word 'earnest' was indeed an in-joke, then in certain respects, it must surely count amongst the most successful ever in its genre. It remained undetected for about a century, and the idea that, in spite of suppression and criminalization, the homosexual community of the 1890s was still able to outwit the mainstream in this way is hugely appealing. When the joke finally came to light, it polarized society. Responses ranged from the indignation of Sir Donald Sinden to the approval of Sir Richard Eyre, former director of the National Theatre. But if this is what success looks like, then all it reveals is the inbuilt failure of the in-joke as a strategy. What did Wilde's joke actually achieve? Nothing. If it aimed to subvert homophobia or heteronormative standards, it failed, because nobody paid it any attention until long after homosexuality was decriminalized, which robbed the joke of its point. That's why I suggested that, even though it's nigh-on a best-case scenario for the in-joke, this joke fell flat.

Indeed, if Wilde did indeed use 'earnest' as a synonym for 'homosexual', the number of people who would have picked up on this reference would have been close enough to zero. That is the conclusion drawn by Alan Sinfield, the world's most authoritative expert on Wilde's homosexuality and its influence on subsequent gay subcultures.[72] This is partly because the chain of allusions is so elaborate as to make decoding it impossible, and partly because if it had been possible to decode the reference, then the play would have been banned and its author disgraced. (For this reason, Sinden was probably right to query whether 'earnest' was common Victorian slang.) The cryptic allusions behind which the in-joke is concealed safeguards Wilde from the consequences of his joke but at the price of robbing his joke of any possible audience or impact.

Thus, in-jokes, by virtue of appealing only to a small minority, tend to be damp squibs. Wilde's in-joke lay dormant, like Sleeping Beauty, for a hundred years. It came to life only *after* (and *because*) society's standards had changed during that time: homosexuality was legalized, standards of taste made it less taboo to portray it, and our sense of humour evolved accordingly. So what this example suggests is that in-jokes are less powerful than, and take second place to, more visible varieties of humour: compare Wilde's in-joke tactics with his mainstream contrarianism as outlined in the previous section, and the strengths of the latter over the former become clear. Hence, if you want your trolling to produce tangible results, obscurely ironic in-jokes are probably how *not* to do it.

[72]See Alan Sinfield, '"Effeminacy" and "Femininity": Sexual politics in Wilde's comedies', *Modern Drama*, vol. 37, no. 1, 1994, pp.34–52.

Let's contrast Wilde's in-joke with a twenty-first-century example that was rather more successful, because its defiant references to homosexuality were rather more mainstream. Unlike the word 'earnest', the word 'pride' is nowadays commonly associated with LGBTQ+ lifestyles and has been since Gay Pride became a rallying point against homophobia in the 1970s and 1980s. Still, it seems unlikely that this sense of the word 'pride' was uppermost in the minds of the ultra-right-wing, violently pro-fascist organization who call themselves Proud Boys. Easy enough, then, for LGBTQ+ activists to appropriate the hashtag #ProudBoys, repurposing it so as to promote tolerance instead of hate. That's what happened in October 2020.[73] A flood of photographs, short videos, and images of gay couples kissing deluged Twitter, all depicting 'boys' (in the colloquial sense of 'guys') showing 'pride' in their gay identity – that is, proud boys. As for the terrorist organization that goes by that name, they were already banned from mainstream social media such as Facebook, Twitter, YouTube, and Instagram, so the hashtag #ProudBoys remained one of very few ways in which the name remained in general online circulation. Swamping it in a veritable online Pride Parade effectively paralyzed it for pro-fascist usages. Whether this prank caused any serious or long-term disruption to the Proud Boys is hard to say.[74] But at the very least, the incident showed how the tactics of trolling can be mobilized for a good cause with hilarious effect.

The hijacking of the #ProudBoys hashtag superficially resembled Wilde's tactics in taking a word that, in a certain context, is associated with homosexuality, and punning on that usage in such a way as to weaponize its meaning in a different context. But fundamentally, the cases are different. These hijackers were trolling with a joke that most people get; its widespread uptake means it wasn't an in-joke. That's why they succeeded where Wilde failed. The great Roman rhetorician Quintilian once wrote that 'the essence of all wit lies in the distortion of the true and natural meaning of words'.[75] But for this kind of wit to succeed, the distortion

[73]See Maija Kappler, 'Gay Twitter Is Taking Back the Term "Proud Boys"', *Huffington Post*, 4 October 2020. Available at: https://www.huffingtonpost.ca/entry/proud-boys-gay-twitter_ca_5f79e852c5b64b480aaf52de. 'When you call your hate group something as silly as "Proud Boys", you have to expect a little trolling', she opines.

[74]For a more cautious interpretation of this incident, see Dani Di Placido, 'Why the Twitter Hijacking of #ProudBoys Isn't Quite the Victory It Seems', *Forbes*, 5 October 2020. Available at: https://www.forbes.com/sites/danidiplacido/2020/10/05/why-the-twitter-hijacking-of-proudboys-isnt-quite-the-victory-it-seems/

[75]Quintilian, *Institutio Oratoria*, ed. and trans. H. E. Butler (Cambridge, MA: Harvard University Press, 1967), vol. 2, p.89.

has to be recognizable as such to your audience. That's how a mainstream sense of humour trumps an in-joke.[76]

By the end of Wilde's career, the theory that incongruity explains laughter was starting to yield to a more socially grounded view of it. In 1900, the year of Wilde's death, French philosopher Henri Bergson published his contribution to the philosophy of laughter, which opined:

> To understand laughter, we must put it back into its natural environment, which is society, and above all we must determine the utility of its function, which is a social one.... Laughter must answer to certain requirements of life in common. It must have a *social* signification.[77]

This is good advice. However contrarian your viewpoint, however incongruous your humour, you can achieve nothing if you don't carry enough people with you. This may suit many trolls – it's not as if they typically want to achieve anything, after all. But the rest of us should remember that in-jokes are designed to exclude society at large, and we do this at our peril.

How to troll like Wilde #2: Aphorisms not arguments

According to Yahia Lababidi, in placing his voice in splendid and implacable opposition to his culture and to the values of the society around him, Wilde's contrarianism was comparable even to that of Friedrich Nietzsche.[78] (It might be coincidental, but Angela Nagle observes that Nietzsche is one of the household gods of the trolling subculture.[79] If Lababidi is right, then Wilde should be too.) One of the main respects in which these two unlikely contemporaries resembled each other was in the style of their writing. Both

---

[76]Now might be the time to confess I remain sceptical about the idea of a hidden, homosexual meaning behind the word 'earnest', for simple reasons. During Wilde's trial, the moral backlash against him was so vicious and pervasive that, had there been even a hint of a homosexual subtext in his best-loved play, somebody somewhere would have spoken up about it, and the prosecution would in turn have latched onto it. Nobody did so. This leaves us with two possibilities: either Wilde made no such joke, or else one of the funniest men in the English language made a joke that literally no one appreciated. The second explanation seems the further fetched to me.

[77]Henri Bergson, *Laughter: an Essay on the Meaning of the Comic*, trans. C. S. H. Brereton and F. Rothwell (London: Macmillan, [1900] 1911), pp.7–8.

[78]See Lababidi, 'Great Contrarians'. Wilde (1854–1900) and Nietzsche (1844–1900) were contemporaries, and the comparisons Lababidi makes between them are truly striking.

[79]See Nagle, *Kill All Normies*, pp.34–5; pp.104–05.

avoided getting bogged down in detailed arguments, because the Western predilection for reason and logic was part of what they were speaking out against. Instead, they both turned to the aphorism, using concise and well-crafted one-liners in which the poetic and the philosophical become indistinguishable from one another. Take Lababidi's challenge, and see if you can differentiate which of the aphorisms in the following pairs is Nietzsche's, and which Wilde's:

> We possess art lest we perish of the truth.
> The telling of beautiful untrue things is the proper aim of art.
>
> What fire does not destroy it hardens.
> What does not kill me makes me stronger.
>
> The simple truth: is that not a double lie?
> The truth is rarely pure and never simple.
>
> Public opinion exists only where there are no ideas.
> To say it again: Public opinions, private laziness.[80]

Aphorisms such as these are hard to compose – it is no mean feat to turn a phrase so neatly. Nevertheless, they are, I would suggest, the perfect form of expression with which to go about trolling, and not just because they are brief enough to fit into a tweet (though that is always a practical consideration).

To explain why, let's look at how the aphorism works as a literary genre – or, to use a better term, a 'microform'.[81] The short length typically has two important effects: on the one hand, it maximizes the punchiness and impact of the expression, while on the other hand, it disconnects the expression from any surrounding context, making it deliberately ambiguous and therefore hard to interpret. The two may well be connected. As literary scholar Andrew Hui puts it, in an insightful discussion of how aphorisms work:

> The very minimal syntax of an aphorism gives it a maximal semantic force. The best aphorisms admit an infinitude of interpretation.... In other words, while an aphorism is circumscribed by the *minimal* requirements of language, its interpretation demands a *maximal* engagement.[82]

---

[80]These remarkable pairings are Lababidi's. See 'Great Contrarians', pp.34–5. The right answers are: Nietzsche/Wilde; Wilde/Nietzsche; Nietzsche/Wilde; Wilde/Nietzsche.

[81]Andrew Hui, 'Aphorism', *New Literary History*, vol. 50, no. 3, 2019, pp.417–21, p.418.

[82]Ibid., p.420.

Hopefully I don't need to spell out why a literary form that carries such a forceful effect on its readers while it resists being pinned down to any single clear meaning would be advantageous to trolls: the combination makes the aphorism a potentially very emotive and/or divisive vehicle.

There's no doubt that Wilde grasped this potential in the aphorism. As Yababidi puts it:

> Vast thoughts condensed could be carried in these deceptively slight vessels which relied on the culture of the reader to release them. Moreover, their pithy phrasing ensured that they were memorable.... 'Our proverbs want rewriting', he had written in *Dorian Gray*, and he set about doing so over the span of his career in oft-repeated epigrams and maxims (with titles like: *A Few Maxims for the Instruction of the Overeducated*, or *Phrases and Philosophies for the Use of the Young*).[83]

Nietzsche, however, had different reasons for embracing aphorisms, which in turn reveal more about the aptness of this literary form for trolling. To understand them, let's take a moment to look over the way that philosophers have tended, over the centuries, to fall in and out of love with aphorisms.

The earliest Greek philosophers – pre-Socratic thinkers such as Heraclitus, Xenophanes, Anaximander, and Parmenides – dealt in aphoristic sayings (*gnōmai*) and were roundly scorned by Plato and Aristotle for it. Such fragmentary one-liners sound like words of wisdom, but contain no clear reasoning or logic to back them up, and, as a result, could be invoked to justify almost anything (compare, perhaps, the use of movie quotes in today's conversation). Thus, Western philosophy was built on rejecting the aphorism in favour of the argument – first the Socratic dialogue, and then the treatise, the discourse, the essay. Over subsequent centuries, the philosophical tide has ebbed and flowed away from aphorisms, then back towards them again. During the Renaissance, René Descartes took philosophical system-building to new heights, in books such as his *Meditations on First Philosophy* and *Discourse on Method*. It's probably no coincidence that two of the best-loved books of aphorisms in the whole of European literature were written in France in the seventeenth century – Pascale's *Pensées* and the *Maxims* of La Rochefoucauld. Both men were clearly unconvinced by Descartes's magisterial argumentation and felt that wisdom and morality were better dispensed in memorable one-liners than in book-length diatribes. By the following century, the pendulum was swinging back: frustration had grown with the woolliness and haphazard nature of the French moralists' aphorisms, and the thinkers of the Enlightenment demanded more rigorously systematic argumentation. They got it, in Kant's monumental three *Critiques*, and in

---

[83] Yababidi, 'Great Contrarians', pp.34–5.

the works of Hegel. Not very far into the nineteenth century, the backlash against macro-argumentation was underway once more and brought on another return to aphorisms, as philosophers like Schopenhauer, and above all his admirer Nietzsche, used short sharp sayings to chip away at the edifice of Kant and Hegel's impenetrable tomes. By the early twentieth century, Wittgenstein's turn to an aphoristic style can be read as a rebuttal of the logical system-building of his mentors Russell and Frege.

All this seems to suggest a pattern: that argument and aphorism are irreconcilably different modes of expression. As Hui puts it:

> The philosopher creates and critiques continuous lines of argument; the aphorist composes scattered yet lapidary lines of intuition. One moves in a chain of discursive logic; the other by arrhythmic leaps and bounds. Much of the history of Western philosophy can be narrated as a series of attempts at the construction of systems. Conversely, much of the history of aphorisms can be narrated as ... a turning away from such grand systems through the construction of literary fragments.[84]

And this, no doubt, was why Nietzsche turned to aphorisms: to construct arguments would be to play into the hands of the rational and logical system-builders, whose very approach to thinking Nietzsche despised. (As did Wilde, come to that.)

Hopefully, this helps us grasp why aphorisms are so well suited to trolling. Aphorisms tend to disrupt logical arguments; so do trolls. They are a perfect match for each other. If that seems like a glib generalization, then let's look at some worked examples. Earlier on, we saw a probable troll called 'exit strategy' trying to start an argument on a divisive issue. He got very short shrift. Let's contrast his argument-based approach with trolling based on aphorism.

'There are only two kinds of people who are really fascinating – people who know absolutely everything, and people who know absolutely nothing'; 'There are only two tragedies in life: one is not getting what one wants, and the other is getting it'; 'There are two ways of disliking poetry, one is to dislike it, the other is to read Pope'; 'There are two kinds of people in this world. People who live with cats and people whose houses don't reek of cat piss'. Three of these aphorisms are by Oscar Wilde. The fourth – and by no means the least witty – is by a troll, posting a comment in response to a *Guardian* article entitled 'Experience: I'm a Fulltime Cat Sitter', dated 24 May 2019. Where 'exit strategy' tried to start an argument and failed to get any trolling off the ground, this troll – referred to below as 'A' – used an aphorism, and all hell broke loose. The discussion is reconstructed in the table below:

---

[84]Hui, 'Aphorism', p.417.

Sender/Addressee	Message
1 A	**There are two kinds of people in this world. People who live with cats and people whose houses don't reek of cat piss.**
2 B → A	Such a stunning insight. Did you come up with that all by yourself?
3 A → B	The first part of the aphorism is quite common. The second part is an observation that a lot of people whose houses don't reek of cat piss tend to experience. So the answer to your question is yes and no.
4 C → B	'Such a stunning insight. Did you come up with that all by yourself?' No, of course not. it's an old internet trope.
5 D → A	Lots of cats will go outside to do their business. They are actually very good at sticking to the same area outside i.e. they don't like to randomly poop all over the place. Some people will put a litter tray outside. But I agree, if you have an indoor cat it's likely there will be at least some cat pee smell as the ammonia is so strong.
6 E → A	But my cats prefer to shit and piss in your garden so I don't know how this can be true.
7 D → D	* an indoor cat that uses an indoor litter tray
8 F → A	I have a cat. My house doesn't reek of cat piss. Perhaps it's the company you keep.[85]

It's instructive that A's second comment refers to his original post as an 'aphorism' – and the insouciant tone of indifference to any controversy or outrage is pure Wilde. However, look closely and you'll see that the second comment didn't really need posting at all. All of the ensuing controversy is caused by the original aphorism. What's more, though all five respondents clearly feel that this aphorism has stung them into replying, they all reply in very different ways, presumably because they have all interpreted the aphorism differently.

B is apparently offended by the post, but doesn't want to give A the satisfaction of showing it. So the reply is a sarcastic rhetorical question, ironically praising A for his insight and originality. C either doesn't appreciate B's irony or thinks that B hasn't gone far enough in repudiating A's

[85]This table is taken from a discussion of this example in Henna Paakki, Heidi Vepsäläinen, and Antti Salovaara, 'Disruptive Online Communication: How Asymmetric Trolling-Like Response Strategies Steer Conversation off the Track', *Computer Supported Cooperative Work*, vol. 30, 2021, pp.425–61, p.441.

aphorism. D, perhaps the most clueless of these respondents, shows precisely what happens when you try to respond to an aphorism with an argument: this intervention may be a well-meaning attempt to defuse the situation by reasoning with A, but all it achieves is to reveal that D hasn't grasped the cutting nature of the original aphorism. That D later feels the need to add further explanation apropos of nothing much only adds to the impression of D's failure to appreciate the force of the aphorism as an aphorism, by responding to it instead as a factual statement. E's response is an attempt to troll the troll – a refutation through an appeal to a tongue-in-cheek logic that implies a personal slight against A. It is, perhaps, the wittiest of all the replies. F uses bald fact and bald logic, followed by a suggested personal slight. Unlike D, this reply is effective at arguing away the aphorism, but unlike E, it is completely humourless.

Though some of these replies aren't bad under the circumstances, none of them really nails a put-down. That they all respond in such different ways underscores my point: because aphorisms are open to such different interpretations, they are divisive, splitting their readership into different ways and kinds of uptake. And how does A respond to all these replies? How does A keep needling the respondents and stoking the flames? A doesn't; A doesn't need to. A understands that arguing about an aphorism is essentially pointless – that it can only detract from the aphorism's force and risk opening up arguments that might easily be lost. All told then, this exchange shows why the aphorism is a better tool for trolling than the argument.

From the troll's viewpoint, there's one more advantage the aphorism has over the argument: it doesn't matter if you screw it up. After all, let's face it: whatever John Cleese might have said, arguing is a tricky business. It requires much intellectual and verbal dexterity, and if you get it wrong, you lose. Aphorisms also require much intellectual and verbal dexterity too, but if you get them wrong, you can still win on trolls' terms. Consider this example – a comment posted by a prolific troll with the username KenM back in 2015, under an AP news article comparing US presidential candidates' fundraising efforts in the build-up to the 2016 election: 'Ben Franklin said politicians are like pampers, they both stink and they act like babies'.[86] It's clearly an attempt at a witty aphoristic one-liner, though it doesn't quite come off (in what sense do pampers act like babies, exactly?) and its obviously anachronistic misattribution to Ben Franklin is jarring – deliberately so. The troll in question, Kenneth McCarthy, says he enjoys

[86]This example is discussed in P. J. Connolly, 'Trolling as Speech Act (or, the Art of Trolling, with a Description of All the Utensils, Instruments, Tackling, and Materials Requisite Thereto: With Rules and Directions How to Use Them)', *Journal of Social Philosophy*, vol. 53, no. 1, 2021, pp.1–17, p.3.

'playing a well-meaning moron on the internet', and it seems that half the fun comes from those who mistake his failed attempts at aphorisms for those of a genuine moron: someone with the username Karl responded to this post by saying: 'ken hate to tell you pampers have only been around 50 years. True moron'.[87] For a troll, this response is as gratifying as the responses A got from respondents B to F.

Conclusion: it doesn't matter if your aphorisms don't live up to those of Wilde and Nietzsche. You can troll with a bad aphorism just as well as with a good one. (As a matter of fact, Wilde himself understood the comic value of the self-defeating, broken-backed aphorism, as in 'To win back my youth ... there is nothing I wouldn't do – except take exercise, get up early, or be a useful member of the community'.[88]) But the same is not true of trolling through arguments. That's why the aphorism, whether good or bad, is a better vehicle for trolling with than the argument – let alone the in-joke. Whereas in-jokes are divisive because they are designed to be exclusionary, aphorisms tend to be divisive because their readers are prone to interpreting them in multiple ways. This is arguably less reprehensible, and definitely more effective, since aphorisms are designed to be striking and impactful, whereas in-jokes are lost on the majority of people.

How not to troll like Wilde #2: Characters not masks

There is, unfortunately, one sizeable obstacle that blots out any clear view of Wilde as a role model for today's trolls. He ended up in jail. This remains an all-too common destination for twenty-first-century trolls, as our final chapter discusses. Furthermore, when Wilde was placed on trial and charged with gross indecency, some of the evidence for the prosecution came from his own writings and expressions. His contrarianism had caught up with him in the end.

Like many trolls, Wilde often maintained that he didn't, or didn't necessarily, mean everything he said. 'I live in terror of not being misunderstood',[89] he once wrote – long before his appearance at the Old Bailey brought this terror to life, and compelled him to clarify his meanings. Prior to this, he had resisted efforts to pin him down to any position or stance: 'I may have said

[87]See ibid., p.3.

[88]Oscar Wilde, *A Woman of No Importance*, in *Complete Plays*, pp.301–77, pp.343–44.

[89]Wilde, 'The Critic as Artist', p.136.

the same thing before', he once remarked. 'But my explanation, I am sure, will always be different'.[90] In justifying his slipperiness, he often appealed to a metaphor which, following the work of Whitney Phillips, we have applied to trolls in each of the last three chapters: the mask. But let's not rush from this to a facile conclusion such as 'Wilde adopted masks; trolls adopt masks; therefore Wilde was a troll'. On the contrary: Wilde's reliance on masks, I'm going to argue, was in fact his undoing. Otherwise put, his use of masks illustrates how *not* to troll.

Phillips's account of trolls and their masks fits Oscar Wilde's case quite neatly. Here's a recap:

> the mask worn by trolls precludes reciprocity; only the troll can wear the mask. The recipient of the trolls' behavior ... is expected to take things seriously, the more seriously the better. If the target does not, then the troll has failed.... While the person can be equated with the profiles he or she creates ('I am David'), the resulting profiles cannot similarly or necessarily be equated with the person ('David isn't *me*'); it is perhaps more accurate to say that trolling profiles, and trolling personas generally, fall somewhere between character and proxy – a sometimes-rupture sometimes-slippage between the offline and the online self.[91]

Wilde routinely used the metaphor of the mask so as to pick and choose when to stand by his words, and when not to. In this respect, the only difference between him and today's trolls was that at least Wilde was explicit, even voluble, about the many advantages of the mask.

The key point, though, is that the mask was not a defence that saved him. Nor is it a defence that saves trolls from a similar fate. To adopt a mask is only to provoke the indignant demand for clarification as to what a troll really stands for. And in Wilde's case, these demands were hard to answer, since, like a true contrarian, he had repeatedly made claims that turned conventional thinking about how to use the persona of a mask on its head. 'A mask tells us more than a face', he wrote.[92] 'Man is least himself when he talks in his own person. Give him a mask, and he will tell you the truth'.[93] In summary: Wilde's example shows that using a mask isn't always the best tactic for trolling. And not only are there better strategies than this, but Wilde also shows us what they are: 'Good taste ... [is] the excuse I've always

---

[90]Wilde, *Epigrams*, p.142.

[91]Phillips, *This Is Why ...*, p.33, p.80.

[92]Oscar Wilde, 'Pen, Pencil and Poison', in *Complete Works*, vol. 4, pp.104–22, p.107.

[93]Wilde, 'The Critic as Artist', p.185.

given for leading such a bad life';[94] 'Heaven is a despotism. I shall be at home there';[95] 'It is perfectly monstrous the way people go about, nowadays, saying things against one behind one's back that are absolutely and entirely true'.[96] When Wilde gave lines like these to the characters of his drama and fiction, it wasn't easy to hold them against him.

However, when he encouraged scandal and controversy by using similar expressions in his own persona – in essays, letters, in conversation, and so on – they could. Looked at from this angle, where Wilde went wrong was in cultivating a persona for himself that was indistinguishable from that of any number of his own characters. True, this had its uses, in promoting his reputation as an aesthete who lived life as art and created art from his aesthete's lifestyle. But it meant that his characters started to look just like his masks, with the result that both were all too easily mistaken for Wilde himself. (For example, readers of *The Picture of Dorian Gray* readily identified Wilde with the decadent dandy Lord Henry Wotton, despite Wilde's protestations that he identified himself more closely with the character of the troubled artist Basil Hallward.)

As we've just seen Phillips observe, the persona of a mask is not a simple proxy for the writer's own self, nor is it quite a separate entity, like a literary character invented by the writer. Wilde's case suggests that trolls are better off going the whole hog and inventing literary characters through whom to troll. In a nutshell: if masks can all too easily be mistaken for the author, then create a character who cannot. But how to create a fictional character through which to troll?

Let me introduce you to two of my favourite Twitterati – Titania McGrath and Adiasistos. The two couldn't be more different: Titania McGrath is a left-wing social justice warrior, a militant vegan, a radical intersectionist poet and activist, an ecosexual whose preferred pronouns are 'variable' and who describes themself as 'nonwhite' (despite a suspiciously Caucasian-looking profile pic). Adiasistos is Greek, male, right-wing, and petty bourgeois, with (very questionable) credentials as a successful businessman. He's socially conservative and economically neoliberal – so much so that he is passionately in favour of the damaging and harmful austerity measures of the mid-2010s, inflicted upon Greece by its government at the insistence of EU leaders such as Angela Merkel, whose wanton economic vandalism he sees as preferable by far to any kind of socialist alternative. The only thing these two very (very!) different people have in common is that they do not exist outside of Twitter (or X as it is now called): they're fictional characters. Both are

[94]Wilde, *Importance of Being Earnest*, p.258.

[95]Oscar Wilde, *Vera, or The Nihilists*, in *Complete Plays*, pp.515–78, p.543.

[96]Wilde, *A Woman of No Importance*, p.310.

prone to saying the most ridiculous things – parodies of so-called 'woke' culture, on one hand, and satirically deluded paeans to the depredations of the most brutal excesses of capitalism, on the other – and doing so in the concise, pithily direct style fostered by X/Twitter. Both therefore combine contrarianism with aphorism, to brilliant comic and political effect. And both are regularly accused of trolling by those who don't get the joke.

Here is Adiasistos serving up some comedy gold in the build-up to the festive season of 2012:

> 9 Dec 2012 @adiasistos Be careful, now with the hard weather poor people may sneak into your yards to protect themselves from the cold. It is illegal and you must kick them out.
>
> 12 Dec 2012 @adiasistos 'It's ok, let them search in the garbage bin, they are poor people'. That's how it starts and then they ask you to pay for their insurance when they work.
>
> 25 Dec 2012 @adiasistos Now that this year reaches to an end, all of you who are unemployed take a moment to think what you did wrong. Perhaps you are a little bit lazy? A little bit ill-mannered?

This concise style, based on the broken-backed aphorism that is so perfectly suited to X/Twitter, gives way in the subtly different media ecology of Facebook to a more chatty, more anecdotal approach, which makes Adiasistos come across more like the character of David Brent from the vintage sitcom *The Office*. But the comic contrarianism is still very much in evidence:

> Monotony definitely does not help workers in the working environment. That's why I am thinking to organize a surprise draw in my company. The three employees whose names will be drawn will receive a reduction in their salaries while the rest will not. I think that this will stimulate my workers' interest and we are all going to have a good time! (Adiasistos, Facebook, 26 May 2017)[97]

Some might object to me comparing Wilde's good-humoured wit with the crass economic cruelty of Adiasistos. They should remember the following Wildean aphorism, from *Phrases and Philosophies for the Use of the*

[97]I am grateful to Yiannis Mylonas and Panos Kompatsiaris, 'Trolling as Transgression: Subversive Affirmations against Neoliberal Austerity', *International Journal of Cultural Studies*, vol. 24, no. 1, 2019, pp.34–55, for bringing to my attention the splendid and hilarious Adiasistos (whose name translates as something like 'the unassailable one').

Young: 'It is only by not paying one's bills that one can hope to live in the memory of the commercial classes'.[98]

Adiasistos is, in any meaningful sense of these terms that I know, both a literary creation and a fictional character. But that needn't stop him from posting inflammatory contrarian aphorisms in the X/Twitter feeds of real-life politicians, journalists, and celebrities. Moreover, Adiasistos would be more than capable of defending those views in reasoned argument, especially since they were sometimes not *that* far from government and EU policy. Whoever the writer/s that created Adiasistos might be, they've found a way of trolling that seems to me to be irreproachable: using a character who gets to say all sorts of controversial things that his creator/s probably don't mean, things that are plugged into some of the most divisive issues Greek society has faced in recent years – but these comments get people thinking and talking as well as laughing. Jonathan Swift would approve; Wilde might respond in kind, with a contrarian aphorism.

Something similar could be said of Titania McGrath, though their politics could hardly be more opposed to those of Adiasistos. Interestingly, Titania's tweets have also drawn comparison to the satires of Jonathan Swift.[99] Arguably, though, a closer match would be with Oscar Wilde. For, to paraphrase Wyndham Lewis's critique of Wilde, Titania's one trick is to reverse the conventional tropes that underpin contemporary identity politics without saying anything very interesting about them. The result is a stream of contrarian aphorisms replete with topsy-turvy Wildean paradox. Here's a more or less representative selection of Titania's tweets:

> 3 Sep 2020 @TitaniaMcGrath How do I know that all straight white males are bigoted? Because they're the only ones who ever make assumptions about people based on their sexuality, race or gender.
>
> 17 Nov 2020 @TitaniaMcGrath I am all for equality, so long as women are valued more than men.
>
> 1 Feb 2021 @TitaniaMcGrath If the government was serious about tackling racial discrimination, it would make it illegal for white people to reproduce.
>
> 8 Apr 2021 @TitaniaMcGrath Burning books is the only way to defeat fascism.

---

[98]Wilde, *Epigrams*, p.186.

[99]See Adam J. Smith and Jo Waugh, 'Titania McGrath: Twitter Parody of "Wokeness" Owes a Lot to Satirists of the Eighteenth Century', *The Conversation*, 15 March 2019. Available at: https://theconversation.com/titania-mcgrath-twitter-parody-of-wokeness-owes-a-lot-to-satirists-of-the-18th-century-113312

9 Apr 2021 @TitaniaMcGrath When a famous straight white male dies, if your first instinct isn't to get on Twitter to gloat and trash his reputation then you clearly have no idea what it takes to be a progressive and compassionate human being.

29 Apr 2021 @TitaniaMcGrath To solve the climate crisis, we must sterilise all living human beings. Believe me, future generations will thank us.

Clearly, there's more to Titania McGrath than just a mask: these tweets reveal a carefully delineated set of characteristics and their own distinctive idiom which, like that of Adiasistos, isn't so very far from what they are spoofing as to make the target unrecognizable. Hence, Titania McGrath is a well-crafted literary character.[100] But Titania is also a troll, regularly attracting angry responses, and regularly engaging commenters who misjudge the tone of these tweets in (often hilarious) mock debate. Like Wilde at his best, Titania's polemical strategies make it impossible to distinguish a contrarian argument from the empty posturing we call trolling.

For example, when Titania tweeted the remark below, as a comment on a news article about a research study from the University of Colorado (which had found that, following the success of the feminist #MeToo movement, men were now less likely to perform CPR on women, for fear of being accused of sexual assault), the following exchange ensued:

@TitaniaMcGrath It is NEVER OKAY for men to give CPR to an unconscious woman.

'Resuscitation' is just a fancy word for 'rape'.

@SC You are stupid aren't you

@TitaniaMcGrath Or maybe I just won't stand for rape apologists like you.

@SC Lol so what you're telling us all is, if you went into cardiac arrest and the paramedics that came to try and save your ass were both men you wouldn't want them to perform CPR on you because you consider that rape? Am I correct?

@TitaniaMcGrath *Finally* you understand.

---

[100]In fact, Titania is an author as well as a character, having published two fairly successful books to date: a mock activist's manifesto called *Woke: A Guide to Social Justice* (London: Constable, 2019) and a spoof children's book entitled *My First Little Book of Intersectional Activism* (London: Constable, 2020).

Some might object to me comparing Titania McGrath with Wilde, perhaps on grounds that Wilde's satire never stooped to such depths of misogyny. They should remember the following Wildean aphorisms: 'The only way to behave to a woman is to make love to her, if she is pretty, and to someone else, if she is plain';[101] 'My dear young lady, there was a great deal of truth, I dare say, in what you said, and you looked very pretty while you said it, which is much more important';[102] 'I don't mind plain women being Puritans. It is the only excuse they have for being plain'.[103] And note that Wilde was careful to place all these reprehensible views in the mouths of his comic characters – just as Titania McGrath's creator, Andrew Doyle, has done.

So, trolls take note: you can get away with voicing outrageous views in maddeningly contrarian aphorisms *provided that* you place them in the mouths of fictional characters whom you have taken trouble to create, and whose views and opinions cannot be easily conflated with your own. The alternative – using a mask – risks following Wilde's example more closely: the result of his love of masks was that he lost everything he had ever built, spent time in jail, faced universal opprobrium, and died in poverty and disgrace, far from a home he could never go back to.

Conclusion

Wilde shows us that controversy is a double-edged sword. It can make you enemies; it can win you admirers. It can bring you fame; it can bring you disgrace. Contrarianism is just as ambivalent. It can be a civic virtue, or it can disrupt the public sphere in negative ways. It can challenge groupthink, or it can degenerate into mindless nay-saying. We knew all this long before internet trolling – even before Wilde. What Wilde reveals, though, is precisely what trolls lack: the need to carry people with you, however contrarian your views, however controversial your humour. His humour was divisive without being exclusionary; he dismissed argumentation neither with violent anti-intellectualism nor by turning debate into self-defeating logical games, as trolls might, but by using rhetorical flair and wit to rise above it. Though, on the face of it, the contempt in which they hold the public seems to link Wilde to the trolls, Wilde's avowed disdain for the public is packaged in ways that make his views attractive to hold, and hard to refute. Generally, then, Wilde harnessed controversy well: by positioning his contrarianism in relation to a mainstream, his witticisms used incongruous humour to manipulate the

[101]Wilde, *Importance of Being Earnest,* p.237.

[102]Wilde, *A Woman of No Importance*, p.331.

[103]Ibid., p.318.

public into siding with him against ... the public. By contrast, trolls' reckless defiance of mainstream taste and mainstream humour alienates so many that they're unlikely to achieve much beyond short-term outrage. If only trolls trolled like Wilde instead, the internet would be a better, funnier place, and a more effective vehicle for change.

Wilde shows us that positioning ourselves rhetorically is all-important – using characters instead of masks, aphorisms instead of arguments, wit instead of in-jokes, and so on. Yet he also shows us that defying the conventions that surround different genres or kinds of writing can all too easily backfire. For example, when a writer publishes an essay, or gives a lecture, or says something in conversation, that writer is normally taken to mean what they say, whereas nobody identifies the lines given to all the various characters in a play with the views of the playwright. Wilde's writings, as we've seen, flouted the conventional relationships between art and life, to the extent that what, in other writers, might have been dismissed as fiction or poetic fancy ended up being used as evidence against him in his trial. He wrote essays in which he claimed to disagree with his own views; he created dialogue for the characters in his plays and novels that was hard to distinguish from his own conversation; and 'in conversation he went so far as to say, only half in jest, that whenever anyone agrees with him, he felt he must be wrong'.[104] In these respects, Wilde's writing is, perhaps, an example of how *not* to troll.

And yet this negative example carries within it an important lesson. If novels and plays, essays and lectures position the writer in such different relations to the public, and implicitly ask and expect different things from writers and readers alike, then the same is true of writing on the internet. X/Twitter, Instagram, Facebook, Wikipedia, and other forums all entail subtly different conventions, and this in turn means that what counts as trolling will be different in each context. It's important to note that the way to troll cat-loving *Guardian* readers is different from the way to troll creepy men on Tinder – as important as the difference between an aphorism when it occurs as dialogue in a playscript and a similar aphorism when it is delivered in a lecture by the playwright.

In the next chapter, then, we will turn to a very specific genre – one more familiar from the field of politics or public relations – that wasn't remotely associated with literature until the early twentieth century. We'll be looking at the fiery impact of the avant-garde manifesto – a genre which was predicated on making clear and bold statements, whether about art or life.

---

[104]Lababidi, 'Great Contrarians', p.40.

6

... or to be provocative or vexatious ...

'A Slap in the Face of Public Taste': Some avant-garde trolls

By the start of the twentieth century, the structures of a modern mass media network were recognizably in place. Daily national newspapers with huge circulations were reaching unprecedented numbers of people. The development of the rotary press in the mid-nineteenth century had accelerated the printing process rapidly, and the newly built railways enabled same- or next-day distribution to all but the remotest communities. Compulsory education meant that literacy had become the norm, while the development of affordable paper, made from cheaper wood pulp instead of cloth, meant almost everyone could access print. Those whose budget didn't stretch to a daily newspaper could easily pick up a discarded one or read one for free in a public library. The media circus, in the form of mass newspaper circulation, had become part of the fabric of everyday life. This brought about all kinds of new opportunities for trolling.

It also redefined what literature was. A generation before Oscar Wilde, most writers were addressing themselves to a readership that was to some degree privileged. A generation after, most writers were feeding the press with text written for the masses. To be a prestigious writer now, you had to establish that you were writing literature, as opposed to journalism. Indeed, one way to understand the horror, disgust, and contempt that Wilde expressed for 'the public', who 'have an insatiable curiosity to know everything, except what is worth knowing',[1] is as a disconcerted reaction to this unfamiliar new mediascape, which democratized reading.

One writer, whose loathing of democracy surpassed even Wilde's, owed virtually all his accomplishments to his uncannily prescient manipulation of the new mass media. This adeptness earns him a place in any history of trolling. His tactics were widely emulated by daring and radical young writers of various stripes all around the world. He was an Italian firebrand named Filippo Tommaso Marinetti, and he spawned a multitude of writers and artists referred to collectively as the avant-garde.

Though Marinetti described himself as a poet, today it is not his verses we read, but his manifestos. These reveal him to be a precociously savvy operator in the realms of PR and media, with a gift for the publicity stunt. But, or so this chapter will argue, Marinetti's legacy lies not in harnessing the power of new media as a new outlet for new forms of new literature but rather in harnessing that power for purposes of provocation, much of it mischievous or downright vexatious. In this way, Marinetti paved the way to internet trolling.

Avant-garde trolling: The manifesto as provocation

France's oldest daily newspaper is the venerable institution that is *Le Figaro*. On 20 February 1909, three columns of its front page were given over to a short text called 'Le Futurisme', written by one F. T. Marinetti. It was a bold, programmatic outline for an artistic movement called futurism, consisting of artists and writers united in their zeal for the futuristic promises of technology, and more so in their hatred of the past. Such was the intensity of this hatred that Marinetti's text exhorted readers of *Le Figaro* to 'set fire to the library shelves!' and to 'flood the museums' for the sheer 'joy of seeing the glorious old canvases bobbing adrift on those waters, discoloured and shredded!' It incites us to 'Take up your pickaxes, your axes and hammers and wreck, wreck the venerable cities, pitilessly!' The rationale – though Marinetti's texts are in general rather short of such things – is that modern writers and artists, whose task should be to 'shake the gates of life, test the bolts and hinges', and wrench open the way into a new future, instead 'wish to waste all [their] best powers in this eternal and futile worship of the past'. Whereas 'we, the young and strong *Futurists!*' have our priorities right: 'we

[1]Oscar Wilde, 'The Soul of Man under Socialism', in *The Complete Works of Oscar Wilde*, vol. 4, ed. Josephine M. Guy (Oxford: Oxford University Press, 2007), pp.229–68, p.255.

want no part of it, the past'. Therefore 'We will destroy the museums, libraries, academies of every kind'.[2]

Perhaps it seems strange to us today that a respectable thoroughbred newspaper should give front-page space to ostensible incitements to violence and vandalism. But Marinetti's text hints that it is trying not so much to incite as to *provoke*. (The two aren't quite the same thing: tellingly, we can say 'I hereby incite you [to do something]', but not 'I hereby provoke you [to do something]', suggesting the relationship between provocateur and provoked is less straightforward, less direct than that between inciter and incitee.) His manifesto is self-conscious about its inflammatory nature: 'we launch through the world this violently upsetting incendiary manifesto of ours', it boasts.[3] It defies and dares its readers to disagree with it, then threatens them with unpleasant consequences if they do: 'You have objections? – Enough! Enough! We know them ... We've understood! ... – But who cares? We don't want to understand! Woe to anyone who says those infamous words to us again!'.[4] Marinetti's manifesto, then, encapsulates one aspect of trolling in a microcosm: it opens with a calculatedly inflammatory position statement, so outrageous as to induce a response, yet it bats any responses away with brusque dismissal, and closes down any disagreement with a menacing threat. This is not trolling by insult or defamation; neither is it related to satire. It isn't quite controversy, either, since Marinetti clearly isn't interested in debate. This is a clear instance of trolling as provocation. As one of the most time-honoured art histories of modernism puts it: 'Marinetti was the first international *agent-provocateur* of modern art'.[5]

At first, 'Le Futurisme' met a rather blasé reception: readers of *Le Figaro* did not rush out to burn down the Louvre. But Marinetti had probably chosen to publish it in this particular newspaper for a reason. Some years earlier, *Le Figaro* had published an article called 'Le Symbolisme', which had championed the new symbolist poetry that would come to dominate France's *fin de siècle* verse. Thereafter, the newspaper gained a reputation for supporting fledgling literary movements that quickly rose to prominence. Marinetti approached *Le Figaro* so as to stand on their shoulders. Yet he seemed determined to outdo them all, using unprecedented tactics for self-publicity and provocation.

Soon after its first appearance in *Le Figaro*, he published an expanded version of 'Le Futurisme' in Italian, under the title by which it is better

[2]F. T. Marinetti, 'The Founding and Manifesto of Futurism', trans. R. W. Flint, in *Futurist Manifestos*, ed. Umbro Apollonio (Boston: MFA Publications, [1909] 2001), pp.19–24.

[3]Ibid., p.22.

[4]Ibid, p.24.

[5]Robert Hughes, *The Shock of the New: Art and the Century of Change* (London: Thames & Hudson, [1980] 1991), p.40.

known today: *Fondazione e Manifesto del Futurismo*, or, in English, the *Foundation and Manifesto of Futurism*.[6] Marinetti would go on to declaim its text from the stages of theatres from London to Moscow; he would get it translated into most of the major European languages, and into Japanese; he would throw copies of it at passers-by from a speeding racing car. But most of all, he would go on to write more manifestos and to cause others to write still more. Within a few years, there were manifestos of futurist painting, music, literature, sculpture, cinema, architecture, and theatre; not to mention futurist manifestos of lust, cookery, and men's clothing. By the time Marinetti died, in 1944, over four hundred different futurist manifestos had been published.[7] All were direct descendants of the short, edited-down text first published in *Le Figaro*.

What Marinetti's new futurist art and literature is actually going to consist of is left as a rather vague threat. 'Art, in fact, can be nothing but violence, cruelty, and injustice'. 'No work of art without an aggressive character can be a masterpiece'. 'Up to now literature has exalted a pensive immobility.... We intend to exalt aggressive action ... the punch and the slap'. 'We will glorify war – the world's only hygiene – militarism, patriotism ... and scorn for woman. We ... will fight moralism, feminism'.[8] Above all, the futurists announced their intentions to celebrate the exhilaratingly modern sensation of speed, made possible by exciting new technologies such as the motor car, express train, and aeroplane. But few of these hymns to speed and violence were ever written, and such poems as the futurists wrote seemed underwhelming compared with the tub-thumping bombast of their manifestos. This point was not lost on cultural commentators at the time. Britain's *Daily Telegraph* opined: 'Marinetti writes like Walt Whitman gone mad. But Whitman sang, instead of telling us what he was going to sing. Why do not the futurists write their poems about railway trains and aeroplanes, their sermons in steam-engines, and books in racing motor-cars,

[6]An authoritative guide to the manifesto's composition and publication history can be found in Jean-Pierre De Villers, *Le Premier Manifeste du Futurisme. Édition critique avec, en facsimilé, le manuscript original de F.T. Marinetti* (Ottawa: Éditions de l'Université d'Ottawa, 1986).

[7]For the whole hog, see the monumental four-volume collection by Luciano Caruso (ed.), *Manifesti, Proclami, Interventi, e Documenti Teorici del Futurismo, 1909–1944* (Florence: Coedizioni SPES-Salimbeni, 1980).

[8]Marinetti's misogyny comes across clearly here; his eventual fascism less so. After the First World War (which Marinetti was in favour of, and clamoured for Italy to join), he abandoned his scarcely even half-serious attempt at forming a Futurist Political Party and threw in his lot with Mussolini's *fascisti*. Some might infer links between his politics and his trolling, since today's incel and alt-right movements seem equally prone to troll-type tactics. Sadly, I lack the expertise necessary to evaluate these connections rigorously.

instead of telling us they mean to write them?' – a reaction that Marinetti proudly reprinted in the poetry magazine he edited, *La Poesia*.[9]

In a sense, these critics missed the point. What they failed to understand was how Marinetti was reinventing the rules of the manifesto as a form of writing. For example, when a political party produces a manifesto, they are committing themselves to a future course of action. By contrast, Marinetti understood that the manifestos he wrote as a poet had their impact in the here and now, and not in the books he might go on to write in some indefinite futurity. (In this sense, his choice of 'futurism' as a strapline is odd.) Political manifestos generally promise a brighter future; Marinetti's were calls for things to happen right now without much regard to whether they would, should, or even could. They were not promises, but provocations.

Marinetti's use of the manifesto as a tool for provocation didn't stop with his coup in taking over the front page of *Le Figaro*. He then spearheaded what Luca Somigli calls:

> a carefully orchestrated campaign that made use of techniques that even anticipated the advertising industry itself, such as the use of the mail to reach a selected target audience of intellectuals, who were invited to join the movement in a personal letter that also included the text of the first manifesto. ... The responses to this invitation—whether negative or positive—in turn became further fuel for the futurist advertising machine.[10]

That's because Marinetti then published a dossier 'with a copious selection of answers to his letters' in his magazine *Poesia*.[11] Here's one example. It's an indignant reply to Marinetti by a bestselling French novelist named Pierre Loti (1850–1923). Loti had been a member of the distinguished *Académie française* for nearly twenty years at this point. He responded: 'I have a passionate cult for the past, and a horror and disgust for modernism. If

[9]Marinetti, 'Le Futurisme et la Presse Internationale', *Poesia*, vol. 53, no. 6, 1909, pp.23–4. Similar reactions greeted the 1912 exhibition of futurist painting in London. Newspaper critics were affronted by the idea that artworks should be introduced with a manifesto. 'Painting that requires literary explanation stands self-condemned', painter Walter Sickert observed in the *English Review*. For a range of first-blush reactions to futurism in the English press, see Luca Somigli, *Legitimizing the Artist: Manifesto Writing and European Modernism, 1885–1915* (Toronto: University of Toronto Press, 2003), esp. p.178.

[10]Ibid., p.159.

[11]Ibid.

you have read a single line of my books, how could you not know that, and how could you ask me in all seriousness to support, even partially, your manifesto?'[12]

It goes without saying that, as Somigli puts it, 'the point of Marinetti's move was not to garner the affiliation of authors such as Loti'.[13] From Marinetti's viewpoint, Loti's outrage is as beneficial as his approval, if not more so, since it suggests that futurism must surely be new and daring, if it can rile up the old establishment like this. In today's parlance, we would undoubtedly say that Marinetti had trolled Loti. He wrote an inflammatory text, targeted it at an individual he must have known would find it upsetting and vexatious, and then published the target's affronted reply for all to see. That he used the printed word instead of a digital platform to do it is neither here nor there. What matters instead is that analogue forms of trolling like Marinetti's letters enable us to sidestep the blind alley of blaming internet technology, and to focus instead on the strategies trolls deploy in their writings. Here, the driving factor behind this interaction is provocation.

Marinetti's *agent provocateur* tactics were astonishingly successful, partly because the art world had seen nothing like them before. He was nicknamed 'the caffeine of Europe', and his outlandish publicity stunts became the stuff of legend. In London, he declaimed against feminism to a meeting of suffragettes, then joined them in smashing shop windows on one of their demonstrations. Days after his *Manifesto of Futurist Cooking* had called for pasta to be banned, he had himself photographed eating spaghetti. But his success is perhaps best measured by his influence, which was truly global. A futurist movement quickly sprang up in Russia, declaring its allegiance to Bolshevism instead of fascism. It was spearheaded by charismatic poet Vladimir Mayakovsky (who, unlike Marinetti, produced a genuinely remarkable body of strikingly modern poetry). Mayakovsky sent his poetry to Einstein by telegram, with the note: 'From the art of the future to the science of the future'.[14] Another movement sprang up in Britain, calling itself vorticism, which derided Marinetti and tried to set itself up as a countermovement to futurism, despite the obvious and unmistakable overlap between the two. Its frontman – a writer, artist, and fascist named Wyndham Lewis – was a literary troll even more unpleasant than Archilochus. Both these spin-off movements, of course, were launched with their own manifestos.

The founding document of Russian futurism was a manifesto entitled 'A Slap in the Face of Public Taste'. The influence of Marinetti's violent

---

[12]The translation is Somigli's (ibid., p.159). His account of Marinetti's voracious self-publicity is fascinating.

[13]Ibid., pp.159–60.

[14]See Martin Puchner, *Poetry of the Revolution: Marx, Manifestos, and the Avant-Gardes* (Princeton, NJ: Princeton University Press, 2005), p.106.

rhetoric – he had, after all, called for a futurist literature that would celebrate aggressive motions like the punch and the slap – is on show in the very title, which 'creates an adversarial relation between the text and its audience, a speech act dreaming of physical combat'.[15] It makes it clear that these writers seek to provoke through confrontation, through defiance of what it calls 'Your "Common sense" and "good taste"',[16] perhaps even through violence. The corresponding document for Lewis's vorticism appeared in a short-lived magazine he edited called *Blast*. His manifesto is preceded by a bizarre list of people and things that vorticists hate and curse – including the personal names of a large number of living people. The list is hard to take seriously: it lacks any logic or coherence, ranging from cricketers to philosophers, journalists to painters, music hall celebrities to politicians. Its purpose is left unclear – and perhaps ominously so, since to publicly list the names of those you hate, without any clear sense of why you are doing this, is a threatening move that anticipates trolling at its very worst. (Admittedly, after the list of people whom Lewis says he wants to 'blast', there follows a list of people of whom he approves. But that's slim consolation if your name is on the first list.) For these followers of Marinetti, then, provocation was not far off from threat – as is often the case in trolling.

After Mayakovsky and Lewis, a thousand flowers bloomed. Writers and artists calling themselves Dadaists, surrealists, suprematists, constructivists, and any number more 'isms' besides inaugurated 'an age of furious competition for cultural shelfspace among artistic movements'.[17] Collectively, these movements are known today as the avant-garde, and almost all of them were launched by manifesto. In various ways, and to differing extents, they exploited the new media ecology of mass print. None went viral quite like 'Le Futurisme', but many newspapers no less prominent than *Le Figaro* gave them space. In England, for instance, a manifesto called 'Futurism and English Art', by Marinetti and his English collaborator, painter C. R. W. Nevinson, appeared in the *Observer*.[18]

Without exaggeration, Martin Puchner shows that 'hundreds and thousands of such art manifestos were printed in daily newspapers, often

---

[15]Ibid., p.101.

[16]D. Burliuk, Alexander Kruchenykh, V. Mayakovsky, and Victor Khlebnikov, 'Slap in the Face of Public Taste' [1912], in *Russian Futurism Through its Manifestoes, 1912–1928*, eds. Anna Lawton (Ithaca, NY: Cornell University Press, 1988), pp.51–2.

[17]Janet Lyon, *Manifestoes: Provocations of the Modern* (Ithaca, NY: Cornell University Press, 1999), p.41.

[18]F. T. Marinetti and C. R. W. Nevinson, 'Futurism and English Art', *Observer*, 7 June 1914, p.7. This manifesto caused a rift between Lewis and Marinetti, since Marinetti appended Lewis's signature to it, calling him a futurist without consulting him first. This in turn obliged Lewis to invent vorticism instead, so as to make clear he wasn't one of Marinetti's acolytes.

on the front page, and in literary magazines'.[19] If a manifesto was too subversive for a newspaper editor's liking, its authors could still use print technology to take matters into their own hands and disseminate its content. Manifestos could be (and were) 'printed cheaply in large quantities in the form of leaflets', or 'brought to the public by pasting them on the street, like advertising posters', using smaller-scale technologies to bypass mainstream distribution networks.[20] This gave 'an unprecedented freedom and directness of publicity' to their art movement and their views.[21] Thus, as on the internet today, a strange and complex intersection of mass media and micromedia tapped into one another, each feeding off the more bizarre forms of user-generated content they found in the other. Then as now, 'the new media are objects of fascination – symbols of a technological modernity that promises a radical transformation ... but they are also, and perhaps most importantly, the tools through which this revolution is carried out'.[22] And, then as now, a febrile atmosphere rendered communications technology vulnerable to the provocations of trolls, like Marinetti and his progeny. Although 'hundreds of movements and schools would rely on manifestos to denounce their predecessors and competitors', we must nevertheless remember that 'Futurism taught everyone how the manifesto worked, and all subsequent movements would profit from this lesson'.[23]

Trolling as provocation

Before we delve any further into these avant-garde manifestos, we first need a better understanding of what exactly provocation is, and how it relates to trolling. The second of these issues is easier to cover than the first, since there's a broad scholarly consensus amongst researchers from different disciplines and various methodological standpoints that provocation is an integral component of trolling.

Two recent studies of trolling give particular emphasis to this aspect: 'In general, trolling is antagonistic. The troll aims to provoke their target in some way';[24] 'trolling is driven by a range of factors, always with the

---

19 Puchner, *Poetry of the Revolution*, p.69.

20 Somigli, *Legitimizing the Artist,* p.159.

21 Ibid.

22 Ibid, p.162.

23 Puchner, *Poetry of the Revolution*, p.70, p.73.

24 Ralph DiFranco, 'I Wrote This Paper for the Lulz: The Ethics of Internet Trolling', *Ethical Theory and Moral Practice*, vol. 23, 2020, pp.931–45, p.933.

ultimate aim of provoking reactions'.[25] This view goes back several years. Claire Hardaker defines trolling 'as the posting of incendiary comments with the intent of provoking others into conflict';[26] Jonathan Bishop as the 'sending of provocative messages via a communications platform';[27] Marta Dynel adds 'sending antagonistic, inflammatory messages with the intent of provoking others into conflict'.[28] For other researchers, trolling is as simple as 'posting messages that are intended to be provocative',[29] while a troll is someone who 'acts provocatively'.[30] If things really are as simple as this, then surely all we need to understand trolling is a clearer understanding of the nature of provocation itself.

That, however, is no mean feat, because 'the concept of provocation is undertheorized and underinvestigated'.[31] Straightaway, it's clear there are two very different – even contradictory – usages of the word, denoting 'two types of communication strategies. One is meant to elicit a nonviolent or beneficial response by the provoked party, such as constructive self-questioning in philosophical provocations. The other is supposed to trigger a conflict or a violent response'.[32] The former sense of the term is held to be an important and salutary activity:

> Philosophers, from Socrates to Nietzsche and Sartre, tended to *provoke* their disciples, in the sense of disputing their preconceived ideas, in order to *provoke* – in the etymological sense of the Latin verb *provocare*, 'to call forth' – an original thinking. The point ... is to incite the disciples

---

[25]Vlad Demsar, Jan Brace-Govan, Gavin Jack, and Sean Sands, 'The Social Phenomenon of Trolling: Understanding the Discourse and Social Practices of Online Provocation', *Journal of Marketing Management*, vol. 37, no. 11–12, 2021, pp.1058–090, p.1080.

[26]Claire Hardaker, 'Trolling in Asynchronous Computer-Mediated Communication: From User Discussions to Academic Definitions', *Journal of Politeness Research*, vol. 6, no. 2, 2010, pp.215–42, p.224.

[27]Jonathan Bishop, 'The Art of Trolling Law Enforcement: A Review and Model for Implementing "Flame Trolling" Legislation Enacted in Great Britain (1981–2012)', *International Review of Law, Computers and Technology*, vol. 27, no. 3, 2013, pp.301–18, p.302.

[28]Marta Dynel, '"Trolling Is Not Stupid": Internet Trolling as the Art of Deception Serving Entertainment', *Intercultural Pragmatics*, vol. 13, no. 3, 2016. pp.353–81, p.358.

[29]Luis Gerardo Mojica, 'Modelling Trolling in Social Media Conversations', *arXiv*: 1612.05310, 2016, np.

[30]Pnina Fichman and Madelyn Rose Sanfilippo, 'The Bad Boys and Girls of Cyberspace: How Gender and Context Impact Perception of and Reaction to Trolling', *Social Science Computer Review*, vol. 33, no. 2, 2015, pp.163–80, p.163.

[31]Sandrine Boudana and Elad Segev, 'Theorizing Provocation Narratives as Communication Strategies', *Communication Theory*, vol. 27, no. 4, 2017, pp.329–46, p.329.

[32]Ibid., p.330.

> to distance themselves from conceptions pregiven by others.... Thus, in philosophy, provocations are mostly conceived as pedagogic tools to enhance critical thinking.[33]

In contrast to this usage, however, there is another sense of the term, which is perhaps more common and is often regarded as synonymous with irresponsible troublemaking, and therefore as reprehensible. Until comparatively recently, society took such a dim view of provocation that it could get you killed: you might even get away with murder if your victim provoked you into violence. (Some countries' legal codes have still not abandoned this legal defence entirely.)

But things are far from as simple as this dualistic, good/bad dichotomy suggests. Provocation as a tactical phenomenon expanded into much more pervasive and more complex forms in the age of mass media. Indeed, provocation became the preferred strategy of many *enfants terribles* of the art world and the music industry (from Duchamp's urinal to Lady Gaga's dress made of raw beef); of political or social justice campaigners agitating for change; and of marketing and advertising creatives seeking to promote brand awareness. A cynic might even say that provocation is the last resort of wannabes down on their luck.

Few would disagree that provocation, far from being reprehensible, can be a worthy strategy when used 'as a tool to awaken people's consciousness regarding specific social or political issues, or to affirm freedom of speech against censors'.[34] We might, perhaps, take a dimmer view of the same provocative activities if undertaken for filthy lucre and financial gain. Thus, one research study tries to differentiate between provocations 'aimed at social or political change' and those 'expressed for commercial or marketing ends'.[35] But this is complicated by the uncomfortable truth that 'the same tactical use of provocation may serve to persuade an audience to buy a product' as to promote 'a political program, a set of ideas, or social change'.[36] Moreover, the motivations behind any given provocation are seldom pure, and often mixed. After all, 'artists and intellectuals may resort to provocation for many reasons. They often combine aesthetic pleasure and amusement with political, social, or even economic interests'.[37] Thus, the moral stakes behind the concept of provocation are cloudy: intuitively, it seems clear there are 'good' and 'bad' provocations, but we're often unable

[33]Ibid., pp.331–32.

[34]Ibid., p.331.

[35]Olivier Driessens, '"Do (Not) Go to Vote!" Media Provocation Explained', *European Journal of Communication*, vol. 28, no. 5, 2013, pp.556–69, p.567.

[36]Boudana and Segev, 'Theorizing Provocation', p.332.

[37]Ibid.

to formulate clear grounds for telling them apart. Perhaps we might try to duck the moral issues by saying it's a question of whether the end justifies the means – whether the desired goal is noble enough, and whether the provocation inflicted is proportionate to it. But the ends that provocateurs have in view aren't always the ends arrived at: 'activists may provoke a violent conflict in the short term but with the ambition of provoking social or political change in the long run; artists and philosophers may try to provoke self-questioning in their audience and get rebuff and moral condemnation in return'.[38]

Trolling, at least in some forms, exploits this ambiguity between 'good' and 'bad' forms of provocation. To recall some examples from previous chapters: asking a question about whether Hong Kong was better under colonial British or communist Chinese rule might be a 'good' provocation – a Socratic invitation to self-scrutiny and reappraisal of one's long-held views – or it might be a 'bad' provocation, simply stirring up the hornets' nest. Equally, arguing that climate change could be averted by eating babies is definitely a provocation, especially at a public meeting called to discuss climate change. But is it done to pick a fight, and therefore 'bad'? Is it done to confront a perceived unthinking dogmatism, and therefore 'good'? Or does the answer depend on whether you think there's a debate to be had about the causal factors driving climate change?

It's important to note that whereas the first two of those questions are about the provocateur's intentions, answering the third question shifts the focus onto the standpoint of their target. These are two very different ways of looking at provocation. Marinetti's incendiary manifesto may have been intended to provoke sincere critical reflection on the need for new, more dynamic artforms to reflect the modern world, or it may have been intended to provoke scandal and uproar by inciting vandalism. But once he singled out Pierre Loti as a target, and sent him a personal copy, then Loti's perspective seems no less important than Marinetti's. Yet neither viewpoint is entirely satisfactory. If what counts is Marinetti's intentions, those intentions are known only to himself, and he is hardly likely to admit to mere pot-stirring. But if what counts is the impact on Loti, then we're basically saying that provocation (and trolling with it) lies solely in the eye of the beholder. The flaws in both these positions are obvious enough, as is their incompatibility. So where does this leave us?

As is the case with trolling, 'intentionality appears to be one of the challenging questions to address when conceptualizing provocation'.[39] But, if the concept of provocation can help us understand how to answer the similarly challenging questions that intentionality poses to the concept of

[38]Ibid., p.334.

[39]Ibid., p.332.

trolling, then it would be worth the digression to look into it, since the question is as important as it is muddled. In Chapter 1, I argued that intentionality was an unhelpful place to start: surely we'd first have to know what trolling was in order to be able to intend to troll, so intentionality can't help us define it. Furthermore, trolls might well lack the self-awareness to understand their real intentions, the honesty to own up to them, or even lack clear intentions in the first place. And yet, in Chapter 4, I was endorsing Angela Nagle's views on confronting trolls about what they actually mean and what they are really trying (i.e. intending) to say. The time has come to square this circle, and the concept of provocation shows us how to do it.

Provocation is not necessarily intentional: as Driessens observes, 'there is an exception when a certain behaviour is perceived to be a provocation by others, although the "provocateur" did not (immediately) intend to provoke'.[40] Thus, for instance, an ignoramus who walks into a mosque with his shoes on might end up provoking some of the worshippers without meaning to. It's plain to see why such cases create difficulties for intentionalism:

> This suggests that interpretation of a message as provocative should come from those receiving, rather than those emitting, this message. ... Yet disregarding the provocateur's intentions is problematic insofar as it is the provocateur who is often held responsible for the provocation and its potentially damaging effects. Here we face a dilemma. On the one hand, as intentions are difficult to assess, they are subject to interpretations by the provoked one as well as by third parties. On the other, the original intentions of provocateurs cannot be ignored, particularly if they are to be accountable for the alleged provocation.[41]

Researchers' studies into provocation seem to have almost unanimously agreed on a solution to this dilemma: the solution is to take the issue out of the hands of both the provocateur and the provoked and place it into its social or behavioural or communicative context. Thus, Paris and Driessens are agreed that provocation is provocation if it '*should* elicit a reaction' in its context.[42] Boudana and Segev concur that this gives us 'a way to reconcile the provocateurs' intentions with the provoked's reception/interpretation'.[43] Hence, 'there is therefore an agreement among scholars that certain reactions are provoked, in the Latin sense of *called for* [*pro-vocare*]. This nuance is

---

[40]Driessens, 'Do (Not) Go to Vote!', p.566.

[41]Boudana and Segev, 'Theorizing Provocation', pp.332–33.

[42]Driessens, 'Do (Not) Go to Vote!', p.558. My emphasis.

[43]Boudana and Segev, 'Theorizing Provocation', p.333.

what allows for the connection, and potentially disconnection, between the provocateur's intentions and the reactions of the provoked one'.[44]

Can a similar solution be applied to trolling – and should it? Wherever possible, yes. In online contexts and communities where there is a reasonable degree of consensus about standards, norms, and etiquette, it shouldn't be difficult to identify and call out trolling that consists of provocation. But still, few online contexts and communities are built on conventions with much clarity or stability to them. And even where they are, provocation as a concept takes us only so far, for reasons we'll look at in the next section.

From the provocative to the vexatious

Let's look more closely at the nature of provocation. A review of research published on this topic yielded the following range of characteristics said to define it: 'Unexpectedness and distinctiveness, questioning or contravention of norms, intentionality, and the elicitation of a reaction'.[45] The overlap with the characteristics used to define trolling back in Chapter 1 is striking: partly the same uneasy tension we just discussed between the responses it evokes and the intentions behind it, but also the same emphasis on disrupting or transgressing against norms. Provocation, then, is a concept closely related to trolling. Yet it's not quite the whole story.

That's because the idea of provocation has the notion of a response built into it. True, 'provocations may not always provoke actual reactions, or at least not the intended ones'.[46] But irrespective of whether they do or not, most of us can still recognize certain behaviour as provocative, even if no response is actually provoked. But is the same true of trolling? The range of examples surveyed in this book suggests otherwise. To ask whether life in Hong Kong was better under the British is indeed to solicit a response, but to answer a personal question on Tinder with an off-topic put-down is to make it clear that no further response is called for or wanted. Moreover, if someone fires off an abusive insult about dead earthquake victims in reply to a film of the carnage, or posts a derogatory comment about cats in response to a newspaper article about them, then it isn't clear whether any response is being asked for, let alone what kind. This, perhaps, was the confused situation in which Loti found himself when perusing the

---

[44]Ibid.

[45]Ibid, p.343.

[46]Ibid, p.333. Dissenting from this view, German sociologist Rainer Paris argued that provocation is a social process defined by its outcome: no response, no provocation. See his 'Der kurze Atem der Provokation', *Kölner Zeitschrift für Soziologie und Sozialpsychologie,* vol. 41, no. 1, 1989, pp.33–52.

copy of the futurist manifesto that Marinetti sent him. Hence his baffled response, asking Marinetti what he could possibly have meant by it. Though Marinetti's action was certainly provocative, it could also, and perhaps more accurately, be termed vexatious.

Distinguishing between the provocative and the vexatious helps us pin down one of the most disconcerting things about trolling: its ambiguity. If a troll posts something insulting about me, I might feel offended, or not; if a troll posts something defamatory or humiliating about me, I might feel embarrassed and ashamed, or not; if a troll posts something obviously provocative, I might respond, or not. But if a troll posts something patently inflammatory, which shouldn't go unchallenged, without any clue as to what an appropriate response might be, then what to do? I might very well *feel* provoked. But what complicates and intensifies this feeling is the lack of any obvious outlet for it – the impossibility of knowing whether or how to respond.

Take perhaps the best-known provocation scene in English literature: when Sampson (a Capulet) bites his thumb at Balthasar and Abraham (both Montagues) in *Romeo and Juliet*, he says, 'I will bite my thumb at them; which is a disgrace to them, if they bear it' (I, i, 31–2). Obviously, Sampson intends his insult to provoke a reaction, and he gets it. This seems to exemplify the kind of interaction that those scholars who try to define provocation have in mind – it meets the definitions of Boudana and Segev, Driessens, and Paris. Now, compare this kind of provocation with a practice in the game of cricket known as sledging, where the fielders try to distract or disconcert the batsman by insulting his batsmanship, cricketing prowess, intelligence, physical appearance, the pedigree of his team, and (often) the fidelity of his wife. The targeted cricketer is seldom in any position to react – engaging in a slanging match is likely to put any batsman off his stroke, and in any case the game must go on. The fielders know this. They do not seriously expect any kind of reaction, and they seldom get it. Does that mean that sledging is not provocation? Or does that make it even more provocative?

Here we can finally grasp an obvious consideration that's missing from the definitions of provocation given out in the scholarly discussions we've looked at – perhaps because it's just too obvious to need pointing out. The act of provocation specifically aims to produce responses that are somehow flustered or wrongfooted. Being provoked means your normal powers of critical judgement and decision-making have been interfered with. (That's why it used to be a legal defence, until we decided that responsible citizens could more reasonably be expected to control their anger than to give it vent through acts of violence.) Simplistically, what's important about provocation is not *being* provoked (i.e. responding) but *feeling* provoked (irrespective of any response). This feeling is likely to be exacerbated in a situation where no apt response is possible.

If a provocateur sets up a situation to which an apt response seems urgent yet impossible, perhaps this is better understood as vexatious than as provocative, since the act of provocation has parted company with the possibility of response. The purpose is to produce the feelings associated with provocation, free from the danger of an effective counter-response. Consider the analogy with vexatious litigation, where a frivolous threat of unfounded legal action places the defendants in an impossible position where a response is completely unnecessary (since the case against them is so obviously bogus) and yet absolutely necessary (since they must follow through with due legal process). The frustration felt by the defendant is the very purpose of the vexatious litigant.

The claim I'm trying to make here is not that trolling is better understood as vexatious than as provocative: on the contrary, we've already seen that trolls deal in provocation all too often. The claim is merely that the concept of provocation doesn't quite capture the grievance of someone whom a troll has provoked in such a way that a satisfactory response cannot be framed. Hence the need, in certain cases, for the additional concept of vexation. Note that the distinction I am proposing here hinges on the nature of the experience involved in being trolled: this isn't to say that trolling lies entirely in the eye of the beholder, but it is to emphasize that how trolling is experienced by the trolled is important.

When Marinetti published a piece on the front page of a respectable newspaper calling upon its readers to burn down museums, he was being provocative. When he sent the same manifesto to a targeted individual with the reputation of Loti, he was being vexatious. (That Loti has no idea how to frame a response to Marinetti can be inferred from the fact that all he does is ask dumbfounded, indignant questions.) The words of the manifesto are exactly the same in both cases, but the contexts make them starkly different things. It can be surmised that trolling provocatively and trolling vexatiously are importantly different from the fact that it's easy enough to see that a gesture of provocation can be made unintentionally. But it's harder to see how someone could be vexatious without meaning or trying to.

The art of pot-stirring

In order to get a clearer understanding of the workings of the provocative and the vexatious, let's turn to the polemical antics of the avant-garde writers of the early twentieth century, so as to see how their manifestos made use of these two closely related strategies. Then, once we have a firmer grasp of them, we can evaluate the role they play in trolling.

Perhaps the easiest tactics to understand are those of Russian futurist Vladimir Mayakovsky. Mayakovsky's aim was undoubtedly to agitate and provoke the Russian people in the build-up to the revolution of 1917 – a publication entitled 'A Slap in the Face of Public Taste' tells us as much. But his way of doing so was surprisingly conventional. This '"Slap in the Face of Public Taste", like the majority of Russian manifestos, appeared as the introductory text to an anthology carrying the same title'.[47] Thus, the provocative 'slap in the face' is implicitly delivered by the poems, with the manifesto positioned as the clarion call announcing the promise of something new. To recoil in outrage from this manifesto, then, is merely to shoot the messenger. This became a standard *modus operandi*: 'most futurist groups in Russia ... presented themselves through anthologies framed by programmatic manifestos', to the extent that 'in Russia manifestos functioned primarily as a frame for collections of poetry'.[48] In this sense, these manifestos worked in a comparatively conventional manner: they promised radical change, while the poems showed how it could be achieved.

'A Slap in the Face of Public Taste' talks up the novelty of its authors' writings by provocatively denigrating the writings of the past: 'To the readers of our New First Unexpected. ... Throw Pushkin, Dostoevsky, Tolstoy, etc., etc. overboard from the Ship of Modernity'. Readers and poets alike are 'ordered' to 'feel an insurmountable hatred for the language existing before their time'.[49] The aim is to make the poetry seem like a revolutionary break with the past. Compare this with the strategy in the preface to a better-known collection of poems that, over a century before, did indeed effect a genuine poetic revolution: Wordsworth and Coleridge's *Lyrical Ballads*, which effectively inaugurated British romanticism. Wordsworth's main aim in writing his famous 'Preface' is, contrastingly, to downplay the novelty of his poetry, by justifying it to the reader and rationalizing it for the critics. *Lyrical Ballads*, according to Wordsworth, is simply new poetry as an inevitable response to a new world, where the Industrial Revolution has broken down social bonds, changed the way people interact and even the language they use, and severed modern life from nature. Whereas Wordsworth goes about explaining and cajoling away any sense of affrontery or provocation caused by his dazzlingly, daringly new poetry, 'A Slap in the Face of Public Taste' does the exact opposite, such that the main value of the poems is framed as their powers of affrontery and provocation.[50]

But at least Mayakovsky's Russian futurists presented their readers with poems. Marinetti's Italian futurists seldom did. Indeed, some literary

---

[47]Puchner, *Poetry of the Revolution*, p.102.

[48]Ibid.

[49]D. Burliuk, Alexander Kruchenykh, V. Mayakovsky, and Victor Khlebnikov, 'Slap in the Face of Public Taste', p. 51–2.

[50]For more on this comparison, see Puchner, *Poetry of the Revolution*, p.69.

historians and critics – foremost among them Marjorie Perloff and Martin Puchner – have argued that to understand the Italian futurists aright, we need to grasp that they regarded the manifesto as itself a literary genre, and not only that, but as their foremost means of expression. That is, 'the Futurist manifesto marks the transformation of what had traditionally been a vehicle for political statement into a literary, one might say, a quasi-poetic construct'.[51] Hence, the artistic output of Italian futurism was first and foremost its manifestos, conceived as a new kind of literary text, and not the poems and paintings those manifestos called for. We might say they took a step from the provocative towards the vexatious, in that these manifestos provocatively disparage the status quo but present their readers with nothing new to judge in its place. It's easy enough to see how this vexatious strategy might unsettle or discombobulate readers, but that is all it does. Unlike Mayakovsky, whose manifestos introduced poems that were indeed a valuable contribution to European modernism, Marinetti's manifestos were comparatively empty gestures in that there was usually nothing further for their readers to respond to. In order to sustain this vexatious strategy, the Italian futurists' manifestos gave voice to progressively more outrageous ideas.

Many notorious examples abound, such as Marinetti's proposal to concrete over the canals of old Venice, turning them into motorways so as to destroy its romantic-era clichés by bringing speeding motor cars into the city to supplant the gondolas. But perhaps the most outrageous of all came from one of the women associated with the futurist movement, Valentine de Saint-Point, whose 1913 'Futurist Manifesto of Lust' made her one of very few (professed) feminists to speak out in favour of rape. This remarkable document starts out by taking up the very same stance that many trolls use today: she begins with the claim that she is only telling the truth where mainstream media prefer to lie, and only daring to say what many others are thinking. Her manifesto begins thus:

> A reply to those dishonest journalists who twist phrases to make the Idea seem ridiculous;
>
> to those women who only think what I have dared to say.[52]

It goes on to claim that, far from being a sin, 'lust is a force', and a powerful one at that, which should be harnessed. Shocking at the time, this idea did

---

[51]Marjorie Perloff, *The Futurist Moment: Avant-Garde, Avant Guerre, and the Language of Rupture* (Chicago: University of Chicago Press, 1986), pp.81–2. See also Puchner, *Poetry of the Revolution*, pp.74–5.

[52]Valentine de Saint-Point, 'Futurist Manifesto of Lust', trans. J. C. Higgitt, in *Futurist Manifestos*, ed. Umbro Apollonio (Boston: MFA Publications, [1913] 2001), pp.70–4, p.70.

not seem quite so outrageous by the 1960s. Saint-Point, however, is merely warming to her theme:

> A strong man must realize his full carnal and spiritual potentiality. The satisfaction of their lust is the conquerors' due. After a battle in which men have died, IT IS NORMAL FOR THE VICTORS, PROVEN IN WAR, TO TURN TO RAPE IN THE CONQUERED LAND, SO THAT LIFE MAY BE RE-CREATED.[53]

Having advocated for the right of the strong to rape the weak, she goes on to assert that this right belongs to artists as much as it does to warriors:

> When they have fought their battles, soldiers seek sensual pleasures, in which their constantly battling energies can be unwound and renewed. The modern hero, the hero in any field, experiences the same desire and the same pleasure. The artist, that great universal medium, has the same need.[54]

She goes on to conclude that 'lust should be made into a work of art',[55] as if perpetrating sexual violence could somehow be justified on aesthetic grounds. (One wonders what Roosh V's followers would make of this idea.)

Inevitably, a point is reached where provocation gives way to shock. Perhaps that point is unique to each of us; perhaps it is culturally constructed – that is not at issue. What's important here is that the experience of shock is qualitatively different from that of provocation. To provoke is, literally, to call forth a response: shock, on the other hand, is a state of mind wherein we typically become unresponsive. It follows that shocking your readers is perhaps not the best way to provoke them. Saint-Point's indefensible defence of rape as a weapon of war is a useful illustration.

And yet the advent of the avant-garde, and of modern art in general, has been characterized by a phrase from distinguished art historian Robert Hughes: 'the shock of the new'. Indeed, one of the most profound cultural commentators on the period in question, German philosopher Walter Benjamin, argued convincingly that the experience of shock is 'the price for which the sensation of modernity could be had'.[56] For Benjamin, not only is shock *the* characteristic of the modern world *par excellence*, but our responses to shock amount to a very specific, because impoverished, mode of receptivity. Drawing on (then) recent work by Freud, Benjamin argues

[53]Ibid., p.71.

[54]Ibid.

[55]Ibid., p.73.

[56]Walter Benjamin, 'On Some Motifs in Baudelaire', in *Illuminations*, trans. Harry Zohn (London: Fontana, 1992), pp.152–96, p.190.

that when reacting to shock, our consciousness tries to protect itself from trauma, in other words to 'parry the shocks'.[57] It does this by shielding itself from the shock stimulus, shutting itself down and detaching itself so that the experience of shock takes on 'the character of an isolated experience [*Erlebnis*]', as opposed to a more integrated experience [*Erfahrung*].[58] According to Benjamin, then, 'giving events the character of a shock' means 'detaching them from the context of experience'.[59] Consider the metaphorical deer in the headlights: stock still, unresponsive, momentarily caught up in a sensory shutdown – this encapsulates what Benjamin means by shock. If he's right, then irrespective of whether we're discussing trolling through avant-garde manifestos or trolling through digital platforms, the upshot remains the same: if the aim of the trolling is to provoke a response (instead of, for example, simply to insult or offend), then shocking readers is not the wisest move.

As if in response to the rather limited value of shock tactics, most avant-garde manifestos in the years immediately following futurism preferred bamboozling their readers to just shocking them. This resulted, naturally enough, in some very bizarre polemical posturing, often more vexatious than provocative. The first step in this direction was taken by Wyndham Lewis, in his manifesto for vorticism, entitled *Blast*. 'Blast presents an art of Individuals', it proclaims.[60] Unlike the futurists, says Lewis, the individuals of *Blast* aren't bound by slavish devotion to Marinetti, nor do they need to toe a party line prescribed by some leader: 'Marinetteism bores us. We don't want to go about making a hullo-bulloo about motor cars, anymore than about knives and forks, elephants or gas-pipes'.[61] What they want to do instead is left unclear – that, apparently, is up to each individual vorticist. Lewis presents his readers with a paradox: this is a manifesto for a movement each of whose members does their own thing.

Manifestos, as a form of expression, are generally predicated on speaking on behalf of a group of people. Indeed, Lewis is as extravagant as Marinetti in what Janet Lyon rightly calls 'the use of the manifesto's signature pronoun "we"'.[62] In this sense, then, *Blast* is a self-negating manifesto, the very premise of which is absurd. (Compare, perhaps, the scene in Monty Python's *Life of Brian* where a mob chants in unison: 'We are all individuals here!'; to which a lone voice dissents: 'I'm not!') To drive home this self-contradiction, Lewis makes it more explicit: he goes on in heated terms to blast, curse, and

[57]Ibid., p.160.

[58]Ibid., p.158.

[59]Ibid., p.194.

[60]Wyndham Lewis (ed.), *Blast*, 20 June 1914, p.8.

[61]Ibid.

[62]Lyon, *Manifestoes: Provocations of the Modern*, p.11.

damn (for example) England and the English sense of humour, France and the French, and the Atlantic Ocean, before going on to bless, praise, and exalt the very same things.

Insofar as it does present a joint programme for co-ordinated action, *Blast* calls for the use of tactics which, incidentally or not, anticipate those of today's trolls. Back in 1914, Lewis described uncannily closely the polarizing antics by which today's trolls sabotage debate and discussion:

> We start from opposite statements.... Set up violent structure of adolescent clearness between two extremes.
>
> We discharge ourselves on both sides.
>
> We fight first on one side, then on the other, but always for the SAME cause, which is neither side or both sides and ours.[63]

Furthermore, he explains the ultimate goal of these tactics, which is to tear down civility and consensus: 'to destroy politeness standardization and academic, that is civilized, vision, is the task we have set ourselves'.[64] Its violent tone and edgy jibing suggest an intention to provoke, but this seems like a subterfuge: *Blast*'s real aim is to baffle its readers, sometimes by resorting to gibberish such as 'Elephants are VERY BIG. Motor cars go quickly'.[65]

What is the purpose of such a strategy? Not simple provocation. If that was Lewis's only goal, he could have more effectively achieved it by insulting the English and the French outright – there is no need (and indeed it would be counterproductive) to go on to praise them. Instead, the purpose is to wrongfoot readers, so they are unsure whether or how to respond, and whether or not they are right to read *Blast* as a provocation. This uncertainty exacerbates the affront of being provoked by muddling, and hence thwarting, an appropriate choice of reaction. *Blast,* in other words, is a vexatious manifesto. As with so many aspects of trolling, the average reader is frustratingly unsure how seriously to take what has been written; furthermore, as in trolling, a division is thereby created between those who see through Lewis's strategy, and those who don't. As Hughes correctly notes: 'the first effect of *avant-gardism* is to create new elites; the difficult work splits its audience into those who understand it and those who do not. This cleavage does not run along political lines and may not conform

---

[63]Lewis, *Blast,* p.30.

[64]Ibid., p.7.

[65]Ibid., p.8.

to existing layers of power'.[66] In other words, these avant-garde manifestos anticipated the way today's trolling works through divisive in-jokes that thrive on the obliviousness of a mainstream readership. For this reason, Lewis's self-negating manifesto is arguably a more stinging slap in the face of public taste than Mayakovsky's, since the public can't tell whether they've been slapped or not.

The definitive self-negating manifesto, however, was written a few years afterwards, in 1918, by Romanian writer Tristan Tzara, principal spokesman for one of the most exuberant avant-garde groups of all time, the Dada movement. Dada was not so much an art movement as an anti-art movement. It regarded the art world and the literary establishment with hostile derision, seeing them as complicit with the powers that be, and responsible for brainwashing bourgeois culture with tawdry idealism, thereby fanning the flames of the First World War. Dada's countermeasures consisted of comedic nihilism – an all-out assault on traditional virtues such as beauty, truth, and logic. Hence, Tzara's Dada manifesto begins thus:

> The magic of a word – Dada – which has brought journalists to the gates of a world unforeseen, is of no importance to us.
> To put out a manifesto you must want: ABC
> to fulminate against 1, 2, 3
> to fly into a rage and sharpen your wings to conquer and disseminate little abcs and big ABCs, to sign, shout, swear, to organize prose into a form of absolute and irrefutable evidence, to prove your non plus ultra and maintain that novelty resembles life just as the latest appearance of some whore proves the essence of God. His existence was previously proved by the accordion, the landscape, the wheedling word. To impose your ABC is a natural thing – hence deplorable. Everybody does it in the form of crystalbluff-madonna, monetary system, pharmaceutical product ...
> At the crossroads of the lights, alert, attentively awaiting the years, in the forest. I write a manifesto and I want nothing, yet I say certain things, and in principle I am against manifestos, as I am also against principles (half-pints to measure the moral value of every phrase too too convenient; approximation was invented by the impressionists). I write this manifesto to show that people can perform contrary actions together while taking one fresh gulp of air; I am against action; for continuous contradiction, for affirmation too, I am neither for nor against and I do not explain because I hate common sense....

[66]Hughes, *Shock of the New*, p.374.

> To be plain: *The amusement of redbellies in the mills of empty skulls.*
> ☞ *DADA DOES NOT MEAN ANYTHING*[67]

This mix of gibberish and logical contradictions takes us a good few steps further down the trail blazed by Lewis's *Blast* five years before.

But, for all this flamboyant nonsensicality, Tzara's manifesto nonetheless defuses its own vexatious and provocative credentials by taking a step that *Blast* did not: not only does Tzara call his readers' attention to the manifesto's self-negating stance, but he also overtly anticipates, and even tacitly endorses, the reactions of those bamboozled readers who simply dismiss it as meaningless prattle: 'If you find it futile and don't want to waste your time on a word that means nothing … ', he says.[68] In describing his manifesto as a futile waste of time, Tzara might well be *trying* to be provocative or vexatious. But a self-negating manifesto that announces itself as such is unlikely to have such effects, because it's harder to feel provoked or vexed by a document that has the honesty of describing itself as much ado about nothing. Thus, though the style, tone, and content of Tzara's manifesto are all noticeably more extreme than in Lewis's, Lewis keeps his cards to his chest, whereas Tzara lays his open for the reader to see. Tzara's text, perhaps, is not so much avant-garde trolling as avant-garde clickbait: a clamour for attention based on 'the love of novelty'[69] that Tzara's manifesto explicitly owns up to.

These, then, are some of the ways in which avant-garde manifestos went about provoking and vexing their readership. From making bald, edgy, taboo-breaking statements designed to shock, to advancing outspoken and impassioned arguments that make literally no sense, they set clear precedents for twenty-first-century trolling on the internet. This, I'm about to argue, is because the manifesto as a genre of literature implicitly shares many of the properties and characteristics of the writing produced for digital platforms.

How manifestos work (and how trolling does too)

In some ways, the manifesto is a paradoxical form of writing. Its paradoxes might explain why manifestos seem to bring out the very worst in people, both proponents and opponents. Let's compare it, briefly, with some other literary

---

[67]Tristan Tzara, 'Dada Manifesto' in *Modernism: An Anthology*, ed. Lawrence Rainey (Oxford: Blackwell, 2005), pp.479–83, p.479.

[68]Ibid., p.480.

[69]Ibid., p.479.

genres. A well-honed lyric poem can craft a sense of personal intimacy with its reader; a play, more obviously, addresses itself directly and/or indirectly to the audience in the theatre; the novel, especially those eighteenth- and nineteenth-century novels that routinely hold forth to their 'Dear Reader', addresses whoever happens to be holding the book in their hands – that is, the purchaser. But to whom is a manifesto addressed? It's addressed to absolutely everyone at once. It typically aims at a universal reach. Few other literary forms do, at least not in the same way. And yet the writing we post online – in comments sections, on social media, even on relatively neutral platforms like Wikipedia – is similarly addressed to the world, with a potentially universal reach. This is a point with important consequences.

Janet Lyon is quite right to observe that 'the manifesto form has much to teach us about the problems of modernity'.[70] It's important to note that the manifesto as we know it today could only come into being once the modern concept of 'the people', to whom the manifesto is addressed, had been established. Without the idea of 'the people' as an entity of some importance, the manifesto makes no sense. Hence, 'the rise of the manifesto is thus coeval with the emergence of the bourgeois and plebeian public spheres in the West'.[71] Traditionally, the manifesto is a political document, which addresses the people as a rational entity able to think for themselves, able to do so in terms intelligible to other people (i.e. according to pervasively accepted standards of reason), and all able to do so equally. Simply put, then, the manifesto is a by-product of modernity, democracy, and the Enlightenment's age of reason: 'when political and economic developments in post-Enlightenment Europe generated the modern concepts of equality and rational autonomy, the manifesto arose as a public genre for contesting or recalibrating the assumptions underlying this newly "universal" subject'.[72]

One of the paradoxes of the manifesto is that whilst it owes its existence to democratic openness, universality, and equality, it often voices a revolutionary critique of the state of these things, as in the most widely read manifesto in history, Marx and Engels's *Manifesto of the Communist Party*. Their revolutionary manifesto (and all subsequent revolutionary manifestos) is a direct appeal to the people: it tries 'to circumvent ordinary parliamentarian avenues of public redress, and to challenge the ostensible universalism that underpins modern democratic cultural formations'.[73] But even though a revolutionary manifesto such as Marx and Engels's lambasts democracy, equality, and universality as bourgeois myths hijacked to suppress the workers, it must paradoxically still retain some level of faith

[70]Lyon, *Manifestoes: Provocations of the Modern*, p.2.

[71]Ibid., pp.1–2.

[72]Ibid., p.3.

[73]Ibid., p.2.

in them, or else why would it, and how could it, urge working men of all lands to unite? In this way, 'the manifesto promulgates the very discourses it critiques: it ... presumes the efficacy of modern democratic ideals'.[74]

Similar paradoxes seem to underpin the attention-seeking behaviour of trolls. The old cliché has it that the internet gives everyone in the world a platform from which to address everyone else in the world. Internet-based communication thus carries with it the implicit promise of equality, democracy, and universality.[75] Trolls set out to destroy these ideals, to tear apart the conventions and consensuses that make online communities possible. They are often thought of as people who use online communities to demolish online communities. But their actions only demonstrate how far they as much as we take the values of online communities for granted. Their refusal to treat their interlocutors as equals underscores the pervasive expectation that internet users do just that; their compulsive need for attention highlights just how attractive the digital utopia's promise of worldwide readership is. Hence, because trolling, like the revolutionary manifesto, is an inherently and necessarily public-facing sort of writing, so too trolls, like those who write revolutionary manifestos, depend upon and derive validation from the very public sphere they seek to destroy.

A further paradox begins to appear when we look more closely at the idea of the manifesto's universal addressee, by which I mean the idea that a manifesto addresses itself in principle to everyone equally. According to Mary Ann Caws, whose authority in the field is such that she has been called 'the unquestioned dean of manifesto studies',[76] the manifesto as a genre addresses its readers in a way that is contradictorily inclusive yet exclusive:

> Couched always in general terms, the manifesto appeals, at least on the surface, to all sorts and conditions of men. As an example, we may take this sentence from the first Surrealist Manifesto: 'Man proposes and disposes. It is up to him alone if he wants to be his own master.' If one chooses to follow the way of Surrealism, he will find such and such a thing to be true. ... All are addressed, and each is invited....
>
> But at the same time ... a certain exclusivity is displayed.[77]

---

[74]Ibid., p.3.

[75]Of course, as with any democracy, these promises are invariably skewed to advantage the privileged, and hence hollow, but that is another matter. Moreover, though the internet is in theory a platform from which anyone can address everyone, the algorithms behind it are in practice likelier to isolate us in divisive echo chambers than to unite us in harmonious communities.

[76]Robert Archambeau, 'Marginality and Manifesto: A Response', *Poetry*, vol. 194, no. 3, 2009, pp.239–43, p.239.

[77]Mary Ann Caws, 'Notes on a Manifesto Style: 1924 Fifty Years Later', *Journal of General Education*, vol. 27, no. 1, 1975, pp.88–90, pp.88–9.

That's because manifestos as a genre also seek to stake out a position or to formulate a credo of some kind. If you disagree with its position, then the manifesto is no longer addressing you as part of the solution, but as part of the problem. So, while it's true to say that manifestos address everyone equally, what they say to everyone is that you're either with us or against us. Hence, they're simultaneously universal yet divisive; written both for everyone, and for 'us' as against 'them', thereby 'claiming for "us" the moral high ground of revolutionary idealism, and constructing "them" as ideological tyrants, bankrupt usurpers, or corrupt fools'.[78]

What this has to do with trolling should be plain enough: we've seen forms of trolling that are similarly double-dealing, saying one thing whilst doing another. We've also seen many times that trolling insinuates division and discord, often through these two-faced rhetorical strategies. We've seen, furthermore, that trolling tends to function as a driver of polarization; so too do manifestos: 'By causing either rejection or embrace, the manifesto managed to polarize the cultural field like a magnet'.[79] When Lyon observes that 'the manifesto refuses dialogue or discussion; the manifesto fosters antagonism and scorns conciliation. ... It conveys resolute oppositionality and indulges no tolerance for the fainthearted', she might as well be describing the writings of a troll.[80] Furthermore, because both manifestos and trolling are by nature oppositional, and tend to alienate as well as to appeal, the tone and the language of both is shrill and intemperate. 'The manifesto is by nature loud, unlike the essay', argues Caws.[81] It uses 'a language that may be extreme, condensed, and ... at times violent', adds Puchner.[82] In this way, too, it offers a prototype for trolling. And, last but by no means least, in its immoderate tone, style, and content, the manifesto 'demands attention',[83] just as trolling is at its root a twisted form of attention-seeking.

So: if the two genres are so very similar, what can the manifesto teach us about trolling? Since manifestos tend to polarize, polarized answers to this question suggest themselves. For fans of modernist literature and art, one such answer might go something like this. The 'manifesto moment' of the early twentieth century gave us a few years of 'glorious madness' which unleashed a fervent mayhem of creativity.[84] What emerged from the chaos, in which rival groupings sought to outdo one another in progressively

---

[78]Lyon, *Manifestoes: Provocations of the Modern,* p.3.

[79]Puchner, *Poetry of the Revolution,* p.109.

[80]Lyon, *Manifestoes: Provocations of the Modern,* p.9.

[81]Mary Ann Caws, *Manifesto: A Century of Isms* (Lincoln: University of Nebraska Press, 2001), p.xx.

[82]Puchner, *Poetry of the Revolution,* p.99.

[83]Caws, *Manifesto,* p.xx.

[84]See ibid., p.xxii.

more radical styles and ideas, was the greatest flowering of Western culture since the Renaissance. Every single artform was transfigured by it, virtually overnight. Modernism gave us abstraction in painting, atonality in music, free verse in poetry, stream of consciousness in fiction, montage in cinema, experimental forms of drama, and daring architecture. These all came about largely because the provocations of the avant-garde goaded new life into our culture. They provoked the thought and the creativity of an entire generation, where 'provoke' is taken both in the positive sense of self-reflection as well as in the term's more antagonistic sense. If hammered out into a lesson for posterity, this view might suggest that trolling could maybe provoke us into ever newer and more inventive ways of communicating through the internet.

For those left unmoved by 'the shock of the new', a very different answer transpires, perhaps along these lines. The belligerence with which each manifesto denounced its rivals and predecessors was unhelpful, even pathetic. It fragmented the art scene into competing groups, robbing it of any direction or coherence. Futurism fractured into its Italian and Russian factions; then constructivism and suprematism split from the Russian faction, while vorticism and the Dada movement sought to distance themselves from Marinetti and the Italians; surrealism then split off from Dada, and so on ad infinitum. None of them lasted. All were ephemeral. And all, to differing extents, failed. In spite of all these slaps in the face, public taste still seemed to prefer novels that told stories, to expect poems to rhyme and scan, to favour paintings that are pictures of things, music with a tune we can hum, and so on. The manifestos called for radical change, yet changed nothing. At the time, no less a commentator than Leon Trotsky argued that 'Monumental proletarian styles cannot be created by means of manifestos'.[85] He was right. If there are lessons for posterity here, they are more nuanced. On the one hand, why get so upset about something as short-lived and directionless as trolling? On the other hand, who knows what a wonderful utopia the internet might be if only we stopped sabotaging it? Who knows what our culture might look like if only those Italian futurists had put their efforts into writing wonderful poetry instead of jibing manifestos that clamoured for a none-too-forthcoming futurist poetry?

As with most polarized views, you are free to take either, but neither is very helpful. A middle ground between the two might look something like this. Probably the most important anglophone writers of the early twentieth century were James Joyce, T. S. Eliot, Virginia Woolf, Ernest Hemingway, Gertrude Stein, D. H. Lawrence, F. Scott Fitzgerald, Katherine Mansfield, and William Faulkner. Not one of them ever wrote or signed a manifesto. Neither did the greatest writer of the age, Franz Kafka. Those whose literary

[85]Leon Trotsky, *Literature and Revolution*, ed. William Keach, trans. Rose Strunsky (Chicago: Haymarket, [1925] 2005), p.172.

reputations relied on provocation generally found that provocation fatigue set in and stalled their careers. Vladimir Mayakovsky found that, after the revolution, the consequences of slapping public taste in the face could be no less serious than under the tsars. Having alienated the Soviet authorities, he shot himself in 1930, leaving behind a heartbreaking suicide note in which he wrote that he had crushed the throat of his own song. Marinetti, whose aggressive nationalistic posturing and warmongering helped Mussolini into power, found that life in a fascist dictatorship obliged him to tone down the provocations on which his career had depended and to direct them only at officially approved targets. It was catastrophic for futurism. Already sidelined before his death in 1944, Marinetti's futurist manifestos lay all but forgotten until their rediscovery in the late twentieth century. Valentine de Saint-Point remains a marginal figure even to this day, though perhaps that is attributable to the marginal position her gender conferred upon her a hundred years ago. This pattern suggests one final paradox that unites trolling with the avant-garde manifestos. Both are loud, shrill, clamouring, short-term forms of attention seeking, yet both often condemn their writers to medium-term failure and oblivion. To wind up this chapter, let's look at one such example more closely.

A troll's tragedy, or, Wyndham Lewis and the dangers of provocation fatigue

Media theorist Olivier Driessens astutely comments that 'provocation fatigue may set in when the audience is confronted repeatedly with the same kind of provocation'.[86] Perhaps this accounts for the shape of Wyndham Lewis's woefully downward career trajectory. Lewis began his career as a polymath of almost unlimited promise: a groundbreaking painter, a gifted draftsman, and an up-and-coming writer of works of fiction, poetry, drama, philosophy, art criticism, and literary criticism. He ended his career a dilettante, a jack of all trades and master of none, who lived much of his later life in penury and semi-obscurity. I maintain that this was largely because of his trolling. If Lewis had criticized Wilde for having just one trick up his sleeve, the same was no less true of Lewis, and his one trick was provocation.

Lewis was amongst the most cantankerous writers of all time. It is said that 'critics have often portrayed [him] as an artist with violent tendencies and extreme political views'.[87] That is because he was. His first quarrel

---

[86]Driessens, 'Do (Not) Go to Vote!', p.561.

[87]Julian Hanna, 'Blasting after *Blast*: Wyndham Lewis's Late Manifestos', *Journal of Modern Literature*, vol. 31, no. 1, 2007, pp.124–35, p.126.

was with the Bloomsbury Group: he stormed out of Roger Fry's Omega Workshop in an argument about the details of an interior design commission he was working on. He turned instead to the futurists, welcoming Marinetti to London, but then fell out with them because his ego wouldn't permit him to be described in the press merely as one of Marinetti's followers. So he set up his own avant-garde group, vorticism. Thus, *Blast* was born.

We have already seen how, in *Blast*, 'Lewis had abused rather than simply used the manifesto'.[88] According to Lewis scholar Julian Hanna, although 'the term "manifesto" occurs regularly in Lewis's writing only during the vorticist period of 1914–15', nevertheless the combative, provocative strategies honed in the *Blast* manifesto remained a constant throughout his career.[89] For Hanna, it makes sense to think of Lewis's subsequent output in terms of the skills he learnt from writing manifestos: later on, Lewis would refer to many of his writings simply as 'blasts', and not without reason. Another way of putting it is that Lewis comported himself as a troll. In the years that followed *Blast,* 'Lewis regularly belittled his enemies by describing them as insignificant, impotent, and amateurish', and thereby 'alienated himself to ever-greater degrees'.[90] His list of targets grew to include most of the major writers of his day: James Joyce, Gertrude Stein, Ernest Hemingway, D. H. Lawrence, the entire Bloomsbury Group, and its offshoot focussed around the Sitwell family. There were few leading writers or artists who did not attract his scorn.

The successor to *Blast* was a magazine Lewis founded called *The Enemy*. It was virtually a one-man band, a vehicle invented by Lewis for Lewis, since he had antagonized so many of the editors and publishers of literary magazines that he could find no other outlet for his work. Its oppositional nature is clear from its title. As a result of having to fill the space of his own magazine, Lewis was now spending so much time on literary journalism that his more creative writing might well have suffered; he was writing such consistently vitriolic invective in his literary journalism that his reputation certainly did. One rival literary magazine that felt his wrath described *The Enemy* as 'seven-tenths bluff'.[91] It was a generous estimate.

That Lewis was full of hot air and unable to restrain his pot-stirring compulsion can be seen from his disastrous ventures from literary into political journalism. Here, he finally found something to praise instead of to disparage. Sadly, that something was Nazism, and he praised it with the same provocative nonchalance as anyone on today's alt-right. His book *Hitler* (1931) has gained notoriety for its crass misjudgement of the political

---

[88]Puchner, *Poetry of the Revolution,* p.118.

[89]Hanna, 'Blasting after *Blast*', p.125.

[90]Ibid., p.131, p.128.

[91]See ibid., p.131.

situation in Germany: 'Hitler is not a gratuitously warlike individual at all'; 'Hitler is The German Man, therefore Hitler is a Man of Peace'; 'I do not think that if Hitler had his way he would bring the fire and the sword across otherwise peaceful frontiers'.[92] In fairness, there was no shortage of people around the world wanting to believe the same thing in 1931. But Lewis went further. He goes on to justify Nazi anti-Semitism:

> it is perhaps only fair to the Nationalsocialist to say that the jew [*sic*] has often lent colour to [Hitler's] accusations.... And as regards, again, the vexed question of the 'antisemitic' policy of his party, in that also I believe Hitler himself – once he had obtained power – would show increasing moderation and tolerance.[93]

He also suggests, against all evidence, that the Nazis are entirely innocent victims of Communist aggression, and even that they are more tolerant of same-sex relationships than the Weimar Republic.[94] He heaps racist abuse upon 'the american [*sic*] fashion of negro-worship, with its basis in the jazz-cult'.[95] And, in closing, he earnestly entreats his readers, 'Sir' and 'Madam', to 'give your best attention to the safeguarding of your famous White Skin'.[96] The sneering superiority of this white supremacist rhetoric suggests an intention to provoke completely inappropriate to the subject matter, then no less than now. Such vexatious writerly techniques are indistinguishable from those of an alt-right troll.

It has been said that Lewis regretted writing the book almost as soon as he finished it. I find that hard to believe; at any rate, his regret did not entail any penitence. He never changed his tone. He used the same sneering jibes when trying to undo the damage he had done. Finally convinced, by 1939, that Nazism was anti-Semitic and that anti-Semitism is wrong, he decided to write a book on the subject, and could think of no better title to give it than *The Jews: Are They Human?* Admittedly, the title was a reworking of *The English: Are They Human?*, a humorous bestseller published in 1931 by émigré Dutch historian Gustaaf Johannes Renier. Admittedly, its takedown of anti-Semitism was favourably reviewed in the *Jewish Chronicle* and panned in the newsletter of the British Union of Fascists.[97] That's not the point. The point is that Lewis had clearly failed to appreciate, even over

[92]Wyndham Lewis, *Hitler* (New York: Gordon Press, [1931] 1972), p.52; p.44; pp.47–8.

[93]Ibid., p.38; p.48.

[94]See ibid., pp.18–19; p.22.

[95]Ibid., p.119.

[96]Ibid., p.121.

[97]For more on this, see Paul O'Keeffe, *Some Sort of Genius: A Life of Wyndham Lewis* (London: Jonathan Cape, 2000).

many years, that sometimes, tactics other than provocation, shock, and in-jokey allusions are called for, especially when discussing serious, sensitive, and intractable problems. By the time his eventual repudiation of Nazism came out (in *The Hitler Cult and How It Will End,* 1939), it would have been a wonder if anyone was still taking Lewis seriously.

Lewis may well have responded that he neither wanted nor expected to be taken seriously. Like many trolls, he repeatedly characterized his provocations as satire, in essays such as 'Satire and Fiction' (1930) and 'Is Satire Real?' (1934). Certainly, satire was a mode Lewis routinely deployed in his novels. His 1930 novel *The Apes of God* lampooned the foremost modernist writers of the 1920s with thinly veiled, highly personal attacks; his 1932 novel *Snooty Baronet* similarly railed against the London literary scene, including some of his own supporters and financial backers; his 1937 novel *The Revenge for Love* lambasted the next generation of more politically committed writers, scoffing at their opposition to fascism in the Spanish Civil War. But this is not quite what Lewis meant by 'satire'. As when trolls (mis)invoke the term, 'Lewis's definition of satire has little in common with the usual meaning of that genre and makes sense only within his own political and aesthetic universe'.[98]

According to Lewis's 'Is Satire Real?', satire should have nothing to do with moral values or with critical judgements. Nor should it have anything to do with the prevailing sense of humour – indeed, Lewis had vilified conventional humour early on in *Blast* and in his first novel *Tarr* (1918). What is left of the concept of satire, by the time Lewis has finished reclassifying it to suit his own purposes, is little more than the concept of provocation for its own sake – something strikingly close to trolling. Unsurprisingly, then, 'Lewis's so-called satires' are almost unreadable today.[99] 'To us', writes Martin Puchner, they are apt to appear:

> beyond the pale, full of grotesque distortions, offensive clichés, racist portraits, patronizing characterizations, sexist obsessions, and tiresome repetitions ... [Lewis] managed to create something ugly: a truly nasty modernism whose value might lie in the fact that it makes *Blast* ... seem, retrospectively, not all that bad.[100]

I'd venture to suggest that the tactic of provocation had driven Lewis to ever more extreme kinds of writing, and from there, in a vicious circle, to ever lower levels of popularity, as he tried harder and harder to provoke a public he found harder and harder to shock. Provocation fatigue had set

---

[98]Puchner, *Poetry of the Revolution,* p.129.

[99]Ibid.

[100]Ibid., pp.130–31.

in. Unsurprisingly, there were times in his later life when he found himself on the brink of destitution and obscurity.

Yet Lewis never learned, never grew up, never changed his ways. 'From his pre-war vorticist interventions to his reinvention as the "Enemy" in the late 1920s, Lewis always played the provocateur'.[101] He spent his entire life abusing and vilifying almost everyone with any literary or artistic credentials, using the same set of provocative tactics. They failed him. In the final analysis, perhaps Lewis ran out of people to provoke. But that was because people had stopped listening, since he'd made it impossible for them to take him seriously. His career is an object lesson in the consequences of trolling. This lesson also reminds us that, as with Lewis's writings on Hitler, history has an uncanny knack for catching out, discrediting, and generally drubbing those prone to shooting their mouths off unthinkingly on controversial topics they only partially understand. Events can all too easily take a turn that transforms trolling from a form of polemical sabotage into abject self-sabotage. We would all do well to keep this in mind before we post anything on the internet.

Towards the start of Lewis's career, the arch-conservative T. S. Eliot had called him 'the most fascinating personality of our time';[102] towards its end, the arch-liberal George Orwell wrote that Lewis had had 'enough talent to set up dozens of ordinary writers'.[103] Yet from the start, Lewis routinely squandered his readers' goodwill through what we now call trolling. He never regained it, and even today he remains at best a peripheral, controversial figure in literary history. That is where an over-reliance on provocation gets you.

Conclusion

An understanding of 'provocation as an aggressive action to which an aggressive reaction would be predictable, if not inevitable' can yield important insight into how trolling works.[104] It helps explain why trolling is so escalationary, and so virulently so. Yet the notion of provocation fatigue also helps explain why trolling is so ephemeral – smarter trolls tend to move on before it sets in, leaving the mess behind them in search of something new

[101]Hanna, 'Blasting after *Blast*', p.133.

[102]T. S. Eliot, '*Tarr*', *The Egoist*, vol. 5, no. 8, 1918, p.106.

[103]George Orwell, 'Good Bad Books', in *The Collected Essays, Journalism and Letters of George Orwell*, vol. 4, eds. Sonia Orwell and Ian Angus (London: Secker and Warburg, [1945] 1968), pp.19–22, p.21.

[104]Boudana and Segev, 'Theorizing Provocation', p.335.

to mess up. Most importantly of all, though, since provocation is a concept that is necessarily grounded in contexts, conventions, and communities, it helps us grasp the vast extent to which trolling is, too.

Generally speaking, we now live in a culture where responding to provocation is no longer as socially acceptable as it was. According to Boudana and Segev, those who overreact to provocation are typically judged more culpable than those who provoke. Once, a man who didn't respond to an insult against his honour by defending it with violence was called a coward; nowadays, he is said to have issues with anger management if he does. Perhaps this is another reason why we are encouraged not to feed the trolls. Maybe – and this is pure speculation – such changes in the way that provocation is supposed to function in our culture can also help account for the emergence of more vexatious trolling strategies. That is, provocation by itself might not be a successful tactic in a world where we are all encouraged to ignore it. A vexatious approach, which does not seriously expect a response and which forestalls unresponsiveness by making the question of how to respond irresolvable, might have thereby evolved as a more effective strategy than mere provocation.

In the next chapter, we're going to look at one of the most celebrated, commendable, and noble provocations in all of literary history. It took place at a time when the mediascape I described at the start of this chapter was already in place, although slightly newer than it was in Marinetti's day. This provocation involved abusing that same communications technology to disseminate a scurrilous message that trolled the most senior members of the government, the judiciary, and the military. It was written at a time when there were still some people who thought an appropriate response to provocation was a challenge to a duel. But that was the least of this *provocateur*'s problems: the legal consequences he faced were far more serious, and it is to this aspect of trolling that we will turn next. The provocation I have in mind is an open letter to Félix Faure, president of France, written by Émile Zola, published on 13 January 1898. It's better known as *J'Accuse…!*

7

… sometimes with legal consequences

Social justice trolling: Émile Zola's *J'Accuse…!*

Trolling can, in certain forms, be tantamount to criminal activity. Throughout this book, we've come across a number of individuals whose writings have brought them to the attention of the police: Sean Duffy, Reece Messer, Anthony Elonis, and Rhodri Colwyn Philipps, to name a few. We have additionally touched upon a number of more famed, more literary authors who have also felt the strong arm of the law. These span a spectrum so broad as to appear ridiculous, ranging from the notoriety of Oscar Wilde, prosecuted for Gross Public Indecency at the Old Bailey, to the piety of Martin Luther, defending his religious beliefs from the charge of heresy levelled against him by the pope at the Diet of Worms. Surely the latter group of writers are too disparate, too far removed from our more tolerant century, to teach us anything meaningful about the former?

On the contrary. In this chapter, we'll explore some of the legal debates that have sprung up in response to trolling. We'll go on to see what light might be shed on them by one of the most flagrant and incendiary examples of literary law-breaking in history: Émile Zola's *J'Accuse…!*, a remarkable piece of trolling which earned its illustrious author a prison sentence and a number of hefty fines. This, I hope, will clarify what's really at stake in the twenty-first-century conflicts over freedom of online expression.

Before we start, though, let me make a few things clear from the outset. This is not a guide to the law, nor to what can and can't be legally posted online. I'm a literary scholar, not a trained lawyer. In any case, the laws that cover trolling are different in each country, and often, as for example in the United Kingdom, vary within different jurisdictions of the same nation state. That's one reason why this chapter contains no recommendations as to what the laws that govern trolling should be. Another is that I'm not an activist trying to change the law; I'm a scholar trying to understand and explicate the principles behind it. Least of all am I offering any kind of legal advice in this chapter: if you are reading this as a victim of trolling wondering what can be done about it, or as a perpetrator of trolling in trouble with the police, then please put the book down and get yourself some proper legal advice from a competent professional, right now.

Freedom of speech; freedom from harm

The internet is an American invention; so too are most of the social media that operate through it. Unsurprisingly, then, the spirit of the First Amendment, stipulating that 'Congress shall make no law ... abridging the freedom of speech', exerts a powerful sway even where Congress has no jurisdiction. An attorney acting for a leader of the American alt-right sets out the position thus: 'You can say any nasty thing you want about any person or group you want and that is protected by the First Amendment.... That's not me saying that, that's the Supreme Court'.[1] This, unsurprisingly, is the interpretation favoured among trolls. Whitney Phillips's research found that 'American trolls in particular ... often cite what they presume to be their constitutionally protected right to irritate strangers on the Internet ... [and] regard any form of online censorship, including on-site moderation policies, as a basic infringement on their civil liberties'.[2]

The counterargument has it that freedom of speech is and ought to be tempered by freedom from harm. This view, too, is easy enough to oversimplify: according to those who decry political correctness, freedom from harm is now (mis)invoked to justify suppressing whatever any given group of individuals might happen to find offensive. Still, free speech doesn't mean unlimited speech, and it never has: threats of violence and incitement to law-breaking have always been curtailed because the right of the individual to live at liberty in a civil society depends upon it. A range

---

[1]Quoted by Bernd Debusmann Jr in 'Charlottesville: Why are the "Unite the Right" organisers on trial?', *BBC News*, 27 October 2021. Available at: https://www.bbc.co.uk/news/world-us-canada-59054166

[2]Whitney Phillips, *This Is Why We Can't Have Nice Things: Mapping the Relationship Between Online Trolling and Mainstream Culture* (Cambridge, MA: MIT Press, 2015), p.132.

of legal safeguards sets certain limits on free speech: laws against sedition protect the state; laws banning incitement to racial or religious hatred protect minorities; libel laws protect the individual; and so on.

The balance between these two viewpoints is something that will probably never be struck: Plato was wrestling with it 2,300 years ago, when brainstorming his ideal republic. (He failed spectacularly, famously banning poetry on grounds that it harmed citizens by appealing to their emotions instead of their reason.) If there's anything new about it today, it's the puritanically shrill tone with which both sides insist on their views. Since the debate tends towards polarization, all we seem to hear about is the excesses of one side or another, as, for example, when the First Amendment is invoked to challenge a school's anti-cyberbullying policies.[3] This example is interesting not because it is particularly egregious – though there is that – but because it seems to suggest that the vehemence of the debate is connected to internet technology. After all, it's hard to imagine anyone seriously objecting to a school tackling bullies in its own playgrounds, let alone invoking the First Amendment to justify playground bullying. Seemingly, it's because the issue involves social media that it becomes inflamed and divisive. Why is this?

One possible reason is that the technology is still new, and that it is constantly so – that is, ever-changing. Zeal for the freedoms that new technology might bring is continually fed with newer technology, while fears that harm may come from newfangledness are never dispelled in an online world that is forever newly newfangled. Another reason might perhaps be the sheer ubiquity of the technology, which makes some feel as entitled to it as they are to any of the other freedoms they enjoy in their daily lives; meanwhile, others, who've been victimized online, feel their sense of injustice amplified by this same omnipresence. A third reason might be that there is as yet simply no consensus as to what kind of speech we're engaging in online. There are some for whom the online world is simply a place for banter, and nothing more. Mr Justice Eady, a High Court judge in England,

[3]'Cyberbullying statutes have been found unconstitutional on numerous occasions where courts have struck them down as overbroad and/or vague'. Fernando L. Diaz, 'Trolling and the First Amendment: Protecting Internet Speech in the Era of Cyberbullies and Internet Defamation', *University of Illinois Journal of Law, Technology and Policy,* vol. 2016, no. 135, 2016, pp.135–59, p.155. The article lists a number of examples. 'In People v. Marquan M., 2014 WL 2931482, Judge Graffeo found Albany County's laws on cyberbullying to be "overbroad and facially invalid under the Free Speech Clause of the First Amendment". See also: Saxe v. State Coll. Area Sch. Dist., 240 F.3d 200, 216-17 (3d Cir. 2001) (invalidating an overly broad school anti-bullying policy); United States v. Cassidy, 814 F. Supp. 2d 574, 576 (D. Md. 2011) (finding federal cyberstalking statutes was a content-based restriction that unlawfully limited speech protected by the First Amendment)' [ibid.].

has ruled that comments on an internet bulletin board run by a financial services company have the same legal status as:

> contributions to a casual conversation (the analogy sometimes being drawn with people chatting in a bar) which people simply note before moving on; they are often uninhibited, casual and ill thought out; those who participate know this and expect a certain amount of repartee or 'give and take.'[4]

In contrast, the Chief Constable of Essex Police 'observed that social media commentary has a permanence, whereas the same comments in "a playground, coffee shop or pub" are transient and forgotten within moments'.[5] Confusingly, they're both right – each to an extent that will depend on the dynamics and culture of whichever of the countless online spaces where we socialize happens to be under discussion.

Perhaps, though, one of the reasons why questions of free speech tend to get so vehement once they involve the internet is because of failed expectation management. There's a long-standing history of equating the ostensibly democratic, open nature of the internet with the First Amendment itself, and doing so in unhelpfully emotive terms. This view has an important legal precedent on its side. In a landmark ruling, dating back to 1996 and still widely cited around the world today, Judge Dalzell explicitly found that the First Amendment applies in cyberspace:

> As the most participatory form of mass speech yet developed, the Internet deserves the highest protection from governmental intrusion.
>
> True it is that many find some of the speech on the Internet to be offensive, and amid the din of cyberspace many hear discordant voices that they regard as indecent. The absence of government regulation of Internet content has unquestionably produced a kind of chaos, but as one of plaintiff's experts put it with such resonance at the hearing:
>
> What achieved success was the very chaos that the Internet is. The strength of the Internet is that chaos.
>
> Just as the strength of the Internet is chaos, so the strength of our liberty depends upon the chaos and cacophony of the unfettered speech the First Amendment protects.[6]

This techno-utopian view shares its optimistic vision of the internet's future with a better-known document published that same year: John Perry

[4]*Smith v ADVFN* [2008] 1797(QB).

[5]House of Lords Select Committee on Communications, *Social Media and Criminal Offences*, 1st Report of Session 2014–15, p.11.

[6]*ACLU v Reno*, 929 F. Supp. 883 (E.D. Pa. 1996).

Barlow's 'Declaration of the Independence of Cyberspace', which proclaimed the internet to be beyond the reach of any terrestrial governments, none of which could claim the legitimacy of the consent of the governed, making the internet its own utopian space, exempt from the tyranny of any laws.

Both these documents, now over a quarter of a century old, epitomize a faith in the boundless possibilities of the internet that was pervasive at the time. If that utopian faith seems strange now, it's not just because hopes for the future were running so high back when computer screens were unliftable cubes and the internet connection cut out whenever the phone rang. It's rather because today's internet has become one of the most heavily, and invisibly, regulated spaces imaginable. Our every keystroke and every clickthrough are captured and scrutinized. The content we see is filtered before it's channelled to us. Search engines are as likely to prevent us from finding what we're looking for as to locate it, returning results more in line with what their algorithms think we should be seeing instead. Accounts can be suspended, frozen, or deleted in an instant. And none of this is because of government legislation. It's because the chaos of the internet that Dalzell and Barlow were so enamoured with was tamed by private corporations, and most of all by social media companies.

It's no longer a question of whether Dalzell and Barlow were heroic libertarian crusaders or irresponsibly naïve idealists: either way, the plain fact is that when using the internet, terms and conditions apply. The only real question left is: since nowadays the internet comes with inbuilt regulation, who should make the laws – the companies who build the kit we use, or democratically elected governments? Those motivated by financial gain, or those motivated by political gain? (That, thankfully, is a question for political philosophers, not for literary scholars.) As for the techno-utopian arguments of Dalzell and Barlow, the question that remains there is merely whether, twenty-five years on, their now quaint views evoke nostalgia or not.

So perhaps the best way to understand the bitterness of debates about freedom of speech and freedom from harm in our digital world is in terms of this nostalgia: the misplaced hopes for the internet, the expectations that were pegged so impossibly high, and the reluctance with which that dream of freedom was confronted with the harsh reality that social media platforms have terms of use. And perhaps the best way to move beyond this acrimony is to uncouple discussions of freedom from discussions of technology. A healthy step in this direction was taken by the House of Lords Select Committee on Communications' 2015 report into 'Social Media and Criminal Offences'. With admirable clarity, it explained that:

> There are two different ways to think about the harmful acts committed using social media: either they are new acts, or they are acts already

prohibited by the criminal law but committed in the new forum of social media as opposed to elsewhere. We have been persuaded that the latter is usually the case.[7]

In support of this view, they quoted the eminently sensible views of expert witnesses that 'social media is simply a platform for human beings to behave or misbehave'; 'It is not about the medium, it is about the offence'; 'what is not an offence off-line should not be an offence online'.[8] This dispels the fog with which our impassioned views on internet technology have shrouded the issue.

With this in mind, and with the aim of achieving a clearer separation between questions of freedom, on one hand, and questions of technology, on the other, let's turn now to a writer who trolled the establishment through the same low-tech, non-digital, offline communication platform as Marinetti – the front page of newspapers such as *Le Figaro* and, later on, *L'Aurore*. Émile Zola's *J'Accuse…!* came about because of a notoriously contentious trial – that of Captain Alfred Dreyfus – and led straight to another – this time, of Zola himself. Oscar Wilde once quipped that 'M[onsieur] Zola … is determined to show that, if he has not got genius, he can at least be dull'.[9] That was seven years before Zola wrote his effervescently spirited *J'Accuse…!*, and suffice to say that Zola got the last laugh, emerging from his libel trial rather more triumphantly than Wilde did from his.

J'Accuse…!: A very short introduction

To describe *J'Accuse…!* as trolling is likely to raise some eyebrows, especially in France, where the text is widely studied by schoolchildren, who are taught to regard Zola as a national hero. He certainly was: he stood up for truth and justice in the face of grotesque racism and the flagrant abuse of power with a bravery and single-mindedness that out-Luthered Martin Luther. He richly deserves his resting place in the Panthéon of Paris, alongside many great politicians, generals, and judges of a more upright character than those he attacked. Yet *J'Accuse…!* is a piece of trolling for all that.

It begins as an open letter to Félix Faure, then president of France. It starts by paying him a handsome set of compliments. It then goes on to lambast

[7]House of Lords Select Committee on Communications, *Social Media and Criminal Offences*, p.8.

[8]Ibid., pp.8–12.

[9]Oscar Wilde, 'The Decay of Lying', in *The Complete Works of Oscar Wilde*, vol. 4, ed. Josephine M. Guy (Oxford: Oxford University Press, 2007), pp.71–103, p.78.

and defame the top brass of the French Army, along with a raft of their underlings, sometimes in scurrilously insulting terms. It did so as publicly as possible – on the front page of a national newspaper – and precisely so as to cause controversy. Finally, it ends with a bold provocation:

> In making these accusations, I am fully aware that my action comes under Articles 30 and 31 of the law of 29 July 1881 on the press, which makes libel a punishable offence. I deliberately expose myself to that law.
>
> As for the persons I have accused, I do not know them; I have never seen them; I feel no rancour or hatred towards them. ... The action I am taking here is merely a revolutionary means to hasten the revelation of truth and justice....
>
> Let them dare to summon me before a court of law! Let the inquiry be held in broad daylight!
>
> I am waiting.[10]

As we'll see, he didn't have to wait for long: Zola was soon handed down the maximum sentence of a year in prison and a fine of three thousand francs, both of which he completely ignored. But we'll come to that. For now, let's note that *J'Accuse...!* ticks all our boxes for trollhood, with the one important exception of Zola's impassioned sincerity in his beliefs. And there's an important twist: although the assertions Zola made in *J'Accuse...!* were all libellous, they were also all completely true, and he knew it. So, paradoxically, Zola was breaking the law so as to do the right thing.

Background: The Dreyfus affair

In the late nineteenth century, France underwent a brutal transformation. It was humiliated by a crushing defeat in the Franco-Prussian War, in which it lost around 140,000 young men. It then found itself stripped of the provinces of Alsace and Lorraine and facing down revolution and civil war against the Paris Commune. All this happened very suddenly, within just a year, and France would never be the dominant power in Europe again. In the years that followed, the aggrieved French responded by lurching towards nationalism, militarism, and populism, personified by figures such as the soldier-turned-politician General Georges Boulanger, a right-wing demagogue who enjoyed huge popularity. Boulanger's promises to abolish the republic, install a dictatorship, and take revenge on Germany came close

[10]Émile Zola, 'J'Accuse...!', in *The Dreyfus Affair: 'J'Accuse' and Other Writings*, ed. Alain Pagès, trans. Eleanor Levieux (New Haven, CT: Yale University Press, 1996), pp.43–53, pp.52–3.

to bringing him to power, both through the ballot box and through a *coup d'état* that never quite materialized. (Indeed, the threat of a coup, with the military at best doing little to hinder it, was never far away in these years.)

As part of this lurch to the right, an ugly wave of anti-Semitism infected French life. Financial scandals were blamed on 'the Jews'; a book denouncing the Jewish presence in France became a runaway bestseller, with 140 printings selling out in just two years; openly anti-Semitic organizations were formed, with their own newspapers, which achieved a wide circulation. One of them, replete with grotesque caricatures and threats of violence that anticipated Nazi propaganda, was entitled *La Libre Parole* (in English, *Free Speech* – why do these things never change?). Mainstream media realized that anti-Semitism was selling newspapers and followed suit. Zola, one of France's most respected novelists at the time, wrote a number of articles for *Le Figaro,* remonstrating against anti-Semitic hatred in the name of the French values of liberty, equality, and fraternity. It was a sad sign of the times that enough readers threatened to cancel their subscriptions that *Le Figaro* had to drop Zola as a columnist. (He wrote *J'Accuse…!* for the newspaper *L'Aurore* instead.)

It was against this background that, in September 1894, a French mole in the German embassy in Paris intercepted a document listing classified military files that had been leaked to the German military attaché by a spy in the French Army. The minister of war, General Auguste Mercier, charged one Major Charles du Paty de Clam with investigating. Du Paty de Clam didn't search very far to find his spy. His suspicions instantly fell on Captain Alfred Dreyfus, for the simple reason that Dreyfus was the only Jewish officer on the General Staff, and a newcomer in his post to boot. When the handwriting expert called in to compare Dreyfus's handwriting with that on the intercepted document found the match to be inconclusive, du Paty de Clam dismissed him and found other experts more willing to confirm his suspicions. He then arrested Dreyfus and began an investigation so farcical that Zola later concluded his 'fuzzy mind' must be 'haunted by implausible plots and indulging in the methods that litter cheap novels' (a subject about which Zola knew a thing or two).[11] Major du Paty de Clam devised ludicrously theatrical stunts with which to embellish his interrogations and at one point 'went out with a dark lantern intending to slip into the cell where the accused man was sleeping and flash the light on his face all of a sudden so that he would be taken by surprise and blurt out a confession'.[12] He was rewarded with promotion to lieutenant-colonel.

Dreyfus's court martial was held behind closed doors. A key witness against him, Major Hubert-Joseph Henry, later committed suicide after

[11]Ibid., p.44.

[12]Ibid.

being exposed as the forger of documents incriminating Dreyfus in order to corroborate his own testimony. Worse still, in advance of the hearing, the judges had – completely illegally and unconstitutionally – been given sight of a secret dossier of evidence, never disclosed to the defence. A guilty verdict was inevitable. Dreyfus was stripped of his rank in a humiliating public ceremony and sent for life imprisonment to the worst penal colony in the world – Devil's Island, where tropical diseases often turned a custodial sentence into the death penalty. He was held at gunpoint and in solitary confinement for most of his five years there. There is no doubt that he was singled out and framed because he was Jewish and that this fact was known to the highest military authorities in France.

Misgivings about Dreyfus's guilt surfaced within a few months, both inside and outside the military. The existence of a secret dossier of evidence (though not, importantly, its contents) was leaked to the press. The leak was intended to place Dreyfus's guilt beyond further public discussion, by insinuating that such a dossier could only mean that the army must have had good reasons for convicting him, and that is how it was spun in most sections of the press. Ironically, though, it gave the Dreyfus family a basis from which to argue there had been a miscarriage of justice. More grounds followed. An investigative journalist named Bernard Lazare began to pick apart inconsistencies in the prosecution, which suggested the military authorities had colluded to secure a guilty verdict. More damningly, according to the intercepted document Dreyfus was supposed to have written, the spy had handed the Germans information that only an infantry officer could have known; Dreyfus had served in the artillery. The Dreyfus family began to canvas support from lawyers, politicians, and writers, in order to reopen the case. Their cause was soon taken up by the eminent novelist and veteran social justice warrior Émile Zola.

Meanwhile, a diligent military intelligence officer named Major Georges Picquart had uncovered the real spy. Having intercepted a telegram from the same German military attaché to an officer on the General Staff named Major Ferdinand Walsin Esterhazy, he inspected Esterhazy's handwriting and was immediately struck by its identical resemblance to the hand that had written the document Dreyfus had been convicted of writing. He opened the secret dossier that had secured Dreyfus's conviction and was astounded at the flimsiness of the evidence therein. He took his findings to his superiors, keen that justice might be served.

Instead, the French Army doubled down. Having stitched up an innocent scapegoat, they embarked on a face-saving cover-up. Picquart was warned by the top brass to keep his suspicions to himself. Then, to get him out of the picture, they transferred his posting from Paris to eastern France and thence to North Africa. Later, after he had heroically spoken out and shared what he knew, he was arrested, court martialled for forging the documents that had exposed Esterhazy as the culprit, and found guilty. Now, two innocent men were in prison, while the real spy was still at large. Only after coming under immense political pressure did the French Army agree to court martial Esterhazy. The trial was held behind closed doors and took less than a day to unanimously acquit him. Three handwriting experts drafted in by the army testified that Esterhazy hadn't written the document from the German embassy; Dreyfus had.

Forty-eight hours later, the front page of *L'Aurore* was ablaze with the headline *J'Accuse…!* Zola's article was an instant sensation, and immediately went viral: Léon Blum, who went on to become France's first Jewish prime minister, recalled that *J'Accuse…!* 'overwhelmed Paris in a single day'.[13] On that day, 13 January 1898, '*L'Aurore* sold between 200,000 and 300,000 copies, ten times the normal number'.[14] A young poet named Charles Péguy recalled the mood: 'All day long, the street vendors in Paris shouted "*L'Aurore*" at the top of their lungs, ran about with huge bundles of *L'Aurore* under their arms, and thrust copies of *L'Aurore* at eager buyers. … The impact was so stunning that Paris was nearly turned upside down'.[15] So what was all the fuss about?

J'Accuse…! is undoubtedly one of the most remarkable pieces of literary journalism ever written. Zola moves nimbly from rational arguments for Dreyfus's innocence, to impassioned pleas for justice, to righteous anger at the army's skulduggery, to disgust that militarism and nationalism could so blind the French to such manifest institutional anti-Semitism, to appeals to a more genuine form of patriotism. But he saves this bombshell to the very end:

> I accuse Lt-Col du Paty de Clam of having been the diabolical agent of a miscarriage of justice … and then of having defended his evil deed for the past three years through the most preposterous and blameworthy machinations.
>
> I accuse General Mercier of having been an accomplice, at least by weak-mindedness, to one of the most iniquitous acts of this century.
>
> I accuse General Billot of having had in his hands undeniable proof that Dreyfus was innocent and of having suppressed it, of having committed this crime against justice and against humanity for political purposes, so that the General Staff, which had been compromised, would not lose face.
>
> I accuse Generals de Boisdeffre and Gonse of having been accomplices to this same crime … perhaps because of the esprit de corps which makes the War Office the Holy of Holies and hence unattackable.

---

[13]Léon Blum, *Souvenirs sur l'Affaire* (Paris: Gallimard, [1935] 1993), p.120.

[14]Alain Pagès, 'Introduction', in *The Dreyfus Affair*, p.xviii.

[15]Charles Péguy, *Les Cahiers de la Quinzaine*, 4 December 1902, p.31.

> I accuse General de Pellieux and Major Ravary of having led a villainous inquiry, by which I mean a most monstrously one-sided inquiry [into Major Esterhazy's guilt] ...
>
> I accuse the three handwriting experts, Messrs Belhomme, Varinard and Couard, of having submitted fraudulent and deceitful reports – unless a medical examination concludes that their eyesight and their judgement were impaired.
>
> I accuse the War Office of having conducted an abominable campaign in the press (especially in *L'Eclair* and *L'Echo de Paris*) in order to cover up its misdeeds and lead public opinion astray.
>
> Finally, I accuse the first court martial of having violated the law by sentencing a defendant on the basis of a document which remained secret, and I accuse the second [Esterhazy's] court martial of having covered up that illegal action, on orders, by having, in its own turn, committed the judicial crime of knowingly acquitting a guilty man.[16]

With that, Zola dares the establishment to bring libel charges against him. And it did – which, remarkably, was just what Zola had wanted all along.

It's essential to understand that defaming someone in a position of public authority was a criminal offence in France at that time. So it was not a question of whether the men Zola had named and shamed were minded to sue him; it was a question of whether prosecuting him would be in the public interest. This was easy to settle, given the fervent militaristic bent of French nationalist opinion. Zola was subpoenaed a week after publishing *J'Accuse...!* His trial began just a couple of weeks after that.

He had not been bluffing: there is no doubt that 'his aim was to bring about a new trial'.[17] Later, he called it 'the trial that I deliberately provoked solely because I wanted it to be the field in which truth would be sown and harvested'.[18] It was a simple enough plan: Zola calculated that, since the courts martial of both Dreyfus and Esterhazy had been conducted in secret, public opinion had been unable to gauge the full extent of these flagrant outrages, because only sketchy accounts of the evidence were available. His trial would call the very same evidence in his defence, bringing it into the public domain for free discussion. (He might even have hoped to force the disclosure of the notorious secret file that had convicted Dreyfus, or perhaps to summon witnesses from the German embassy, but if so, this was naïve optimism.) This is what Zola meant by saying he had broken the law to provoke a trial that would in turn bring injustice to light. So, to sum things up: Zola's *J'Accuse...!* had made a public statement full of insult,

---

16 Zola, *J'Accuse...!*, pp.52–3.

17 Pagès, 'Introduction', p.xviii.

18 Zola, 'Justice', *L'Aurore*, 5 June 1899, in *The Dreyfus Affair*, p.126.

defamation, and controversy to provoke his opponents into a response, and they had risen to his bait. What else can we call this but the most successful piece of trolling in literary history?

Trolls and activists

Let's pause here to ask what we can learn from Zola's story so far. The first lesson, I hope, is clear enough: if there was any remaining doubt that trolling can be carried out in the furtherance of a good cause, then *J'Accuse…!* surely shatters it. Secondly, it follows from this that trolling shares some (though by no means all) of its characteristics with activism, and Zola's example highlights the main areas of overlap. That both trolling and activism necessarily involve making public statements scarcely needs pointing out. Both thrive on controversy, and both often favour provocation as a strategy (recall Zola's comment on 'the trial I deliberatively *provoked*'). And, for obvious reasons, both activists and trolls have a larger than average stake in the question of freedom of speech and so tend to be vociferous in debates about it.

So it makes sense that calls to clamp down on troublesome abuses of the internet tend to meet with resistance from a strangely broad coalition that includes some of its noblest users as well as its ignoblest. Their fears are easy to understand: 'Attempt to smoke out the trolls', writes Whitney Phillips, 'and you simultaneously smoke out the activists'.[19] Social media companies have been very vocal in making this case – perhaps because it's easier for them to make high-principled statements about freedom than to solve the difficulties involved in enforcing their own rules. When giving evidence in parliament, for example, 'Twitter drew to attention the value of anonymity for human rights workers, dissidents, and journalists working in conflict areas: it enables them to publish information and opinion without placing themselves at risk'.[20] To back up this claim, we could adduce the events of the Arab Spring, where social media platforms enabled a younger generation of activists to bypass censorship, mobilize large numbers of protestors, defy curfews, and coordinate resistance in ways that had been impossible for the previous generations who had grown up under the same dictatorships. At the same time, though, it's worth pointing out that the same technology used by pro-democracy activists in the Arab Spring also

---

19 Phillips, *This Is Why …*, p.155.

20 House of Lords Select Committee on Communications, *Social Media and Criminal Offences*, p.16.

enabled a grotesque attempt to overturn the result of a democratic election: it helped a mob of delusional conspiracy theorists and opportunistic fascists, galvanized by high-profile far-right trolls with pseudonyms such as Baked Alaska or Ali Akbar, to orchestrate their storming of the Capitol building on 6 January 2021.

Both these groups of people were passionate about their right to freedom of speech. But are they both talking about the same thing? Or do they rather mean different things by the same phrase? What does freedom of speech even mean? For the protestors of the Arab Spring, it meant the same thing it meant to the Enlightenment-era philosophers who framed the concept in the seventeenth and eighteenth centuries; the same concept that inspired the French and American revolutionaries who enshrined it in the Rights of Man and the First Amendment. It was, in essence, an amplification of *habeas corpus* – it meant that no despot could execute, imprison, torture, or fine the citizens they ruled for speaking truth to power. For people living in, for instance, Muammar Gaddafi's Libya, this possibility was all too real. But it goes without saying that practically none of those who marched on the Capitol in 2021 had known life lived under such brutal repression. Yet the trolls amongst them claimed that all of them did, and they were believed. So what did the phrase 'freedom of speech' mean to them? What is 'free speech'?

Freedom from and freedom to

In a famous essay written in 1958, philosopher Isaiah Berlin differentiated between two concepts of liberty: 'freedom from' and 'freedom to'. He characterized the former of these as 'negative liberty', because it's defined by the absence of constraints, and the latter as 'positive liberty', because it's defined by the presence of self-determination, as in the condition of being master in your own house. Perhaps phrases such as 'freedom of speech', or just 'free speech', cause such heated debate because the phrases themselves leave it awkwardly unclear which of these kinds of freedom they refer to.

In its positive sense, the kind of freedom we have in freedom of speech would seem to lie in the freedom to seize hold of our own voice and use it freely to formulate our freest thoughts in words that set free their full potential. This sounds very appealing – it makes us all sound like great writers and romantic poets. I would venture to speculate that this is the kind of freedom most people have in mind when we debate freedom of expression. But this kind of 'freedom to' is never actually under threat: from the moment you acquire the mastery of a language, you are free to construct sentences to articulate any thought your language is capable of expressing.[21] If that doesn't suffice, you can use poetic experimentation to expand the horizons of what can be expressed, and you can even invent new terms or figures of speech for whatever ideas your language lacks. In this sense, all speech is – always, already – free speech.

Obviously, then, the kind of freedom that freedom of speech consists in is a negative liberty: it consists in freedom from being arrested, imprisoned, tortured, or executed for what you have said. Instead of a freedom to speak, it's rather a freedom from the consequences of having spoken. For those advocating for the right to troll, freedom of speech means not just the freedom to say whatever we like about whatever we like to whoever we like: it includes the freedom to do so without any ramifications whatsoever.

This is an idle fantasy. It's a dream of an imaginary world of make-believe based not on freedom of speech but on freedom from responsibility. In this world, the German car manufacturers who, back in 2015, were found to have fabricated data on emissions to sell their cars could have escaped their one-billion-dollar fine by claiming that free speech meant they could use whatever numbers they liked in their advertising. The men who, back in 2013, put horse meat into the convenience food of thirteen European countries and called it beef could have said that freedom of speech gave them the right to do just that. Not so. It is an inescapable fact, both of society and no less of language itself, that words have consequences and that the speakers of those words are responsible for them. The trolls' idea of unfettered free speech is just a daydream of a deranged world – which *might* explain why trolls find it so attractive.

Extrapolating from the fact that our words have inevitable consequences in the same way any of our deeds do, influential literary scholar Stanley Fish drew the disconcerting conclusion that there's no such thing as free speech: 'insofar as the point of the First Amendment is to identify speech separable from conduct and from the consequences that come in conduct's wake', he writes, 'there is no such speech and therefore nothing for the First Amendment to protect'.[22] As Fish sees it, the very idea of free speech is predicated on an illusory distinction:

> the distinction, essential to First Amendment jurisprudence, between speech and action. This distinction is essential because no one would think to frame a First Amendment that began 'Congress shall make no law

---

[21]That is a potentially ableist statement. Those who lose the power of speech and/or writing, or those who cannot acquire it, plainly do not enjoy freedom of speech in the same ways as the rest of society.

[22]Stanley Fish, *There's No Such Thing as Free Speech ... and It's a Good Thing, Too* (Oxford: Oxford University Press, 1994), p.106.

> abridging freedom of action', for that would amount to saying 'Congress shall make no law', which would amount to saying 'There shall be no law', only actions uninhibited and unregulated. If the First Amendment is to make any sense, have any bite, speech must be declared not to be a species of action, or to be a special form of action.[23]

For Fish, however – as for philosophers such as Ludwig Wittgenstein and J. L. Austin before him – speech is just another kind of the many actions we humans perform in our daily lives.

To the trolls who backed Anthony Elonis's right to say whatever he liked, or to those devil-may-care libertarians who 'declare up front that total freedom of speech is our primary value and trumps anything else, no matter what', Fish's response is that:

> freedom of expression would only be a primary value if it didn't matter what was said, didn't matter in the sense that no one gave a damn but just liked to hear talk. There are contexts like that, a Hyde Park corner or a call-in talk show where people get to sound off for the sheer fun of it. These, however, are special contexts, artificially bounded spaces designed to ensure that talking is not taken seriously.[24]

And with that, Fish has clinched the distinction between what a troll means by free speech and what an activist means by it. Trolls want the internet – and perhaps even the whole world – to be precisely such a space where they can sound off for the sheer fun of it, and where nothing is taken seriously. Activists, on the other hand, aren't just sounding off; they demand their speech be taken seriously.

To be fair, there are indeed some trolls for whom the phrase 'freedom of speech' also entails the right for their speech to be taken seriously. The prototype here would be the Twitter troll I likened to Martin Luther in an earlier chapter – Donald Trump. Trump has regularly made up 'alternative facts' – about anything from the size of the crowd at his inauguration, to climate change being a Chinese hoax, to immigrants being rapists, to Covid-19 being cured by drinking bleach, to having won the election of 2020 – and instead of presenting any evidence to substantiate them, he would instead simply insist on his unconditional constitutional First-Amendment-protected right to say them. Trolls in this vein take 'freedom of speech' to mean something different to freedom from consequences. (Maybe this is because Trump's privileged position means he is typically insulated from any consequences of his words and actions anyhow.)

---

[23]Ibid., p.105

[24]Ibid., pp.106–07

For trolls of this stripe, freedom of speech seemingly means the right to have their words respected. Apparently, this respect is unconditional – it's not contingent on the words being true. It's hard to know whether this is a form of negative liberty that consists, basically, in freedom from contradiction, or whether it's some twisted, bogus variant of 'freedom to' – a form of positive liberty in which the bare fact of stringing a sentence together entitles you to the right to success in argument. It's too simple to call it freedom to lie, because trolls like these would merely retort that they believe in the truth of what they're saying. It is, perhaps, a view of freedom of speech as *equality* of speech, a view in which whatever hunch Joe on Facebook has just had about Covid-19 or climate change is automatically afforded the same footing as research by Nobel Prize–winning scientists.

Here, once again, we get to see how trolls and activists part company in their respective takes on freedom of speech. Activism becomes pointless in a world where all views are equally valid. Why risk your life for civil rights if the segregationists have a fair point? Why confront anti-Semitism if the neo-Nazis are entitled to their view? Why overthrow dictatorships if tyrants' lives matter? A world in which freedom of speech means equality of speech, or freedom from contradiction, is just as deranged and impossible as a world in which it means freedom from consequences. That may be what trolls want, but it isn't what activists want. Activists of whatever stripe have a vision of a world that's a better place, on whatever terms their vision of 'better' might be. They campaign to convert people to their vision because they know their vision has no automatic entitlement to respect or success – usually, they have to fight for it every step of the way.

It's been some pages since we last talked about Zola. But he is the perfect writer to turn to in this context because he was such a dedicated activist, convinced in his marrow that 'Truth itself and justice itself have been slapped in the face'.[25] He was certain of being in the right: the last words he spoke to the jury at his trial were a prediction that 'one day, France will thank me for having helped to salvage its honour'[26] – a prediction that came true. And he had an unwavering commitment to his cause irrespective of personal cost. He told his jurors that 'He who suffers for the sake of truth and justice becomes august and sacred'.[27] He *could* have just scoffed 'Free speech!' and insisted this was a freedom afforded to him by the Rights of Man as set out

[25]Zola, 'J'Accuse…!', p.43.

[26]Zola, 'Statement to the Jury', *L'Aurore*, 22 February 1898, in *The Dreyfus Affair*, pp.55–61, p.61.

[27]Ibid., p.58.

during the revolution of 1789.[28] He could have told them that as an artist, he was entitled to express himself however he saw fit. Or he could have tried to worm his way out of trouble by claiming that, as one of France's foremost novelists, everyone knew he was in the business of making up elaborate stories, so no one could possibly have taken *J'Accuse…!* literally, and hence no libel had taken place.

He did nothing of the sort. The idea that free speech meant freedom from his responsibilities or freedom from their consequences would never have occurred to him. Not only was he unafraid to face those consequences and responsibilities, but he had deliberately sought a court hearing to establish the truth of what he had said, and he welcomed the opportunity to do so. So the idea that his accusations should be held as true just because he thought, felt, and said they were would also never have occurred to him. In short, Zola's example demonstrates that arguments grounded in freedom of speech pale into insignificance alongside arguments grounded in truth and fact.

This in turn suggests that Zola's example also softens the somewhat extreme conclusions drawn by Stanley Fish. Though Fish shows us convincingly enough that the idea of unfettered freedom of speech is a will-o'-the-wisp, the lesson he urges us to take from this is pragmatic to the point of being cynical: '"Free speech" is just the name we give to verbal behavior that serves the substantive agendas we wish to advance'.[29] Zola's principled stance shows us that the names of truth and justice serve our substantive agendas much better, which might in turn suggest that 'free speech' is rather the name we give to agenda-serving verbal behaviour that's lacking in other, more solid and upright kinds of justification.

Indeed, Zola's credentials as an activist of such impeccable rectitude are precisely what makes his case so illuminating. Zola was no troll. Though he made use of nearly every trick in the trolling book, combining defamation, provocation, and controversy in a very public statement, his use of these tactics depended – and this is the key point – on the fact that everything he said was true. Admittedly, to get yourself prosecuted for defamation when it's obvious that the defamatory things you have said are all perfectly true is to bring about a ridiculous paradox that anticipates the pranks we associate nowadays with trolling. But this was no empty hoax: on the contrary, it had painfully real consequences for Zola. And as he faced these consequences

---

[28]In point of fact, it's just as well he didn't opt for this line of argument. The relevant article in the Rights of Man – Article 11 – reads 'The free communication of ideas and opinions is one of the most precious of the rights of man. Every citizen may, accordingly, speak, write, and print with freedom, but shall be responsible for such abuses of this freedom as shall be defined by law'. Stanley Fish would no doubt point out that the strength of this 'but' confirms his argument that speech is not and never has been entirely free.

[29]Fish, *There's No Such Thing as Free Speech*, p.102.

down, he discovered how dangerous those who prefer carping platitudes about free speech can be. So let us now pick up his story again and look more closely at some of those consequences.

Freedom of speech as freedom to shout down your opponents

Zola's trial was no less of a travesty than Dreyfus's or Esterhazy's. The only plausible way to explain the farce is that the politicians had interfered, illegally, in the conduct of the trial and placed pressure on the presiding judge, Président Albert Delegorgue. He buckled under it. He refused to admit any line of argument touching upon the Dreyfus or Esterhazy verdicts, insisting that both matters were closed, and forestalling – even at the cost of due process – any possibility of a hint that either case might have involved a miscarriage of justice. The transcript of the trial is peppered with a refrain that Delegorgue repeated dozens of times: 'The question will not be put'. From the start, then, the trial's outcome was a foregone conclusion. Zola's lawyer, the heroic Fernand Labori, fought on valiantly, jousting with the judge's baffling reasoning in exchanges that might be mistaken for a skit by the Marx Brothers if the context were not so very serious.

The asymmetry of the trial was striking: the judge did nothing to intervene or prevent the military authorities from tampering with the proceedings. At one point, General Raoul Le Mouton de Boisdeffre, the chief of the General Staff, whom Zola had called an accomplice to the crimes of his underlings, stood at the bar in his dress uniform and was allowed to berate and threaten the jurors. He told them: 'You are the jury, you are the nation. If the nation has no confidence in the chiefs of its army, in the men who are responsible for the nation's defence, those men are prepared to hand over that grave task to others'.[30] The judge did not rebuke him, though de Boisdeffre was saying, in effect, that if the jury dared acquit Zola, they would be personally responsible for leaving their defenceless country at the mercy of the hated Germans.

In a sense, the trial was the least of Zola's worries. What was happening outside the courtroom was even worse. Every session of the trial was picketed by an angry mob of nationalist bigots, and Zola had to run the gauntlet of these right-wing extremists twice a day, at immense personal risk. They were literally baying for his blood; stones were thrown at him as well as insults. He described them in an interview with a journalist as 'a gang of fanatics and braying bullies' who were 'shouting and yelling death

[30]Cited by Pagès, 'Introduction', p.xx.

threats in the hope of drowning out our voices'.[31] In an open letter to the new prime minister, Henri Brisson, which was also published in *L'Aurore*, he went into more detail:

> Every single insult was allowed, every single threat as well, all of them filthy and despicable; no one was arrested. The demonstrators were even allowed to come close enough to constitute a genuine danger. And the police did not step in and save me until the very second when things threatened to get out of hand ...
>
> Well, M. Brisson ... in addition to your authority as Prime Minister, you are Minister of the Interior as well. It is you who are responsible for maintaining law and order. So we are going to find out what conditions you think should prevail when a defendant is to appear in court; whether you think people should be allowed to insult and threaten him, whether such a barbaric sight does not dishonour France totally. ... Since anything is possible, M. Brisson, I hereby declare in advance, that if we are murdered on Monday [the day of the verdict], the murderer will be you.[32]

Zola was not hamming up his situation: his life was in genuine danger from a hate-filled pack of rabid anti-Semites. Georges Clemenceau, then an outspoken journalist whose support of Dreyfus and Zola launched a political career that would later make him prime minister of France, looked back on those times in no uncertain terms:

> I saw Zola close up during those dreadful hours. I was with him at the end of each session before the Assize Court, each time he had to flee from the abominable crowds; they were hurling stones, hissing, booing, shrieking for his death. I was there when he was sentenced ... and I must admit I had not expected such a ferocious display of hatred. If Zola had been acquitted that day, not one of us would have left the courtroom alive. That is what this man did. He braved his times. He braved his countrymen.[33]

Nor was Clemenceau's assessment of the situation biased by his support for Zola: Arthur Meyer, another journalist in the crowd that day with right-wing anti-Dreyfus sympathies, agreed with Clemenceau that the crowd was

---

[31]P. Dubois, 'M. Émile Zola at Home', *L'Aurore*, 25 February 1898, in *The Dreyfus Affair*, pp.61–2, p.62.

[32]Zola, 'Letter to Prime Minister Brisson', *L'Aurore*, 16 July 1898, in *The Dreyfus Affair*, pp.66–73, p.72.

[33]Cited by Pagès, 'Introduction', p.xxvii.

riled up enough to have taken matters into its own hands and lynched Zola in the event of his acquittal.[34]

Hate, violence, and death threats – by no means empty ones – dogged Zola and his supporters both during the trial and on into its aftermath. While the appeal against his conviction was pending, Zola was set upon and beaten up by a gang of soldiers while out riding his bicycle near Versailles. His ally Octave Mirbeau, a celebrated novelist in his own right, was challenged to a duel by right-wing extremist Lucien Millevoye. Worst of all, his lawyer, the valiant Fernand Labori, narrowly escaped with his life after being shot in an assassination attempt. (The gunman was never apprehended.) On top of this, Zola was ostracized from literary circles and suspended from the Legion d'Honneur. During the Dreyfus affair, his allies twice proposed him for membership of the *Académie française*: although he was the best-known writer in France at that time, he received not one single vote. A motion for a vote of support at the *Société des gens de lettres* was denied the floor, rebuked with a strongly worded vote of condemnation, and almost came to fisticuffs. 'It was not healthy to be seen with him', writes Alain Pagès.[35]

Mirbeau remarked that Zola took it all in his stride:

> Those howls and shouts demanding his death which pursue him every time he enters or leaves the Palais have not even got on his nerves.... When I see this strong and simple man who has not once flinched throughout these tragic hours, whose soul has become greater and greater with every insult, every threat, my heart overflows with emotion.... Now I know what the word 'heroic' means.[36]

All told, then, if ever an activist had good cause to protest about freedom of speech, Zola surely did. But, irony of ironies – and the Dreyfus affair was riddled with multi layered ironies, at once bitter and ludicrous – it was the angry mob, clamouring for Zola's blood, and calling for death to stop his libellous, traitorous tongue from telling the truth, who were being incited to this behaviour by their newspaper of choice: the ultra-nationalistic, anti-Semitic *La Libre Parole*, or, *Free Speech*.

Threatening to kill a writer in the name of free speech might seem rather odd. But such things still happen today, and they're evidence of how pernicious, warped, and fundamentally empty the concept of freedom of speech can all too easily become, especially when pressed into the service of a populist agenda. Consider the following example. In August 2018, a mob of a dozen far-right extremists barged into a socialist bookshop near

---

[34]See Arthur Meyer, *Ce que mes yeux ont vu* (Paris: Plon, 1912), p.149.

[35]Pagès, 'Introduction', p.xx.

[36]Cited by Pagès, 'Introduction', p.xxvii.

the British Museum in London, abusing the customers, threatening the staff, and trashing the shop. One was wearing a Donald Trump mask; three were members of the extreme right-wing political party UKIP, including a member of its National Executive Committee who had recently stood for the position of party leader.[37] It would appear from the placards they were carrying that they had attacked the bookshop while dispersing from a demonstration in support of InfoWars, the online vehicle for Alex Jones, a prominent right-wing conspiracy theorist who has been described in the press as 'King of All Trolls'.[38] InfoWars – which Jones describes as libertarian in outlook – had just been taken down from Facebook, YouTube, iTunes, and Spotify; in the weeks that followed, it would be removed from Twitter, Vimeo, Pinterest, and LinkedIn too, in all cases for violating terms of use.[39] Jones's followers considered this an attack on his freedom of expression, and so, apparently, the UKIP supporters who stormed into that bookshop in London had just been protesting for free speech. It would appear that, somehow, the culture around alt-right trolling sees no contradiction between clamouring for freedom of speech and wrecking a bookshop whose politics they happen to disagree with. In this context, it's hard to disagree with Stanley Fish's assessment that '"free speech" is just the name we give to verbal behavior that serves the substantive agendas we wish to advance'.[40]

But if the turmoil surrounding Zola's trial still has lessons for us today, then those lessons are perhaps somewhat more constructive than Fish's shoulder-shrugging conclusion that there's no such thing as free speech. Here's a more nuanced takeaway point. Whether in the Paris of 1898 or the London of 2018, freedom of speech has often been warped into meaning freedom to break the law. Lawbreakers then try to claim the moral high ground by saying that the law is depriving them of their free speech. Rightly looked at, though, it is the rule of law that provides them and us with free speech in the first place. Otherwise, free speech belongs to those

---

[37]See Henry Zeffman, 'UKIP Suspends Activists after Raid on Socialist Bookshop', *The Times*, 8 August 2018, and Alison Flood, 'UKIP Suspends Three Members over Socialist Bookshop Attack', *The Guardian*, 7 August 2018. Available at: https://www.thetimes.co.uk/article/ukip-suspends-activists-after-raid-on-socialist-bookshop-bookmarks-in-bloomsbury-sl906f27n and https://www.theguardian.com/books/2018/aug/06/socialist-bookshop-support-after-rightwingers-attack-bookmarks respectively.

[38]See Ken White's Op-Ed 'Is Alex Jones an Extreme Conspiracy Theorist or a Giant Troll? Here's Why the Answer Matters', *Los Angeles Times*, 19 April 2017, and Jennings Brown, 'Infowars' Alex Jones, King of All Trolls, Relishes His Moment', *New York Magazine*, 11 November 2016. Available at: https://www.latimes.com/opinion/op-ed/la-oe-white-alex-jones-character-20170419-story.html and https://nymag.com/vindicated/2016/11/alex-jones-king-of-all-trolls-relishes-his-moment.html respectively.

[39]Note that, as I pointed out earlier, this protest was therefore about access to technology, and not about freedom of speech.

[40]Fish, *There's No Such Thing as Free Speech*, p.102.

with the loudest mouths and the hardest fists. Hence, the idea that freedom of speech is some natural harmonious condition to which we could revert by repealing the laws that have been imposed upon it is nonsense. Simply put, legalizing the kind of death threats to which Zola was subjected, or to which some followers of InfoWars have subjected its targets, is more akin to legalizing vigilante censorship than it is to broadening freedom of speech. Counterintuitive though it may seem to supporters of Alex Jones or Anthony Elonis, the law is primarily what creates their freedom of speech rather than what restricts it.

I can imagine that this line of argument might seem a little rich to some. After all, a counterargument might run, Zola was a lawbreaker himself, with spectacular disregard for what he wasn't allowed to say. *J'Accuse…!* without its libellous content is not *J'Accuse…!* This is true, but only superficially. Zola's conduct during and after his trial (of which more is to follow) revealed he had a profound understanding of the law rather than a contemptuous disregard for it. Not only was he, as he put it, 'a defendant who of his own free will had chosen to appear in his country's courts of justice',[41] but, as I'll show later, his every move was calculated so that the legal process would amplify and advance his cause. In a nutshell, the shambles of Zola's trial, the dignity with which he faced it, and the resourcefulness with which he turned the charade of its verdict to his advantage all underscore the point that a competent grasp of legal frameworks is more than a match for vapid sloganeering about freedom of speech.

From censorship to citizenship

True, Zola flouted the law blatantly, and was then handed down a flawed verdict by a court that had been nobbled by the powers that be (as were Dreyfus and Esterhazy before him). So much for the rule of law, you might think. But of course, these grand-scale abuses of the legal system show how important respect for due legal process is: disrespecting it during the Dreyfus affair toppled successive French governments and ended the careers of some top politicians, judges, and generals. Sadly, though, there are still lessons to be learnt about the importance of an even-handed, independent judiciary in the twenty-first century, as several trolls have found out. In fact, if the trolls have a grievance about the legal consequences of their actions, it is more a grievance about the fairness of the legal system than a grievance about being subjected to laws in the first place. Let me explain.

Researcher Jonathan Bishop has written prolifically about the legal consequences of trolling and the laws covering it in the United Kingdom.

---

[41] Zola, 'Letter to Prime Minister Brisson', p.71.

Writing back in 2013, he concluded that 'the current legal system resembles a pre–Henry II legal system where decisions are not based on precedence but expedience. This has resulted in unfair outcomes where in virtually identical situations people have been treated completely differently by the authorities'.[42] To understand why, let's look at one of the examples he cites.

On 6 March 2012, a huge improvized explosive device killed six British soldiers in Afghanistan. It was the deadliest attack on British forces serving there for over ten years, and it sent a shockwave through the country. Two days later, a young man named Azhar Ahmed wrote on Facebook: 'People gassin about the deaths of Soldiers! What about the familys [*sic*] who've been brutally killed. The women who have been raped. The children who have been sliced up!' After some abusive comments about the British Army, he concluded that 'All soldiers should die and go to hell'.[43] He was from the same community in Yorkshire as some of the deceased; he must have witnessed first-hand the outpouring of grief there and must have known what an emotive topic this was. Later, he claimed he had deleted the message as soon as he realized how much pain it was causing and that he'd apologized to several people who had replied to his post, telling him they had lost loved ones in Afghanistan. But all this was too little, too late. He was prosecuted for making a grossly offensive communication and sentenced to 240 hours of community service and a £300 fine. This wasn't good enough for an angry crowd of far-right protestors who had gathered at the courtroom: some heckled the judge with cries of 'Disgusting!' when the sentence she handed down didn't include a term in jail. Ahmed, for his part, admitted that the message was likely to prove upsetting or distressing but denied it had been grossly offensive.

Ahmed might have had a point. The very same words he typed into Facebook could just as easily have been written forty years earlier, during the conflict in Vietnam, in leaflets or placards by particularly militant anti-war protestors. This wouldn't have resulted in any kind of prosecution. And it's hard to see why writing such things on Facebook should make them liable to criminal proceedings when 'what is not an offence off-line should not be an offence online'.[44] Ahmed's judge, like Zola's, had taken a heavy-handed

[42]See Jonathan Bishop, 'The Effect of Deindividuation of the Internet Troller on Criminal Procedure Implementation: An Interview with a Hater', *International Journal of Cyber Criminology*, vol. 7, no.1, 2013, pp.28–48.

[43]See Helen Carter, 'Man Gets Community Sentence for Facebook Post about Dead Soldiers', *The Guardian*, 9 October 2012, available at: https://www.theguardian.com/uk/2012/oct/09/community-sentence-facebook-dead-soldiers

[44]House of Lords Select Committee on Communications, *Social Media and Criminal Offences*, p.12.

view of insulting the military.[45] Moreover, Bishop's research into this incident contrasts it with a disturbing comparator: a case involving a campaign of harassment and domestic abuse, which went on for quite some time, and which the victim described as violent, abusive, manipulative, and coercive throughout. Its perpetrator, sentenced around the same time as Ahmed, got 140 hours of community service compared with Ahmed's one-off comment getting 240. There is something worryingly disproportionate here.

Bishop's research uncovers much that is alarming about the way trolling is handled by UK criminal justice systems. He cites the remarks of several judges when sentencing trolls, all of whom have said that the sentence they passed was reflective of 'public outrage'. This implies the trolls in question were punished more severely because the media covered their actions with a tone of moral outcry.[46] Perhaps more disturbing is Bishop's finding that in Scotland, a worryingly high number of police officers – both male and female – had faced disciplinary charges for abusing social media, including writing posts about in-progress police activities on public platforms. Some had been ordered to undergo diversity awareness training for some of their more offensive posts, which suggests they involved hate speech. But none had been prosecuted. Still, these same police forces will have arrested people for posting (what those arrested called) jokes on the same social media platforms – jokes that were likely no more offensive than the comments written by serving police officers. Bishop rightly summarizes this skewed situation by observing that 'The criminal justice system can be its own worst enemy'.[47]

Given all this, it is perhaps understandable that certain trolls feel strongly about free speech. The threat of prosecution is one thing, but the threat of a trial that is in thrall to public opinion, that has been politicized by the media, and that dishes out draconian sentences to certain *personae non gratae* while turning a blind eye to the misdeeds of those in positions of public authority – all this seems to recall what happened to Zola. One wonders whether those in the trolling subculture might rather improve society, and do themselves some good in the process, by dedicating their considerable energies to calling out injustices and inconsistencies in the courts. However, since this would necessitate them recognizing and engaging with the legal system as they find it, rather than carping vague platitudes about free speech, we are unlikely ever to find out.

---

[45]A similar view was taken in a Scottish court in January 2022, when one Joseph Kelly was sentenced to 150 hours of community service for tweeting that 'the only good Brit soldier is a deed [*sic*] one'. See Chiara Giordano, 'Man Guilty of Sending "Grossly Offensive" Tweet about Captain Sir Tom Moore', *Independent,* 1 February 2022. Available at: https://www.independent.co.uk/news/uk/crime/captain-tom-moore-tweet-guilty-b2004800.html

[46]See Bishop, 'The Effect of Deindividuation', p.38.

[47]Ibid., p.36.

At the end of the day, however, there is more to the rule of law than law enforcement. After all, 'the law is rarely the most effective tool for changing behaviour: effective law tends to reinforce, rather than in itself change, social attitudes'.[48] We need to keep in mind, in discussions like these, that the rule of law depends for its smooth running at least as much on a law-abiding citizenry as it does upon a fair and fairly administered legal code.[49] If we rely on law enforcement alone for the health of our communities, then we will have unhealthy communities. Online communities are no exception to this rule.

'It is important to recognise that when an action can be labelled criminal that criminal procedure is not necessarily the best way of handling it', writes Bishop.[50] We need to remember this. Prosecution might not always be the most effective way to deal with trolls. For one thing, it gives them more of the publicity and notoriety they crave. For another, the punishments for the offences they typically commit are comparatively light: 240 hours of community service is likelier to embitter and entrench a troll than to lead to them mending their ways. Combined, these two things can easily create a vicious circle: an embittered troll is likelier to reoffend if the notoriety is worth the slight punishment. At any rate, there is little incentive for them to stop trolling. As Bishop puts it, 'current criminal procedure forces defendants to remain in denial and does almost nothing to cultivate their expressions of remorse and apologies and victims' forgiveness'.[51] We need a way of responding to trolling that is proactive as well as reactive, that involves communities as well as individuals, and that is about betterment as well as punishment. In essence, we need to think of this issue less in terms of censorship and more in terms of citizenship.

The concept of digital citizenship is still very much in its infancy. Disappointingly, its uptake seems confined largely to those working in education, whose laudable aim is to teach the next generation how to be responsible, ethical, critically aware, engaged citizens in a digital world. This is all very important, but the concept means so much more than this. Because digital communities are vastly more participatory than even the most democratic of nation states, and because participating in them is such a fluid, ever-changing process, we are constantly making and unmaking

---

[48]House of Lords Select Committee on Communications, *Social Media and Criminal Offences*, p.20.

[49]That is not to say we should all become mindless sheep, blindly obedient to whatever the law tells us. A good citizen can tell the difference between justice and legality, and a great citizen is unafraid, when the need arises, to break unjust laws in the name of justice: Émile Zola, like Mahatma Gandhi or Rosa Parks, is a case in point here.

[50]Bishop, 'The Effect of Deindividuation', p.36.

[51]Ibid.

the communities we share in online. The risk is that this makes them more fragile and parlous communities; the potential is that this makes them more robust and responsive, since their members are constantly and directly involved in them. It is up to us what kind of communities we want to build online, and we make these choices in and through the micro-acts of digital citizenship that comprise our online lives.

Many of us seem content with allowing platform moderators, and hence the terms of use of private, for-profit corporations, to take care of matters of digital citizenship for us. We consider we have done our duty if we flag or report inappropriate content and leave it at that. (Indeed, that is often a best-case scenario and already more than many internet users bother with.) This does nothing to tackle the source of the problem, to confront its perpetrator, or to prevent the perpetrator from doing exactly the same thing again under another username, from another account. In particularly dire cases, we might involve law enforcement. But none of this is asking very much of us as digital citizens. If we are to move beyond the hotly polarized non-debates between 'free speech' libertarians and their opponents in the so-called cancel culture, we need to do better than this.

One of the most eloquent and oft-cited defences of freedom of speech makes this point very clear. Back in 1927, a milestone ruling by Justice Louis D. Brandeis of the US Supreme Court wisely stated: 'If there be time to expose through discussion the falsehood and fallacies, to avert the evil by the processes of education, the remedy to be applied is more speech, not enforced silence'.[52] Libertarians are fond of quoting the 'more speech, not enforced silence' part. They tend to overlook the force of the 'if', and the hard graft entailed by it, probably because that would make free speech look more like a privilege that is earned than a right that is inalienable. And it is indeed an easy oversight, when so few of us these days have the time, let alone take it, to educate our opponents by exposing falsehood and fallacies through discussion. It's much easier to flag or report objectionable content, and thereby risk strengthening the perception of a 'cancel culture'. It's easier still to do nothing. (No doubt that is one reason why 'Do not feed the trolls' is such a popular slogan.) But, if we're serious about defending our online communities from the damage done by trolling, we might need to become more engaged, more proactive, and more creative than this in our roles as upstanding digital citizens.

Perhaps this sounds a bit like hard work. And indeed, confronting trolls isn't easy and is often futile. Taking the trouble to put right a defamation, to make a considered and measured contribution to a controversy, or to write a response to provocation that's deflationary rather than escalationary: these things are all difficult, and take time – much more time than it takes to bash

[52] *Whitney v California*, 274 U.S. 357, 377 (1927).

out a piece of trolling. So the odds are on the trolls' side. Furthermore, it may well be asking too much of their victims to engage with them. Some insults and defamations might be just too painful to respond to. But if digital citizenship is about ethical community membership, then they shouldn't have to: in an ideal world, there should be plenty of upstanding digital citizens willing to jump to their aid, thereby enabling us to crowdsource our fightback against trolls. Here's a brief example of what I mean by this.

Anti-Semitism is, nauseatingly, just as common on today's internet as it was in Zola's nineteenth-century France. One of many brave, Zolaesque figures to confront it is British comedian David Baddiel. On X/Twitter – to which he confesses an addiction – his bio reads simply 'Jew', though his distinguished career in broadcasting gives him plenty of other accolades to boast about. Baddiel makes a point of challenging anti-Semitism whenever he finds it – which is disturbingly frequently. One particular example, however, springs to mind as a comedic triumph and a wonderful way of galvanizing the support of digital citizens in fighting back against anti-Semitic trolling.[53]

During the Chanukah festivities of December 2017, after Sadiq Khan – the Muslim mayor of London – joined in with the Jewish community's celebrations, Baddiel tweeted this: 'Multiculturalism, despite all you may have heard recently, is mainly fucking great'.[54] A Twitter user with the handle @evaluhater tweeted a cutting reply: multiculturalism 'seems to suit a certain band of rootless cosmopolitans'.[55] In case you aren't familiar with this phrase, 'rootless cosmopolitans' was a term coined by Stalin. It meant 'Jews'. He coined the term to conceal the anti-Semitic nature of some of his purges, which specifically targeted Jews in prominent positions in the Soviet Union. Today, it's a term revived by the alt-right for similar purposes of concealment. Until recently, few hate speech filters picked up on it, and relatively few people were aware of its anti-Semitic meaning. Hence, its use often enables the alt-right to hide anti-Semitic hate speech in plain sight.

Some of us might have reported or flagged a tweet like this; most of us would likely have ignored it. But Baddiel wasn't about to lose this chance to make a troll look ridiculous. His reply challenged @evaluhater's choice of words – but *not* the anti-Semitic slur. Ingeniously, Baddiel wrongfooted @evaluhater by picking him up on his use of a different word: 'What band *is* that, @evaluhater? Oy Division? The Stone Moses? Black Shabbos?'[56] Baddiel's followers took this as their clarion call, and what happened next was a small-scale Twitterstorm following his lead: 'Hannukah Montana',

[53]The incident is discussed by Baddiel in his show *Trolls: not the dolls*, which I was lucky enough to see live (Grand Opera House York, 1 November 2021).

[54]@Baddiel, 12 December 2017.

[55]@evaluhater, 14 December 2017.

[56]@Baddiel, 14 December 2017.

'Rabbi Williams', 'Schmuck Berry', 'Semite Be Giants', 'Torah Amos', 'Rita Menorah', 'Talmuddy Waters', 'Duran Shmuran', 'The Bagel City Rollers', 'Chasid Vicious', 'Oy vey-sis', 'Motley Jew', 'Dreidel of Filth', 'Tallis Cooper', 'Limp Brisket', 'Florence and the Meshuganah', 'Goyz II Mensch', 'Jew2', 'SO many great Heavy Shtetl bands ... '[57] The outpouring of puns (of which this list is simply a 'greatest hits' compilation) kept coming all day. All of them were replies not just to Baddiel, but to @evaluhater too, who was thereby made to witness a continuous stream of irrefutable proof that multiculturalism, as encapsulated in these wisecracking juxtapositions and intersections between traditional Jewish culture and contemporary secular music, *is* mainly fucking great. Eventually, @evaluhater was stung into a disgruntled reply – 'high levels of verbal IQ on display' – and was roundly pilloried for such 'high and grand sarcasm'.[58]

This is, of course, a far cry from Zola's way of tackling anti-Semitism. And it's far beyond the scope of this book – let alone my expertise – to judge which is the better way of confronting racism.[59] The point I'm trying to make here is instead one about digital citizenship. By choosing to stand up against a troll, contributors to this thread left the internet a better place than it was when they logged on. These good-humoured puns are micro-acts of digital citizenship: they are pro-active, positive contributions that protect an online community from someone trying to destroy it and that defend an individual from unwanted and unwarranted aggression. It's a wittier, kinder take on the so-called 'dogpile': collectively, they establish and assert unity in the face of divisiveness, through a shared sense of humour. Rather than inflaming aggression, they de-escalate it – without letting it go unchallenged. Thus, a vexatious insult ends up being made to look ridiculous under the weight of an onslaught from a counter-humour that is unprovocative, uncontroversial, non-insulting, and sincere. This encapsulates one of the lessons we learned when discussing Oscar Wilde: that mainstream humour is likelier to succeed on a larger scale than the lulzy jibes, taunts, and in-jokes of trolls. But it's also a great example of modelling context-specific, responsible, and upright digital citizenship.

I'm not suggesting that Baddiel's tactics can be straightforwardly emulated. After all, he has over 800,000 followers on X/Twitter; few of

---

[57]Respectively: @missbekirk1, @DavidButtPhilip, @A_Waller1, @CrazyAlify, @jjunglejim, @Nick_Pettigrew, @RachelDelahaye, @drjtreml, @balrogz, @jared_za, @toffeegod, @metzbo, @danhett, @metzbo, @robertdee, @djhazydave, @metzbo, @djhazydave, @gjoutteridge. All dated 14–15 December 2017.

[58]@evaluhater; @Baddiel, both 14 December 2017.

[59]For a useful discussion of calling out anti-Semitism, I refer readers to Baddiel's own admirable book *Jews Don't Count: How Identity Politics Failed One Particular Identity* (London: TLS Books, 2021).

us could muster so large a pool of support in a similar situation. But the incident is nevertheless instructive, because in the online world it is rare for hate to call forth a response involving ridicule rather than anger, and rare for it to be challenged by proactive citizenship instead of reactive censorship. Given that we have seen often enough in this book that trolling aims at divisiveness, it's surprising how seldom we have seen online communities uniting against it on such a scale, in such a good-humoured way. Coming to one another's aid in defence of the values we share is something we can all do at any time, not just when prompted by a celebrity. It's a tool that online networks and social media give us that was unavailable to earlier champions of multicultural civic-mindedness, like Zola, who had to face the music by himself. Let's pick up his story again, and see how he turned defeat into victory.

Zola's last stand

Naturally enough, Zola's first move was to appeal the verdict against him. The authorities tried to transfer the case from Paris to Versailles, partly to get away from the angry mob, partly to get away from the glare of publicity, but mostly because the jurors there were likely to be more conservative and pro-government. Zola and his legal team resisted these manoeuvrings, but their strategy now was to play for time. Zola's trial had brought the Dreyfus affair under the spotlight and made it the biggest news story in Europe; his best hope was that, given time and the pressure of public opinion, new witnesses or new facts would eventually emerge and bring the truth to light. After these legal wranglings came to an end, the appeal came up in court, and the court confirmed that the original trial had followed correct procedure. It was inevitable that the guilty verdict would be upheld, so Zola knew he had to do something drastic. His lawyer, Labori, and his ally, Clemenceau, suggested to him a radical course of action: although he could be found guilty *in absentia*, he couldn't be sentenced *in absentia*. If he went into hiding, his case would remain open, and the cause of the Dreyfusards, though hanging by a thread, would be kept alive. Zola packed some belongings into a bag, so hastily that the only underwear he took was what he was wearing, and caught the boat train from Paris to London that same night, before anyone could come looking for him when he failed to appear in court the next morning.

At the time, and occasionally in the years since, there have been those who have sought to paint Zola's English exile as an act of moral cowardice. Newspapers such as *La Libre Parole* went further still: for them, Zola's exile was proof of an international Jewish conspiracy against France. Looking back, Zola would write: 'As for the silly people who think I went away to avoid going to prison and to have a good time abroad with Jewish gold to support me – all I can feel for them is a little disgust and a great deal of pity'.[60] There is no doubt that Zola's only motive was to keep the Dreyfus affair going. His letters home to his wife and lawyer from his very first weeks in exile regularly lament his hasty departure, and express his preference for coming back to face the music, and to get his jail term over with. It took quite some effort to dissuade him from this course of action and to reconcile him to exile. But Zola's allies were of one mind in telling him to stay right where he was: he was the only card left up the Dreyfusards' sleeve.

Zola began his English exile at London's Grosvenor Hotel, not far from his point of arrival in Victoria Station, under the assumed name of Pascal. He was almost instantly recognized, having been to London on a successful tour just a few years earlier. Fearing that a French official could easily locate him and serve him notice of his sentence, thus closing his case in spite of everything, he fled a second time. He spent the first half of his exile at three addresses in leafy Surrey, and the second half in the south London suburb of Upper Norwood. Zola went by the name of Beauchamp at first, then later under the name of Richard. Ironically, his life began to be shaped by manoeuvres resembling the elaborate world of espionage he had poured scorn on in *J'Accuse…!* His letters were placed inside two envelopes, so they couldn't be tampered with, and sent via intermediaries. His wife was told to feed misinformation to their domestic staff, and his English translator helped concoct a variety of smokescreens locating Zola in Norway, or on a bicycling holiday in Switzerland, or living undercover in France. Importantly, Zola obeyed one golden rule: he published nothing whatsoever about the Dreyfus affair until he was fully vindicated and back in France, and not for want of pleading from the English newspapers. (He began work on his next novel, *Fécondité*, instead.)

The dénouement did not take long. Zola had succeeded in bringing matters to a boiling point. In 1898, the year of *J'Accuse…!*, two French governments fell within little more than four months. Additionally, the third minister of war resigned, to be reinstated days later. A parlous, ugly mood gripped the nation: anti-Semitic riots flared up across the country. Pressure mounted on the establishment to settle a matter that wasn't going away. Their counter-efforts to refute Zola's allegations led them to make public some of the documents that, in their eyes, confirmed Dreyfus's guilt. But doing so meant highlighting that some of these documents had, indeed, been kept secret and not disclosed to Dreyfus's defence. Meanwhile, Esterhazy – a pantomime villain if ever there was one – was, according to some accounts, openly bragging to his associates that 'I put Dreyfus in prison, and all of

[60]Zola, 'Justice', p.128.

France cannot get him out!'[61] These associates included an undercover, pro-Dreyfus journalist from Ireland named Chris Healy and Healy's friend – a famous writer who, like Zola, was living in exile after an infamous libel trial: none other than Oscar Wilde. By coincidence, one of Wilde's few remaining friends had also befriended a confidant of German military attaché Maximilian von Schwartzkoppen and was well aware that Dreyfus was utterly blameless. According to some accounts, Wilde passed what he knew on to Zola, thereby giving him the encouragement he needed that matters were coming to a head.[62]

Coming to a head they certainly were. Close examination of the documents in the secret file revealed they had been tampered with: slightly different coloured inks betrayed the presence of forgery, which in turn exposed the machinations of the General Staff. Colonel Henry, who had testified against Dreyfus at his court martial, owned up to the forgery. Placed

---

[61]See Nigel Jones, 'Dreyfus and Oscar Wilde: A Tale of Two Scandals', *History Today*, vol. 61, no. 2, 2011, np.

[62]For more on this, see J. Robert Maguire, 'Oscar Wilde and the Dreyfus Affair', *Victorian Studies*, vol. 41, no. 1, 1997, pp.1–29; see also Maguire's *Ceremonies of Bravery: Oscar Wilde, Carlos Blacker, and the Dreyfus Affair* (Oxford: Oxford University Press, 2013). For a more concise and accessible account, which differs in some respects from Maguire's, see the final chapter of Gregor Dallas's *Metrostop Paris* (London: John Murray, 2009).

As writers, Zola and Wilde seem like polar opposites: Wilde went into exile in Paris in 1897 after an unsuccessful libel trial in London; Zola went into exile in London in 1898 after an unsuccessful libel trial in Paris. The latter cultivated the image of a political progressive dedicated to gritty social realism, the former that of a decadent aesthete interested only in art for its own sake.

They met at least twice: once in the early 1890s, when Zola's biographer introduced Wilde to him, which Zola esteemed 'a great honour' (See Richard Ellmann, *Oscar Wilde* [London: Hamish Hamilton, 1987], p.304); and again in 1893, when Zola was in London on a writer's tour, and was, he wrote, called on by 'the very charming and remarkable poet Oscar Wilde, who had very thoughtfully sent a basket of flowers to my wife' (see Colin Burns, 'Le voyage de Zola à Londres en 1893', *Les Cahiers Naturalistes*, vol. 60, 1986, pp.41–73, p.65).

Though I'm no expert on this, I have my doubts about the extent of Wilde's importance to Zola in the Dreyfus affair. Had Wilde been instrumental in Zola's vindication, he would likely have boasted about it. Instead, he boasted about the very opposite: about his friendship with Esterhazy, whom Wilde knew to be an anti-Semite, a spy, and a traitor. Like a troll, Wilde crowed that all this was what made Esterhazy so interesting to befriend and that he would have had no interest in Esterhazy whatsoever had he been innocent. Wilde added that, since his own disgrace, companions such as Esterhazy were the only society he was fit for.

Additionally, Wilde was intimately associated with a number of people who held eye-wateringly anti-Semitic views, most notably his lover, Lord Alfred 'Bosie' Douglas. He created characters who expressed such views, most notably Dorian Gray. And he might have held a grudge against Zola, who had refused to sign a petition in support of a reprieve for Wilde, since he regarded the sordid details of Wilde's sex life as immoral.

There is certainly a fascinating story about a fascinating set of coincidences here, but readers who consult the above sources should make up their own minds about whether there is more to it than that.

under arrest, he committed suicide the next day, using his razor to cut his own throat. Though *La Libre Parole* tried to argue he had been hounded to his death by traitors in the pay of an international Jewish conspiracy, the tide had unmistakably turned. Zola, at his hideout in Addlestone, Surrey, received a simple telegram: 'Victory. Tell Beauchamp immediately'. He had to cycle over to the next village to buy an English newspaper, and decode it laboriously with his dictionary, to find out what had happened.

But still the authorities stalled: though Dreyfus's family had submitted a petition to review his conviction, the military, judicial, and political establishments preferred to pass it back and forth to one another, commissioning inquiries that sought to blame each other rather than do anything for Dreyfus or Zola. General Émile Zurlinden, the new minister of war, publicly said that to reopen Dreyfus's case 'means war', and indeed nationalist leader Paul Déroulède was telling his followers in *La Libre Parole* to prepare for civil war. Meanwhile, Esterhazy, having confessed his guilt in secret to one of these inquiries, was allowed to flee France in safety, scot-free – ironically, to the same sanctuary Zola had sought: London.

This logjam began to break up early in 1899, about a year after Zola's letter had been published. Félix Faure, the president of the Republic to whom Zola had addressed *J'Accuse…!*, died suddenly and unexpectedly. He had been a bulwark of conservatism, shielding the establishment from much of the furore around the Dreyfus affair.[63] (Whether or not this was because he had taken umbrage at Zola's *J'Accuse…!* is unclear). Fearing for their cause without his presidential protection, the nationalists and anti-Semites panicked. On the day of Faure's funeral, Déroulède launched a nationalist uprising, hoping to topple the new president and install himself as dictator. He had come from a military background and clearly expected the army to join him in a *coup d'état,* if only to protect their reputation. Thankfully, they didn't, and his insurrection quickly foundered, turning into a spectacular own goal that began to turn the tide of popular opinion away from militant nationalism and towards moderation.

At long, long last, the Supreme Court of Appeal quashed the verdict of Dreyfus's court martial on 3 June 1898, ordering a retrial. Word reached Dreyfus on Devil's Island two days later, by which time Zola had already packed his bags and headed back to Paris in triumph. Dreyfus's return took a little longer: his ship did not reach France till July, whereupon he was immediately incarcerated in the military prison of Rennes to await his retrial. There was every reason to believe this would lead to his full exoneration. By the time his second court martial began, Henry had confessed to perjury

[63]Another of the bitter ironies in this sorry episode of history is that Faure, who was fully aware that Dreyfus was an innocent victim of institutional anti-Semitism, and who found it easier to overlook or condone institutional anti-Semitism than to let justice be done, died in the arms of his mistress, who was Jewish.

and forgery, Esterhazy had confessed to being the real culprit, du Paty de Clam had been arrested, many of the conspirators in the War Office and the General Staff had resigned or been replaced, and even some of his original judges were proclaiming his innocence. It looked like plain sailing.

Upon returning to France, Zola rushed straight back into print. The very day after Dreyfus's conviction was overturned, *L'Aurore* carried an article called 'Justice', in which Zola wasted no time in picking up the provocative thread of *J'Accuse…!*:

> I am at home. Thus, whenever it may please the public prosecutor, he can officially notify to me the verdict from the Assize Court in Versailles, which sentenced me, in absentia, to one year in prison and a fine of three thousand francs. And once again we shall come before the jury.[64]

He was in fine form and had lost none of his knack for trolling. Humblebrags abounded:

> Every one of the accusations I had made in my 'Letter to the President of the Republic' was borne out. … I have no desire and no need to crow triumphantly. Yet I cannot help noting that the events have borne out all my accusations. The guilt of every single man I accused has been demonstrated in the glaring light of the investigation. Everything I announced, everything I predicted stands before us, unmistakable. And something else from which I derive a sweeter pride is that my letter was dignified, worthy of me, indignant but not violent. It contains not one insult, not one word that is uncalled for.[65]

While the voice of the establishment was calling for calm, reconciliation, healing, and national unity, Zola was having none of it. Christopher Hitchens, another great contrarian who regarded Zola as his inspiration, describes the 'caustic and brilliant epistolary campaign' that was *J'Accuse…!* as '*saeva indignatio* of a quality not seen since Swift himself' – but Zola's follow-up is even more angry than Swift at human weakness and folly.[66] He clearly relished metaphorically rubbing the noses of his opponents and fair-weather friends in it:

> Does anyone recall the abominable chorus of protests that greeted my 'Letter to the President of the Republic'? I had insulted the army; I

---

[64]Zola, 'Justice', p.132.

[65]Ibid., p.129, p.131.

[66]Christopher Hitchens, *Letters to a Young Contrarian* (New York: Basic Books, 2001), p 5, p.8.

> was a traitor; I was devoid of patriotism. Literary friends of mine were appalled.... Articles were written which will now weigh heavy on their authors' consciences. Never had any writer, no matter how coarse, or mad, or blinded by self-importance, sent to any head of state a more unrefined, more fallacious, more criminal letter. And now, let them re-read that poor letter of mine. I must confess that by now I am a little ashamed of it – ashamed to see how discreet it was.... I might almost say, how cowardly. ... I toned down that letter considerably.... And now my poor letter no longer hits the mark and looks altogether childish, a mere mawkish tale dreamt up by a timid novelist, compared with the fierce and awe-inspiring reality![67]

Playing down the import of *J'Accuse…!* by describing it, in effect, as some kind of modest proposal is another Swiftian move, superficially disarming yet calculated to inflame. And yet Zola was gloating too soon. The Dreyfus affair still had a few more twists of the knife to come.

Dreyfus's second court martial was perhaps the world's first mass-media event. Hundreds of journalists and photographers attended from across the globe. Early filmmakers came too, but were excluded. To the shock of the world's press, and in spite of everything that had transpired, Dreyfus's judges refused to acquit him; he was found guilty a second time. They were almost certainly ordered to do so from on high. For window-dressing, they reduced his sentence to ten years, owing (supposedly) to extenuating circumstances. This is perhaps the hardest part of the whole sorry saga to understand. Zola was incredulous: 'Jesus was convicted only once!', he scoffed.[68] It had been established beyond any doubt that junior officers, acting out of anti-Semitism, had conspired to frame an innocent man and that the top brass, not invulnerable from such bigotry, had preferred to collude with their subordinates so as to cover their own backs, further their political ambitions, and safeguard the reputation of the army, than to stand up for liberty, equality, and fraternity. All the court martial had to do was set the record straight. Instead, the army, tasked with marking its own homework, chose to give itself an A+. The civil unrest that was gripping France rose to fever pitch. Anti-French protests broke out in dozens of cities all over the world. Zola summed up the mood in *L'Aurore*: this was 'overwhelming proof that military justice is powerless to be just since it is not free and it ... prefers to convict an innocent man all over again rather than place its own infallibility in doubt.... It has pronounced sentence on itself'.[69]

---

[67]Zola, 'Justice', pp.130–31.

[68]Zola, 'The Fifth Act', *L'Aurore,* 12 September 1899, in *The Dreyfus Affair,* pp.136–43, p.139.

[69]Ibid.

Belatedly, the government stepped in to broker a political solution. They offered to pass a law of amnesty pardoning Dreyfus, Zola, and Major Picquart, who was still in prison for having dutifully conducted an impartial investigation whose findings had brought the army into disrepute. All the government wanted in turn, as a sop to the bigots, nationalists, and anti-Semites, was for Dreyfus to admit his guilt. With a heavy heart, and faced with the alternative of going straight back to Devil's Island, he acquiesced – to the fury of many of his supporters, including Picard, Labori, and Clemenceau.

Zola was incandescent with rage. 'It was truly a monstrous ploy to refuse me the trial that I have been seeking', he wrote in an open letter to the Senate.[70] He had been looking forward to the showdown that would clear his name, even boasting about it. Deprived of his day in court, he decided to vindicate himself in the press and repeated the gesture he first made in *J'Accuse...!*: an open letter to the president. In both these open letters, Zola once again rolled out the big guns from his arsenal of trolling tactics. Humblebrags abound ('I am merely a poet, a solitary teller of tales who works away in his corner but who works with a will').[71] So do provocations ('I am writing this letter simply for the great honour of having written it. I am doing my duty, and I doubt that you will do yours') and statements so wilfully contrarian they can hardly be sincere ('the Dreyfus Affair ... was the best thing that could have happened to France; ... without the Dreyfus Affair, France today would be, no doubt, in the hands of the reactionaries').[72] Perhaps the most entertaining part is when Zola gives President Émile Loubet a run-through of the charge-sheet from *J'Accuse...!*:

> I accused Lt-Col du Paty de Clam 'of having been the diabolical agent of a miscarriage of justice (though unwittingly, I am prepared to believe), and then of having defended his evil deed for the past three years through the most preposterous and blameworthy machinations'. Now that is discreet and courteous, is it not? compared with the report by the formidable Captain Cuignet, who accuses him outright of committing forgery.
>
> I accused General Mercier 'of having been an accomplice, at least by weak-mindedness, to one of the most iniquitous acts of this century.'— Now, here, I apologize; I withdraw the 'weak-mindedness'. But then, if General Mercier does not have the excuse of being feeble-minded, that

[70]Zola, 'Letter to the Senate', *L'Aurore*, 29 May 1900, in *The Dreyfus Affair*, pp.154–64, p.155.

[71]Zola, 'Letter to M. Émile Loubet, President of the Republic', *L'Aurore*, 22 December 1900, pp.164–75, p.175.

[72]Zola, 'Letter to the Senate', p.164; 'Letter to M. Émile Loubet', pp.171–72.

> means he is entirely responsible for the actions which he committed … which the legal Code classifies as criminal.[73]

And so on down the list. Zola's arch tone, contrarian stance, and heavy irony had lost none of their barb:

> Can you picture it? … an inquiry by the highest Court! I would have spent a few enjoyable hours, for it would have been a pleasure to be acquitted; and if I had been condemned a second time; well, cowardly stupidity and blind passion have a special beauty of their own that has always fascinated me.… Therefore, I ask you … don't you agree that your government's law which grants me amnesty – I, an innocent man among the heap of guilty persons I denounced – is truly a villainous law?[74]

But, sadly, this would be the last time Zola picked up the cudgels for the cause of Dreyfus. He did not live to see the matter fully resolved.

Zola died in the early hours of 29 September 1902. He may very well have been murdered by an anti-Semitic arch-nationalist: we'll never know for sure, but it would fit the strange facts surrounding his final hours.[75] He died of carbon monoxide poisoning, but curiously, when the inquest into his death ordered that his chimney be tested, they could find nothing obviously wrong with it, and it emitted no toxic fumes. Years later, in 1927, a Parisian roofer with far-right sympathies is said to have made a deathbed confession in which he admitted to Zola's murder, having deliberately blocked the chimney while working on the adjacent building, and then unblocking it again the next day. This didn't come to light until 1953 – far too late to investigate its reliability. But finding an alternative explanation for a deadly chimney that showed no sign of blockage and never malfunctioned again isn't easy. Either way, Zola was laid to rest in Montmartre Cemetery, with Dreyfus in attendance as an honoured guest.

Meanwhile, the political tide had turned against the nationalists. A left-leaning government under Jean Jaurès, himself a veteran Dreyfusard, was returned in 1902, largely because the right wing had disgraced itself so badly in its handling of the Dreyfus affair. The following year, Jaurès commissioned yet another inquiry, which, this time, would leave no stone unturned. A couple of years and an 800-page report later, the verdict of Dreyfus's second court martial was overturned by the Supreme Court, which ordered his full reinstatement. Dreyfus was re-admitted to the French

---

[73]Ibid., pp.172–73.

[74]Ibid., pp.172–74.

[75]For a balanced, succinct, and accessible account of these events, see Richard Cavendish, 'The Strange Death of Émile Zola', *History Today*, vol. 52, no. 9, 2002.

Army at the rank of major in July 1906 – twelve years after the epaulets had been ripped from his shoulders in the ceremony that marked his public disgrace. He went on to serve his country in the First World War, sometimes using the very artillery whose secrets he had been convicted of leaking to the country he was fighting. The appalling discrimination with which the French Army had victimized him for so long never dented his loyalty to it. He was awarded the Croix de Guerre and the Legion d'Honneur, and he died in 1935, in time to avoid betrayal and murder by the nationalists and anti-Semites of the Vichy era. But he'd had an even more fortunate escape than that. In 1908, when Zola was awarded the distinction of being re-interred in Paris's Panthéon – an honour bestowed only on the greatest of France's citizens, and which places him for all posterity literally by the side of Victor Hugo – the newly reinstated Major Dreyfus was shot in the arm in a botched assassination attempt by a far-right terrorist. The gunman, it transpired, had been a long-standing friend and trusted employee of the man who ran the 'free speech' newspaper *La Libre Parole*. In yet another botched trial, he was acquitted of all charges, and an anti-Semitic mob celebrated by rioting in the streets.

Conclusion

Zola's age was a harbinger of our own, which it resembles uncomfortably closely. Reacting to a downturn in their country's prestige, insecure mobs, egged on by populist politicians unashamed to resort to hate speech, were manipulated by the far right into embracing a nationalism poisoned by bigotry. They used violence to intimidate those who tried to reason with them and shouted down moderate voices under the self-contradicting slogan of free speech. For a sense of the scale of this problem nowadays, readers are referred to a 2019 survey of 181 British MPs: amongst the female respondents, over two thirds reported being threatened with physical violence; almost as many reported threats of violence towards their loved ones; around half had received death threats; and nearly a third had been threatened with rape (69.45%, 62.2%, 48.81%, and 30.5%, respectively). Four in five (79.6%) had experienced mental or emotional stress as a direct result of online abuse. This study describes such abuse as 'trolling'.[76]

The most worrying lesson of Zola's age is that it teaches us loud and clear that speech like this has consequences. We ignore this lesson at great risk.

[76]See Shazia Akhtar and Catriona M. Morrison, 'The Prevalence and Impact of Online Trolling of UK Members of Parliament', *Computers in Human Behavior*, vol. 99, 2019, pp.322–32. Predictably, the proportions of male MPs who reported being subjected to such threats was dramatically lower.

Where death threats become normalized, murders will follow. The shootings of Dreyfus and Labori, and the possible murder of Zola himself, warn us against turning a blind eye and dismissing incitements to violence as empty blather. It is depressing, if unsurprising, that right-wing populists steadfastly refuse to learn this lesson. When reminded by Paula Sherriff MP that 'We should not resort to using offensive, dangerous or inflammatory language for legislation that we do not like ... We must moderate our language, and it has to come from the prime minister first', UK Prime Minister Boris Johnson notoriously retorted: 'I have to say, Mr Speaker, I've never heard such humbug in all my life'.[77] One can only assume that it suits the right wing to stoke the fires of populist sentiment and to keep their opponents living in fear for their lives. Zola didn't mince his words with politicians of this stripe: his open letter to the Senate reminded them that 'The future will tell who was right'.[78]

The real-world consequences of trolling are what is most disturbing about it. This is what drives calls to police what is said on the internet more closely. For some commentators, the spillover from online hate to offline harm suggests there is something categorically new, different, and dangerous about our twenty-first-century world of social media. I agree about the danger, but disagree about its novelty. Laws against hate speech predate the internet because we have never lived in a world where words have no consequences. What readers of *La Libre Parole* did to Zola and his allies demonstrates that this spillover was operative on a viral scale back in the 1890s.

That is not to say there is nothing to fear. Rather, the precise opposite. If meaningful parallels can be drawn between the foment of Zola's time and our own – and we find in both the coupling of elaborate conspiracy theories with insurrectionist rhetoric, that in both cases is anti-Semitic at its heart – then we should be gravely concerned for the state of our public sphere, no less so than at the parallels we found earlier between the turmoil Martin Luther left behind him and that of the present day. But we should not allow that fear to cow us, or to prevent us from being good, responsible digital citizens, who confront abuses when we see them. Equally, we could follow Zola's example by standing up for truth and justice with a bit of social justice trolling. His case strongly suggests that neither new legislation nor existing law enforcement can be relied upon to fix the fractious state of the public sphere. Change from below is likelier to succeed than change from above.

[77]See 'MPs' Fury at Boris Johnson's "Dangerous Language"', *BBC News*, 25 September 2019. Available at: https://www.bbc.co.uk/news/uk-politics-49833804

[78]Zola, 'Letter to the Senate', p.157.

J'Accuse...! brought about profound positive consequences. These consequences rocked a nation, confronted an epidemic of bigotry and prejudice, freed an innocent man, disgraced a corrupt establishment, and toppled multiple governments. That's impressive for one page of small typeface print. And it shows there's no reason, in principle, why some well-thought-out trolling cannot bring about positive and beneficial change. An academic study from 2016 points out that legislative moves towards the criminalization of trolling rely on the assumption that 'trolling is universally undesirable'.[79] If *J'Accuse...!* was trolling, then this assumption is flawed. That should be at the forefront of our minds when deciding how to regulate our digital lives, whether through legislation in our parliaments or through digital citizenship in our online communities.

Above all, Zola's case is exemplary in one vital respect: for him, the truth of what he wrote was sacrosanct, and he never let his zeal for the cause of justice eclipse it. Notably, both Émile Zola and Alex Jones have been found liable for defamation, but at the time of writing, only the former has been exonerated.[80] That's the difference between activists and trolls. Indeed, it has been argued that 'trolling is about triumph over truth rather than producing truth itself.'[81] It's no coincidence that our anxieties about trolling have flourished at the same time as our anxieties about the post-truth world. In this, as in so much else, Zola's age was a forerunner to ours. As Christopher Hitchens put it:

> Zola did not in fact require much intellectual capacity to mount his defense of one wronged man. He applied, first, the forensic and journalistic skills that he was used to employing for the social background of his novels. These put him in the possession of the unarguable facts. But the mere facts were not sufficient, because the anti-Dreyfusards did not base their real case on the actual guilt or innocence of the defendant. They openly maintained that, for reasons of state, it was better not to reopen the case. Such a reopening would only serve to dissipate public confidence in order and in institutions. Why take this risk at all? And why on earth take it on behalf of a Jew? The partisans of Dreyfus therefore had to face the

[79]Bryn Alexander Coles and Melanie West, 'Trolling the Trolls: Online Forum Users' Constructions of the Nature and Properties of Trolling', *Computers in Human Behavior*, vol. 60, 2016, pp.233–44, p.243.

[80]See Bevan Hurley, 'Alex Jones Guilty in All Four Sandy Hook Defamation Cases', *Independent*, 15 November 2021. Available at: https://www.independent.co.uk/news/world/americas/alex-jones-sandy-hook-infowars-b1957993.html

[81]Benjamin Aspray, 'On Trolling as Comedic Method', *JCMS: Journal of Cinema and Media Studies*, vol. 58, no. 3, 2019, pp.154–60, p.156.

> accusation not that they were mistaken as to the facts, but that they were treacherous, unpatriotic, and irreligious.[82]

If Zola has a lesson for us here, then it is as admirable as it is paradoxical: what better way to troll a post-truth world than by insisting on telling it the truth? This gives us a clue as to why the populists of both Zola's time and our own were so drawn to slogans about free speech. It's not censorship they fear; rather, what threatens their 'free' speech is true speech. They find a world in which truth takes no precedence over drivel and in which threats and harassment are afforded the dignity of legitimate speech, to be congenial. In such world, they can persecute whom they please. Yet truth may well prove more effective than legislation in dismantling their carefully constructed, asymmetric rhetorical impregnability. Zola teaches us how to be steadfast in the face of such collective psychosis.

[82]Hitchens, *Letters to a Young Contrarian*, p.4.

Conclusions

Conclusion #1: We (still) can't define trolling

I began this book by trying to argue that no one knows exactly what trolling is; I am ending it almost none the wiser. That is not, I hope, because our journey through Western literary history has been a wild goose chase. Rather, it's because the range of textual, rhetorical, and polemical strategies we've looked at upholds the idea that 'trolling' is an umbrella term, covering an extremely broad spectrum of writers' tactics, all of which are highly context-specific. The idea that everything we call trolling must share a distinctive common characteristic unique to trolling turns out not to stack up.

Still, without defining what trolling is, I hope nevertheless to have elucidated how it typically works. This, I think, is more important. Posing an important question in the form of 'What is [X]?' is all too often unhelpful, and conducive only to pseudo-philosophical hair-splitting. Asking how things work, whether things have always been this way, how they might have functioned in the past, and what that might teach us – a roundabout way of asking 'What is our understanding of [X]?' – gives a clearer picture both of what we already know and of what we still need to understand better, and it saves us running round in circles about definitions.

When we look at the many different ways in which trolling works, the one most salient thing that stands out about them all is that none of them is particularly new. From flaming and 'slut'-shaming to RIP trolling and disaster trolling, we have seen again and again that, however shocking the writings of trolls may be, they are not without precedent in the Western literary classics.

Conclusion #2: There is nothing new under the sun

To say that there's nothing new about trolling is apt to come across as glib and dismissive, downplaying one of the major issues of our time. In fact, it might sound like a piece of trolling in itself. After all, trolls often set to work by treating big problems as small, and small issues as big – thus said the great Aristotle (or was it Rachel Barney?).[1]

To say, on the other hand, that trolling lies right at the heart of Western literature and culture, and draws upon a broad and complex range of rhetorical strategies and textual devices with a collective pedigree that goes back many centuries, is to give a more proper sense of the scale and the seriousness of the trolling phenomenon.

These are two ways of putting the same thing. But they seem to entail different consequences. Saying that trolling is nothing new seems to imply that nothing needs to change; that it's trivial or insignificant. And it's not: trolling is often deeply offensive, profoundly hurtful, and positively dangerous. If anyone doubts the seriousness of its real-life consequences, look at the centuries of sectarian bloodshed that Martin Luther's trolling unleashed.

Trolling is based on divisiveness, polarization, and victimization. It is, potentially, a deadly serious problem. But it is not a technological problem. We need to understand this key point if we are to stand any chance of solving it. So as to clinch it, we'll see how the technological claims made about trolling weigh up in the scales of literary history.

Conclusion #3: It's not about the technology

Let's evaluate some of the most common claims made about the links between digital technology and trolling. The best-known ones include: (1) that the digital world fosters anonymity; (2) that it produces an online disinhibition effect; (3) that its instantaneous speed results in ill-thought-out words being posted without due reflection; and (4) that its global reach sidesteps effective law enforcement. All these aspects of digital technology have been said to facilitate or exacerbate trolling. So let's consider them in turn.

[1] Rachel Barney, '[Aristotle], *On Trolling*', *Journal of the American Philosophical Association*, vol. 2, no. 2, 2016, pp.193–95, p.193.

Conclusion #3.1: Anonymity

It's often said that trolling is enabled by the anonymous environment of the online world. That is simply false. We have looked at trolling over many centuries, and, of all the writings we've surveyed, only Swift's *A Modest Proposal* was published anonymously; from the Renaissance onwards, all the other writers trolled nonymously. True, this suggests that online anonymity is indeed new. But it simultaneously disproves the idea that anonymity breeds trolling. As Whitney Phillips puts it, 'there is no guarantee that an anonymity-free Internet would be a kinder, gentler Internet. History has proven again and again that people are perfectly capable of being atrocious to each other under their real names'.[2]

Conclusion #3.2: Online disinhibition

It is also widely claimed that trolling comes about because of an online disinhibition effect. Research suggests that electronic communication dehumanizes those we communicate with, reducing them to digital texts instead of real people. As a result, we do not curb our outpourings as we would in face-to-face communications.[3] Sometimes, this is comparatively benign, as in inappropriately oversharing deep emotions or personal experiences with strangers; too often, though, it is 'toxic disinhibition', leading to rude, angry, hateful communication, with little remorse for offence given.

While such an analysis may be true, it is too poorly described to evaluate. It doesn't even start to explain what is new or unique about digital communication. That's because it fails to consider that writing itself is dehumanizing.

Take the works of almost any poet in the Western tradition, and you'll see that many of their verses say things in writing they would never say to their readers' faces. Consider the case of love poetry: we don't, in casual conversation, describe the pain of unrequited love to random strangers. But that is just what plenty of great love poems do. Is that because they bypass face-to-face conversation? Would we say that writing disinhibits poets? Would we go so far as to say that the disinhibition effect brought about by writing is what makes poetry possible? Maybe; maybe not. But if so, that would suggest that disinhibition is an effect not of digital technology but of writing itself. And if not, then that would suggest that the absence of face-to-face contact is a red herring and that online disinhibition must be driven

---

[2]Whitney Phillips, *This Is Why We Can't Have Nice Things: Mapping the Relationship Between Online Trolling and Mainstream Culture* (Cambridge, MA: MIT Press, 2015), p.156.

[3]See John Suler, 'The Online Disinhibition Effect', *CyberPsychology and Behavior*, vol. 7, no. 3, 2004, pp.321–26.

by other factors. Either way, it turns out that explanations of trolling based on online disinhibition need more work.

Distrust of communication by text isn't new. Ancient Greek philosophers, such as Plato and Aristotle, denounced handwriting for the same reasons: it deprives us of the presence of the speaker we are trying to converse with; it is a poor substitute for the fullness of the individual voice. Medieval theologians denounced print on the same grounds: it emptied writing of the thoughtfulness that scribes put into their calligraphy over many hours of devotion. A printing machine like Gutenberg's, they reasoned, since it lacked a human soul, could produce only empty babble, and never the meaningful, beautiful words of a scribe.

When the great literary critic Wolfgang Iser observed that 'with reading there is no face-to-face situation',[4] he was merely pointing out the obvious. This is simply what writing does to communication, whether Sumerian cuneiform, Egyptian hieroglyphs, Kanji calligraphy, or Facebook Messenger. It's certainly possible that the last of these might have some digital characteristics that make it more susceptible to trolling than the first three, but what those characteristics might be is not (yet) clear.

Conclusion #3.3: Speed

Claims are also made for the instantaneous speed of digital communication as an aggravating factor behind trolling. These claims are impressive, since electronic communication that moves at the speed of light is itself impressive. But they are not unprecedented.

The argument here is that digital technology facilitates communication so quick we don't take time to weigh our words and reflect on their consequences. This may well be true. But though the speed of the internet is indeed unprecedented, communicating at unprecedented speeds is most certainly not. Whenever we look at a pre-internet revolution in communications technology, we find writers making the same mistakes. Martin Luther, caught out by the fast tempo of the Gutenberg press, published in haste and repented at leisure, as did Wyndham Lewis four hundred years later.

Conclusion #3.4: Ineffective law enforcement

Finally, there's the argument that trolling happens because the global reach of the internet amounts (seemingly) to legal impunity: if a troll targets a victim

[4]Wolfgang Iser, *Prospecting: from Reader Response to Literary Anthropology* (Baltimore, MD: Johns Hopkins University Press, 1993), p.32.

in another country, then traditional law enforcement is usually powerless to act if the troll breaks the law. This in turn creates the impression of a free-for-all, encouraging trolls to troll whoever and however they please.

Here, the argument for the novelty of the digital age strikes me as pretty sound: no other form of communications technology has ever before offered instant worldwide publication, beyond the reach of most countries' police and censors. But the argument about legal impunity doesn't hold water. On one hand, we've come across plenty of digital-era trolls who've been in trouble with the law; on the other, Zola was neither the first nor the last great writer to escape the law by fleeing into exile. So it's not as if impunity was unavailable in the past (albeit at the price of international exile) or complete in the present (since it doesn't exist at intranational level).

All told, then, not only have we seen centuries of literary evidence that trolling predates the internet; we've also seen how the arguments that trolling is enabled or worsened by digital technologies are (at best) patchy. So perhaps the real question to ask is not 'How do digital technologies cause/facilitate/exacerbate trolling?' but rather 'Why do we think they do?'

Conclusion #4: Beware the moral panic

Every innovation in communications technology seems to bring with it a moral panic. Back in my schooldays, the fear was that the VCR was bringing so-called video-nasties into the homes of children like me, and, compounded with the first home computer games, would corrupt our minds irretrievably with violence. Next, the advent of mobile phones was blamed for allowing gangsters to organize illegal raves in the English countryside. Later, buying your child a phone was briefly considered dangerous, because it somehow turned privileged children into targets for muggers. In reality, by pinpointing its location, a mobile phone is the best safety feature a child could have.

Such moral panics are not always without foundation. We've seen respected historians argue that the Reformation couldn't have happened without Gutenberg's printing press. But the fear is always the same. It is a fear of technology in the wrong hands. This means that there are, apparently, right hands for the technology to be in. And those hands are always 'ours', while the wrong hands are those of a 'they' who are generally less privileged – less powerful, wealthy, educated – and are said to lack 'our' moral compass.

Since buying into these moral panics buys you into the moral high ground, it's easy enough to see why they catch on. They also give those with an instinctive fear of the new the perfect justification for recoiling from it, or for proselytizing against it. But if there's to be a moral backlash against trolling, then it needs to proceed from a sounder moral basis than such 'them'/'us'-driven thinking. Clearly, we cannot chide trolling for its divisive and polarizing nature while speaking from such a divided and polarized viewpoint.

This doesn't mean that the moral panic is completely unfounded. On the contrary, there are plenty of morally sound objections to trolling. But none of them involves technology. Trolling is a human problem, not a technological one. It follows that arguments rooted in technology serve at best to muddy the waters, in terms both of the moral issues at stake and of the practical solutions to them.

Arguments rooted in technological determinism are familiar enough. Often there's much to be said for them: no doubt the human experience was profoundly changed by the advent of railways, motor cars, or aeroplanes, just as the neolithic way of life was ended by the technological development that was bronze. But technologically deterministic arguments all share one common weakness: they reduce human beings to puppets manipulated by the very technology they think they master. They thereby downplay our agency and have even been said to rob us of our humanity. That's not to say that they're wrong. But it is to say that, in the context of a debate about the moral status of trolling, they are utterly self-defeating.

The problem with arguments to the effect that trolling is caused by technology is that they provide trolls with the perfect excuse for the very behaviour our moral panics decry. Trolls need take no personal responsibility for their actions whatsoever if they were only bending to the influence of technology. Instead, trolls are cast as a natural by-product of digital communication, from which it isn't such a far stretch for them to claim the status of victim rather than aggressor. This is what I mean by technology muddying the ethical waters in this debate.

Worse still, technological problems seem inevitably to call for technological solutions – which in this context implies algorithms, artificial intelligence, and such like. We should shrink from this prospect. If this book has demonstrated anything, it has shown that the writings of some of the finest authors in Western literature were tantamount to trolling or else depicted scenes of trolling in ways that glorify and glamourize it. To what ignominious oblivion would artificial intelligence confine Zola's *J'Accuse…!*, Swift's *A Modest Proposal*, or Luther's *Ninety-Five Theses*? If it's true that some aspects of literature and some aspects of trolling are simply indistinguishable, then what good is an algorithm?

The alternative, which I've been advocating throughout this book, is to regard trolling as a kind of writing, consisting of various literary and rhetorical strategies. When we do so, both the practical and the moral issues it raises begin to appear in clearer focus.

Conclusion #5: Clarifying the moral stakes

There is much to deplore about trolling. It's typically aggressive and/or divisive; it tends towards victimization and/or polarization. True, aggression is sometimes justified: certain behaviours may call for stern confrontation, for example. Similarly, polarization is sometimes unavoidable: for instance, either vaccines work, or they don't; there's scant middle ground to be found here. Divisiveness, though seldom a virtue, may become one where an unthinking consensus enforces a monopoly on thought. But though there are circumstances under which the more reprehensible aspects of trolling might seem legitimate, there is one aspect common to both deceptive trolling (as in the angling metaphor) and aggressive trolling (*à la* Scandinavian monster) which clarifies why trolling is at rock bottom an unethical activity.

Philosopher Ralph DiFranco nails it when he writes that, ethically, trolling is 'wrong, because the troll fails to respect their target as an equal conversational participant'.[5] This is no trite, simple point about courtesy and respect: impoliteness is not exactly immoral, after all. It's rather a point that derives from something we established early on: the deep-seated asymmetry in trolling. To cite Phillips again: 'trolls exercise what can only be described as pure privilege – they refuse to treat others as they insist on being treated'.[6] Trolling therefore strikes at the fundamental principles of reciprocity and even-handedness that underpin not just conversation but even civility itself. This helps clarify some of the moral stakes around trolling, and, as DiFranco points out, several important practical considerations follow from it.

The first of these is that a clear understanding that trolling is something that's wrong in itself is important, because 'it shifts the moral burden of proof off of targets and victims of trolling to prove that they have been harmed and onto the trolls themselves to show that the provocation they are engaged in is morally justified'.[7] This helps us, both in our online communities and in society at large, to direct our attention to root causes rather than their outcomes; to focus on the aggression while shielding the victims from further scapegoating.

Secondly, it follows from DiFranco's view that, as the above quotation implies, there might be some occasions where trolling is neither wrong nor uncalled for. There is, of course, a broader moral debate here about whether noble causes may resort to ignoble tactics without compromising their nobility: that is a question for philosophers to decide. But if Zola was right to use trolling to expose anti-Semitism, if Swift was right to verge

---

[5]Ralph DiFranco, 'I Wrote This Paper for the Lulz: The Ethics of Internet Trolling', *Ethical Theory and Moral Practice*, vol. 23, 2020, pp.931–45, p.932.

[6]Phillips, *This Is Why …*, p.26.

[7]DiFranco, 'I Wrote This Paper ….', p.932.

on trolling in remonstrating against man-made famine, and if Luther was right to expose church-sanctioned extortion through trolling, then there is such a thing as morally justifiable trolling. In fact, there are times when treating your conversational participant as a respected equal is itself morally questionable. We are under no obligation to treat bigotry with even-handedness and reciprocity, for example.

Scrutinizing the moral justifications (if any) for the act of trolling draws attention to a third aspect of DiFranco's account that helps us reframe the ethics of trolling. Trolls, when called out for their trolling, will often shrug their shoulders and claim they were 'only trolling', as if that excused their behaviour. The recognition that trolling is by nature unethical helps us to see that this is no excuse. As DiFranco says, it 'does not excuse online derogators simply because they protest that they themselves do not endorse the attitudes they express'.[8] In fact, another philosopher argues that the excuse of 'only', 'just', or 'merely' trolling not only doesn't hold, it actually makes matters worse:

> abuse should not be considered somehow more acceptable as a component of an act of trolling ('mere trolling'); it is in fact even more questionable when used in such a way. Once we see that an act of trolling is by nature divisive and manipulative, an act of abusive trolling is, therefore, better thought of not as *mere* trolling, but as abusive *and* divisive *and* manipulative. Just as if I do something wrong and lie about it I would be held liable for two wrongs should the lie be discovered (the lie and the act I lie about), so too using racist speech, for example, does not somehow become more acceptable when used as a means of trolling. The moral implications, therefore, are cumulative not diminishing.[9]

Rightly looked at, then, there is no such thing as 'only' trolling.

The upshot of DiFranco's arguments carries a fourth implication, which he himself doesn't pursue. Collectively, these three insights entail an important change of moral emphasis in the way we regard trolling. This goes back to the distinction this book has drawn between trolls and trolling – between the people and the activity. The current media discourse tends to favour stigmatizing and demonizing individuals as trolls, without looking at what it is they do that is so reprehensible. This is utterly counterproductive: at best, it means we fail to learn from trolls' mistakes.

---

[8]Ibid.

[9]P. J. Connolly, 'Trolling as Speech Act (or, the Art of Trolling, with a Description of All the Utensils, Instruments, Tackling, and Materials Requisite Thereto: With Rules and Directions How to Use Them)', *Journal of Social Philosophy*, vol. 53, no. 1, 2021, pp.1–17, p.4.

At worst, it means the moral panic around trolling itself fuels the very cultural climate that makes trolling possible – a climate of hostility and derision targeted at individual victims. 'Don't blame the technology; blame the people', says the technophile to the technophobe. But blaming the people does not improve matters much. A more constructive approach to the (im)morality of trolling would involve recognizing that 'by focusing on the "doing" of trolling rather than who does it, we may derive a more comprehensive understanding of the processual enactment of trolling in the context of social dynamics within online communities'.[10] Less wordily, 'removing individuals from the center of analysis and instead focusing on the socially shared elements of behaviors has important implications for how trolling is understood'.[11]

Decentring the individual and foregrounding the context is simultaneously a way of emphasizing the importance of digital citizenship. 'What is broadly referred to as digital citizenship is usually concerned with ethical behaviour in online environments and takes aim at problematic or aberrant forms of participation'.[12] Defining digital citizenship more specifically is as difficult as defining trolling, and for similar reasons: what counts as good digital citizenship is highly context-specific and changes from forum to forum. (It seems likely – though this hunch would need another book to explore it – that the notions of digital citizenship and of trolling are symbiotically linked: probably, an example of bad digital citizenship in any given context would also be regarded as trolling in that context.)

This is why it's so important to reframe trolling as a kind of writing. The emphasis on its techniques and strategies helps remind us that trolling is a very particular activity. If we want to overcome it, then railing and ranting at those who engage in it, however morally justified or satisfyingly cathartic that may be, is going to be less effective as a strategy than getting to grips with what it is about such writing that's harmful and dangerous. Perhaps the next step is to reflect on what kind of digital world we want to live in. If what we 'put out there' is ill-thought-out, hastily composed, poorly written, and emotionally raw, then we forfeit the right of complaint if that's what we get back. We can all raise the tone of the social media we participate in, all the time. And so we should.

---

[10]Angela Gracia B. Cruz, Yuri Seo, and Mathew Rex, 'Trolling in Online Communities: A Practice-based Theoretical Perspective', *The Information Society*, vol. 34, no. 1, 2018, pp.15–26, p. 18.

[11]Ibid., p.17.

[12]Anthony McCosker, 'Trolling as Provocation: YouTube's Agonistic Publics', *Convergence: The International Journal of Research into New Media Technologies*, vol. 20, no. 2, 2014, pp.201–17, p.201.

Conclusion #6: Be careful who you call a troll

Many myths and stereotypes have sprung up around trolling. No doubt many of them are well founded. But others, it seems, could well be rather less so. As good digital citizens, we would do well to take a good, hard look at who we're calling trolls before we start pointing fingers.

Giving evidence before the House of Lords Select Committee on Communications, barrister John Cooper QC said: 'The vast majority of people who use the social media are like society. The vast majority are decent, intelligent, inspiring people. The problem comes with a small minority, as in society, who spoil it for everyone else'.[13] Needless to say, this small minority are the trolls. In this conception, they are simply bad people. They have no moral compass and are only happy when they're making the rest of us miserable. Or, as a team of researchers recently put it, 'one popular recurring narrative in the media suggests that ... trolls [are] a small number of particularly sociopathic individuals'.[14] Jonathan Bishop has gone so far as to suggest that trolls have something wrong with them and that there might be a correlation between trolling and ASPD (anti-social personality disorder).[15] This has given rise to a belief that 'trolls are born, not made' – that they are, as it were, a breed apart.[16] Furthermore, though they are thought to be just a tiny proportion of the internet's massive population, 'trolls are widely regarded as the primary obstacle to a kinder, gentler, and more equitable Internet'.[17]

In 2014, a study appeared that garnered a fair amount of press attention. Entitled 'Trolls Just Want to Have Fun', it seemed to offer stark proof of all these stereotypes.[18] Surveying a sample size of 1,215 people, and asking them a range of questions both about their internet habits and their personalities, it found that just a small minority of this sample (5.6%) listed their preferred online activity as trolling (as opposed to debating, chatting, socializing, etc.). This small minority seemed to exhibit personality traits

---

[13]House of Lords Select Committee on Communications, *Social Media and Criminal Offences*, p.7.

[14]Justin Cheng, Michael Bernstein, Cristian Danescu-Niculescu-Mizil, and Jure Leskovec, 'Anyone Can Become a Troll: Causes of Trolling Behavior in Online Discussions', *Proceedings of the 2017 ACM Conference on Computer Supported Cooperative Work and Social Computing*, 2017, pp.1217–230, p.1218.

[15]See Jonathan Bishop, 'The Effect of Deindividuation of the Internet Troller on Criminal Procedure Implementation: An Interview with a Hater', *International Journal of Cyber Criminology*, vol. 7, no. 1, 2013, pp.28–48.

[16]Cheng et al., 'Anyone Can Become a Troll', p.1218.

[17]Phillips, *This Is Why ...*, p.10.

[18]Erin E. Buckels, Paul D. Trapnell, and Delroy L. Paulhus, 'Trolls Just Want to Have Fun', *Personality and Individual Differences*, vol. 67, 2014, pp.97–102, p.98.

consistent with what the authors of the study call a 'Dark Tetrad' (comprising narcissism, sadism, Machiavellianism, and psychopathy). Admittedly, a more sophisticated survey, using a more detailed questionnaire, partially modified these findings: it revealed that really, 'narcissism was actually negatively associated with trolling enjoyment' and 'was instead positively correlated with enjoying debating', while psychopathy 'was unrelated to trolling enjoyment'.[19] Nevertheless, those who enjoy trolling appear to be thoroughly Machiavellian sadists, with the association between trolling and sadism in particular 'so strong that it might be said that online trolls are prototypical everyday sadists'.[20]

These findings, as disturbing as they are impressive, would seem to offer proof positive of our stereotypes: that trolls are no-good reprobates bent on spoiling things for everyone else, and that the best that can be said of them is that they are few in number. Yet the study strikes me as flawed, for reasons we covered early on. It makes much of the deceptive and Machiavellian nature of trolling, yet it nevertheless (and preposterously) assumes that no deception or underhand Machiavellianism could be taking place when these trolls are filling out the researchers' questionnaires, which ask them to agree or disagree with such personality-testing statements as 'In video games, I like the realistic blood spurts', or 'Hurting people is exciting', or 'It's not wise to tell your secrets', or 'I enjoy making jokes at the expense of others'.[21] Are we quite sure that everyone, let alone a troll, has both the self-knowledge and the honesty to answer reliably?

More importantly, though, its findings are challenged by a later study, which ought to give us pause for thought. It set out to ask questions such as 'is trolling caused by particularly antisocial individuals or by ordinary people? Is trolling behavior innate, or is it situational? ... Can trolling spread from person to person in a community?'[22] Remarkably, their research studied a corpus of no fewer than sixteen and a half million posts (16,500,603 to be precise) by 865,248 users commenting on the CNN.com website between December 2012 and August 2013, during which time 20,197 of these users were banned, 3,801,774 posts were deleted by moderators (that's 23 per cent of all posts), and 571,662 (3.5 per cent) were 'flagged' for abusing the community or its users. Flaggings and bannings, the researchers argue, can be taken as fairly reliable proxy indicators of trolling. Thus, at first glance, the low percentage of banned users suggests that there is indeed a small minority bent on wrecking online communities. And yet, the researchers thought, the large numbers of posts deleted for inappropriate content – nearly a quarter

[19]Ibid., p.101; p.100; p.100.

[20]Ibid., pp.100–101.

[21]Ibid., pp.98–9.

[22]Cheng et al., 'Anyone Can Become a Troll', p.1217.

of all posts, in fact – and the sheer 'prevalence of antisocial behavior online suggests that these trolls, being relatively uncommon, are not responsible for all instances of trolling'.[23] Looking into things a little more closely, they found that one in four 'flagged' comments was written by a user with no previous history of being flagged. So they asked: 'Could ordinary individuals also engage in trolling behavior, even if temporarily?'[24]

Their findings were nothing short of fascinating. Assume you're just an ordinary user who's never been publicly rebuked by having one of your comments flagged before. Once this happens to you, you're much likelier to have your next comment flagged. Even if your next comment is in a completely different discussion on a wholly unrelated topic, the likelihood that you'll write another nasty post more than doubles as soon as your nastiness is called out. (To modify the old saying: you might as well be flagged for a sheep as for a lamb.) Interestingly, time is also a factor in this. You're much likelier to go on to write other flagged comments if you do so within five minutes of being flagged – three times likelier, in fact, than if you write your next comment a week later. Even the difference between five and ten minutes results in a huge reduction in the likelihood of getting flagged – a clear lesson (if one were needed) never to post anything in the heat of the moment.

The study also found that 'trolling behavior can spread from user to user'.[25] Statistically, if the initial post that starts a discussion is flagged, subsequent posts are much likelier to be flagged too, and throughout the duration of the whole discussion at that, that is, not simply in reply to the initial post. It seems, unsurprisingly, that lowering the tone infects the rest of the debate. The researchers liken this to the so-called broken window hypothesis – the social theory behind 'zero tolerance' thinking, which says that whilst most people would just walk past an empty building, if one of its windows is broken, then the chances of further vandalism or break-ins go up dramatically. Hence, the idea goes, antisocial behaviour spreads if untended, eventually becoming normalized. The digital equivalent of a broken window is a flagged post: the probability of newcomers to a discussion writing something objectionable enough to get flagged goes up considerably in relation to whether the previous few posts were flagged or not – and to how many of them were flagged. The odds of someone's first contribution to a discussion getting flagged approach fifty/fifty where the previous four posts were flagged. Furthermore, users who'd never been flagged before were found to be likelier to write their first offending post after having participated in a discussion where other people's posts were

[23]Ibid., p.1218.

[24]Ibid., p.1218.

[25]Ibid., p.1219.

flagged. In other words, if your discussion is trolled, you are likelier to go on to troll someone else's, even if you've never trolled before, and even if the discussion is on a separate topic. 'Anger begets more anger', the researchers suggest. 'Our findings suggest that trolling, like laughter, can be contagious, and that ordinary people, given the right conditions, can act like trolls', they conclude.[26]

Some scholars have claimed to demonstrate that people troll out of boredom, to vent, or for fun. This study found that flagged posts go up in number at the end of the working day, that there is a marked onset of users having posts flagged on a Friday, and that Mondays generate the highest volume of flagged posts. While the first point could be explained away ('trolls may simply wake up later than normal users',[27] the study meticulously observes), the others are pretty revealing: trolling patterns seem to correlate with the workaday routines and patterns of mainstream, middle America.

Is it possible, then, that much of what gets flagged as trolling comes about simply because everyday people are not above stumbling into an acrimonious discussion and letting that acrimony get the better of them, taking it with them into their next discussions? Or because of the crowd mentality that means we let our guard down when surrounded by others who've cast aside their inhibitions in defiance of social norms? Or because sometimes, we're simply not capable of rising above the frustrations of our twenty-first-century lives? Do these findings imply that we troll because we're only human?

Claiming this is going a bit far: much of the trolling we've come across in this book, far from being 'only human', is downright inhumane. Certainly, then, there seems to be a small number of trolls who apparently lack any sense of humanity. But if trolling 'is a serious issue that undermines the operation of social networks and media, and their role as a global channel of communication',[28] then can a tiny number of sadists and sociopaths really add up to a global threat? I wonder how much of this debate is in fact a scientifically grounded, evidence-based inflection of the Viking/angler schism explored in the first chapter. According to the one study, trolls are a small, mysterious group of sinister creatures: not only are 'they' different from all of 'us', they are a menace, too. Whereas according to the other study, trolling is an activity that anyone might partake in from time to time, so if you want to find a potential troll, you could do worse than look in the

[26]Ibid., p.1217.

[27]Ibid., p.1223.

[28]Paraskevas Tsantarliotis, Evaggelia Pitoura, and Panayiotis Tsaparas, 'Defining and Predicting Troll Vulnerability in Online Social Media', *Social Network Analysis and Mining*, vol. 7, no. 1, 2017, pp.1–15, p.1.

mirror. The thing is that each of these very different ideas implies a very different way of dealing with the problem of trolling.

If trolls are thought of as a small faction of incorrigibles, as undesirable elements with nothing redeemable about them, then, the argument goes, we simply need to get rid of them, by banning their profiles, closing down their platforms, and perhaps jailing them once they've gone so far as to break the law. Presumably we'll all be safer, and life on the internet will be so much better, without them. But what if trolling is also a bad habit shared by a large number of people no different from people like you and me? What if there simply was no 'them' and no 'us'?

History ought to have made us wary of patterns of thought that brand a small number of people as evildoers who have something innately wrong with them that sets 'them' apart from the rest of 'us' in the moral majority. History ought to have taught us to be suspicious when the tiny size of the minority seems out of any proportion to the vast extent of the problems blamed on them. And above all, history ought to have left us in no doubt that wanting to get rid of a small group of people because of some defect in their make-up, or because they were 'born, not made' different to everyone else – a subspecies, as it were – is a mindset as reprehensible as it is dangerous.

That is not in any way to suggest we should excuse or tolerate trolling: I am no troll apologist. It is merely to ask that we think critically about how we label trolls and the discourse in which we frame them. If there are findings that 'suggest that ordinary users are responsible for a significant amount of trolling behavior, and that many may have just been having a bad day', then 'interpreting [their] snarky remarks as resulting from general mean-spiritedness' seems itself a bit mean-spirited, and diagnosing them as psychologically defective is pretty extreme.[29] Exercising our critical faculties, and a bit of restraint, seems a better course. To see why, let's look at one last study.

Here's a devastatingly simple experiment carried out in 2015.[30] Take a random sample of one hundred students at an American midwestern college. Give them a description of three fairly familiar scenarios: (1) a Wikipedia page is suddenly rewritten by a brand new contributor, who provides no sources or references for the contentious information added, leading to heated debate among the other editors; (2) in a Q&A platform (such as Yahoo! Answers), a new user shows up and starts posting answers with politically inflammatory comments, resulting in off-topic, polarized political debate; (3) on a popular multiplayer gaming site called *League of*

[29]Cheng et al., 'Anyone Can Become a Troll', p.1223; p.1227.

[30]See Pnina Fichman and Madelyn Rose Sanfilippo, 'The Bad Boys and Girls of Cyberspace: How Gender and Context Impact Perception of and Reaction to Trolling', *Social Science Computer Review*, vol. 33, no. 2, 2015, pp.163–80.

Legends, a new player materializes who keeps asking questions at crucial moments while the game is in play. Now: here's the intriguing part. Give the description of the mysterious new contributor/user/player one of the following usernames – either Todd, or Emily, or AbcD. Thus, all the subjects in the experiment are asked to comment on the activity of an apparently male user, an apparently female user, and a gender-neutral user. Which of the three usernames was attached to which of the three activities was randomly assigned for each participant in the experiment.

You can probably guess the results: even though what they wrote was word-for-word identical, Todd was far more likely to be perceived as a troll than Emily, with AbcD sitting in the middle position. Of course, it goes without saying that the gender of a username or avatar offers no indication whatsoever as to the gender of the real-life person behind it. But still, male usernames seem to invite accusations of trolling much more readily than female ones. (Interestingly, the study also found that men are more likely to respond to trolls, whether by confronting them or blocking them, whereas women are likelier to just ignore them.)

So: is it really the case that trolls are overwhelmingly male? Or is it rather the case that we, as a society, are prone to gender profiling, and that we tend to perceive men as potential aggressors, and thus regard trolling as a masculine pursuit? How else to explain why Emily isn't called a troll when she does exactly the same things, verbatim, as Todd? That's not to suggest, however, that men are getting a rough deal in these scenarios. When someone with the username Emily spoils a gaming session by asking a badly timed, stupid question, she's written off as a 'clueless newbie'; when she makes barbed digs about politics in a politically neutral discussion space, she is thought to be ideologically sincere (if perhaps overzealous), or else confused about the site's purpose.[31] In other words, women are just as likely to be negatively stereotyped in their online behaviour as men are; it's just that the male stereotypes involve potential malevolence, whereas the stereotypical female is well-meaning and in earnest, but clueless.[32] Sadly, the patterns of thinking that we bring to the internet from mainstream, offline society tend to skew the way we think about trolls.

What this experiment really shows us, I think, is that at least some aspects of trolling lie in the eye of the beholder. Whether something counts as trolling or not, then, is in part down to the way readers interpret it. We saw, towards the start of this book, that the intentions of an author are not enough to determine whether their writings belong to a certain genre; we're ending it by suggesting that the interpretations of their readers play an

---

[31]Ibid., p.174.

[32]Or, as Whitney Phillips puts it, 'Trolling behaviors are gendered male'. See Phillips, *This Is Why ...*, p.42.

important part. That, I'd hope, ought to give a final indication that studying trolling in the light of studying literature is an instructive and illuminating task.

Conclusion #7: And finally …

A closing thought: if trolling is a writerly problem, then it has writerly solutions. And the literary classics are a storehouse of them. Rhetorical flourishes, witty ripostes, scornful rejoinders, deft turns of phrase – literature has everything you need to defend yourself against the trolls. And, if you feel you lack the time and/or wit to compose, for example, an unanswerable aphorism in the Wildean vein, then it doesn't matter – the internet is awash with wonderful quotations from the literary classics and, as we saw towards the start, you can wear them like a mask while flinging them back in a troll's face. Whether you want to argue like Cicero or insult like Falstaff, or if you prefer to repay bile with beauty and disarm provocation with disingenuity, the classics of literature can show you how. In these parlous, fractured, insecure times, they stand out as the best possible social network you can join.

INDEX